First World War
and Army of Occupation
War Diary
France, Belgium and Germany

11 DIVISION
Headquarters, Branches and Services
General Staff
1 July 1916 - 30 April 1917

WO95/1787

The Naval & Military Press Ltd
www.nmarchive.com
Published in association with The National Archives

Published by

The Naval & Military Press Ltd

Unit 10 Ridgewood Industrial Park,

Uckfield, East Sussex,

TN22 5QE England

Tel: +44 (0) 1825 749494

www.naval-military-press.com

www.nmarchive.com

This diary has been reprinted in facsimile from the original. Any imperfections are inevitably reproduced and the quality may fall short of modern type and cartographic standards.

© **Crown Copyright**
Images reproduced by permission of The National Archives, London, England, 2015.

Contents

Document type	Place/Title	Date From	Date To
Heading	11th Division General Staff Jly 1916-Apl 1917 From Egypt		
Heading	G.S. 11th Division War Diary July 1916		
War Diary	At Sea.	01/07/1916	03/07/1916
War Diary	Marselles	04/07/1916	04/07/1916
War Diary	On Train.	05/07/1916	06/07/1916
War Diary	Flers.	07/07/1916	14/07/1916
War Diary	Flers Le Gauroy.	15/07/1916	15/07/1916
War Diary	Le Cauroy Duisans.	16/07/1916	16/07/1916
War Diary	Duisans.	17/07/1916	29/07/1916
War Diary	Warlus	30/07/1916	31/07/1916
Operation(al) Order(s)	11th Division Operation Order No. 17	19/07/1916	19/07/1916
Miscellaneous	Movement Table Issued With 11th Division Operation Order No. 17		
Operation(al) Order(s)	11th Division Operation Order No. 18		
Heading	Cover for Documents. Nature of Enclosures. "G" Branch XIth Div		
War Diary	Warlus.	01/08/1916	21/08/1916
War Diary	Le Cauroy	22/08/1916	31/08/1916
Operation(al) Order(s)	11th Division Operation Order No. 18 Appendix "A"	15/08/1916	15/08/1916
Heading	11th Division. Scheme Of Defence. Appendix B		
Miscellaneous	Scheme Of Defence. 11th. Division.		
Miscellaneous	Index of Maps forwarded With 11th Division Defence Scheme.		
Miscellaneous	11th Division Defence Scheme.		
Miscellaneous	Table Showing Disposition Of 11th Division. Appendix 1		
Miscellaneous	Appendix 5 Organisation Of The Artillery For Defence.		
Miscellaneous	Instructions As To Action in The Event of A Gas Attack. Appendix 4		
Miscellaneous	Medical Arrangements. Appendix 5		
Miscellaneous	Orders For Divisional Battle Posts. Appendix 6		
Miscellaneous	Traffic Orders. 11th Division. (Issue With D.R.O. 201) Appendix 7		
Miscellaneous	Secrets. Appendix 8		
Miscellaneous	Appendix 9 Distribution Of Grenades And Establishment Of Grenade Posts		
Miscellaneous	Distribution of Shall Arm Ammunition Appendix 10		
Miscellaneous	Appendix 11. Garrisons Of Defended Localities For Which Reserve Ammunition And Rations Are Required.		
Map	Plan Of Brewery Post.		
Map	Petit Moulin Keep.		
Map	Wailly Keep		
Map	Map No 2 (d)		
Map	Mill Post.		
Map	Plan Of Agny Defences.		
Map	Achicourt.		
Map	Ronville Defences.		
Map	F. Sector.		

Map	G Sector		
Map	H. Sector		
Miscellaneous	Units On 6th Corps Exchange.		
Map	11th Division Communications Diagram Of Circuits Up To Brigades		
Map	Visual Communications. 11th Divn.		
Miscellaneous	11th Divisional School Of Instruction. Appendix "C"	23/07/1916	23/07/1916
Miscellaneous	Programme.	03/08/1916	03/08/1916
Miscellaneous	List of Lectures to be given at 11th Divisional School of Instruction	12/08/1916	12/08/1916
Miscellaneous	Sports Programme Friday And Saturday 25th And 26th August 1916	25/08/1916	25/08/1916
Miscellaneous	Standing Orders 11th Division School Of Instruction.		
Miscellaneous	11th Division Training Programme. Appendix "D"		
Operation(al) Order(s)	Appendix "E" 11th. Division Operation Order No. 19	30/08/1916	30/08/1916
Miscellaneous	Move Of 11th Division (less Artillery). Appendix "A"		
Miscellaneous	Appendix "B"	31/08/1916	31/08/1916
Miscellaneous	Reference 11th. Division O.O. No. 19	31/08/1916	31/08/1916
Heading	War Diary Of 11th. Division, General Staff, For Month Of September, 1916		
War Diary	Le Cauroy.	01/09/1916	01/09/1916
War Diary	Doullens.	02/09/1916	02/09/1916
War Diary	Acheux.	03/09/1916	06/09/1916
War Diary	Camouflage V.16.d.	07/09/1916	07/09/1916
War Diary	Camouflage.	08/09/1916	08/09/1916
War Diary	Camouflage Senlis.	09/09/1916	14/09/1916
War Diary	Camouflage. Senlis V. 16.d.	15/09/1916	21/09/1916
War Diary	Camouflage V.16.d.	24/09/1916	26/09/1916
War Diary	Donnet Post. W.12.d.9.2	26/09/1916	30/09/1916
Operation(al) Order(s)	11th Division Order No. 21	12/09/1916	12/09/1916
Miscellaneous	Proposed Artillery Programme For "X" Day Appendix 1		
Miscellaneous	Appendix II.		
Miscellaneous	Administrative Instructions. Appendix III		
Miscellaneous	Secret.	13/09/1916	13/09/1916
Operation(al) Order(s)	11th. Division Order No. 22	14/09/1916	14/09/1916
Operation(al) Order(s)	11th Division Order No. 23 Appendix D	15/09/1916	15/09/1916
Operation(al) Order(s)	11th Division Operation Order 24. Appendix E.	15/09/1916	15/09/1916
Miscellaneous	Table Of Moves On 6th September 1916	06/09/1916	06/09/1916
Operation(al) Order(s)	11th Division Order No. 25 Appendix F	16/09/1916	16/09/1916
Miscellaneous	11th. Division Order No. 26. Appendix G.	20/09/1916	20/09/1916
Operation(al) Order(s)	11th Division Order No. 29 Appendix J.	24/09/1916	24/09/1916
Miscellaneous	Appendix 1		
Miscellaneous	Administrative Instructions Appendix II		
Operation(al) Order(s)	Addendum To 11th Division Order No. 29	25/09/1916	25/09/1916
Operation(al) Order(s)	11th Division Order No 30 Appendix K	27/09/1916	27/09/1916
Operation(al) Order(s)	11th Division Order No 31. Appendix L	27/09/1916	27/09/1916
Miscellaneous	Reference Operation Order No. 27	21/09/1916	21/09/1916
Operation(al) Order(s)	Reference Operation Order No. 27	21/09/1916	21/09/1916
Operation(al) Order(s)	Ammendment To 11th Division Order No. 27		
Operation(al) Order(s)	11th Division Order No. 27 Appendix H	21/09/1916	21/09/1916
Operation(al) Order(s)	11th Division Order No. 28 (Preliminary). Appendix I	24/09/1916	24/09/1916
Miscellaneous			
Operation(al) Order(s)	11th Division Order No. 32 Appendix M.	27/09/1916	27/09/1916
Operation(al) Order(s)	11th Division Order No. 33 Appendix N	28/09/1916	28/09/1916
Operation(al) Order(s)	11th. Division. Preliminary Order No. 34 Appendix O	29/09/1916	29/09/1916

Miscellaneous	Table Of Moves.		
Operation(al) Order(s)	11th. Division Order No. 35 Appendix P.	30/09/1916	30/09/1916
Miscellaneous	11th. Division Order No. 35 Table Of Moves.	30/09/1916	30/09/1916
Miscellaneous	Plan For Minor Operation To Be Carried Out On 30th. Inst.	30/09/1916	30/09/1916
Miscellaneous	Mouquet Farm Operations Against		
Miscellaneous	34th. Inf. Bde.	21/09/1916	21/09/1916
Operation(al) Order(s)	32nd Infantry Brigade Order No. 23	24/09/1916	24/09/1916
Miscellaneous	32. Brigade Report On Situation	24/09/1916	24/09/1916
Miscellaneous	R.B.		
Miscellaneous	11th Division.	24/09/1916	24/09/1916
Miscellaneous	32 Brigade.	23/09/1916	23/09/1916
Miscellaneous	32nd Inf. Bde. C.R.A. For Information.	24/09/1916	24/09/1916
Miscellaneous	Order For Clearing Up Of Mouquet Farm.	21/09/1916	21/09/1916
Miscellaneous	The Adjutant. 11th Manchester Regt.	22/09/1916	22/09/1916
Miscellaneous	Orders For Clearing Up Of Mouquet Farm.	21/09/1916	21/09/1916
Heading	War Diary Of "G" Branch. 11th. Division. For October 1916. G.S. Vol 5		
War Diary	Donnet Post W.12.d.9.2	01/10/1916	01/10/1916
War Diary	Acheux.	01/10/1916	01/10/1916
War Diary	Berneville	02/10/1916	03/10/1916
War Diary	Domart-en-Ponthieu	04/10/1916	17/10/1916
War Diary	St Ouen.	18/10/1916	31/10/1916
Miscellaneous	Location Table showing position of units of 11th. Division at 6 a.m. day after date Return is rendered. Appendix "A"	05/10/1916	05/10/1916
Operation(al) Order(s)	11th Division Order No. 36 Appendix C	23/10/1916	23/10/1916
Miscellaneous	March Table To Accompany 11th Division Order No. 36		
Miscellaneous	Location Table showing Position of units of 11th Division at 6 a.m. day after date return is rendered. Appendix "D"	31/10/1916	31/10/1916
Heading	War Diary "G" Branch 11th Div. Vol 6		
Heading	War Diary General Staff. 11th Division. November 1916		
War Diary	St. Ouen	01/11/1916	10/11/1916
War Diary	Yvrench.	11/11/1916	13/11/1916
War Diary	Canaples.	14/11/1916	15/11/1916
War Diary	Conty	16/11/1916	16/11/1916
War Diary	Hedauville	17/11/1916	25/11/1916
War Diary	Hedauville and Q. 26.c.o.4	26/11/1916	26/11/1916
War Diary	Q. 26.c.0.4	27/11/1916	30/11/1916
Operation(al) Order(s)	11th Division Order No. 37 Appendix "A"	10/11/1916	10/11/1916
Miscellaneous	A Form. Messages And Signals		
Operation(al) Order(s)	11th. Division Order No. 38 Appendix "B"	12/11/1916	12/11/1916
Miscellaneous	March Table To Accompany 11th. Division Order No. 38		
Miscellaneous	Appendix "C" Location Table showing position of units Of 11th. Division At 6a.m. Day After date Return Is Rendered. 12th. November 1916	12/11/1916	12/11/1916
Operation(al) Order(s)	Appendix "D" 11th Division Order No. 39	13/11/1916	13/11/1916
Miscellaneous	March Table To Accompany 11th Division Order No. 39		
Miscellaneous	Reference Divisional Order No. 40	14/11/1916	14/11/1916
Operation(al) Order(s)	11th Division Order No. 40	14/11/1916	14/11/1916

Miscellaneous	March Table Of Accompany 11th Division Order No. 40		
Miscellaneous	Location Table showing probable disposition of units of 11th Division at 5 p.m. 14/11/16. Appendix "F"	14/11/1916	14/11/1916
Miscellaneous	Location Table showing disposition of troops of 11th. Division at 6 a.m. day after date return is rendered. Appendix G	15/11/1916	15/11/1916
Miscellaneous	Appendix "H" Location Table showing position of units Of 11th. Divn. At 6 A.m Day After Date Return Is Rendered Appendix "H"	17/11/1916	17/11/1916
Miscellaneous	Location Table showing position of units of 11th. Division at 6 a.m. day after date return is rendered. Appendix "I"	18/11/1916	18/11/1916
Operation(al) Order(s)	11th Division Order No. 4 Appendix "J"	19/11/1916	19/11/1916
Miscellaneous	March Table to accompany 11th Division Order No. 41		
Operation(al) Order(s)	11th Division Order No. 42 Appendix "K"	20/11/1916	20/11/1916
Miscellaneous	Table "A" Referred To In 11th Division Order No. 42		
Operation(al) Order(s)	11th Division Order No. 40. Appendix "L"	20/11/1916	20/11/1916
Miscellaneous	March Table Referred To In 11th Divl Order No. 43		
Operation(al) Order(s)	11th Division Order No. 44	25/11/1916	25/11/1916
Miscellaneous	March Table to accompany 11th Division Order No. 44		
Operation(al) Order(s)	11th Division Order No. 45 Appendix "N"	27/11/1916	27/11/1916
Miscellaneous	Table Referred To In 11th Divisional Order No. 45		
Miscellaneous	Appendix "O". 11 Corps.		
Map	France		
Miscellaneous	Glossary		
Heading	General Staff 11th Division December 1916		
Heading	War Diary General Staff. 11th Div. Vol 7		
War Diary	Q. 26.c.0.4	01/12/1916	24/12/1916
War Diary	W. 26.c.0.4	25/12/1916	31/12/1916
Heading	Summary. Casualties. Killed, Wounded, Missing.		
Operation(al) Order(s)	11th Division Order No. 46. Appendix "A"	07/12/1916	07/12/1916
Miscellaneous	March Table Referred To In 11th Division Order No. 46		
Miscellaneous	11th Div. No. G.S. 73 Appendix B	07/12/1916	07/12/1916
Miscellaneous	11th Division Provisional Defence Scheme. Appendix "C"	13/12/1916	13/12/1916
Miscellaneous	Operation Report For Week Ending 15th Decr. 1916 Appendix "D"	15/12/1916	15/12/1916
Operation(al) Order(s)	11th Division Order No. 47 Appendix E	15/12/1916	15/12/1916
Miscellaneous	11th. Division No. G.S. 377. Appendix E		
Miscellaneous	Appendix G. 32nd. Inf. Bde.	23/12/1916	23/12/1916
Miscellaneous	Relief Of 34th. Inf. Bde. By 32nd. Inf. Bde. Nights 24th/25th. And 25th/26th		
Miscellaneous	11th Division. Appendix H		
Map	France.		
Map	France		
Miscellaneous	Glossary.		
War Diary	Q. 26.c.0.4	01/12/1916	19/12/1916
War Diary	Marieux	20/12/1916	20/12/1916
War Diary	Marieux Bernaville	21/12/1916	21/12/1916
War Diary	Bernaville Yvrench	22/12/1916	22/12/1916
War Diary	Yvrench	23/12/1916	31/12/1916
Miscellaneous	11th Division No. G.S. 50	22/01/1917	22/01/1917
Operation(al) Order(s)	11th Division Order No. 56	18/01/1917	18/01/1917

Miscellaneous	Move Table "A" Issued With 11th Division Order No. 56		
Miscellaneous	Billetting Accommodation Area.		
Map	Divisional Area.		
Miscellaneous	Artillery Orders fellow later.		
Operation(al) Order(s)	11th Division Order No. 55	15/01/1917	15/01/1917
Operation(al) Order(s)	Reference 11th. Division Order No. 55	16/01/1917	16/01/1917
Miscellaneous	Following Amendments and Additions in March Tables Issued With 11th Division Order No. 54 of 14th January Are Published.	18/01/1917	18/01/1917
Operation(al) Order(s)	Provisional Amendments To 11th Division Order No. 54	16/01/1917	16/01/1917
Operation(al) Order(s)	11th. Division Order No. 54	15/01/1917	15/01/1917
Miscellaneous	Move Table "A" Issued With 11th D.O. No. 54		
Miscellaneous	11th. Division No G.S. 714	09/01/1917	09/01/1917
Operation(al) Order(s)	11th. Division Order No. 52	09/01/1917	09/01/1917
Miscellaneous	Heave Artillery Tasks. Appendix "A"		
Operation(al) Order(s)	11th. Division Order No. 51	08/01/1917	08/01/1917
Operation(al) Order(s)	11th Division Order No. 50	05/01/1917	05/01/1917
Heading	Defence Scheme		
Miscellaneous	11th. Division Defence Scheme. Index.		
Miscellaneous	Appendices.		
Miscellaneous	Headquarters.		
Miscellaneous	11th Division Defence Scheme January 1917	00/01/1917	00/01/1917
Miscellaneous	Chapter II. Instruction As The Action Of The Troops.		
Miscellaneous	Chapter III Action Of Corps Reserve.		
Miscellaneous	Chapter IV Administrative Arrangements.		
Miscellaneous	Appendix I. Boundaries Of Areas And Distributions Of Troops.		
Miscellaneous	Appendix II (A).		
Miscellaneous	Appendix II (B).		
Miscellaneous	Appendix II (C).		
Miscellaneous	Appendix II (D).		
Miscellaneous	Appendix II (E).		
Miscellaneous	Special Schnapps Barrage.		
Miscellaneous	Appendix III Supply Of R.E. Stores And Materials.		
Miscellaneous	Appendix IV. Standing Orders On Action To Be Taken During "Gas Alert" And During Hostile Gas Attacks.		
Miscellaneous	Appendix VI Liaison Between Infantry And Artillery.		
Heading	Dug-Outs. South of River Ancre and North of River Ancre Appendix V		
Miscellaneous	North Of River. Appendix 5		
Miscellaneous	Appendix V South Of River.		
Heading	G S 11 Divn January 1917		
Map	Trenches Corrected To 27-11-16		
Miscellaneous	Glossary.		
Map	First Edition		
Map	France.		
Miscellaneous	Glossary		
Map	France		
Miscellaneous	Glossary.		
Map	Trenches Corrected To 14-10-16		
Miscellaneous	Glossary.		
Map	France.		
Miscellaneous	Trench Map. France.		
Map	France.		

Miscellaneous	Glossary.		
Map	Bois D'Hollande		
Heading	War Diary 11th. Division "G" February 1917. Vol 9		
War Diary	Yvrench	01/02/1917	19/02/1917
War Diary	Yvrench Canaples.	20/02/1917	20/02/1917
War Diary	Canaples.	21/02/1917	22/02/1917
War Diary	Canaples Marieux	23/02/1917	23/02/1917
War Diary	Marieux	24/02/1917	28/02/1917
Operation(al) Order(s)	11th Division Order No. 57	13/02/1917	13/02/1917
Miscellaneous	Movement Table to accompany 11th Div. Order No. 57		
Operation(al) Order(s)	11th. Division Order No. 58	18/02/1917	18/02/1917
Miscellaneous	March Table To Accompany 11th. Division Order No. 58		
Miscellaneous	Proposed Location In Canaples Area.		
Miscellaneous	11th. Division No. G.S. 304	19/02/1917	19/02/1917
Miscellaneous	11th. Division Preliminary Entraining Order.	19/02/1917	19/02/1917
Miscellaneous	11th. Division Supplementary Entraining Order.	20/02/1917	20/02/1917
Miscellaneous	Programme Of Move Of 11th Division No. 1	19/02/1917	19/02/1917
Miscellaneous	Programme Of Move Of 11th Division No. 2	19/02/1917	19/02/1917
Miscellaneous	Table "D" 11th Division.		
Miscellaneous	11th. Division Location Table showing position of units At 6 a.m. day after date return is rendered.	20/02/1917	20/02/1917
Operation(al) Order(s)	11th Division Order No. 59	22/02/1917	22/02/1917
Miscellaneous	March Table To Accompany 11th Division Order No. 59		
Miscellaneous	Proposed Distribution Of Billets In New Area.		
Miscellaneous	11th. Division Location Table showing position of units At 6 a.m. day after date return is rendered.	23/02/1917	23/02/1917
Operation(al) Order(s)	11th. Division Order No. 60	24/02/1917	24/02/1917
Operation(al) Order(s)	March Table To Accompany 11th. Division Order No. 60		
Heading	War Diary. General Staff. 11th Division March 1917		
War Diary	Marieux.	01/03/1917	04/04/1917
Heading	War Diary. March, 1917. Appendix I Location Of Units.		
Miscellaneous	11th. Division Location Table showing position of units At 6 a.m. day after date return is rendered.	05/03/1917	05/03/1917
Miscellaneous	11th. Division Location Table showing position of units At 6 a.m. day after date return is rendered.	06/03/1917	06/03/1917
Miscellaneous	11th. Division Location Table showing position of units At 6 a.m. day after date return is rendered.	07/03/1917	07/03/1917
Miscellaneous	11th. Division Location Table showing position of units At 6 a.m. day after date return is rendered.	08/03/1917	08/03/1917
Miscellaneous	11th. Division Location Table showing position of units At 6 a.m. day after date return is rendered.	09/03/1917	09/03/1917
Miscellaneous	11th. Division Weekly Location Table showing position of units at 6 a.m. Sunday March 11th 1917	10/03/1917	10/03/1917
Miscellaneous	11th. Division Location Table showing position of units At 6 a.m. day after date return is rendered.	11/03/1917	11/03/1917
Miscellaneous	11th. Division Location Table showing position of units At 6 a.m. day after date return is rendered.	12/03/1917	12/03/1917
Miscellaneous	11th. Division Location Table showing position of units At 6 a.m. day after date return is rendered.	13/03/1917	13/03/1917
Miscellaneous	11th. Division Location Table showing position of units At 6 a.m. day after date return is rendered.	14/03/1917	14/03/1917

Type	Description	Date From	Date To
Miscellaneous	11th. Division Location Table showing position of units At 6 a.m. day after date return is rendered.	15/03/1917	15/03/1917
Miscellaneous	11th. Division Location Table showing position of units At 6 a.m. day after date return is rendered.	16/03/1917	16/03/1917
Miscellaneous	11th Division Weekly Location Table Showing Position of Units at 6 a.m. Sunday, 18th March, 1917	17/03/1917	17/03/1917
Miscellaneous	11th. Division Location Table showing position of units At 6 a.m. day after date return is rendered.	18/03/1917	18/03/1917
Miscellaneous	11th. Division Location Table showing position of units At 6 a.m. day after date return is rendered.	19/03/1917	19/03/1917
Miscellaneous	11th. Division Location Table showing position of units At 6 a.m. day after date return is rendered.	20/03/1917	20/03/1917
Miscellaneous	11th. Division Location Table showing position of units At 6 a.m. day after date return is rendered.	21/03/1917	21/03/1917
Miscellaneous	11th. Division Location Table showing position of units At 6 a.m. day after date return is rendered.	22/03/1917	22/03/1917
Miscellaneous	11th. Division Location Table showing position of units At 6 a.m. day after date return is rendered.	23/03/1917	23/03/1917
Miscellaneous	11th Division Weekly Location Table showing position of units At 6 a.m. Sunday 25th. March 1917	24/03/1917	24/03/1917
Miscellaneous	11th. Division Location Table showing position of units At 6 a.m. day after date return is rendered.	25/03/1917	25/03/1917
Miscellaneous	11th. Division Location Table showing position of units At 6 a.m. day after date return is rendered.	26/03/1917	26/03/1917
Miscellaneous	11th. Division Location Table showing position of units At 6 a.m. day after date return is rendered.	27/03/1917	27/03/1917
Miscellaneous	11th. Division Location Table showing position of units At 6 a.m. day after date return is rendered.	28/03/1917	28/03/1917
Miscellaneous	11th. Division Location Table showing position of units At 6 a.m. day after date return is rendered.	29/03/1917	29/03/1917
Miscellaneous	11th. Division Location Table showing position of units At 6 a.m. March 31st 1917	30/03/1917	30/03/1917
Miscellaneous	11th. Division Weekly Location Table showing position of units At 6 a.m. Sunday April 1st. 1917	31/03/1917	31/03/1917
Miscellaneous	Appendix 2 Headquarters, 11th. Division.	16/03/1917	16/03/1917
Operation(al) Order(s)	11th. Division Operation Order No. 61	22/03/1917	22/03/1917
Miscellaneous	March Table Showing Moves 24th March Issued With 11th Div Operation Order No 61		
Operation(al) Order(s)	11th Division Operation Order No. 62. Appendix IV.	24/03/1917	24/03/1917
Miscellaneous	62nd. Division "G" Appendix V	25/03/1917	25/03/1917
Heading	11th Division "G" War Diary April 1917 Vol. IX		
War Diary	Marieux	01/04/1917	11/04/1917
War Diary	Acheux.	12/04/1917	20/04/1917
War Diary	N. 11 Central Near Bapaume.	21/04/1917	30/04/1917
Heading	Divisional Instructions & Miscellaneous Appendix II		
Miscellaneous	11th Division Instruction No. 1. Appendix II	28/04/1917	28/04/1917
Miscellaneous	11th Division No. G.S. 946. Appendix II	23/04/1917	23/04/1917
Miscellaneous	11th Division Instructions No. 2 Appendix II	28/04/1917	28/04/1917
Heading	Defence Scheme (Provisional)		
Miscellaneous	Headquarters.		
Miscellaneous	11th Division. Defence Scheme (Provisional)	28/04/1917	28/04/1917
Miscellaneous	Appendix 1. Morchies - Beaumetz Line. Machine Gun Emplacements		
Miscellaneous	Dispositions of 11th Division. Appendix II		
Miscellaneous	Reserve Brigade Holding Beaumetz-Morchies Line.		
Miscellaneous	Appendix III. Supply Of R.E. Materials.		

Miscellaneous	Supply Of Ammunition Supplies Water And Ordnance Stores		
Miscellaneous	Medical Arrangements. Appendix V		
Heading	Operation Orders Appendix III		
Miscellaneous	A Form. Messages And Signals Appendix III		
Operation(al) Order(s)	11th. Division Order No. 64. Appendix III	18/04/1917	18/04/1917
Miscellaneous	March Table Issued With Operation Order No. 64 Dated 18/4/17		
Operation(al) Order(s)	11th. Division Order No. 65. Appendix III	19/04/1917	19/04/1917
Miscellaneous	March Table Issued With 11th Division Order No. 65 Dated 19/4/17		
Miscellaneous	Issued With 11th D.O. No. 65 Appendix I		
Miscellaneous	Appendix II Administrative Instructions. Issued With C.O No 65		
Operation(al) Order(s)	11th. Division Order No. 66 Appendix III	22/04/1917	22/04/1917
Miscellaneous	Table To Accompany 11th. Division Order No. 66		
Miscellaneous	Administrative Instruction No. 12	22/04/1917	22/04/1917
Operation(al) Order(s)	11th. Division Order No 67. Appendix III	25/04/1917	25/04/1917
Operation(al) Order(s)	11th Division Order No. 68. Appendix III	27/04/1917	27/04/1917
Operation(al) Order(s)	11th Division Order No. 69. Appendix III	29/04/1917	29/04/1917
Operation(al) Order(s)	11th Division Order No. 70 Appendix III	30/04/1917	30/04/1917
Map	France		
Miscellaneous	Glossary.		
Map			
Miscellaneous	Make for war diary.		

11TH DIVISION

GENERAL STAFF
JLY 1916 - APL 1917

FROM EGYPT

G.S. 11th Division

Mons Dean

July 1916
—
Sept 1917.

Army Form C. 2118.

WAR DIARY
or
INTELLIGENCE SUMMARY

JULY 1916.

Place	Date	Hour	Summary of Events and Information	Remarks and references to Appendices
At SEA.	1st		Calm and uneventful. Stayed SCIROCCA BAY, MALTA for 5 hours.	
do.	2nd.		Much cooler.	
do.	3rd.		Arrived off MARSEILLES. Tied up at Hangor 7 at 1400. Major General FANSHAWE, C.B. ordered to Command V Corps and proceed there. Troops either go straight to station or else to rest camp near.	
MARSEILLES.	4th.		Occupied in train journey to concentration area around St.POL. Lieut-General Sir Charles WOOLCOMBE, K.C.B. assumed Command of the Division.	
On train.	5th.		Do.	
do	6th.		Do.	
FLERS.	7th.	1600.	Divl. Hd.Qrs. arrived and billetted. Heavy rain. The Division joined the 6th Corps of the Third Army.	
do.	8th.		32nd Brigade concentrated round BLANGERMONT. Orders received for 32nd Brigade to move up and	

Army Form C. 2118.

WAR DIARY
or
INTELLIGENCE SUMMARY

(Erase heading not required.)

Instructions regarding War Diaries and Intelligence Summaries are contained in F.S. Regs., Part II. and the Staff Manual respectively. Title Pages will be prepared in manuscript.

Place	Date	Hour	Summary of Events and Information	Remarks and references to Appendices
FLERS.	8th contd.		take over eventually from 55th Division a portion of the trench line held by that Division. Party of officers and N.C.O's from 32nd Brigade sent up into trenches for instruction.	
do	9th.		32nd Brigade moved by march route to MAZIERES and vicinity. Two battalions 33rd Brigade arrived and billetted about BUNEVILLE.	
do	10th.		32nd Brigade moved by march route to vicinity of DUISANS, coming under orders and administration of 55th Division from to-day inclusive. 33rd Brigade H.Qrs. arrived at St.POL.	
do	11th.		NIL.	
do	12th.		"F" Sector reconnoitred by Divisional General and G.O.C. 33rd Brigade.	
do	13th.		Divl. Signal Section arrived. 34th Bde. Hd.Qrs. arrived at St.POL.	
do	14th.		6th E. Yorks arrived, billetted at HAUTE COTE and BLANGERMONT. Orders received for 32nd Brigade less 1 Battalion and working party to move to BERNEVILLE and vicinity. 33rd Brigade to DUISANS and vicinity and Divl. Hd.Qrs. to LE GAUROY.	

2449 Wt. W14957/Mg0 750,000 1/16 J.B.C. & A. Forms/C.2118/12.

Army Form C. 2118.

Instructions regarding War Diaries and Intelligence
Summaries are contained in F. S. Regs., Part II.
and the Staff Manual respectively. Title Pages
will be prepared in manuscript.

WAR DIARY
or
INTELLIGENCE SUMMARY

(Erase heading not required.)

Place	Date	Hour	Summary of Events and Information	Remarks and references to Appendices
FLERS. LE GAUROY.	15th.		Divisional Report Centre closed at FLERS at 3 p.m. and reopened at LE CAUROY at same hour. 32nd and 33rd Brigades moved as indicated above.	
LE CAUROY. DUISANS.	16th.		Divisional Report Centre closed at LE CAUROY at 3 p.m. and reopened at DUISANS at same hour. 33rd Bde. Hd.Qrs. to BERNEVILLE. 32nd Bde. Hd.Qrs. to DAINVILLE. 32nd Brigade commenced relieving 166th Brigade in "G" Sector to-night.	
DUISANS.	17th.		Light Trench Mortar Batteries 33rd and 34th Infty. Bdes., Medium Trench Mortar Batteries 58th, 59th, and 60th F.A. Bdes to T.M. School for instruction. Relief of 166th Bde. by 32nd Bde. in "G" Sector completed during the night. 34th Brigade sent parties of officers and N.C.O's to reconnoitre "F" Sector.	
do	18th.		Head Quarters and 3 Battalions of 34th Inf. Bde. moved from GRAND ROOLECOURT and SOMBRIN to BEAUMETZ and SIMENCOURT. Bde. M.G. Coy. moved to SIMENCOURT. Divl. Train marched to billets W. of MOYELLETTE.	
do.	19th.		34th Inf. Bde. commenced to relieve the 165th Inf. Bde. in "F" Sector trenches. Divisional Artly commenced to relieve the 55th Divl. Artly. One section per Battery R.F.A. being completed at a time.	
do	20th.		Relief of the 165th Inf. Bde. by the 34th Inf. Bde. completed. Situation normal on our front.	

Army Form C. 2118.

WAR DIARY
or
INTELLIGENCE SUMMARY

(Erase heading not required.)

Instructions regarding War Diaries and Intelligence Summaries are contained in F.S. Regs., Part II. and the Staff Manual respectively. Title Pages will be prepared in manuscript.

Place	Date	Hour	Summary of Events and Information	Remarks and references to Appendices
DUISANS	21st.		The 33rd. Inf. Bde. commenced to relieve the 42nd. Inf. Bde. in H.Sector trenches. The 11th.Divn. Artillery commenced relieving the 14th.Divnl. Artillery in H.Sector area. The day was quiet on our front. G.O.C. assumed command of the line at 10a.m.	O.O.No.17 d/19.7.16. attached.
do.	22nd.		Quiet day on our front.	
do.	23rd.		The 33rd. Inf. Bde. completed the relief of the 42nd.Bde. by 1.55.a.m. The Division now holds F.G.&H.Sectors of the line with the 46th. Divn. on our right and the 14th. Divn. on our left. About 10 p.m. the enemy bombarded a portion of the 14th. Divn. front and attempted to raid front trenches in I.Sector, but were repulsed by Infantry fire. Some of G.Sector trenches were bombarded with Gas Shells which caused an alarm of Gas to be given, which proved to be false. By 11.30 all normal again along our front.	
do.	24th.		Quiet day on Divnl. front. Enemy artillery Artillery & trench mortars showed activity. Weather fine but overcast.	
do.	25th.		Situation normal. Z.11. medium T.M. Batty. and 34th. Inf. Bde. light T.M.Batty. returned from training at the Third Army School.	,, ,, ,, ,,
do.	26th.		Situation normal. Enemy shelled portions of F.& G. Sectors with 5·9 shell between 11a.m. and 12.30p.m. Our Artillery retaliated with good effect.	,, ,, ,, ,,
do.	27th.		Situation normal. Fine with N.N.E. breeze. On the night 27th./28th. the 9th. Lancashire Fusiliers 9th Bn. Notts.& Derby, 4 machine Guns from No.18 Machine Gun Batty., 2 M.Guns from 33rd. Inf. Bde. all under the command of Lt.Col. E.C.DA COSTA, 9th. Lancashire Fus. relieved the 42nd. Inf. Bde. 14th. Divn. in I. Sector. Relief was completed by 4.30.a.m. when G.O.C. Divn. assumed command of the Sector. The Divn now holds "F.G.H.& I" Sectors of 6th. Corps front.	O.O.No.18 d/25.7.16. attached. ,, ,,

Army Form C. 2118.

WAR DIARY
or
INTELLIGENCE SUMMARY

(Erase heading not required.)

Instructions regarding War Diaries and Intelligence Summaries are contained in F. S. Regs., Part II. and the Staff Manual respectively. Title Pages will be prepared in manuscript.

Place	Date	Hour	Summary of Events and Information	Remarks and references to Appendices
DUISANS	28th.		Situation normal. Fine day. Wind N.N.E.	
do	29th.		Quiet day. Fine with N. wind.	
Warlus.	30th.	10am 3-4p.m.	Divl. Hd.Qrs. moved to WARLUS. Situation normal. Fine day with Northerly breeze. Enemy trench mortars shelled "H" Sector. Our trench mortars retaliated and silenced the enemy mortars.	
do.	31st.		Artillery of both sides inactive. Enemy trench mortars fired into "H" Sector, but ceased when our trench mortars retaliated. About 2 a.m. a German patrol of about 10 men attacked one of our listening posts in "I" Sector, and enemy were driven off by our rifle fire. Fine day. Wind N.N.W.	

CASUALTIES.

	Killed.		Wounded.		Missing.	
	O.	O.R.	O.	O.R.	O.	O.R.
20th July.	1.	2.	1.	12.		
21st "	–	3.	–	12.		
22nd "	–	2	2	14		
23rd "	–	–	–	4		
24th "	–	1	2	7		
25th "	–	2	–	9		
26th "	–	4	1	16		
27th "	–	1	1	3		
28th "	–	–	1	4		
29th "	–	–	1	9		
30th "	–	3	–	9		
31st "	–	4.	1	10		
Total.	1.	21.	8.	109.	NIL	

Army Form C. 2118.

WAR DIARY
or
INTELLIGENCE SUMMARY
(Erase heading not required.)

Instructions regarding War Diaries and Intelligence Summaries are contained in F. S. Regs., Part II and the Staff Manual respectively. Title Pages will be prepared in manuscript.

Place	Date	Hour	Summary of Events and Information	Remarks and references to Appendices
WARLUS.	31st.	6p.m.	SUMMARY FOR JULY 1916.	

1. The Division arrived at MARSEILLES on the 3rd. July from EGYPT and proceeded by rail to a concentration area about ST.POL. being allotted to the 6th. Corps of the Third Army.

2. On the night of the 16th/17th. July the 32nd. Inf Bde. completed the relief of the 166th. Inf.Bde. of the 55th. Divn. in G.Sector 6th. Corps front.

3. On the night of the 19th/20th. July the 34th. Inf. Bde. completed the relief of the 165th. Inf. Bde. 55th. Divn. in F. Sector.

4. On the night of the 22nd/23rd. July the 33rd. Inf. Bde completed the relief of the 42nd. Inf Bde 14th. Divn. In H.Sector.

5. On the night of the 21st./22nd. July the 11th. Divn Artillery completed the relief of the 55th. Divl. Artillery in F.& G.Sector and of the 14th. Divl. Artillery in H.Sector.

6. On the night 27th./28th. July the 9th. Lanc. Fus.,9th. Notts. & Derby, 4 M.Guns,(all under the command of Lt.Col. E.C.Da Costa 9th.Lanc.Fus) of No.18 Machine Batty. relieved 43rd. I.B. in I.Sector as a tempory measure.

7. The Division is now holding "F.G.H.& I" Sectors with one attached Group of the 14th.Divnl. Artillery covering I.Sector. The line held lies to the South & East of ARRAS. The Divisional defences consist of:—

(a) Front line.
(b) Support line.
(c) Line of defended villages and localities.

WAR DIARY
or
INTELLIGENCE SUMMARY

(Erase heading not required.)

Summary of Events and Information

SUMMARY Continued:-

All the above lines are protected by barbed wire entanglements. They are in fair repair, but there is a good deal of work to be done in the line and working parties are busy nightly.

8. **Policy of the Division.**

Although on the defensive the Units of the Division were offensive in their action during the month, our patrols and snipers were active, and our Artillery and Trench Mortars retaliated vigorously whenever necessary.

9. **Attitude of the Enemy.**

The enemy has been very inactive along our front during the month, he used his Artillery very little, his Trench Mortars were slightly more active. Enemy patrols reconnoitred our trenches on several occassions, but attempted no raids.

H.Q. 11th. Division
31st. July, 1916.

[signature]
Lieut. General.
Com'g. 11th. Division.

SECRET   Copy No. 13

Reference Map Sheet 51c 1/40,000

11th Division Operation Order No.17.

19th July 1916.

1. The 11th Division will continue the relief of the 55th Division in the line.

2. (a) The Infantry relief and the relief of one section a battery of R.F.A. will be completed by the morning of the 21st July.
The completion of the infantry relief and other moves in connection with the relief will be carried out in accordance with the attached table - details being arrangd in the case of infantry between the Brigadiers concerned.

   (b) The relief of the remainder of the artillery will be completed by the morning of 22nd July - details being arranged between the two Brigadiers Generals C.R.A.

3. The Command of the line will pass to the 11th Division at 10 a.m. on 21st.
The Brigadier General C.R.A. - Brigade and Battery Commanders 55th Division will retain Command until completion of the artillery relief - on the morning of the 22nd.

4. The 55th Division will for the present leave in action two batteries of trench mortars.

5. Completion of all reliefs will be reported to 11th Divl. H.Q.

Issued at 9 a.m.

Major.
G.S. 11th Div.

Copy No. 1.   VI Corps.
        2.   55th Divn.
        3.   46th Divn.
        4.   32nd Inf. Bde.
        5.   33rd Inf. Bde.
        6.   34th Inf. Bde.
        7.   Divl. Art.
        8.   Divl. Eng.
        9.   A.A. & Q.M.G.
       10.   Signals.
       11.   A.D.M.S.
       12.   A.P.M.
       13.   War Diary.
       14.   G.S.
       15.   File.
       16.   G.O.C.
       17.   Train

SECRET.

Reference Map
Sheet 51.c. 1/40,000.

Movement Table issued with 11th Division Operation Order No. 17.

Date.	Unit.	From	To.	Remarks.
19th July.	1 Battn. 34th Inf. Bde.	GRANDRULLECOURT	GOUY exchanging stations with one Battn. 166th Inf. Bde.	
From 19th July to be completed by 6 a.m. 21st July.	34th Inf. Bde.	BEAUMETZ and SIMENCOURT	"F" Sector in the line exchanging positions with the H.Q., M.G.Co. and 3 Battns. 165th Inf. Bde.	
	1. Battn. 34th Inf. Bde.	GOUY.	BRETENCOURT relieving 1 Battn. 165th Inf. Bde. attached 165th Inf. Bde.	

Reference 1/10000 Sheet 51.B, S.W.1.
1/40000 Sheet 51 B & C.

SECRET.

Copy No. 17

11th Division Operation Order No. 18.

1. The 14th Division, less Artillery, is being withdrawn from the line.

2. The 14th Division, less Artillery, will be relieved by the 11th Division in "I" Sector, and by the 21st Division in "J" and "K" Sectors

3. The 9th Bn. Lancashire Fusiliers.) under the Command of
   9th Bn. Notts & Derby Regt.) Lieut. Colonel E. C. Da COSTA,
   4 Motor Machine Guns.) 9th Bn. Lancashire Fusiliers
   will relieve the 42nd Inf. Bde. in "I" Sector by the night of the 27th/28th July under arrangements to be made direct between Commanders concerned. The troops mentioned above will remain under the tactical command of Lt. Col. Da COSTA and will be under the B.G.C. 33rd Inf. Bde. for administrative purposes.

4. On completion of relief G.O.C. 11th Division will assume command of "I" Sector including the Artillery Group, 14th Division covering that Sector.

5. All trench maps, defence schemes, log books and Intelligence reports will be taken over by relieving Units from out-going Units.

6. Completion of all reliefs will be reported to D.H.Q.

Issued at 4 p.m.

Major.
G.S. 11th Div.

Copy No. 1. 6th Corps.
2. 14th Div.
3. 21st Div.
4. 46th Div.
5. G.O.C.
6. G.S.O.1.
7. A.A. & Q.M.G.
8. G.O.C. R.A.
9. C.R.E.
10. 32nd Inf. Bde.
11. 33rd Inf. Bde.
12. 34th Inf. Bde.
13. Signal Co.
14. A.D.M.S.
15. Train.
16. Lt. Col. Da Costa.
17. War Diary.
18. Office.

Army Form W. 3091.

Cover for Documents.

Nature of Enclosures.

Congress

G Branch

XIth DIV

Notes, or Letters written.

Army Form C. 2118

WAR DIARY
or
INTELLIGENCE SUMMARY

(Erase heading not required.)

11th. DIVISION "G".

AUGUST 1916.

Instructions regarding War Diaries and Intelligence Summaries are contained in F. S. Regs., Part II. and the Staff Manual respectively. Title Pages will be prepared in manuscript.

Place	Date	Hour	Summary of Events and Information	Remarks and references to Appendices
WARLUS.	1st.		A quiet day, fine with N.N.E. wind. Situation normal with rather less enemy artillery fire. Gas alert was put on in Divisional Area at 10 a.m.	
"	2nd.	3 a.m. to 5 a.m.	Enemy active with trench mortars, rifle grenades and M.Gs. against "G" Sector trenches. Our artillery replied with success.	
		2 p.m. to 3 p.m.	Enemy fired 50 rounds 105 M.M. shells into "I" Sector. Our artillery replied.	
			A quiet day generally. Fine with N.E. breeze. Enemy aircraft were rather more active than usual.	
"	3rd.		An exceptionally quiet day, enemy showing distinctly less activity. The aircraft of both sides were active. A hostile aeroplane dropped several bombs on ARRAS, one bomb causing 9 casualties. Fine day with N.W. wind. " Gas Alert ", was taken off at 10 a.m.	
"	4th.	7.15 a.m.	Enemy blew a Camouflet opposite our gallery in trench "H" 33. No damage was done to our gallery.	
		12 noon.	The Kite Balloon W. of DAINVILLE was brought down by enemy shell fire. Both occupants descended safely by parachute.	
		7 p.m.	Twelve shells were fired into and about GOUY causing very slight damage.	
			A quiet day generally with increased enemy artillery activity against the back areas. Fine day with N.W. wind.	
"	5th.		Enemy artillery was rather more active against "F" Sector. Enemy artillery, trench mortars and rifle grenades were active against "H" trenches but little material damage was done and the casualties were slight.	
		4 a.m.	A soldier of the 3rd. Company 1st Battalion, Bavarian Reserve Infantry Regiment was shot near our wire opposite "G" Sector. The body was brought in and buried. Enemy were more active during the day than usual probably as a reply to the fire of our artillery and trench mortars. Fine day with N.W. wind.	

Army Form C. 2118

WAR DIARY
or
INTELLIGENCE SUMMARY
(Erase heading not required.)

11th. DIVISION "G".

AUGUST, 1916.

Instructions regarding War Diaries and Intelligence Summaries are contained in F.S. Regs., Part II. and the Staff Manual respectively. Title Pages will be prepared in manuscript.

Place	Date	Hour	Summary of Events and Information	Remarks and references to Appendices
WARLUS.	6th.		A quiet day. Divisional artillery fired on several targets during the day. Fine day with N.W. wind.	
		6 pm.	The 1st. Class of 26 Officers and 26 N.C.O's from Infantry Battalions of the Division assembled at the Divisional School of Instruction GOUY EN ARTOIS. Classes of Instruction in Bayonet Fighting and precautions against enemy poison gas are also being held.	
"	7th.	7 am.	Eight 5.9 shells fell about GOUY without causing any damage.	
		1.15 pm.	Seventeen 5.9 shells fell about GOUY doing very slight damage. A quiet day with a slight increase in the number of rifle grenades fired into "F" Sector. Our artillery, trench mortars and snipers were active, Latter had few targets. Fine day with N.W. breeze.	
"	8th.		Enemy artillery was more active during the day along our front, ACHICOURT and GOUY both being shelled with 5.9 shells. Our artillery and trench mortars were also active against various parts of the enemy lines. On night 7/8th. August the 6th. S.Staffords in Right Sub-sector trenches of "H" Sector. Border Regiment relieved the 7th. S.Staffords in Right Sub-sector	
		10. am	Wind changed to N.E. and "Gas Alert" was ordered in Divisional Area. Fine day.	
"	9th.		A quiet day. Enemy trench mortars were active in "G" and "H" Sectors, probably as a retaliation for the use of our own. Fine day with N.N.W. wind.	
		4 pm	"Gas Alert" cancelled.	
		11.45 pm.	A fighting patrol of the 6th. Lincolns consisting of 1 Officer and 20 O.R. and 10 bombers was sent out to attack a sap-head at point M.5a.9.8. with the object of clearing out the enemy there and to obtain an identification. On arriving close to the sap the party of 4 Germans was seen out mending the wire protecting the sap. An attempt to surround and capture the enemy failed but the patrol killed two, badly wounded another, while the fourth crawled away with a wounded leg. The patrol brought back the bodies of two men to our trenches and the marks of identification from the wounded man. The Germans belonged to the 27th. Infantry Regiment 7th. Division. 4th. Corps which relieved the 5th. Bavarian Division probably on 7th. August last in the enemy line opposite our front. The identification obtained a valuable one. Our patrol had no casualties.	

Instructions regarding War Diaries and Intelligence Summaries are contained in F.S. Regs., Part II. and the Staff Manual respectively. Title Pages will be prepared in manuscript.

Army Form C. 2118

WAR DIARY
or
INTELLIGENCE SUMMARY
(Erase heading not required.)

11th. DIVISION "G".

AUGUST 1916.

Place	Date	Hour	Summary of Events and Information	Remarks and references to Appendices
WARLUS.	10th.		Quiet day. Enemy artillery was inactive, his trench mortars only fired as a retaliation for the fire of our mortars. The enemy is working hard in his saps and front line trenches, his work is hampered daily by the fire of our trench mortars and machine guns.	
		6.30 to 7 pm	A concentrated bombardment by the Divisional Artillery, one 6 inch Howitzer Battery, Medium and Light Trench Mortars was carried out on enemy trenches and support trenches about M.15c & d and M.4d. Our machine guns also assisted. Our fire appeared accurate and effective. The enemy retaliation was very feeble causing very few casualties and little material damage. The remainder of the day and night passed quietly. Rained in the morning from 8 am. to 11 am. afterwards fine.	
"	11th.		A very quiet day. Enemy artillery and trench mortars were inactive, probably as a result of our bombardment of the afternoon of the 10th. Night patrols were hampered by a thick mist which descended about 1.30 am. A Patrol of 1 Sergeant and 3 O.R. under Lieut. Holloway,9th. West Yorks lost their way and entered the German trenches. Lieut. Holloway was captured, the Sergeant is still missing and the 2 men returned to our lines at midnight having gone out at 1 a.m. on the 10th. inst. On the night of 11/12th. patrols were out along the whole Divisional Front but no enemy were seen outside his wire. Fine day with light N.W. wind.	
"	12th.		Situation quiet. Our patrols were active at night but encountered no enemy patrols. Enemy artillery and trench mortars were much less active than usual. There was an increase in the number of fish tail bombs fired by enemy and a decrease in the number of their rifle grenades. Fine day, wind N.W. changed to N.E. at 10 a.m. when "Gas Alert" was put on.	
"	13th.		Situation quiet. Our patrols were active at night.	
		4.5am.	A party of 6 Germans supported by M.G. fire and rifle grenades tried to approach and bomb our trench at M.15a. They were easily repulsed without doing any damage.	
		2.6pm.	Enemy fired about twenty 150 M.M. shells into ARRAS setting a house on fire near the HOTEL DE VILLE.	
		2 pm.	Our Medium Trench Mortars fired with good effect on enemy sap at R.29b.9.5. The enemy is still working hard strengthening his wire and his front line trenches generally. Fine day. Wind N.W. "Gas Alert" taken off 11 a.m.	

Army Form C. 2118

WAR DIARY
or
INTELLIGENCE SUMMARY

(Erase heading not required.)

11th. DIVISION.

AUGUST 1916.

Instructions regarding War Diaries and Intelligence Summaries are contained in F.S. Regs., Part II. and the Staff Manual respectively. Title Pages will be prepared in manuscript.

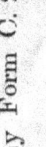

Place	Date	Hour	Summary of Events and Information	Remarks and references to Appendices
WARLUS.	14th.		With the exception of the intermittent of shelling of ARRAS with 150 M.M. and 77 M.M. shells, the enemy artillery was inactive. A number of shells fired during past 24 hours by the enemy were blinds. Our medium and Stokes T.Ms. were active, also our snipers and patrols. Fine day, Wind S.W..	
"	15th.		Situation quiet with exception of intermittent shelling of ARRAS and some enemy trench mortar activity against "H" Sector Trenches. On night 14/15th. a raiding party of 1 Officer and 16 O.R. 6th. Border Regiment attempted to raid an enemy's sap about M.4d. 9.5 and to blow up a M.G. emplacement. Owing to the the bright moonlight and the fact that a strong enemy wiring party was encountered the enterprise was abandoned after a bomb-fight. Our casualties were NIL.	O.O.No.18 for relief of the Division by 12th. and 21st. Divisions issued.
		5/5.30 pm.	59th. Group D.A. Medium and Light T.M.s. carried out a concentrated bombardment on enemy defences at BEAURAINS with the particular object of destroying the T.M. positions there. Enemy trenches were seen to be damaged and opposite "H" 2 his wire was cut. Enemy retaliation was feeble and his heavy T.Ms fired less than usual and no material damage or casualties occurred in our line. Showery day, cool with squally S.W. wind.	Appendix "A".
"	16th.	10/10.30 pm.	Some desultory shelling of our trenches by hostile artillery and trench mortars, little damage done. An organised bombardment of the enemy front and support trenches in M.14d. and M.20b. was carried out by the Divisional Artillery, Medium and Light T.Ms. The enemy's reply was feeble. Three bombs were dropped by a hostile aeroplane on the extreme left of "I" Sector about 6 p.m. but no damage was done. Fine day N.W. wind.	

WAR DIARY 11th. DIVISION.

or

INTELLIGENCE SUMMARY AUGUST 1916.

(Erase heading not required.)

Army Form C. 2118

Instructions regarding War Diaries and Intelligence Summaries are contained in F.S. Regs., Part II. and the Staff Manual respectively. Title Pages will be prepared in manuscript.

Place	Date	Hour	Summary of Events and Information	Remarks and references to Appendices
WARLUS.	17th.	3 pm and 6 pm 7 pm to 7.20 pm. 9.15 pm.	Situation normal. Enemy's trench mortars and artillery inactive. 58th. Group D.A. and Medium T.Ms. carried out a concentrated bombardment of enemy's saps and trenches in M.20a and also on the wire entanglements there. The wire in front of "B" sap was reported to have been cut by our fire. 60th. Group D.A., Medium and Light T.Ms carried out a concentrated bombardment on enemy trenches and wire in areas in R.30a, M.19d., and M.25b. Our fire appeared effective. Two raiding parties of the 6th. Yorks & Lancs. Regt. attempted to enter enemy's saps in M.20a but found the wire insufficiently cut for penetration. Parties withdrew after a bomb-fight with slight casualties. One patrol brought back alive and unwounded a Sergeant of the 9th. West Yorks who had been missing from a patrol sent out on the 11th. inst. Showery day wind S.W.	
	18th.	6 am. 10 am.	Enemy artillery and trench mortars showed little activity, about 15 150 M.M. shells were fired into ACHICOURT doing little damage a few trench mortar bombs fell in "G" Sector trenches. Our Stokes Mortars bombarded sap"C" M.20a. 80 bombs were fired with apparent effect. Our Medium T.Ms. fired on wire surrounding enemy saps in M.30a. and cut gaps in it. Our patrols were out along the front and again reported the complete absence of hostile patrols. The 9th. Lancashire Fusiliers, 9th. Notts and Derbys and 4 guns, 18th. M.G. Service were relieved in "I" Sector by the 62nd. Infantry Brigade, 21st Division by 8.30 p.m. Showery day, wind S.W.	
"	19th.		Enemy artillery and trench mortars generally inactive. The right of "H" Sector was intermittently shelled during the afternoon with a variety of shells and trench mortar bombs, causing some damage to our trenches. During the night of 19/20th. a party of 2 Officers and 16 O.R. of the 8th.Northd. Fusiliers raided an enemy sap at R. 29b. 9.5. Part penetrated about 50 yards down the sap and after a brief bomb-fight captured a wounded prisoner whom they brought back to our lines. The party suffered no casualties. The prisoner was a L/Cpl. of the 78th.Landwehr Regiment, attached to 111th. Division. Showery day, wind S.W.	

Army Form C. 2118

WAR DIARY
or
INTELLIGENCE SUMMARY
(Erase heading not required.)

11th. DIVISION "G"   AUGUST 1916.

Instructions regarding War Diaries and Intelligence Summaries are contained in F.S. Regs., Part II. and the Staff Manual respectively. Title Pages will be prepared in manuscript.

Place	Date	Hour	Summary of Events and Information	Remarks and references to Appendices
WARLUS.	20th.	10 am	Situation generally quiet. The 60th. Group D.A. and Medium and Light T.Ms bombarded the enemy's front lines and sap-heads in R.29b and R.29d. Enemy defences were considerably damaged and his wire was cut in places. Enemy retaliated by firing about 100 105 M.M. and 77 M.M. shells into out trenches, little damage occurred. Between 12.45 p.m. and 1.15 p.m. enemy fired 12 77 M.M. shells into ACHICOURT and HAVANNAH. Eight of these shells were "duds". The 32nd. Bde. was relieved in "G" Sector during the night of 20/21st. by the 36th. Infantry Brigade 12th. Division without incident. Fine day, wind S.W.	Divnl. Defence Scheme issued. Appendix "B"
"	21st	11 am to 11.30 am	Enemy showed little activity beyond shelling our front system of trenches East of ACHICOURT and RONVILLE during the day. Only slight damage was done. 59th. Group Howitzers and Medium T.Ms bombarded the enemy's O.P. and suspected Field Gun positions in the house at M.10d. 8.3. with good effect. Fine day, wind N.W. The 34th. Infantry Bde. was relieved in "F" Sector by the 37th. Inf. Bde. Relief was carried out by day and was completed by 4 p.m. On the night of the 21/22nd. the 33rd. Inf. Bde. was relieved in "H" Sector by the 35th. Inf. Bde.	
LE CAUROY.	22nd.	10 am	Command of "F", "G" and "H" Sectors was handed over to the G.O.C. 12th. Division and D.H.Q. moved to LE CAUROY. The moves and distribution of the Division are given in the attached D.O. No. 18 d/15/8/16. Fine day, Wind West.	
"	23rd.		The relief of the Divisional Artillery by the Artillery of the 12th. Division commenced on the night of the 22/23rd.	
"	24th		The relief of the Divisional Artillery by the Artillery of the 12th. Division was completed by 6 am. Divisional Artillery moved to LIENCOURT Area with Headquarters at LIENCOURT.	

Army Form C. 2118

WAR DIARY
or
INTELLIGENCE SUMMARY

(Erase heading not required.)

11th. DIVISION "G"   AUGUST 1916.

Instructions regarding War Diaries and Intelligence Summaries are contained in F.S. Regs., Part II. and the Staff Manual respectively. Title Pages will be prepared in manuscript.

Place	Date	Hour	Summary of Events and Information	Remarks and references to Appendices
LE CAUROY	25th		The Infantry Brigades commenced a Course of Training in a training area about AMBRINES-AVESNES-LE-COMTE-GRANDRULLECOURT (Sheet 51c 1/40,000 map). The relief of the 6th. E. Yorks (Pioneers) and the Field Comapnies R.E. in the line by similar units of the 12th. Division commenced. Fine day with N.W. wind.	Training programme Appendix "D"
"	26th		The relief of the Pioneer Battalion and the Field Companies R.E. in the line by similar units of the 12th. Division was completed by 6 am. Pioneer Battalion moved to AMBRINES and the Field Companies R.E. moved to DENIER and SARS-LES-BOIS. The 21 day Course at the Divisional School of Instruction finished. 26 Officers and 26 N.C.O's attended the Course and derived considerable benefit from it.	Appendix "C" Programme of Instruction at the Divnl School.
		6 pm	The Chemical Adviser Third Army, gave a demonstration with a captured German Flammenwerfer Machine to the 33rd. Inf. Bde. and 100 men per Battalion of the 34th. Inf. Bde. Showery day with W.wind.	
"	27th	10 pm	No change in the dispositions of the Division. Orders were received from the Third Army that the Division (less Artillery) would be transferred to the Reserve Army on the 3rd.September. The Divisional Artillery will march direct to V Corps area on 28th. inst. Showery day with W.Wind.	
"	28th	8.15 am.	The Divisional Artillery and H.Q. Coy. Train marched from LIENCOURT area to join the 5th. Corps of the Reserve Army in area BUS_LES-ARTOIS-COUIN. The Medium T.M. Batteries were conveyed to same area in lorries. The training of units was interfered with in the morning by heavy rain but was continued in the afternoon when the weather improved. Wind S.W.	

Army Form C. 2118

WAR DIARY
or
INTELLIGENCE SUMMARY
(Erase heading not required.)

11th DIVISION "G"

AUGUST 1916.

Instructions regarding War Diaries and Intelligence Summaries are contained in F.S. Regs., Part II and the Staff Manual respectively. Title Pages will be prepared in manuscript.

Place	Date	Hour	Summary of Events and Information	Remarks and references to Appendices
LE CAUROY.	29th	10am	The 33rd. Infantry Brigade Group moved by march route from billets in GOUY and FOSSEUX area to billets in the area about LIENCOURT-BERLENCOURT-ETREE WAMIN-HOUVIGNEUL. Brigade Headquarters were established at LIENCOURT.	
		3.30 pm.	Heavy thunderstorm broke over the Divisional area and the rain continued for the remainder of the day. Wind S.W.	
"	30th	9.30 am	The 34th. Infantry Brigade Group moved by march route from billets in SOMBRIN and GRAND ROLLE-COURT to billets in the area about BOUVIN HOUVIGNEUL, MAGNICOURT GOUY EN TERNOIS. Brigade Headquarters moved to HOUVIN HOUVIGNEUL. Very wet day. Wind S.W.	O.O. No. 19 of 30/8/16. Appendix "E"
"	31st	10.30 am	The 6th. E.Yorks (Pioneers) moved by march route from AMBRINES to GROUCHES. Fine day. Wind. W. Training continued.	

WAR DIARY
or
INTELLIGENCE SUMMARY
(Erase heading not required.)

11th. DIVISION "G"   Army Form C. 2118

AUGUST 1916.

Place	Date	Hour	Summary of Events and Information	Remarks and references to Appendices
			SUMMARY FOR AUGUST 1916.	

The Division continued to hold "F","G""H" and "I" Sectors of VIth. Corps Front, E. and S.E. of ARRAS.

Normal trench warfare conditions obtained, the enemy artillery and trench mortars were generally inactive unless provoked into retaliation by the organised bombardments of our Divisional Artillery and Trench Mortars.

Our patrols were active nightly having but encountered no enemy patrols, the enemy seldom venturing outside his own wire.

2. Infantry raiding parties carried out raids on the German trenches on several occasions. On the night of the 9/10th August a raiding party of 1 Officer and 10 O.R. of the 6th. Lincolns was sucessful in obtaining an important identification by killing two and capturing three Germans. On the night of the 19/20th. the 8th. Northd. Fusiliers raided an enemy sap and captured a wounded prisoner.

3. The action of the Divisional Artillery and Medium Trench Mortars was generally confined to organised concentrated bombardments on selected portions of the enemy defences. This system was found to be much more effective than the previuos system of allowing the artillery to expend its allowance of ammunition in small isolated shoots, generally by request of the Infantry as "retaliation" for enemy fire.

4. Strong working parties were continuously at work improving the fire trenches and C.Ts and in strengthening the wire.

5. On the night of the 18/19th. August the troops in "I" Sector were relieved by the 62nd. Infantry Brigade, 21st Division.
By 6 a.m. on the 22nd. the Infantry Brigades of the Division were relieved in the line by the Infantry Brigades of the 12th. Division.
By 6 a.m. on the 24th. the Divisional Artillery was relieved by the Artillery of the 12th. Division.
By 6 a.m. on the 26th. the Field Companies R.E. and Pioneer Battalion were relieved by similar units of the 12th. Division.

Army Form C. 2118

WAR DIARY
or
INTELLIGENCE SUMMARY
(Erase heading not required.)

11th. DIVISION "G"

AUGUST 1916.

Place	Date	Hour	Summary of Events and Information	Remarks and references to Appendices
			SUMMARY FOR AUGUST 1916. continued.	
			6. On relief by the 12th. Division the Division moved in billets about AVESNES le COMTE training area and carried out training from the 25th. August to date.	
			7. The total casualties in the Division during the month were :-	
			KILLED. WOUNDED. MISSING.	
			O. O.R. O. O.R. O. O.R.	
			2 24 9 110 1 4	
			8. The following APPENDICES are attached:-	
			Appendix "A". O.O. No. 18. Relief of Division by 12th. and 21st.Divisions.	
			" "B". Divisional Defence Scheme and Maps.	
			" "C". 11th. Divisional School of Instruction, Standing Orders and Training Programme.	
			" "D". 11th. Division Training Programme, August 25th. to Sept.2nd. 1916.	
			" "E". O.O. No. 19. Move to Reserve Army.	
	31st. August 1916.		Lieutenant General, Commanding 11th. Division.	

Ref: 1/40,000 Sheet 51.e.
Maps 1/10,000 Trench Maps
51.B.S.W.1. & 51.B.N.W.3.

APPENDIX "A".

SECRET.

15/8/16.

11th Division Operation Order No. 18.

1. The 11th Division will be relieved in "I" Sector by the 21st Division and in "F"., "G"., and "H" Sectors by the 12th Division. Reliefs will take place in accordance with attached Table of Moves.

2. The 62nd Inf. Bde. will relieve the 9th Lancashire Fusiliers and 9th Notts and Derbys under Command of Lt-Col. Da COSTA 9th Lancs. Fusiliers in "I" Sector by 6 a.m. on the 19th August under arrangements to be made direct between Commanders concerned.

3. (a) The 32nd Inf. Bde. Group will be relieved in "G" Sector by the 36th Inf. Bde. by 6 a.m. on the 21st inst.

   (b) The 34th Inf. Bde. Group will be relieved in "F" Sector by the 37th Inf. Bde by 6 a.m. on the 22nd inst.

   (c) The 33rd Inf. Bde. Group/will be relieved in "H" Sector by the 35th Inf. Bde. by 6 a.m. on the 22nd inst.

   All reliefs under arrangements to be made direct between Brigadier Generals concerned.

4. The 11th Division Field Companies R.E. and Pioneer Battalion will be relieved at a later date. Further orders will be issued for the relief.

5. The Divisional Artillery will be relieved by the Artillery of the 12th Division on the nights of August 22nd/23rd., and August 23rd/24th under arrangements to be made direct between C.R.A's.

6. Light Trench Mortar Batteries will accompany the Brigades to which they belong.
   Orders for the relief of Heavy and Medium T.M's will be issued by the C.R.A. 11th Division.

7. All trench maps, air photos, defence schemes and log books will be handed over to relieving troops. Trench stores will also be handed over and receipts for same sent to D.H.Q.

8. Machine and Lewis Gun personnel, snipers, bombers, observers and telephonists of in-coming Divisions will take over 24 hours before the commencement of Infantry relief.
   One officer and one N.C.O. per Company in the front line will be left with the relieving battalion for 24 hours after the completion of the relief. (VI Corps G.X. 405. dated 13/8/16.).

9. Separate orders will be issued for the move of the Divisional Train.

10. Divisional Headquarters will close at WARLUS at 10 a.m. on the 22nd inst. and will re-open at LE CAUROY at the same hour.

11. Completion of all reliefs will be reported to D.H.Q.

Issued at 9 p.m.

Major.
G.S. 11th Division.

Copy No. 1. C.R.A. 11th Div.
2. C.R.E. 11th Div.
3. 32nd I.B.
4. 33rd I.B.
5. 34th I.B.
6. 8th E. Yorks R.
7. Signals.
8. A & Q Branch.
9. A.D.M.S.
10. A.P.M.
11. War Diary.
12. File.

Copy No. 13. 6th Corps.
14. 12th Div.
15. 21st Div.
16. 43rd Div.
17. 11th Div. Train.
18. Divisional School.
19. Town Major. ARRAS.
20. I Sector

MOVE OF 11th. DIVISION (less Artillery).

Unit.	Date.	From.	To.	Route.	Remarks.
1 Infantry Brigade.	September 2nd.	PREVENT.	ACHEUX.	By Rail.	Move by tactical trains.
11th. Divn.(less 3 Infantry Brigades. Pioneer Bttn. and R.A.).	September 2nd.	VIth.Corps area.	DOULLENS. HAUTE VISEE GROUCHES.	To be arranged between VIth. Corps and VIIth. Corps direct.	The places named will not be available before 12 noon.
Pioneer Battalion.	September 2nd.	VIth. Corps area. (AMBRINES)	Area O.	To be arranged between VIth. and VIIth.Corps direct as far as Southern boundary of Third Army area. Beyond that as Reserve Army may direct.	By bus. 52 busses will be at AMBRINES at 10 a.m.
2 Infantry Brigades.	September 3rd.	PREVENT.	ACHEUX.	By Rail.	Move by tactical trains.
11th. Division.(less 3 Infantry Bdes, Pioneer Bttn. and R.A.).	September 3rd.	DOULLENS. HAUTE VISEE GROUCHES.	Area O.	As Reserve Army may direct.	

Copy. No. 6.

11th DIVISION.

SCHEME OF DEFENCE.

Copy No. 6.

SCHEME OF DEFENCE.

11th. DIVISION.

CONTENTS.

1. General Descroption.

2. Distribution of forces and system of command.

3. System of defence and method of dealing with probable forms of attack.

APPENDICES.

1. Disposition of 11th Division.

2. "S.O.S". messages and signals.

3. Organization of Divisional Artillery with Tables.

4. Instructions as to action in the event of a Gas Attack.

5. Medical arrangements.

6. Orders for Divisional Battle Posts.

7. Traffic Orders for Divisional Area.

8. Instructions concerning firing on British Aircraft at night.

9. Distribution of Grenades and Establishment of Grenade Posts.

10. Distribution of Small Arm Ammunition.

11. Garrisons of Defended Localities for which Reserve Ammunition and Rations are required.

INDEX OF MAPS

forwarded with

11th DIVISION DEFENCE SCHEME.

MAP. 1.   Showing Divisional Boundaries and Lines of Defence.

MAP. 2. (a) BREWERY POST.

(b) PETIT MOULIN.

(c) WAILLY KEEP.

(d) PETIT CHATEAU.

(e) HILL POST.

(f) Defences of AGNY.

(g) Defences of ACHICOURT.

(h) Defences of RONVILLE.

MAP. 3. (a) Trenches and Machine Gun Positions in "F" Sector.

(b) "   "   "   "   "   "   "G"   "

(b) "   "   "   "   "   "   "H"   "

11th DIVISION DEFENCE SCHEME.

SECRET.

Copy no 6.

(1) GENERAL DESCRIPTION.

1. Boundaries of the 11th Divisional Area.

The 11th Division holds the VIth Corps line South East of ARRAS. The Sectors held are F. G. H. and the front roughly 9,000 yards. The 46th Division is on our right and the 21st Division on our left.

Southern Boundary.

R.28.c.8.0 - R.27.c.7.8 - R.27.a.6.2 - R.26.d.3.3 -

R.26.c.2.1 - R.26.c.1.3 - R.25.d.7.2 - R.25.a.0.0 -

due West.

Northern Boundary.

G.35.b.8.0, RUE GAMBETTA - RUE ERNESTALE - RUE ST AUBERT -

RUE d' AMIENS - For boundary further West see Map 1.

2. General Description of 11th Division Front.

From the right of "F" Sector the front system of defence runs in a North Easterly direction as far as ARRAS. It is situated on the right bank of the CRINCHON Stream half way up the North Western slopes of the hills forming the Valley of the stream. On the left bank, the ground slopes gently upwards to the DOULLENS-ARRAS Railway and main road, and it is along these slopes that positions can be procured whence good views can be obtained of the hostile lines.

Viewed from one of these positions (Hill 105) the most striking features in the German lines are the villages of BEAURAINS and BLAIRVILLE, the woods round those two villages, and the ruins of FICHEUX Mill. The ground between the two villages is high and reaches its culminating point (Contour 120) at the North Eastern corner of BLAIRVILLE Wood.

The German front system runs along the high ground between the two villages and rather North West of them, and thus commands our front system giving the enemy opportunities for observation, which though good are no better than ours as described above.

Both systems are dug in chalk soil, which causes all excavations, unless carefully hidden, to be most conspicuous.

The CRINCHON is a sluggish stream average 15' wide and 2' deep, the actual banks of the stream are steep and require ramping for any fords that it may be desired to make use of. Owing to the small size of the stream bridging presents few difficulties and sound approaches are ensured.

2.

The South Eastern portion of the town of ARRAS and its suburbs RONVILLE - ACHICOURT - FAUBOURG d' AMIENS are included in the 11th Divisional area. The town is shelled from time to time, but despite this, contains valuable billetting areas, and there is much cellar accommodation which affords good shelter. There are some 1,800 civil inhavitants. living in the town.

Details for the inner defences of ARRAS will be found in APPENDIX 1.

3. **Most Probable Lines of Hostile Attack.**

It would be possible for the enemy to try and attack ARRAS directly from the East, but more probable lines of advance would be North and South of the town, and as far as the Division is concerned the most valuable ground from an enemy's point of view would be the high ground in R.11. South Westwards (Hill 105 etc), which would endanger the town from the South East.

4. **The Main Lines of Defence.**

Obstacle and firing line vide attached

The nomenclature used to denote the various lines of defence in the front line system varies with each Division. The Corps Commander wishes to establish a uniform system throughout the Corps front. The following terms will therefore be used in future :-

1. Obstacle Line. To be used for those portions of the line where obstacle trench exists.

2. Firing Line. The first line of resistance.

3. Support Line. The second line of resistance.

4. Reserve Line. The third line of resistance.

5. The Village Line. The defensive line formed by the villages of BELLACOURT, BRETENCOURT, WAILLY, AGNY, ACHICOURT, RONVILLE, ST. SAUVEUR, and the CEMETERY.

6. Redoubt Line. The Line extending from the OILWORKS (inclusive) to ROCLINCOURT (inclusive).

There will be no reserve lines in those cases where the Village, or Redoubt Lines, form the third line of resistance.

The rear is closed in with 2 sections of fire trench.
Dug-outs in the centre for the garrison.

2. **PETIT MOULIN.** R.12.d.3.9

Garrison. 1 Platoon - 2 Machine Guns.
Is in two portions about 100 yds. apart.
The S.W. Portion has fire trench running round the edge and firing S.E. & S.W. and a M.G. emplacement firing S.W.
The N.E. portion is the larger and has fire trench running round the edge of two small enclosures and firing N.E. & S.E.
At the North corner in a house is position for a M.G. with two alternative emplacements, and a position for a Lewis Gun at the cross roads covering the rear.

2.

The South Eastern portion of the town of ARRAS and its suburbs RONVILLE - ACHICOURT - FAUBOURG d' AMIENS are included in the 11th Divisional area. The town is shelled from time to time, but despite this, contains valuable billetting areas, and there is much cellar accommodation which affords good shelter. There are some 1,800 civil inhabitants living in the town.

Details for the inner defences of ARRAS will be found in APPENDIX 1.

3. **Most Probable Lines of Hostile Attack.**

It would be possible for the enemy to try and attack ARRAS directly from the East, but more probable lines of advance would be North and South of the town, and as far as the Division is concerned the most valuable ground from an enemy's point of view would be the high ground in R.11. South Westwards (Hill 105 etc), which would endanger the town from the South East.

4. **The Main Lines of Defence.**

(i) **The first position.** Obstacle and firing line vide attached instructions from VI Corps.

(a) The first line trenches consisting of the fire trenches in F. G. H, and the immediate support trenches. The support trenches vary in quality, but as a rule have fire stops and are wired. A great deal of work is still required on this support line, especially the construction of deep dug-outs for shelter of garrisons.

(b) **The Second or Support Line.** This line exists in G and H Sectors and is on the whole in good condition; in F Sector it is practically non existant, and is to be taken in hand.

(c) **The ~~Wancourt~~ Village Line.** This line consists of a series of defended localities and field works connected throughout by wire, and in places by trenches which are as a rule in bad condition.

The defences of the Defended Localities are as under :-

1. FACTORY POST. (or BREWERY POST) R 25.a.1.9.

   Garrison. 1 Platoon - 2 Machine Guns.
   Consists of 3 sections of fire trench firing to the front and flanks and two machine gun emplacements, one on each flank.
   The rear is closed in with 2 sections of fire trench.
   Dug-outs in the centre for the garrison.

2. PETIT MOULIN. R 22.d.3.9

   Garrison. 1 Platoon - 2 Machine Guns.
   Is in two portions about 100 yds. apart.
   The S.W. Portion has fire trench running round the edge and firing S.E. & S.W. and a M.G. emplacement firing SMW.
   The N.E. portion is the larger and has fire trench running round the edge of two small enclosures and firing N.E. & S.E.
   At the North corner in a house is position for a M.G. with two alternative emplacements, and a position for a Lewis Gun at the cross roads covering the rear.

3. **MAILLY.** R.29.a.2.4

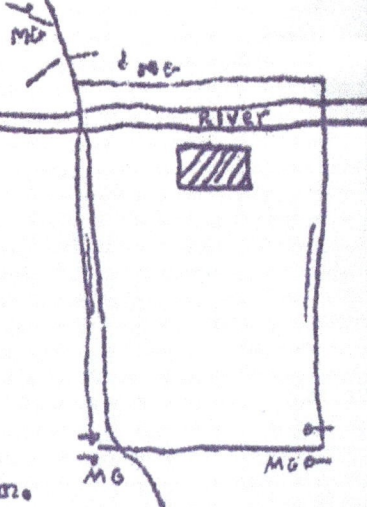

Garrison. 1 Platoon – 3 Machine Guns.
Situated round detached buildings on the S.E. side of the village and consists of several sections of trench connected by communication trench giving all round defence.

There is one machine gun emplacement firing East and two emplacements for a machine gun firing West. Accommodation for the garrison in the cellars of the houses.

4. **PETIT CHATEAU.** R.18.a.1.2

Garrison. 2 Platoons – 3 Machine Guns
It is proposed to construct a new position 150x further to the front at the junction of CHATEAU Street with the old disused communication trench by running out T head trenches from these communication trenches.

The present defences consist of trenches round the CHATEAU enclosure with emplacements for five machine guns firing to the front and flanks.

5. **MILL POST.** M.7.d.3.1.

Garrison. 1 Platoon – 1 Vickers, 1 Lewis Gun.
Consists of two machine gun emplacements connected by a fire trench so arranged as to provide for fire to both front and rear.

6. **AGNY.**

Garrison. 1 Coy. & 3 Platoons Infantry. 3 Sections Field Coy.
Details Tunnelling Coy. 4 Vickers Guns.
The village forms a rectangle 1,000 yards square with a salient at S.E. Corner.

Communications good, cellars numerous, water from wells and R. CRINCHON good and plentiful.

Perimeter 2,500 yards. Fire trench all round. Wire good. Field of fire good on the whole, but much clearing required at Eastern end.

Inner line of defence almost complete.
4 Machine Gun emplacements prepared.
Lewis Gun positions selected.
Bombing posts to protect the Communication trenches which run through the village have been constructed.

7. **ACHICOURT.**

Garrison. 1 Company Infantry – 2 M.G's 1 Lewis Gun.
Consists of a series of trenches round the Southern end of the village, and there are :–
Two machine gun emplacements outside this line of defence –
Sites for three other emplacements have been selected but not yet made.

8. **RONVILLE.**

Garrison. 1 Company Infantry – 2 M.G's – 1 Lewis Gun.
Situated round the cross roads in G.34.B.
There is an outer line of defence covered by an inner line of posts, consisting of trenches and loopholed walls.

Two machine gun emplacements have been constructed and sites for two more selected.

D. The ARRAS Defences :
   (i) The outer line extending from the CITADEL along the railway - MAISON LOVARGIE - MAISON BLANCHE- River SCARPE, at the ST. NICHOLAS Bridge.

   (ii) BOULEVARD line from CITADEL (inclusive) to the bridge on the BOULEVARD de la SCARPE, G.22.a.5,7.

   (iii) Inner Defences, i.e., those defences of the town, exclusive of the BOULEVARD line.

In addition, the following lines will be specially named :-

A. WAILLY Switch.

B. AGNY Switch.

C. The CRINCHON line, N. of the CRINCHON, along the road from WAILLY to AGNY Chateau.

4.

(d) The outer line of the ARRAS Defences.

Other defences in the Corps Area in rear of the First Position are :

2. The Inner Defences of ARRAS.

3. The Corps Line running from Q.35.c.1.8. through Wood 105 in R.10.d. East of DAINVILLE, to junction of Roads in L.22.d. thence North to ST VAAST in G.7.

4. The AGNEZ SWITCH from Q.17.d. - East of BERNEVILLE and WARLUS - K.18.d. - AGNES LES DUISANS.

5. The Army Line from P.30.d.8.1, East of GOUY -EN-ARTOIS East of WANQUETIN - GOUVES - to the R. SCARPE about K.4.a.6.2.
The Division is responsible for the construction, maintenance, and defence of all works of the 1st Position. The VIth Corps is responsible for the maintenance and construction of the Inner Defences of ARRAS and the Corps Line.

II DISTRIBUTION OF FORCES AND SYSTEM OF COMMAND.

(a)   The Division will be distributed as per attached Table, APPENDIX I.
In the event of the Division being called upon to find troops for other Sectors, the Divisional Reserve Battalions of 33rd and 34th Infantry Brigades will be taken for the purpose.

Artillery.

(b)   For positions and zones of fire, combined aggressive action against enemy etc., see APPENDIX 3.
The support of the VIth Corps Heavy Artillery can be obtained when required. Infantry Brigadiers applying to CRA. ~~the O.C. Group of supporting~~ Artillery.
Artillery positions selected for the defence of the Corps and Army Lines have been communicated to the C.R.A.

Divisional Reserve.

(c)   The Battalions composing the Divisional Reserve will reconnoitre all roads leading from their respective Head Quarters to Divisional and all Brigade Head Quarters and to Hill 105 (R.10.d.). Attention should be given to the reconnaissance of tracks hidden fro hostile observation and capable of use by day. Hd. Qrs. of these Battalions will be connected to D.H.Q. by Telephone direct.

III SYSTEM OF DEFENCE AND METHOD OF DEALING WITH PROBABLE FORMS OF ATTACK.

1. The following principles will be adopted in holding the line.

Units will be distributed in depth in spite of the length of front occupied.

The front line trenches will be lightly occupied.
They will be protected mainly by
(a). Strong obstacles.
(b). The artillery barrage.
(c). The fire of machine and Lewis guns.

No more infantry than are necessary to protect the machine guns or special points in the line not protected by Machine or Lewis guns against a coup-de-main, are to be employed in holding the first line trenches.

The remainder of the troops available for the defence of the Sector will be echeloned in rear as Supports and Reserves ready for use in the counter-attack.

Supporting points will be held by permanent garrisons which will on no account be used for any other purpose.

In case of attack the B.G.C. 33rd Infantry Brigade is responsible for the defence of the Outer Line of the ARRAS Defences within the Brigade boundary and for the defence of the Citadel.

The Inner defences of ARRAS will be arranged for by the VIth Corps.

2. The intention is that we should hold our present position in the face of all attacks, and no trench or part of a trench is to be abandoned by the garrison allotted to it without orders.

(a) The front trenches form the first line of resistance against minor attacks and raids, which may or may not be combined with the use of gas or smoke.

Good obstacles and vigilance on the part of the sentries should enable such attacks to be repelled by the fire of rifles, Machine and Lewis guns, and by artillery fire.

Should the enemy succeed in getting into a portion of the front line, he is to be immediately counter-attacked. Brigade, Battalion and Company Commanders must consider and work out the action to be taken in the event of any portion of the line being broken, so that there may be no delay in delivering a counter-attack in any circumstances.

<u>Companies must be prepared to assist the companies on their flanks</u> by immediately delivering bombing attacks on the flanks of the enemy should he succeed in penetrating the line held by a neighbouring company.

Should the counter-attack fail, the lost portion of the trench or trenches must be isolated by blocking the fire trench on both flanks, blocking the communication trenches <u>as far possible as possible,</u> and holding the support trenches in rear until sufficient reinforcements arrive and more deliberate preparations be made. Meanwhile the artillery will establish a barrage on the German trenches.

As regards the advisability of bringing artillery fire to bear on the lost trenches, no general rule can be laid down. It must be left to Infantry Brigadiers and Artillery Brigade Commanders to consider possible cases beforehand and decide on the action which it may be most advisable to take.

Fire should not be opened on the lost trenches without the sanction of the Infantry Brigadier.

(b) For the purposes of meeting a general attack, preceded by a heavy bombardment, which will, in all probability destroy the defences of the First Line, the Second or B Line will be the main line of resistance.

In the event of an attack of this nature, nothing will be gained by reinforcing the front line with a view to retaining our hold on it.

The B. Line and supporting points will be held at all costs until sufficient reserves are available for the offensive to be assumed.

(c). In view of the length of front held by the Division and the number of communication trenches existing in the area, it is of great importance that arrangements for rapidly blocking and defending such trenches in the event of a hostile attack penetrating our line at any point, should be capable of being put into operation without any delay. (Attention is drawn to Third Army No. S.G.410/26 dated 3/8/16).

3. The division of the front line into 3 sectors appears to be a suitable one.
   The 34th Inf. Bde. has the FICHEUX Area to deal with.
   The 32nd Inf. Bde. has LE CHAT MAIGRE Area, which is very strong, to deal with.
   The 33rd Inf. Bde. had the BEAURAINS Salient, which is also strong, to deal with.

Provided the front line wire is constantly repaired and maintained, a surprise attack should not be possible if proper vigilance is exercised.

Gas attacks and mining must be carefully guarded against.

In the event of a general attack, vide para. 1 (3), the closest possible touch with the Divisions on both flanks, would be a matter of special importance.

4. The possibility of improving our positions should always be considered and it would be advantageous if the Front Line was advanced from F.179., R.29.b.7.5 (along the roadway running parallel to our frony trenches in "No mans land") Northwards to G.8., M.14.d.2.5, as this road runs along the crest of the ridge and gives good Command. The enemy is attempting to reach this line of road, and has run out 16 saps towards it. A system of counter sapping should, therefore, be put in hand, and Russian saps run out from our front line towards the heads of the enemy's saps, with a view to facilitating advance towards the road in question.

5. All previous instructions on the subject of S.O.S. messages and signals from the infantry in the trenches to obtain artillery support, are cancelled and the following instruction are substituted.

6. Every sector of trenches has been given a distinctive letter which will be its "Trench Call".
   Artillery units must know the "Trench Calls" of their own Division, and the calls of the sectors on either flanks of their own Division.

APPENDIX I

TABLE SHOWING DISPOSITION OF 11TH DIVISION.

Divisional Headquarters - WARLUS. ADVD: H.Q. Q.29.b.4.4

Brigade or Battn.	POSITION.	SECTOR.	TRENCHES.	HEAD QUARTERS.	No. of Bttns employed.	REMARKS.
34th Bde.	Bde. H.Q. F.Line and Supports.	F.	167-192	BRETENCOURT.	2	86th Fd. Co. less 1 Section and all Pioneers in Sector attached.
	Bde. Reserve.			Bde. arrangements.	1	60th & 1 Btty. 133rd F.A.B. in support.
	Divl. Reserve.			SIMONCOURT.	1	
32nd Bde.	Bde. H.Q. F.Line and Supports.	G.	G.1-24.	DAINVILLE.	2	67th Fd. Co. less 1 Section and all Pioneers in Sector attached.
	Bde. Reserve.			Bde. arrangements.	1	58th and 1 Btty.133rd F.A.B. in support.
	Divl. Reserve.			BERNEVILLE.	1	
33rd Bde.	Bde. H.Q. F.Line and Supports.	H.	H.25-42.	RUE de FOURS. ARRAS. ARRAS.	2	68th Fd. Co. less 1 Section and all Pioneers in Sector attached.
	Bde. Reserve.			Bde. arrangements.	1	59th and 1 Btty. 133rd F.A.B. in support.
	Divl. Reserve.			DAINVILLE.		
6th E. Yorks (Pioneers)	Divl. Reserve.			GOUY EN ARTOIS.	1*	* Battalion less detachments attached to Brigades.
C.R.A., C.R.E.	Hd. Qrs.			WARLUS.		R.E. Workshops 1 Sec 68th Fd.Co. DAINVILLE. 1 Sec 86th Fd.Co. LABRET. 1 Sec. 67th Fd.Co. GOUY. Water Duties

S. O. S.   APPENDIX 2.

1.   Reference Third Army letter S.G. 107/9 of the 2nd August, the instructions contained in forwarding minute G.X.31/41 are cancelled, together will all previous instructions on the subject of "S.O.S." messages and signals from the infantry in the trenches to obtain artillery support, including the "ROCK" scheme, Vl Corps G.X.138.

2.   (The following instructions will be substituted)

2.   The front line system on the Divisional front is at present divided into three sectors, known as F, G, H, each corresponding with an Infantry Brigade front. Each of these sectors will be sub-divided further into two sub-sectors F.1. F.2., G.1., G.2., H.1., H.2., corresponding to normal battalion frontages. These will be the recognised "Trench Calls" when calling for artillery support.

     Artillery must know the trench calls of their own Division and those of the sectors on either flank of their Division.

3.   In the event of immediate support being required by the infantry in any sector or sub-sector, the following signals will be sent or made :-

     (a)   <u>By telephone or visual signalling.</u>

         "S.O.S" with-out/preamble, followed by the trench call of the sector or sub-sector in question, e.g. S.O.S.G., S.O.S. G.2., etc.

     (b)   <u>By coloured rockets.</u>

         (i) <u>By Day.</u> Shells daylight Japanese 4-inch liberating figures of animals, will be fired in groups of three in quick succession.

         (ii) <u>By night.</u> Rockets will be fired in groups of three- 1 red - 1 white - 1 red - in quick succession.

     The above signals will be repeated with a pause between each Signal message, or group of rockets, until the Artillery barrage is opened.

     Changes in the colour of the rockets to be fired by night will be made periodically by Army Headquarters.

4.   The S.O.S. signal denotes that certain portions of our lines have been or about to be attacked, i.e. that it is thought that the enemy are massing in their front line for attack, or are advancing from their front line trenches.

5.   Rockets will be kept at Company Headquarters and will be fired by order of the Company Commander.

6.   In each Battery position a written record will be kept showing the position of Rocket Stations that concern the battery.

     Arrangements will also be made to enable a sentry to detect by means of a fixed "Rake", battery director, or any other means from which of these stations the rockets are being sent up.

2.

7.   On the receipt of the S.O.S. Signal the field guns and Howitzers immediately supporting the portion of the line attacked and batteries on either flank will at once open fire on their "Night" or "Barrage" Lines.

40 rounds per field gun and howitzer will be fired at a rapid rate of fire, after which a slower rate of fire will be maintained until further information is received.

Siege howitzers and heavy guns, which can bear on the sections concerned will open a steady rate of fire on their counter-battery lines.

In order that arrangements may work smoothly in an emergency, the targets to be engaged and the zones to be kept under observation by each individual battery in the Division and Corps Heavy Artillery when any section of the lines is attacked will be previously determined, and laid down in the scheme of defence.

8.   If it is desired to carry out a trial of this system the word "TEST" will be employed instead of "S.O.S", which will only be used in cases of emergency.

Such tests will be carried out frequently.

During tests, instead of 40 rounds per field gun and howitzer being fired, one round per battery of Field Artillery should be sufficient. Siege howitzers and heavy guns will not fire but will report to Divisional Headquarters by priority telegram immediately they are ready to fire, stating the target on which the guns are laid.

9.   The day signal mentioned in para. 3, (b), (1), will be taken into use on and from August 13th.

NIGHT LINES

SECTOR.	F.	G.	H.
BATTERY.			
122	M.28.c.84.47.	M.26.c.84.47.	M.26.c.84.47.
	S. 4.b.33.73.	S. 4b.33.73.	M.30.c.20.50.
Lowland.			
(Q.36.c.	X.10.c.75.70.		
	M.33.b.78.35.	M.33.b.78.35	M.26.c.40.36.
(R.7.b.		M.24.c.22.95.	M.24.c.22.95.
N.MID.	M.23.d.40.15.	M.23.d.40.15.	M.23.d.40.15.
	N.13.c.98.78.	N.13.c.98.78.	N.13.c.98.78.
	N. 8.c.13.41.	N. 8.c.13.41.	N.14.b.96.84.
123	X. 5.d.90.76.	M.28.c.40.36.	M.28.c.40.36.
	M.28.a.20.14.	M.28.a.20.14.	M.28.a.20.14.
30	N.16.c.97.20.	N. 8.d.57.72.	N. 8.d.57.72.
	N.14.b.96.84.	N.25.a.58.58.	N.25.a.58.58.
88	N.13.a.83.40.	N.13.a.83.40.	N.13.a.83.40.
	N.13.b.45.03.	N.25.a.34.83.	N.25.a.34.83.
139		M.24.d.40.40.	M.24.d.40.40.
9			N.38.d.59.76.
			N.20.b.55.78.
102		M.13.b.45.03.	

NOTE:.Batteries concerned fire on the batteries shown in the columns for the sector or receipt of message S.O.S. for that Sector. The batteries shown have all been reported active on the Sectors concerned lately.

APPENDIX 5.

ORGANISATION OF THE ARTILLERY FOR DEFENCE.

(1). ALLOTMENT OF ARTILLERY.

The Divisional Artillery has been divided into 3 groups each consisting of 4 18 - Pr: batteries and one 4.5" Howitzer Battery.

Each of these groups is affiliated to an Infantry brigade.

58th Group affiliated to 32nd Infantry Brigade covers "G" Sector.
59th Group affiliated to 33rd Infantry Brigade covers "H" Sector.
60th Group affiliated to 34th Infantry Brigade covers "F" Sector.

(2) Details of each group are shown on attached TABLES.

(3) Mutual support between Divisions on either flank is arranged as follows :-

    (a) By 11th Divisional Artillery for 46th Division.

        8   18 - pdrs.
        4.   4.5" Howitzers.

    By 46th Divisional Artillery for 11th Division.

        4   18 - pdrs.
        4   4.5" Howitzers.

    (b) By 11th Divisional Artillery for 21st Division.

        4   18 - pdrs.
        2   4.5" Howitzers.

    By 21st Divisional Artillery for 11th Division.

        4   18 - pdrs.
        2   4.5" Howitzers.

(4) Battalion Commanders will call direct on their supporting 18 - pdr. Batteries, through Inf.Bde.Hd.Qrs. vide para III & 5.

    If the support of 4.5" Howitzers is required Battalion Commanders will apply to the Infantry Brigadier who will obtain the required support through the Group Commander.

    In the event of the support of Heavy Artillery being required, Infantry Brigadiers will apply through the Group Commanders to the C.R.A. who will call for necessary support from the VIth Corps Heavy Artillery.

"F" Sector   60th Group.   Group Headquarters at R.23.d.3.8.

BATTERY.	Regt. No.	POSITION.	BARRAGE ZONE.	MAXIMUM ARC OF FIRE.	O.P'S.	REMARKS.
B/135.	1	R.27.c.88.95. alternative R.31.b.59.46.	R.34.b.50.60 - M.20.a.50.30	130° - 80°	R.14.d.68.25.	Alternative O.P's not in use at present.
A/60.	7	R.14.c.22.82 alternative R.14.c.0.6 R.14.d.2.8.	R.34.b.50.65 - R.29.d.48.80	153° - 113½°	R.14.d.75.15.	A/60:— R 4.d.30.15. R.14.d.20.10.
B/60.	13	R.9.c.2.7. Alternative R.9.c.15.65	R.29.d.37.7.2-M.19.d.1.1.	158° - 120°	R.9.c.40.20.	B/60:— R.15.a.80.25. R.15.a.65.15. R.9.c.35.10.
C/60	19	R.9.d.90.99 Alternative R.10.a.4.8.	M.19.d.0.5 - M.20.a.50.30.	151° - 116°	R.16.b.4.8.	
D/60	25	R.9.b.9.9 alternative R.4.c.15.20	R.34.b.30.05 - M.20.a.42.22	205° - 120°	R.10.c.75.30.	

NIGHT LINES.

No.1: R.35.a.2.3.
No.2: R.35.c.50.75.
No.3: M.25.b.6.4.
No.4: M.20.c.7.9.

"G" SECTOR.   58th GROUP.   Group H.Q. at Ref.11.1/100,000.
                                               S side of road due S of 2 CATADELLE.

Battery.	Reg. No.	POSITION.	BARRAGE ZONE.	MAXIMUM ARC OF FIRE.	O.P's.	REMARKS.
A/58.	33.	(Present position). R.4.b.50.30. (Next Position). Alternative M.2.b.64.45	M.19.b.88.18 – M.14.d. 42.08.	117° – 157°	(1) R.11.a.80.40 (2) M.14.c.35.06.	
B/58	39	G.33.b.70.70 Alternative G.27.d.80.10 (Section position)	M.15.c.36.52 – M.15.b. 84.24	164° – 205°	(1) G.33.b.70.60 (2) M.15.c.20.90	
C/58	34 38	(Present position) R.5.a.70.60 (Next position) Alternative {G.33.a.60.30 {R.5.d.40.90	M.15.b.62.12 – M.10.c. 86.12	106° – 166°	(1) M.3.a.44.51 (2) M.9.d.22.22	
D/58	35	M.2.d.60.80	M.20.c.22.94 – M.10.c. 86.12	123° – 199°	M.8.d.80.20	
C/133	31	R.5.c.75.60	M.14.d.35.00 – M.15.c. 80.62		R.5.d.50.00	
D/58			Night Lines. No.1. M.16.a.16.95. No.2. M.19.c.80.70. No.3. M.15.c.60.70. No.4. M.14.c.95.10.			

"H" Sector.　　　　58th Group.　　　　Group H.Q. Rue des Capucines,
　　　　　　　　　　　　　　　　　　　　　　　　ARRAS. G.27.b.7.6.

BATTERY.	Reg. No.	POSITION.	BARRAGE ZONE.	MAXIMUM ARC OF FIRE.	O.P.'s.	REMARKS.
A/59	61	G.51.d.0.1. Alternative (18 pr) G.31.d.8.7.	M.10.b.5.2 – M.4.d.5½.7.	80° – 140°	M.4.c.0.1. G.54.c.9½.9. M.3.a.½.6½.	Gun pits are being re-constructed Maximum Arc will then be re-taken when pits are finished.
B/59	63	G.26.c.6.9 Alternative : G.25.c.5½.1½.	M.5.b.½.8 – G.56.c.2.7.	103° – 140°	G.28.c.2½.2. G.35.a.6½.9½. G.54.b.6.3½.	do
C/59	64	G.52.b.10.5.	M.10.c.8½.½ – M.10.d.4.9½	110° – 170°	M.3.a.5.7. G.54.a.1½.2. G.54.c.2.6	New O.P. which will be best O.P. for this battery is being construct-ed, at G.54.c.2½.5½.
D/59	65	G.27.c.7½.2. Alternative (4.5" How) G.27.d.1½.3½.	No.1. M.4.d.7½.1½. No.2. M.5.a.1.1½. No.3. M.5.a.7½.6½. No.4. M.5.b.6.9½.	70° – 180°	G.28.c.8.6½. M.3.c.1.7. G.54.c.2.4	Tall Chimney.
A/153	66	G.26.c.7.9. Alternative G.22.b.1.2.	L.4.d.5.10 – M.5.a.5½.7.	110° – 150°	G.35.a.6½.9½. G.54.c.2.2½. G.35.a.½.3½.	

NOTE.   These are the co-ordinates of the night line of flank guns of Batteries.

APPENDIX 4.

INSTRUCTIONS AS TO ACTION IN THE EVENT OF A
GAS ATTACK.

GENERAL

1. All gas attacks made by the enemy prove beyond question that the tube helmets provided as a perfect safeguard, provided it is looked after and the instructions as to its use are strictly observed.

This should be constantly impressed on all ranks, who should now have every confidence that in the event of a gas attack, followed by an infantry attack, they will inflict on the enemy very severe losses.

As the enemy may possibly use smoke, or smoke and gas combined, to give the impression of a real gas attack, and there will not be time at the moment to ascertain the exact nature of the cloud, the instructions contained in the following paragraphs will be observed whenever the enemy makes use of any gas or smoke cloud.

It should be remembered that in a gas attack, no immediate infantry attack is likely to follow, whereas a smoke attack may be immediately followed by an infantry attack.

WARNING SIGNALS.

2. As troops may be affected by gas even to a distance of 9,000 yards behind the front trenches, there must be adequate warning signals throughout the whole Divisional Area and every Brigade Area, as well as in the front trenches.

A certain number of Electric, Compressed Air and Strombos horns have been provided which will be disposed by Brigadiers in the most suitable places.

In addition, Brigadiers will instal in their trenches and throughout their Area, wherever troops are quartered, gas gongs made of 18 pr. cartridge cases or railway iron. All such warning signals will be placed under the charge of sentries who will be responsible for sounding them in the event of a gas attack. On no account, however, is reliance to be placed solely on these warning signals.

Officers and N.C.O's must at once take active steps to rouse their men and to see that every man is at his post and all dug-outs cleared. One or two N.C.O's per platoon should always be told off for this duty whenever the "Gas Alert" period is in operation.

The distinctive signal to give the alarm in case of a gas attack is G.A.S.

This Signal will be sent without preamble by every telephone operator who hears the alarm gong, or other signal, and will be repeated two or three times.
This Signal will be passed from front to rear in the same manner as the S.O.S. Signal and will not be distributed laterally.
The Signal will be passed from front to rear by all operators who receive it, until it reaches Divisional H.Q.

P.T.O.

2.

the letter denoting the Sector

The letters G.A.S. will be followed by ~~R or L. according to the Sector~~ from which the message emanates ~~R. Right, L. Left~~ G.A.S. C

The G.A.S. signal will only be employed in the event of a gas attack from cylinders. If gas shells only are being used, the signal G.A.S. will not be employed.

ADJUSTMENT OF SMOKE HELMETS.
5. On the warning being given, all ranks will at once adjust their tube helmets, and will stand to their appointed places.

Orders as to putting on tube helmets apply equally to Artillery personnel and to troops in Reserve. Neglect of this precaution may deprive the Infantry of Artillery support at the moment when it is most needed.

WARNING NEIGHBOURING TROOPS.
4. Brigadiers and Artillery Group Commanders will at once warn neighbouring Brigades and Groups, it being most important that enfilade fire be brought to bear on the gas locality.

ACTION OF TROOPS IN TRENCHES.
5. (a) Troops will at all costs remain at their posts, and are forbidden to remain in or get into dug-outs, or to move to a flank or rear.

(b) A steady rifle, machine gun, and trench mortar fire will at once be opened through the gas cloud against the German trenches.

(c) Men in charge of Vermorel Sprayers will prepare to use them as soon as the gas cloud has passed, so as to admit of tube helmets being removed.

(d) The Artillery will at once open a quick rate of fire ~~against~~ on to the gas zone.

(e) Battalion Commanders will post guards at the heads of all communication trenches, to prevent straggling to the rear.

MACHINE GUNS; PROTECTION OF-
6. To prevent damage to machine and Lewis guns during a gas attack, it is necessary that all working parts should be kept thoroughly oiled always; Lids of ammunition boxes not in use will be kept closed; and the gun and any ammunition not used is to be thoroughly cleaned as soon as possible after the gas has dissipated.

STRAGGLERS POSTS.
7. On receipt of information that a gas attack is being made, the A.P.M. will at once post Stragglers Posts.

APPENDIX 5.

MEDICAL ARRANGEMENTS.

1. ADVANCED DRESSING STATIONS.

    (a)   "F" Sector................GROSVILLE.

    (b)   "G","H",& "I" Sectors.....Convent of ST. SACREMENT ARRAS.

2. COLLECTING POSTS.

    (a)   "F" Sector................LE FERMONT.

    (b)   "F", "G", & "I" Sectors...ACHICOURT.

3. DIVISIONAL COLLECTING STATIONS.

    (a)   "F" Sector................BEAUMETZ.

    (b)   "G","H", & "I" Sectors....L.29.d.33.
                (East end of DAINVILLE village, junction of roads running West from ARRAS and N.W. from ACHICOURT).

4. MAIN DRESSING STATION.

    (a)   "F" Sector................ BARLY.

    (b)   "G","H",& "I" Sectors.....WANQUETIN.

===

APPENDIX 6.

APPENDIX "A".

ORDERS FOR DIVISIONAL BATTLE POSTS.

1. On the Posts being ordered out, the N.C.O. and 3 men detailed will take up their positions without delay and will come under the orders of the A.P.M. They will on no account leave their posts without written orders from the A.P.M.

2. They will take with them the unconsumed portion of the current day's ration and 1 extra day's ration.

3. The duties of the Posts are to stop and collect all stragglers.

4. Formed bodies of troops under an officer or N.C.O. only will be allowed to pass.

5. Any wounded man should be directed to the nearest dressing station.

6. 1 Sgt. and 1 Cpl. M.M.P. will take charge of the Divisional Collecting Station at ....

   1 Cpl. M.M.P will be on duty at each of the 3 Divisional Battle Posts.

   1 Sgt. and 3 Cpls. M.M.P. will be detailed to patrol the Divisional Battle Posts and conduct stragglers to Divisional Collecting Station

7. The M.M.P. at Battle Posts and Collecting Station will carry note books and collect details of all stragglers.

        (a) Name.
        (b) Unit.
        (c) If armed or unarmed.

APPENDIX 6, Contd

SECRET.

....
....

The following Battle Posts will be established forthwith:-

1. DIVISIONAL BATTLE POSTS.

Post.	Place	Detailed by
1.	RIVIERE. Entrance to communication trench.	A.P.M.
2.	BEAULITZ.	"
3.	BAC du NORD - BERNEVILLE Road.	"
4.	Railway Station, DAINVILLE.	"

(a) Each Post will consist of 1 N.C.O. and 4 Men.

(b) The Posts are to be detailed ready to take up their positions when required and are to be shewn their exact positions and the nearest way to them.

(c) The men detailed are not to be employed outside the villages in which they are billetted.

(d) A copy of the orders to be given to each Post is attached, Appendix 'A'.

Divisional Collecting Station will be established:

BERNEVILLE. R.1 D.37.

2. In addition to the Divisional Battle Posts, INFANTRY BRIGADES will establish Posts and Collecting Stations at the following points:-

"F" SECTOR, 34th BRIGADE.

Post.		Position.
1	Wood Street	R.27 A 49.00
2	Brewery Street	R.22 C 22.07
3	Tite Street	R 22 D 38
4	Wailly	R 22 A 35
5	James Street	R.17 C 95.19
6	Maxim Street	R 17 D 25.55
	Chateau Street	R 18 B 05.80

Collecting Station.		Position.
1	Wailly	R.23 A 35

"G" SECTOR, 32nd BRIGADE.

Post.		Position.
1	Bridge over CRINCHON at Mill	M.8 c 24
2	Sunken road, entrance to AGNY	M.8 d 33
3	Bridge over CRINCHON at Mill	M.2 d 73

Collecting Station.		Position.
1	Main road N.E. entrance to AGNY	M.8 B 52

"H" SECTOR, 33rd BRIGADE.

Post.	Position.
1	Junction of roads W. of ACHICOURT M.2 B.40.95.
2	Junction of roads and railway N.E. of ACHICOURT. ~~G.33 B 38.40~~
3	400 yds. S. of ARRAS Goods Station..... G.33 B 95.75
4	Junction of roads 100 yds S. of RONVILLE Railway Bridge........... G.28 C 94.

Collecting Station.   Position.

1 .... Goods Station, ARRAS................. G 33 B 9575

"I" SECTOR, TWO BATTALIONS.

Post.	Position.
1	G.28 B 41.
2	G.23 C 83.
3	Imperial Street } ST. SAUVEUR Redoubt.
4	Iris Street
5	Infantry Lane }
6	Ivy Street } Cemetery Posts.
7	Railway Bridge off INTERPRETER Street. }

Collecting Station.

1 .... G.28 B 87.

(a) Each post will consist of 1 N.C.O. and 3 men.
(b) Posts will be detailed ready to be posted immediately when required and should be shewn exact location of their posts.
(c) Collecting patrols will be detailed to visit the posts at intervals and conduct stragglers to Brigade Collecting Stations.
(d) If possible, an officer should be detailed to supervise the collection of stragglers.
(e) Any modification in number or position of Brigade Battle Posts will be notified at once to Divisional Headquarters.

APPENDIX 7

TRAFFIC ORDERS, 11th DIVISION.

(Issued with D.R.O. 201)

(1) No formed bodies of troops or traffic, except single motor cars or ambulances may proceed East of the BEAUMETZ - DAINVILLE Railway during the hours of daylight, unless the driver is in possession of a pass issued by the A.P.M. 11th Division.

A.P.M. 11th Division will only issue these special passes <u>on requisition by an officer of the Staff</u> of the VI Corps or of a Division.

The control posts at WARLUS and BERNEVILLE have orders to stop all formed bodies of troops and traffic at the outlets of these villages leading to ARRAS or DAINVILLE, unless they have the necessary pass.

(2) Vehicular traffic for trenches and gun positions and large parties of troops will not pass the undermentioned places before the following hours:-

    WARLUS.   9-15 p.m.
    BERNEVILLE. 9-15 p.m.
    BEAUMETZ. 9-30 p.m.

These hours also apply to all traffic for DAINVILLE and ARRAS.

(3) No motor, lorry, wagon, horseman, bicycle or foot passenger is allowed to go along the ARRAS - DOULLENS road during the hours of daylight.

(4) The road leading from BEAUMETZ cross-roads to GROSVILLE and RIVIERE is closed to all traffic during daylight. Exemptions are made for dispatch riders with urgent messages.

-----------oOo-----------

SECRET.   Third Army No. Ga.4/11.

O.B./1769.
                                                   APPENDIX 8

Third Army.

1.   All previous orders concerning firing from the ground
at British aircraft by night will be cancelled from 8 p.m. on
the 4th August.

2.   From the above mentioned hour the following orders
will come into force :-

3. PROHIBITED AREA:

        The following is constituted a "prohibited area" for
all aircraft between the hours of sunset and sunrise :-
        The area lying between the sea and a line drawn through
BOULOGNE - WATTEN - BOURBOURG - GRAVELINES.
        Gun, rifle and machine gun fire will be opened without
warning and without delay on any aircraft flying over this area
between the hours of sunset and sunrise.

4. DEFENDED AREAS:

        In addition to the "prohibited area", certain areas
are defended against aircraft by anti-aircraft guns and machine
guns.   These areas will be designated "defended areas".
        Should Armies or the I.G.C. wish to make any other
areas "defended areas" three clear days notice must be given
to G.H.Q.
        A list of "defended areas" is attached.

5. Firing against aeroplanes by night.

    (a) Rifle and machine gun fire.

        (i)   "Prohibited area":   For orders regarding fire in
the "prohibited area" see para. 3 above.

        (ii)   "Defended areas":   Aeroplanes will as far as
possible avoid flying over the "defended areas" by night.
In cases where such flights are unavoidable, a Klaxon horn
will be sounded by the aeroplane at frequent intervals, as a
warning against fire from friendly guns. Rifle and machine
gun fire will be opened on any aeroplane crossing a "defended
area" by night, which does not sound its Klaxon horn.
        N.B.   As an additional precaution, aeroplanes when flying
               6 miles or more behind our own trenches at night,
               should, if possible, light their navigation lights,
               which are on the outer edge of bottom planes and on
               the tail. The fact that a machine is not showing
               navigation lights is not, however, to be taken as
               proof that it is an enemy machine.

        (iii) " Other areas: In areas other than "prohibited" and
"defended" areas no rifle or machine gun fire will be opened
on aeroplanes by night, unless they disclose their hostile
identity unmistakably by dropping bombs, or opening fire.

    (b) Anti-Aircraft gun fire.

        The following will be the procedure in connection with
night flights by Aeroplanes :-

        When a night flight by aeroplanes is contemplated,
R.F.C. Brigades and independent wings will notify the H.Q. of the
Army concerned, in sufficient time to permit of all Anti-Aircraft
Artillery being warned. At the same time R.F.C. Brigades and
independent wings will inform the H.Q. of the Army whether they
wish this information passed on to neighbouring Armies.

If there is a probability of machines flying in the neighbourhood of BEAUQUESNE at night, R.F.C. Brigades and independent wings will notify the O.C. 23rd A.A. Battery direct.

Whenever warning of a night flight has been given, a further report will be sent to the H.Q. of the Army concerned when all machines have returned to their aerodromes.

Between the time of the first intimation regarding the despatch of a flight, and the receipt of the report as to its return to the aerodrome, no fire by Anti-Aircraft guns against aeroplanes is to take place, unless the aeroplane unmistakably proves itself to be hostile by dropping bombs or opening fire.

After the receipt of the latter report, fire will be opened on all aeroplanes unless they comply with the provisions of paragraph 5 (a) (ii) above.

6. Fire against airships by night.

   (a) Rifle and machine gun fire.

      (i) "Prohibited area": For orders regarding fire in the "prohibited area" see para. 3 above.

      (ii) "Defended and other areas": Rifle and machine gun fire against any airship is prohibited unless the airship has revealed its hostile character unmistakably by dropping bombs.

   (b) Artillery fire.

      (i) Intimation will be given by General Headquarters from time to time to Armies for communication to all concerned as to the area through which the Allied airships are likely to pass during specified periods. All troops occupying that area will be warned by the Army concerned that during the period specified no firing against airships will take place.

      (ii) As it will not always be possible to define the exact route to be followed, and in order to convey the identity of the airships, and to act as a warning against fire by from our own artillery, airships will be provided with signal rockets or various coloured lights. The colouring of the lights will be changed from time to time under instructions to be issued by General Headquarters.

      Until further orders the colour of the lights will be red, or the colour of the day as given in the French Daily Table of colours forwarded to Armies from time to time.

      (iii) Except in the areas and during the periods referred to in para. 6. (b)(i) above, the artillery will regard all airships as hostile, unless they make the specified signal referred to in para. 6.(b) (ii).

7. In future no orders regarding firing at or signalling to aircraft by night are to be issued by Armies or the I.G.C. without previous reference to General Headquarters.

8. The French regulations remain in force in the French area and must be made known to all concerned so that any French aircraft which may fly over the British area may be recognised as such.

GENERAL HEADQUARTERS.

BEAUQUESNE (N.2, Sht.57d).

MONTREUIL.

HESDIN.

FIRST ARMY.

HOUDAIN (J.33.Sht. 36b).

LAPUGNOY (D.15.Sht.36b).

ST. VENANT (P.4.Sht.36a).

TREIZENNES (N.6.Sht.36a).

SECOND ARMY.

CAESTRE (W.3.Sht.28).

ABEELE (L.26.Sht.28).

STRAZEELE (W.29.Sht.28).

THIRD ARMY.

MONDICOURT (C.2.Sht.57d).

AVESNES le COMTE (J.31.Sht.51c).

SAVY (D.4.Sht.51c).

LIGNY ST FLOCHEL (T.30.Sht.36b).

FOURTH ARMY.

FLESSELLES (7 miles N.N.W. of AMIENS).

CONTOY (U.26b.27A, Sheet57d)

RESERVE ARMY.

PUCHEVILLERS (N.27.Sht.57d).

AUTHIEULE (B.25.Sht.57d).

BOUZINCOURT (W.7.Sht.57d).

HEDAUVILLE (P.34.Sht.57d).

LINES OF COMMUNICATION.

DUNKIRK.

CALAIS.

AUDRUICQ.

ST. OMER.

BOULOGNE.

ETABLES.

ABBEVILLE.

ABANCOURT.

ROUEN.

HAVRE.

FRENCH.

AMIENS.

Sheet 11-1/100,000

PERNES   DIEVAL   TINQUES

PREVENT   HUMIERES. All within a radius of from 5 to 8 miles of St.Pol.

APPENDIX. 9.

DISTRIBUTION OF GRENADES AND ESTABLISHMENT OF GRENADE POSTS:

1. 48,000 No. 5 (Mills) hand grenades are held on charge by the Division.

2. Of these, 4,452 for a Divisional Store and 15,504 form the mobile reserve, to be carried as follows :-

	BOXES.	GRENADES.
Each Battalion, including Pioneer Battalion on one limbered wagon, in Regimental Reserve.	64	768
Each Infantry Brigade, in Echelon "A", D.A.C., on three G.S. wagons.	115	1380
In Divisional Ammunition Column, Echelon "B", on one G.S. wagon.	115	1380
In Divisional Store.	371	4452
Total for Division	1663	19,956

When the Division is in the line, these grenades will not be left on wheels, but will be removed from the vehicles, and placed in stores at their wagon lines, to be constructed by units concerned and passed as "dry" by D.A.D.O.S.

These grenades will NOT be detonated unless specially ordered.

The remainder of the 48,000 hand grenades on charge of the Division, viz., 2337 boxes, or 28,044 grenades, are for use in the Front Line System.

They are allotted as follows :-

	BOXES.	Grenades.	
Right Brigade.	687	8,244	(Including 768 in Supporting Points)
Centre Brigade.	750	9,000	(Including 672 in Supporting Points)
Left Brigade.	900	10,800	(Including 864 in Supporting Points)
	2337	28,044	

3. The distribution of the grenades allotted to Brigades for trench use will be determined by Brigadier Generals Commanding, subject to the following conditions:-

(a) Not more than 2 boxes will be kept in any one store in a front line trench.

3(contd).

(b) The bulk of the grenades will be kept at grenade posts arranged in echelons, generally speaking as follows:-

<u>1st ECHELON</u>. In each communication trench
between Front Line and Subsidiary
Line. Each post about. . . . . 6 boxes.

<u>2nd ECHELON</u>. In communication trenches
between Subsidiary and 2nd Divisional
(or Village) Line. Each post about. . . . 15 boxes.

<u>3rd ECHELON</u>. In 2nd Divisional (or Village)
Line, near entrance to communication
trenches leading to the front.
Each post about. . . .150 boxes.

The positions of these posts and reserves, when fixed, will be shown on sketch maps to be attached to Brigade Defence Schemes.

The object of the above system of distribution is:-

(i) In case of the enemy penetrating our trench line, to limit his advance by communication trenches, and to facilitate counter-attack.

(ii) To provide for supply of grenades to the front.

4. The above posts and reserves must be properly constructed so as to preserve the grenades from damage by weather.

5. At the junction of a main communication trench with a line of defence, there should be a grenade post. These posts should consist of at least four grenadiers and a grenade store. The numbers of grenadiers and grenades will depend on the importance of the locality. Splinter-proof dugouts for the grenadiers, and proper recesses for the grenades should be constructed close to the point of junction.

The communication trench leading from the front should be straightened for a distance of 40 yards previous to its junction with a line of defence. At this point a loopholed traverse should be constructed so as to enable rifle fire to be brought to bear along the straight piece of communication trench.

Arrowhead bombing posts should also be constructed at this point :-

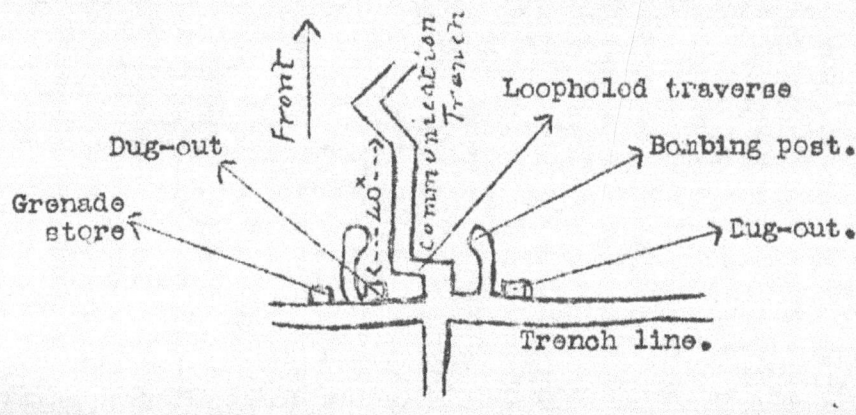

3.

6. Grenadiers will always be located at every grenade post, ready to use the grenades if required.

   The Brigade trench reserve will be under the care of a permanent caretaker.

7. Sufficient waistcoats and grenade carriers will be kept at selected posts and stores for equipping the squads who are to use the grenades, or for carrying them forward.

8. At each grenade post provision will be made for blocking the trench quickly if required.

9. Brigade Grenade Officers will frequently inspect all grenades and posts, and will see that the proper number of grenades is kept up in each post and store; that they are protected from the weather; that a sufficient number of grenadiers are present and understand their duties; that grenades are in good condition; and that waistcoats or carriers are available.

10. All grenades in 1st, 2nd, and 3rd echelons will be kept detonated at all times. Not less than half the grenades in the Brigade trench reserve will be kept detonated. There must be men at hand to detonate the remainder at short notice if required.

11. Any expenditure of grenades in trenches will normally be made good by replenishment from the mobile reserve, to in para.2, in the same way as S.A.A. This reserve will then be referred replenished from the Divisional Ammunition Column.

12. There are also available for issue to Brigades on demand No.1 (Hales) hand grenades, and No.3 (rifle) grenades.

    These will be supplied as demanded by Brigades, who will be responsible for their storage under the same precautions as No.5 (Mills) hand grenades.

APPENDIX 10.

DISTRIBUTION OF SMALL ARM AMMUNITION

A. **IN FRONT LINE SYSTEM.**

    120 rounds per rifle, on the man.

    50 " " " in S.A.A. boxes in front line and support trenches in recesses protected from weather.

    5,500 rounds per machine gun and Lewis Gun.

B. **STORED IN SUPPORTING POINTS.**

    300 rounds per rifle of approved garrison.

    10,000 rounds per machine gun and Lewis gun.

C. **BRIGADE RESERVES.**

    Dump of 128 boxes S.A.A. at any convenient spot.

N O T E.

Of the above:-

A. (in excess of 120 rounds per rifle and 3,500 rounds per Machine Gun),

    and

B. will be made up from Ammunition Park.

C. Will be made up from Divisional Ammunition Column.

APPENDIX 11.

Garrisons of Defended Localaties for which reserve
Ammunition and Rations are required.

11th Divisœn.

Defended Locality.	Garrison.	Machine Guns.	S.A.A.	Rations.
BREWERY POST.	1 Platoon.	2	7,000	100.
PETIT MOULIN.	1 Platoon.	2	7,000	100.
VAILLY KEEP.	1 Platoon.	3	9,000	100,
PETIT CHATEAU POST.	2 Platoons.	3	11,000	200.
AGNY.	2 Companies.	4	30,000	800.
ACHICOURT.	1 Battalion.	8	61,000	1,600.
RONVILLE.	2 Companies.	4	30,000	800

Units holding supporting points will at once complete their points to the above scale. All ammunition and rations surplus to this scale are to be removed.

Arrangements are to be made that rations stocks are turned over regularly.

Scale of rations as laid down in G.R.O. 1235 (amended) and in addition 3 ozs. of jam per man.

SECRET

Map No 2 (a)

Copy......6......

PLAN OF BREWERY POST.

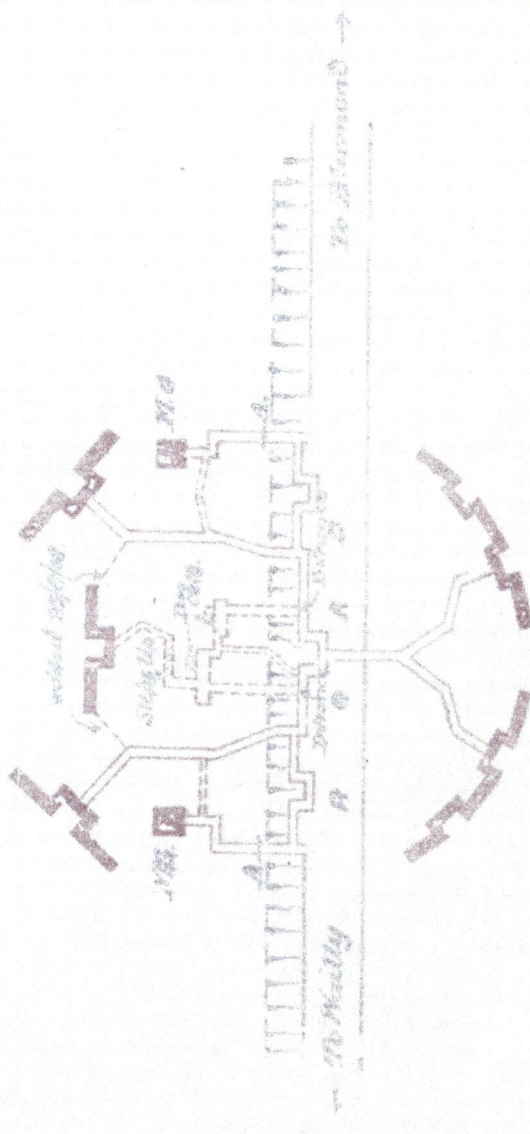

SECRET
MAP 2(b)
Copy 6

"PETIT MOULIN" KEEP.

ONE INCH = 20 YARDS.

SECRET.
Map. 2(c).
Copy. No. 6

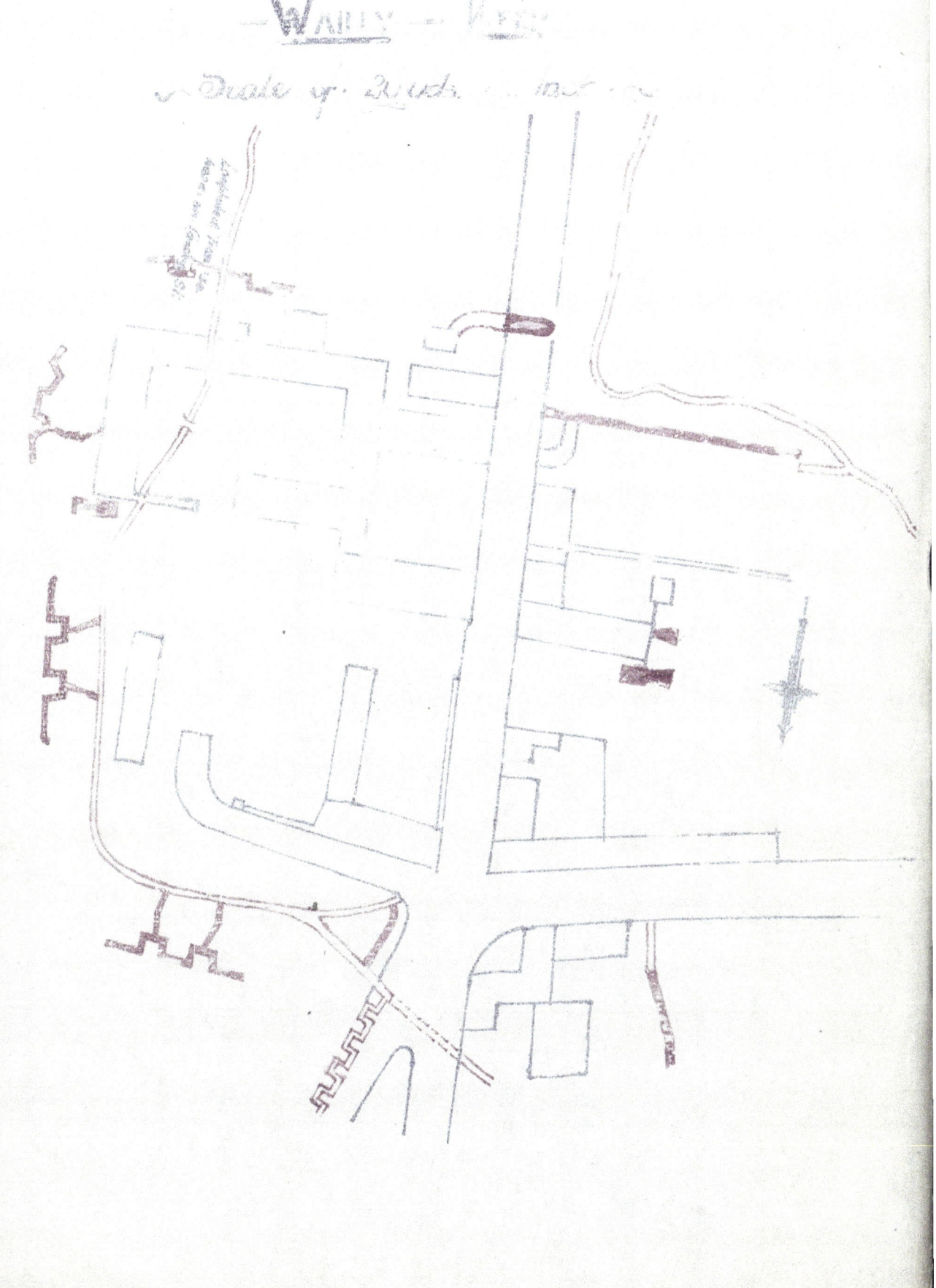

SECRET
MAP N° 2(a)
Copy 6

LA PETITE CHATEAU KEEP

Scale - 20 yds
to 1 in

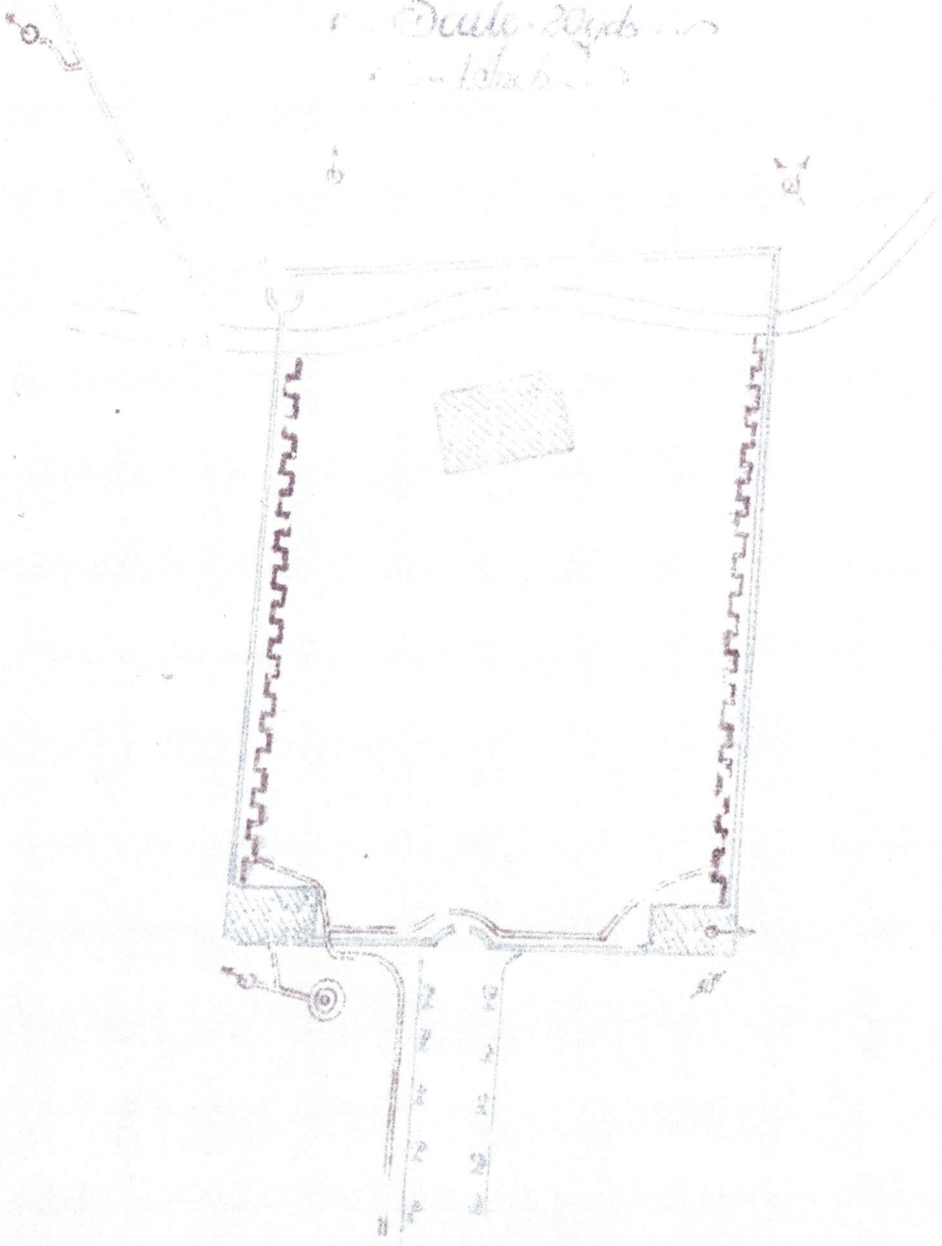

Mill Post.

SECRET
Map No 2 (e)
Copy. 6

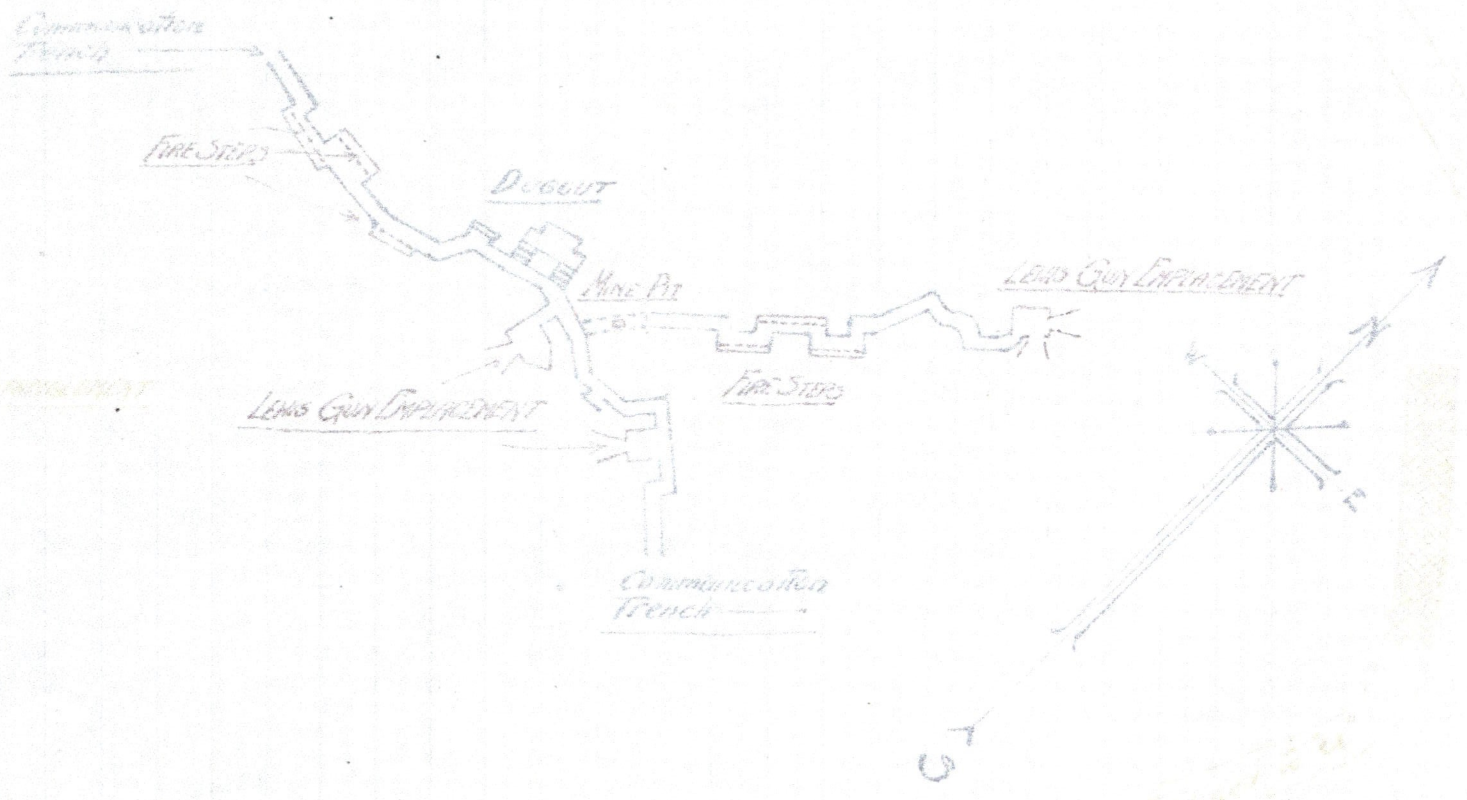

Communication Trench
Fire Steps
Dugout
Mine Pit
Lewis Gun Emplacement
Fire Steps
Lewis Gun Emplacement
Communication Trench
N
E
S

Scale 50 Feet to 1 Inch

SECRET

Map No 2(9)

Copy 6

ACHICOURT.

Scale 1:5,000.

SECRET
MAP N° 2(d)
Copy 6

RONVILLE DEFENCES.

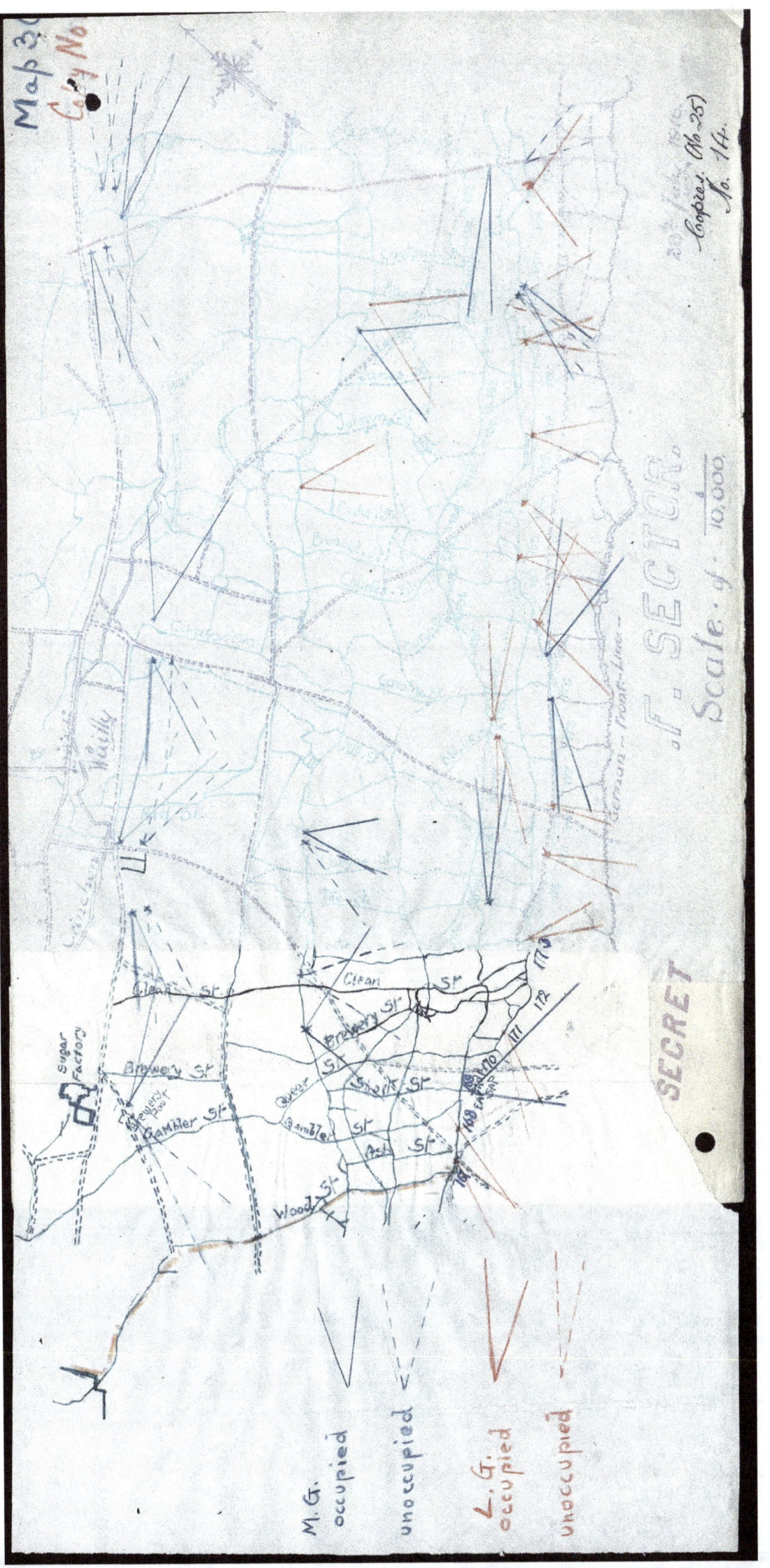

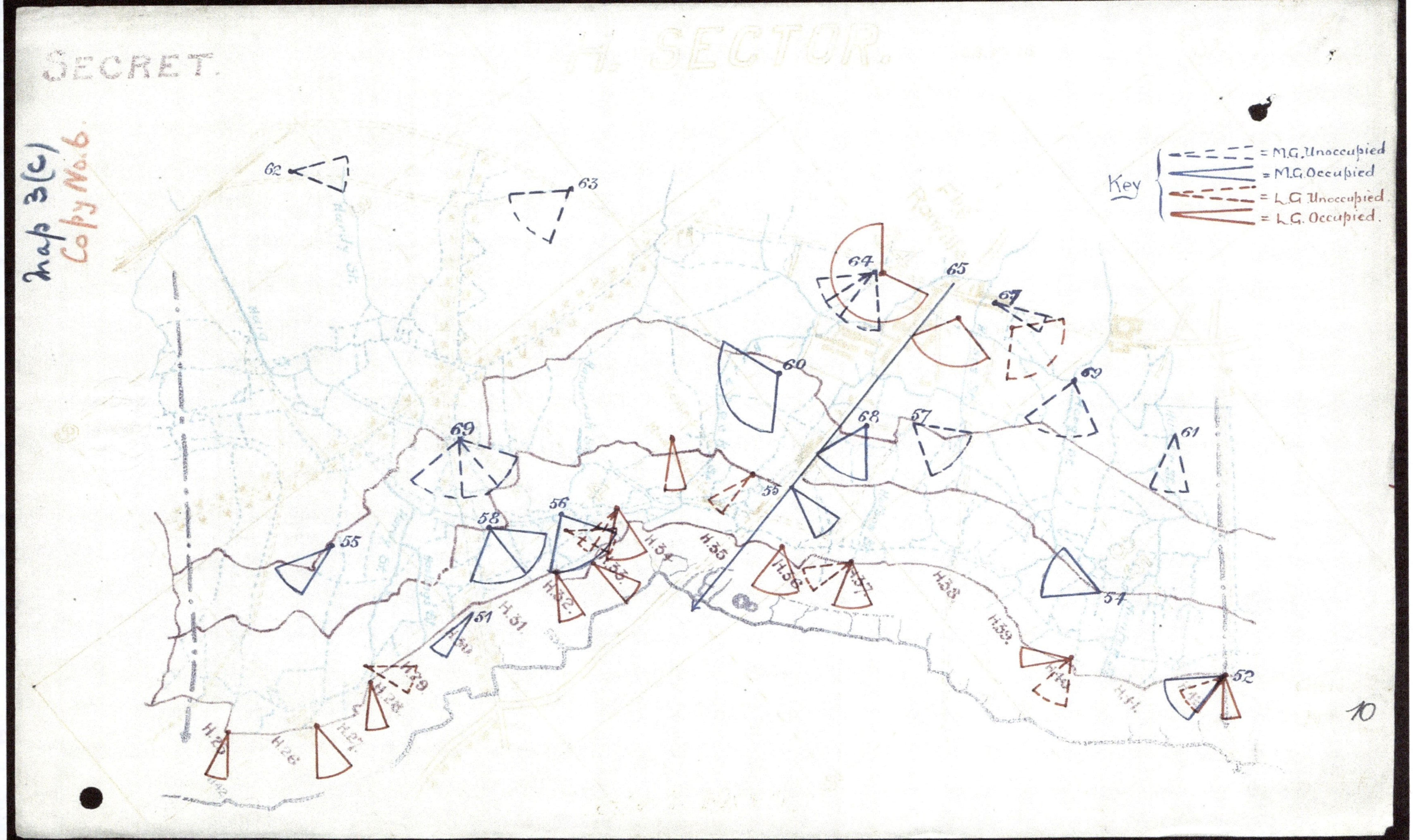
SECRET.
H. SECTOR.
Map 3(c)
Copy No. 6
Key
= M.G. Unoccupied
= M.G. Occupied
= L.G. Unoccupied
= L.G. Occupied.
62
63
64
65
60
68
57
61
69
58
56
55
51
54
52
H.25
H.26
H.27
H.28
H.29
H.31
H.32
H.33
H.34
H.35
H.36
H.37
H.38
H.39
H.41
10

UNITS ON 6th CORPS EXCHANGE.

6th Corps
6th Corps., G., Q., R.A., A.D.O.S., A.D.A.S., D.D.M.S., I.O.M.,
A.P.M., FRENCH MISSION., FIELD CASHIER., 3rd Army., 7th Corps.,
17th Corps., 46th Div., 11th Div. Train., 11th D.S.C., 11th D.A.C,
11th R.E. Park.,(Thro' 46th Div.)., 6th Corps H.A., AVESNES.
All Sqyadrons R.F.C.

UNITS ON 32nd BDE. EXCHANGE.

32nd Bde. Staff., 32nd Advd. Hd.Qrs., 34th Bde., 58th F.A.B.,
6th Yorks Regt., 6th York & Lancs., 9th W. Riding R., 6th W.Yorks.

Units ON 33rd Bde. EXCHANGE.

33rd Bde. Staff., GENDARMERIE ARRAS., 33rd M.G.Co. Artillery
Exchange., 7th S. Staffs. R. 6th Border R., 6th Lincolns.,
Test Station., 59th F.A.B., "I" Sector.

UNITS ON 34th BDE. EXCHANGE.

34th Bde. Staff., 32nd Bde., 139th Bde., 8th North'd Fus.
5th Dorsets R., 5th Manch. R., 34th M.G.Co., T.M.Btty.,
60th F.A.B., 133rd F.A.B., Advd. Dressing Stn., C.Co.E.Yorks.
60th Co. R.E., 6th E. Yorks R.

UNITS ON 6th CORPS H.A. EXCHANGE.

6th Corps., H.A. SOUTHERN and NORTHERN H.A.

UNITS ON GENDARMERIE EXCHANGE.

TOWN COMMANDANT ARRAS., INTELLIGENCE ARRAS., 33rd Inf. Bde.,
62nd Inf. Bde., 110th Inf. Bde., 96th F.A.B., 65th A.O.S.,
TOWN MAJOR, H.Q. "I" Sector., TOXIN BELL., N.Z. TUNNELLING CO.

UNITS ON 11th Div. H.Q. EXCHANGE.

Q., G., C.R.E., C.R.A., A.D.M.S., A.D.V.S., D.A.D.O.S.,
21st Div., R.E. Workshops., 6th Corps H.A., GENDARMERIE.,
Signal Co., 32nd Bde., 33rd Bde., 34th Bde.

SECRET

11TH DIVISION COMMUNICATIONS
MAP No 4.
DIAGRAM OF CIRCUITS
UP TO BRIGADES

REFERENCE

Sounder
Vibrator
Telephone
Telephone on Exchange
Sounder superimposed on Phone

Lines of Visual Communication Station
Wireless Station

Aerial Lines
Buried or Trenched
Under Construction

GENDARMERIE
33RD BDE
53rd R.F.A.
33rd Bde Batt.d H.Q.
32ND BDE.
58th R.F.A.
32nd Bde Batt.d H.Q.
R.E. Workshops
11TH DIV.
6th Corps H.Q.
II DA
3rd Bde Batt.d H.Q.
3rd General Visual St.
34TH BDE.
60th R.F.A.

To 6th Corps
To 46th Div.
To 2nd Div.

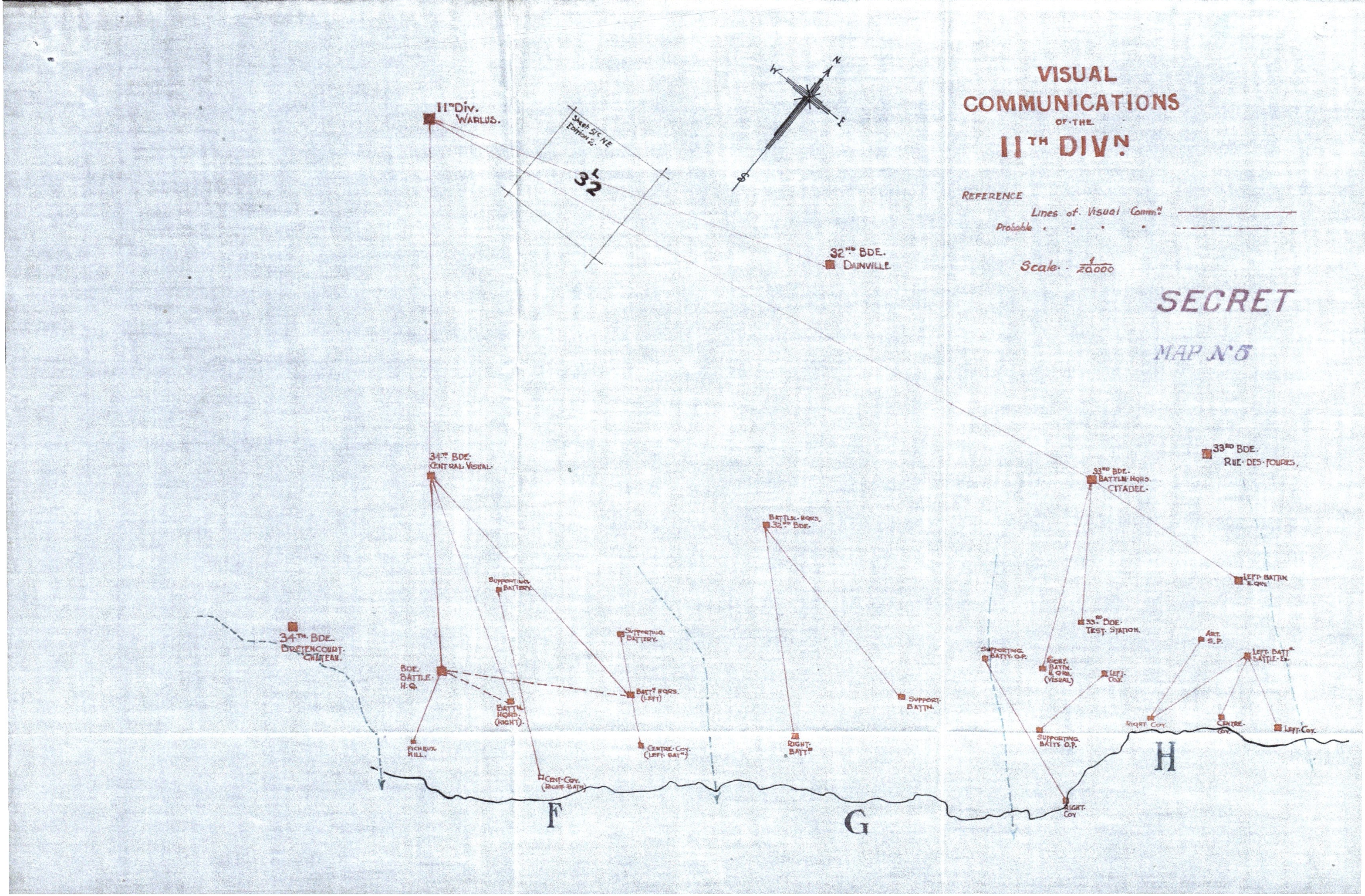
VISUAL
COMMUNICATIONS
OF THE
11TH DIVN.
REFERENCE
Lines of Visual Commn.
Probable
Scale 1/20000
SECRET
MAP No 5
11th Div. WARLUS.
Sheet 51C NE Edition 2.
32
32nd BDE. DAINVILLE.
33rd BDE. RUE-DES-FOURES,
33rd BDE. BATTLN. HQRS. CITADEL.
34th BDE. CENTRAL VISUAL.
BATTLE HQRS. 32nd BDE.
LEFT. BATTN. H.QRS.
33rd BDE. TEST. STATION.
34th BDE. BRETENCOURT CHATEAU.
BDE. BATTLE. H.Q.
SUPPORTING BATTERY.
BATTN. HQRS. (RIGHT).
BATTn. HQRS. (LEFT)
FICHEUX MILL.
CENT. COY. (RIGHT BATTN)
CENTRE COY. (LEFT BATTn)
RIGHT BATTn
SUPPORT. BATTN.
SUPPORTING BATTY. O.P.
RIGHT. BATTN. H.QRS. (VISUAL)
LEFT. COY.
ART. S.P.
LEFT. BATTn. BATTLE H.
RIGHT COY.
CENTRE COY.
LEFT. COY.
RIGHT COY.
F
G
H

APPENDIX "O".

11th Divisional SCHOOL OF INSTRUCTION.

(1). A Divisional School of Instruction for Officers and N.C.O's will be established at GOUY-EN-ARTOIS. The first class will assemble on 31st July. Students to report to Adjt. by 4 p.m.

(2) The following will compose the School Staff :-

		Commandant.	6th E.York.R. ESTRIDGE.Major.
OFFICERS.	N.C.O's.	1st Wing.	32nd Inf.Bde.
		2nd Wing.	6th E.York.R.
Commdt.	S.M.	Bomber.	33rd Inf.Bde.
Adjutant.	Q.M.S.	Gasser.	34th Inf.Bde.
1st Wing.	Asst.Bomber	Adjt.	32nd Inf.Bde.
2nd Wing.	Physical Training.	S.M.	33rd Inf.Bde.
Bomber.	Asst. " "	Q.M.S.	34th Inf.Bde.
Gasser.	Musketry.	1st Asst.)	
		Musketry.)	6th E.York.R.

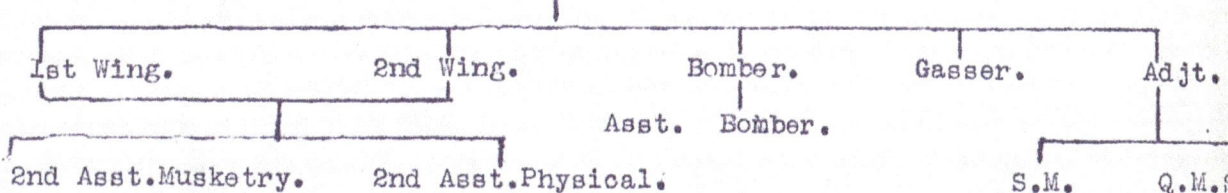

(3) Classes will consist of :-

2 Officers per Infantry Battalion. (Batmen will accompany Officers
2 N.C.O's or selected Privates per Infantry Battalion.
Officers & N.C.O's will be sent to the School under Regimental arrangements.

(4) Each class will last 14 days divided into periods of 3 - 4 - 4 - and 3 days.

(5) The aim of the course is to give officers and N.C.O's a foundation which will enable them to command their men in the conditions peculiar to the present war. The importance of discipline will be especially emphasized, and instruction will be given in special subjects such as grenade work, precautions against gas, bayonet fighting, siting of trenches, sand-bagging, revetting, wiring, and telling off of working parties, (especially at night). Instruction in interior economy and regimental duties will also be given.

Lectures will be given by Officers of the Divisional Staff - R.E. and R.A; and efforts will be made to procure the services of officers outside the Division in this respect.

(6) The School Staff, as detailed in para: 2, will report to the Commandant at GOUY at 4 p.m. on the 26th July.

In order that the School may be a success it is of the greatest importance that only specially selected Officers and N.C.O's should be sent to it as Instructors, the School is being established in the interests of the Infantry Brigades, and Brigade and Battalion Commanders are earnestly requested to select the best Officers and N.C.O's available in their commands to staff it.

H.Q. 11th Division.
23rd July 1916.

Major.
G.S. 11th Div.

PROGRAMME.

NOTE. D.W.O. = At disposal of Wing Officers.
There will be <u>Voluntary</u> Bayonet Fighting daily
from 6 - 7 p.m.

1st WEEK.

HOURS.

1st Day.
- 9- 0 a.m. Inspection by Commandant.
- 9-30 " D.W.O. Explanation of Syllabus, Standing Orders, etc.,
- 11- 0 " Opening address by Commandant.
- 11-45 " P.T. and Bayonet.
- 2- 0 p.m. Parade.
    Lecture on Drill with Demonstration & practice.
- 4- 0 " Lecture "DISCIPLINE".

2nd Day.
- 6-45 a.m. Drill.
- 9-15 " Parade.
- 9-30 " P.T. and Bayonet.
- 11-30 " Demonstration Extended Order Drill, Signals etc.,
- 2- 0 p.m. Battle drill (normal) Demonstration Artillery Formations followed by Practice.
- 4- 0 " Lecture "Trench Orders and Routine".

3rd Day.
- 6-45 a.m.)
- 9-15 ") As before.
- 9-30 " Lecture Entrenchments (revvetting, laying out trenches) and Demonstration.
- 11-30 " Battle drill (normal) 2 practices.
- 2- 0 p.m. Lecture "P.T. and Bayonet" Major CAMPBELL.
- 3- 0 " P.T. and Bayonet.

4th Day.
- 6-45 a.m.)
- 9-15 ") As 2nd day.
- 9-30 ")
- 11-30 " Battle drill (normal) last practices,
- 2 to
- 2-45 p.m. D.W.O.
- 4- 0 " Lecture.
- 9-30 " Explanation and Demonstration "Telling off working parties, laying out trenches".

5th Day.
- 6-45 a.m.)
- 9-15 ") As before.
- 9-30 ")
- 11-30 " D.W.O.
- 2- 0 p.m. Battle drill (abnormal) Explanation, Demonstration and Practice. (1st half).
- 4- 0 " Lecture.

6th Day.
- 6-45 a.m.)
- 9-15 ") As before.
- 9-30 ")
- 11-30 " Lewis Gun. (Officers).
    Telling off working parties, laying out trenches
    (N.C.O's).
- 2- 0 p.m. Battle drill (abnormal) 2nd half. Explanation, Demonstration and Practice.
- 4- 0 " Short revision of week's work.

	HOURS.	2nd WEEK.

7th Day.
- 6-45 a.m.)
- 9-15 ") As before.
- 9-30 ")
- 11-30 "   Fire Control, Fire Orders, Explanations and Demonstration.
- 2- 0 p.m. Attack (normal) first 3 stages. Lecture and Demonstration.
- 4- 0 p.m. Lecture. Reports and Orders. (G.S.O.1)?

8th Day.
- 6-45 a.m.)
- 9-15 ") As before.
- 9-30 ")
- 11-30 "   Fire Control, Fire Orders practised.
- 2- 0 p.m. Attack (normal) last 3 stages. Lecture and Demonstration.
- 4- 0 "   Lecture "The Horse and Horse Mastership" (A.D.V.S.)

9th Day.
- 6-45 a.m.)
- 9-15 ") As before.
- 9-30 ")
- 11-30 "   Telling off working parties, laying out Trenches. Lewis Gun. (N.C.Os).   (Officers).
- 2- 0 p.m. Attack normal. (1st 3 stages) Practice.
- 4- 5 "   Lecture.

10th Day.
- 6-45 a.m.)
- 9-15 ") As before.
- 9-30 ")
- 11-30 "   Demonstration "Mounting Guard" etc.,
- 2- 0 p.m. Lecture and demonstration "Rapid Wiring" followed by practice.
- 4- 0 "   Lecture "Musketry Training " (G.O.C.) ?.

11th Day.
- 6-45 a.m.)
- 9-15 ") As before.
- 9-30 ")
- 11-30 "   Judging distance, description of Targets.
- 2 to
- 3-30 p.m. Gas helmet drill, Bivouac Drill, Demonstration and Practice.
- 9-30 "   Night work. Relieving a Co. in Trenches.

12th Day.
- 6-45 a.m.)
- 9-15 ") As before.
- 9-30 ")
- 11-30 "   Obstacles. Explanation and Practice.
- 2- 0 p.m. Attack (abnormal) 1st Stage. Explanation, Demonstration, followed by Practice.
- 4- 0 "   Short revision of week's work and discussion.

3rd WEEK.

13th Day. Hours.

- 6-45 a.m.)
- 9-15 ") As before.
- 9-30 ")
- 11-30 " Musketry Training, Demonstration and explanation.
- 2- 0 p.m. Attack (abnormal) 2nd Stage. Demonstration, followed by Practice.
- 4- 0 " Lecture.

14th Day.

- 6-45 a.m. D.W.O.
- 9-15 " Parade.
- 9-30 " P.T. and Bayonet.
- 11-30 " Compass, Map reading, takinh bearings.
- 2- 0 p.m. Advanced Guard Scheme.
- 4- 0 " Lecture.

15th Day.
- 6-45 a.m.)
- 9-15 ") As 13th day.
- 9-30 ")
- 11-30 " Musketry Training.
- 2- 0 p.m. Fire Control Scheme.
- 4- 0 " Lecture.

16th Day.

- 6-45 a.m. D.W.O.
- 9-15 ") As before.
- 9-30 ")
- 11-30 " Musketry.
- 2- 0 p.m. Scheme "Defence of Locality".
- 4- 0 " Lecture.

17th Day.

- 6-45 a.m. D.W.O.
- 9-15 " Parade.
- 9-30 " "Outpost" Scheme.
- 2- 0 p.m. Bayonet and Wiring Competitions. (heats).
- 4- 0 " Lecture.

18th Day.

- 9-15 a.m. Inspection by Commandant.
- 11- 0 " Closing address.
- 2- 0 p.m. Competitions (finals) and Sports.
- 9- 0 " Concert.

****

H.Q. 11th Division,

3rd August 1916.

Major.

G.S. 11th Division.

List of Lectures to be given at 11th Divisional

SCHOOL OF INSTRUCTION.

DATE.	NAME.	SUBJECT OF LECTURE.
Saturday Augt.12th.	Colonel SHANAHAN. A.D.M.S. 11th Divn.	Sanitation and Hygiene.
Sunday Augt.13th.	Major HALAHAN. Comdg. 12th Squadron R.F.C.	Aircraft (at 12th Squadron Aerodrome.)
Monday. Augt.14th.	Lt-Col. COLERIDGE. D.S.O. G.S.O.1. 11th Divn.	Reports and Orders.
Tuesday. Augt.15th.	Major MACAULEY. A.D.V.S. 11th Divn.	Horsemastership.
Wednesday Augt.16th.	Captain WOOLEY. V.C. G.S.O.3. 3rd Army.	Bombs and bombing tactics
Thursday Augt.17th.	Sir. C. WOOLCOMBE, K.C.S. Comdg. 11th Divn.	Musketry Training.
Tuesday Augt 22nd.	— — — An officer from 21st Divn.	The Battle of the SOMME.
Thursday Augt 24th.	Captain PEMBERTHY, 3rd Army Sniping School.	Sniping and front line intelligence work.

All lectures at 4 p.m. unless otherwise stated.

H.Q. 11th Division.

12th August 1916.

R.F.Guy

Major.

G.S. 11th Divn.

SPORTS PROGRAMME

Friday and Saturday 25th and 26th August 1916.

2 p.m. each day.

1. BAYONET FIGHTING.

			1st Prize.	2nd P...
(a)	Individual.	(i) Officers	Medal.	Meda...
		(ii) N.C.O's	Medal.	Meda...
(b)	Inter-Bttn.	(Team 2 Officers) (2 N.C.O's.)	Medals.	---
(c)	Inter-Wing.	(Student Officers) (v) (Student N.C.O's.)	---	---

2. WIRING COMPETITION.

    Rapid Wiring. (Student Officers)
                        (v)
                        (Student N.C.O's.)

3. RELAY RACE.

    Teams. Student Officers.   Francs 2 each.
             Student N.C.O's.
             Permanent Staff & duty men.
             Servants.

4. BLINDFOLD DRILL.   N.C.O.   Men.
    Teams. 1 Squad Leader &)   Francs 5.   3:50 ea...
          Squad of 8 men.)

5. SACK BUMPING.
    Teams of 6.   Francs 5 each.

6. TUG O' WAR.
   (If rope can   Teams of 8 (representing officer Students)
    be got).   (N.C.O. Students, Permanent   Francs 3.5...
                        (Staff. Servants).

                                                       1st.   2nd.   3r...
7. BAND RACE.   If the Band attends the Sports. Fr:10. - 7. - 3.

Heats of Events 1 and 6 will be run off on Friday.

8. BEER & BISCUITS RACE.
                                             1st.   2nd.
        Open to Servants and Dutymen) Pr: 5 each. 2'50
                (Teams of 2).   )

STANDING ORDERS.
11th Division School of Instruction.

1. The School is known as the 11th Division SCHOOL OF INSTRUCTION.

2. <u>POSTAL ADDRESS.</u>   do   do   do

3. <u>STAFF.</u>

OFFICERS.	N.C.O's	Attached.
Commandant.	School S.M.	R.E. Officers.
Chief Instructor.	" Q.M.S.	Gas Officer.
(2nd in Command).	Sergt. Instructor.	Bombing Officer.
Adjutant.	(P.T. & Bayonet).	
2 Wing Officer	Asst: do do	
Instructors.	2 Wing N.C.O	
	Instructors.	

The senior Instructor acts as 2nd in Command.

4. <u>CLASSES.</u> Will be divided into 2 Wings, one composed of Officers, one of N.C.O's, each with 1 Officer and 1 N.C.O. instructor.

5. <u>PERIOD.</u> A Course will last 21 days.

6. <u>SYLLABUS.</u> The subjects to be studied will be found hung up in the Messes.

7. <u>STANDING ORDERS.</u> On the day succeeding that of joining, the Standing Orders will be read out on the first parade by Wing Officers to their Wing.

8. <u>WORKING HOURS.</u> According to weekly programme.

9. <u>OFFICIAL TIME.</u> The School time will be taken from the Orderly Room.

10. <u>STAFF CONFERENCE.</u> Officer Instructors will meet the Commandant daily (except Sundays) immediately after noon lecture, or at 4 p.m. if there is no lecture.

11. <u>ORDERLY ROOM.</u> 8-45 a.m. daily.

12. <u>BOUNDS.</u> No Officer, N.C.O., or Man will leave the village without leave from the Commandant.

13. <u>DRESS.</u> (1). <u>OFFICERS.</u> On Drill or Training parades, unless otherwise ordered, Canvas Clothing (if provided) and SAM BROWN Belts with sling and frog, or equipment Belts with slings.
(2). <u>N.C.O's & MEN.</u> Drill Order, and if leather equipment, without pouches. N.C.O's and men walking out will be properly dressed, putties and belts being worn. Overcoats if worn will be properly buttoned up.

14. <u>DUTIES.</u> (a) An Officer of the Instructional Staff will be detailed daily by the Adjutant who will not leave the vicinity of the School H.Q's except for purposes of instruction.

(b) <u>Officers Wing.</u> The Officers Wing Commander will detail a Student Officer daily for duty. Whose duties are :-
   (1) Parade and Inspect the Officers Wing.
   (2) Take charge of the Wing on all parades if an Officer of the Instructional Staff is not present.
   (3) Carry out any other duties which may be assigned to him.

14. DUTIES Contd. (c) **N.C.O's WING.** The senior N.C.O. is responsible for the discipline of the Wing, and for the general care and cleanliness of the N.C.O's quarters.

He will not allow smoking during hours of instruction except by permission of the Senior Officer.

He will not allow any intoxicating liquors to be taken into the quarters.

The School S.M. will detail daily a Student N.C.O. as Orderly Sergt. whose duties will be as follows:-
  (a) Call the Wing at Reveille.
  (b) Be present at all meals, reporting any complaints to the Senior N.C.O. of the Wing.
  (c) Take orders to the Senior N.C.O. who will be responsible that they are posted in the N.C.O's Mess.
  (d) Parade and inspect the Wing and march it to and from the place of parade, calling the roll 5 minutes before the hour of parade.
  (e) Call the roll at Tattoo and report to the School S.M.
  (f) Make out sick reports 30 minutes after Reveille.
  (g) See lights out at the correct time.

15. ADDRESSES. All officers before leaving the School will write their addresses in the Officers address book in the Orderly Room.

16. ROUTINE. Till further orders the following hours will be observed :-
REVEILLE. 5-45 a.m. TATTOO. 9-30 p.m. LIGHTS OUT. 10 p.m.
BREAKFAST. 7-45 a.m. DINNER. 1-0 p.m. TEA. 5 p.m.
MESS 8-0 p.m.

17. SERVANTS AND DUTY MEN'S LINES. The Instructional Officer on duty and the Q.M.Sgt. will visit these daily.

18. SICK. The M.O. will hold sick parade at such time as may be notified. Any N.C.O. or man reporting sick will report to the Wing Orderly Sergt. 30 minutes after Reveille. The M.O. will notify the Adjutant who will report to the Wing Officers the name of any N.C.O. excused parade.

Any officer wishing to report sick will do so in writing to the Adjutant.

19. WING ORDERLY OFFICER & SERGT. Duties are on no account to interfere with the Instructional Training.

20. RATIONS. Will be drawn from the Q.M.Stores at an hour to be notified.

21. QUARTERS. All quarters will be clean and tidy by 9-30 a.m.

22. POST. Student N.C.O's letters will be franked by their Wing Officer, those of Servants and duty men by the Adjutant. All letters will be collected daily at 8 p.m.

23. DISCIPLINE. For the purpose of discipline Student N.C.O's will be under their Wing Commander, all other N.C.O's & men under the Adjutant. These officers will investigate all charges.

24. AMMUNITION. On the day of assembly of each course all ammunition except 20 rds. per man will be handed in to Q.M.Stores.

25. LEAVE. Application for leave on Sundays will be made in the book kept at the O.R. for that purpose, not later than 12 noon Saturday.

25. SPIES. ALL RANKS ARE PARTICULARLY CAUTIONED AGAINST CONVERSING WITH STRANGERS ON MILITARY MATTERS.

APPENDIX "D"

11th Division TRAINING PROGRAMME.

1st and 2nd Day.	3rd and 4th Day.	5th and 6th Days.	7th and 8th Days.
Platoon instruction under Platoon Commanders.	Company instruction under Company Commanders.	Company instruction under Company Commanders.	Battalion instruction under Battalion Commanders.
HOURS.	**HOURS.**	**HOURS.**	**HOURS.**
Running drill with obstacles. ½	Running drill with obstacles.	As in 3rd and 4th days. 2	As in 3rd and 4th days. 1½
Physical Drill ½ hour twice a day. ½	Physical Exercise.		
Grenade Throwing.	Bayonet Fighting.		
Musketry. Rapid Loading} 1½ Loading lying } down. } Fire Control. }	Grenade Throwing.	Attack on Trenches. } 1. Open warfare. } 2. Trenches. }	Outposts. } Battle Drill. } Practice on improvised } 5 Ranges, falling targets} bottles etc. }
Bayonet Fighting ½ hour twice a day. 1	Company Drill. Close Order.} 3 " " Extended Order.} Fire control & discipline. } Passage of Obstacles. } Wood Fighting. } Battle Drill. } Consolidation of positions } Won. }	Consolidation of Positions. } 3 Rapid wiring. } Battle Drill etc. }	
Signals, passing messages ½			
Close Order drill. } Extended Order drill. } Passing of Obstacles. } Battle Drill. } Cross Country marching } in various formations. } Moving through woods. } 2 Attack Practice from } Trenches. }	Rapid Wiring. } Cross Country Marching. } in various formations. }	Cross Country Marching } in various formations. } 3	Route marching with } packs, combined with } 3½ attack (day and night) }
Route marching 5/7 miles }2 without packs. }	Route Marching with packs 10 miles. 3	Route Marching with packs combined with advanced and rear guards. 3	
			9th and 10th Days.
			Brigade instruction under Brigadiers.

NOTES. The following points also require consideration. Instruction of Machine and Lewis Gunners, Signallers and other Specialists, Lectures on Regimental History, Causes of the War, Care of Arms, Avoidance of Waste, Health, Sanitation, Checking Gas and Fire Attacks.

R.Hurry Major
G.S
11th Division.

APPENDIX "E".

SECRET.

Copy No. 12

30th August 1916.

11th. Division Operation Order No.19.

1. The Division (less Artillery) will be transferred to the 2nd. Corps, Reserve Army on the 3rd. September and will be concentrated in area "O", Reserve Army.

2. Details of the move are shown in Appendix A.
   Train timings are given in Appendix B.

3. Dismounted R.E. personnel will travel by train under the orders of the B.G.C.'s of Infantry Brigades they are affiliated to.

4. Transport and personnel moving by road will do so by routes laid down in Appendix A.
   Train will move as ordered by A.A. & Q.M.G.

5. Lists of billets in Area "O" will be issued separately.

6. Supply Railhead for the 11th Division will change from TINCQUES to BOUQUEMAISON on 3rd September.
   Supply Railhead for 4th September will be in Reserve Army area.

7. Completion of all moves will be reported to D.H.Q.

8. On 2nd September D.H.Q. will close at LE CAUROY at 10 a.m and will re-open at DOULLENS at 12 noon.
   3rd September D.H.Q. will close at DOULLENS at 10 a.m. and will re-open at ACHEUX at 12 noon.

for Lieut-Colonel
Gen. Staff.11th Di

Issued:-

Copy No. 1. C.R.A. 11th Div.	Copy No. 12 War Diary.
2. C.R.E. 11th Div.	13 File.
3. 32nd Inf. Bde.	14 Third Army.
4. 33rd Inf. Bde.	15 Reserve Army.
5. 34th Inf. Bde.	16 6th Corps.
6. 6th E. Yorks R.	17 2nd Corps.
7. Signals.	18 D.A.D.O.S.
8. A & Q Branch.	19 Ell Corps.
9. A.D.M.S.	
10. A.P.M.	
11. 11th Div. Train.	

APPENDIX "A".

MOVE OF 11th DIVISION (less Artillery).

Unit.	Date.	From.	To.	Route	REMARKS.
6th E. Yorks.(Pioneers), with 1st line Transport and baggage wagons.	Augt. 31st.	AMBRINES	BOUQUEMAISON	Any.	Present billets to be vacated by 10 a.m. By route march.
6th E. Yorks.(Pioneers)	Sept. 1st.	BOUQUEMAISON.	ACHEUX.	BOUQUEMAISON.-DOULLENS-MARIEUX.	By bus. 52 busses will be at BOUQUEMAISON at 10 a.m. 1st.
1st line Transport.	do	do	do	do do	By route march.
33rd Infantry Brigade.	Sept. 2nd.	LIENCOURT. area.	ACHEUX. via PREVENT.	Route march to PREVENT thence by tactical trains.	Vide Appendix "B".
1st line Transport. 33rd Inf.Bde.	do	do	ACHEUX.	BEAUDRICOURT - IVERGNY-LUCHEUX-HOLLOY-THIEVRES-VAUCHELLES.	By route march.
32nd Infantry Brigade. with transport.	do	AMBRINES-IZEL area.	Billets vacated by 33rd Inf.Bde. Bde. H.Q. LIENCOURT.	Any.	33rd Inf. Bde. billets will not be available before 12 noon.
11th Division (less 3 Inf.Bdes.,Pioneer Bn. R.A. & dismounted R.E. personnel).	do	VIth Corps area.	DOULLENS HAUTE VISEE GROUCHES.	Any.	Places named will not be available before 12 noon. Billetting areas will be arranged by 11th Divl. "Q" Staff and communicated to Units concerned on 31st August 1916.
1st line Transport 34th Inf. Bde.	do	do	PUCHVILLERS	BEAUDRICOURT-IVERGNY-LUCHEUX-HOLLOY-THIEVRES-VAUCHELLES.	To be at PUCHVILLERS by 8 a.m. 3rd September.

P.T.O.

APPENDIX "A" continued.

Unit.	Date.	From.	To.	Route.	Remarks.
34th. Infantry Brigade.	Sept. 3rd.	Present billets.	PUCHVILLERS ACHEUX.	Route march to FREVENT thence by Rail.	Vide Appendix "B"
32nd. Infantry Brigade.	do.	LIENCOURT area.	ARQUEVES RAINCHEVAL	do.	do.
1st. Line Transport 32nd. Infantry Brigade.	do.	do.	ARQUEVES RAINCHEVAL	BEAUDRICOURT— IVERGNY—LUCHEUX— HOLLOY—THIEVRES— VAUCHELLES.	To be at ARQUEVES and RAINCHEVAL by 1 p.m. By route march.
11th. Division (less 3 Inf. Bdes., Pioneer Batt., and R.A. and dismounted R.E. personnel.).	do.	DOULLENS. HAUTE—VISEE. GROUCHES.	ACHEUX. LEALVILLERS. ARQUEVES RAINCHEVAL. PUCHVILLERS	Any.	By route march. 68th. Field Co. wagons and 33rd. F.A. to LEALVILLERS. 86th. Field Co. wagons and 34th. F.A. to PUCHVILLERS. 67th. Field Co. wagons and 35th. F.A. to ARQUEVES.

APPENDIX "B".

The following will be the train timings for the tactical move of the 11th. Division Infantry Brigades from FREVENT to ACHEUX on the 2nd. and 3rd. proximo :-

2-9-16.
TRAINS.
No.1.
FREVENT .... dep. 11:38 T.) 33rd. Infantry
ACHEUX. .... arr. 15:50   ) Brigade and
) dismounted
) R.E. personnel
No.2.   ) 86 a.Field
FREVENT. .... dep. 12:38 T.) Company R.E.
ACHEUX. .... arr. 16:20

No.3.
FREVENT. .... dep. 15:11 T.P.)
ACHEUX. .... arr. 20:40   )

3-9-16.
No.4.
FREVENT. .... dep. 4:38   T.
ACHEUX. .... arr. 8:20
) 34th.
) Infantry
) Brigade and
No.5.   ) dismounted R.E.
FREVENT. .... dep. 5:38   T.) personnel 86th
ACHEUX. .... arr. 9:25   ) Field Company
) R.E.

No.6.
FREVENT. .... dep. 8:38   )
ACHEUX. .... arr.13:35   T.P.)

No.7.
FREVENT. .... dep.14:38   T.
ACHEUX. arr.18:50
) 32nd.
) 34th. Infantry
) Brigade and
No. 8.   ) dismounted
FREVENT. .... dep.18:38   T.) R.E.personnel
ACHEUX. .... arr.23:25.   ) 67th. Field
) Company R.E.

No.9.
FREVENT. .... dep.23:38   T.P.
ACHEUX. .... arr. 4:05.4/9/16.)

All troops should be at the station one hour before entraining time in cases of Trains Nos.1, 2, 4, 5, 7 and 8 and three hours before entraining time in cases of trains Nos.3, 6 and 9.

To:-.................  S E C R E T.

Reference 11th. Division O.O. No. 19.

Erase para.3 and insert :-

September 2nd.   The 67th., 68th., and 86th. Field
                 Companies R.E. with 1st. Line Transport
                 will proceed under orders of the C.R.E.
                 11th. Divn. by route march to GROUCHES
                 and thence to billets in area "O" on
                 September 3rd.

                 Routes. as laid down for the 1st. Line
                 Transport of Brigades./ R.E. Coys are
                 affiliated to.

APPENDIX "B".   Erase " and dismounted R.E. personnel
                 Field Company R.E."

31st. August 1916.
                                          Major,
                                  General Staff, 11th. Divn.

W. 15517—M. 141. 250,000. 1/16. L.S.&Co. Forms/W 3091/2.   Army Form W. 3091.

Cover for Documents.

Nature of Enclosures.

WAR DIARY

of

11th. DIVISION, GENERAL STAFF,

for month of

SEPTEMBER, 1916.

Notes, or Letters written.

Army Form C. 2118.

WAR DIARY
or
INTELLIGENCE SUMMARY

11th Division. "G"

SEPTEMBER 1916.

(Erase heading not required.)

Instructions regarding War Diaries and Intelligence Summaries are contained in F.S. Regs., Part II. and the Staff Manual respectively. Title Pages will be prepared in manuscript.

Place	Date	Hour	Summary of Events and Information	Remarks and references to Appendices
LE CAUROY.	1st.	10a.m.	6th East Yorks (Pioneers) moved from BOUQUEMAISON to ACHEUX by motor bus. Fine day. Wind N.W.	
DOULLENS.	2nd.		33rd Inf. Bde. marched to FREVENT and entrained there for ACHEUX. Marched thence to billets at LEALVILLERS and ACHEUX. Brigade H.Q. opened at LEALVILLERS at 5 p.m. 1st line Transport moved by road to ACHEUX.	Vide O.O. No.19.a/ 30/8/16.
		10a.m.	32nd Inf. Bde. moved from AMBRINES. IZEL area into billets vacated by the 33rd Inf. Bde. about LIENCOURT.	
		10am.	Divl. Hd. Qrs. closed at LE CAUROY and moved to DOULLENS.	
		2 pm.	34th Inf. Bde. 1st line Transport moved by road to PUCHEVILLERS via LUCHEUX-HOLLOY-VAUCHELLES. The Field Companies R.E. moved by route march to GROUCHES.	
ACHEUX.	3rd.		34th Inf. Bde. marched from HOUVIN area to FREVENT and commenced entraining there for ACHEUX at 4-30 a.m. Marched from ACHEUX to billets at PUCHEVILLERS. 32nd Inf. Bde. marched from LIENCOURT area to FREVENT and commenced entraining there for ACHEUX at 2-30 p.m. Marched from ACHEUX to billets at RAINCHEVAL and ARQUEVES with Bde. Head Qrs. at the latter place.	
		9-30am.	67th Field Coy. R.E. 35th Fd. Ambulance. } Marched from GROUCHES to ARQUEVES.	
		do	68th Field Coy. R.E. 33rd Fd. Ambulance. } Marched from GROUCHES to LEALVILLERS.	
		do	86th Field Coy. R.E. 34th Fd. Ambulance. } Marched from GROUCHES to PUCHEVILLERS.	
		10am.	Divl. Hd. Qrs. closed at DOULLENS at 10 a.m. and reopened at ACHEUX at 12 noon. The Division now belongs to the 2nd Corps, Reserve Army.	
ACHEUX.	4th.		No change in the disposition of the Division. Showery day. Wind. N.W.	

Army Form C. 2118.

WAR DIARY
or
INTELLIGENCE SUMMARY

SEPTEMBER 1916.

(Erase heading not required.)

Instructions regarding War Diaries and Intelligence Summaries are contained in F. S. Regs., Part II. and the Staff Manual respectively. Title Pages will be prepared in manuscript.

Place	Date	Hour	Summary of Events and Information	Remarks and references to Appendices
ACHEUX.	5th.	10am.	Orders were received that the Division (less Artillery) was to relieve the 25th Division (less Artillery) in the line S. of THIEPVAL, relief to be complete by the 8th September. 33rd Inf. Bde. marched from ACHEUX and LEALVILLERS to BOUZINCOURT and passed under the orders of the G.O.C. 25th Division. Pioneer Battalion marched to dug-outs in W.18.b. and passed under the orders of 2nd Corps.	APPENDIX A. O.O. No.20. d/ 5-9-16.
ACHEUX.	6th.	2am.	33rd Inf. Bde. relieved the 74th Inf. Bde. 25th Division in right sector trenches R.33.c.6.8. to R.32.c.9.9 from 1500 yards to 2000 yards South of THIEPVAL.	
		8-30am.	Two Battalions 32nd Inf. Bde. marched from ARQUEVES to SENLIS. Fine day with N.W. wind.	
CAMOUFLAGE V.16.d.	7th.	2 am.	Two Battalions 32nd Inf. Bde. 6th Yorks and 6th York & Lancs. relieved the 75th Inf. Bde. in left sector trenches from R.31.a.0.5 to R.31.b.7.4.	
		8-30am.	Head Qrs. and two Battalions 32nd Inf. Bde. (8th W. Riding & 9th W. Yorks) marched from RAINCHEVAL to SENLIS. Bde. Hd. Qrs. moved to W.12.c.6.8 and took over command of left sector trenches at 2 p.m.	
		9 am.	Divl. Hd. Qrs. moved from ACHEUX to huts at CAMOUFLAGE V.16.d. ½ mile S. of SENLIS and G.O.C. took over command of the line from 25th Division. 67th Field Coy. R.E.) 68th Field Coy. R.E.) Marched to AVELUY. 86th Field Coy. R.E. Marched to W.19.d.9.6.	
CAMOUFLAGE.	8th.	8 am.	34th Inf. Bde. marched from PUCHEVILLERS to BOUZINCOURT where the Brigade is in Divisional Reserve. 2 Battalions 32nd Inf. Bde. marched from SENLIS to BOUZINCOURT and BLACK HORSE CORNER dug-outs. There was considerable activity on both sides during the night of the 7th/8th and early morning. The vicinity of left sector Head. Qrs. was shelled with lachrymatory shells. The remainder of the day passed quietly with intermittent shelling of our front line trenches with Artillery and Trench Mortars.	
		10-30am.	The relief of the 25th Divl. Artillery by our Divl. Artillery was completed. Fine day. N.E. wind.	

Army Form C. 2118.

Instructions regarding War Diaries and Intelligence Summaries are contained in F. S. Regs., Part II. and the Staff Manual respectively. Title Pages will be prepared in manuscript.

WAR DIARY
or
~~INTELLIGENCE SUMMARY~~

(Erase heading not required.)

11th Division. "G".

SEPTEMBER 1916.

Place	Date	Hour	Summary of Events and Information	Remarks and references to Appendices
CAMOUFLAGE SENLIS.	9th.		Considerable artillery activity on both sides. During the morning the enemy shelled our front and support lines with H.E. and Shrapnel. From 12-30 p.m. - 2-30 p.m. enemy steadily shelled BLIGHTY CORNER and POPLAR BRIDGE. The enemy Infantry were very nervous, they sent up a large number of VERY lights and various coloured rockets and used their Machine Guns a good deal. Fine day. Wind. N.E. BOUZINCOURT was shelled with 8" shells and some damage was done.	
do	10th.		A quieter day, in the right sector enemy Artillery inactive. In the left sector the enemy shelled our front, support and C.T's at intervals from 5 p.m. until midnight with H.E. and shrapnel. Enemy snipers were also more active, particularly against SKINNER STREET. Our artillery was active during the day and with the H.A. destroyed certain enemy trenches and dug-outs. Enemy working parties were seen working in R.31 and R.32 and were dispersed by our Artillery. Enemy continues to fire a large number of coloured rockets at night. Fine day. Wind N.E.	
do.	11th.		The Artillery of both sides was active throughout the day. Our Artillery bombarded enemy front and support trenches opposite the Divisional front. Enemy bombarded our front line trenches particularly SKYLINE & BRIMSTONE trenches. Between 8 p.m. and 11 p.m. he bombarded the right Brigade line with gas shells. The gas hung about the trenches and dug-outs for fully two hours after the bombardment. About 9 p.m. AVELUY & AUTHVILLE were heavily shelled. About 9-15 a.m. a German aeroplane was driven down by one of our machines and fell in flames behind POZIERES. Showery day. Wind. S.W.	
do	12th		Our Artillery and Corps H.A. continued to ~~xxxit~~ bombard the enemy front line and support trenches at intervals during the day and night. Enemy replied on our trenches notably HINDENBURG and LEMBERG trenches. AUTHVILLE was shelled from 11 a.m. to 1 p.m. and again at 4 p.m. Orders were received from Reserve Army that the line R.31.d.9.8 - WONDER WORK - b.23 - 91 - 78 should be captured on the 14th instant. (vide attached O.O.). Fine day. Wind Westerly.	APPENDIX B O.O. No.21 d/ 12/9/16.

Army Form C. 2118.

WAR DIARY
or
INTELLIGENCE SUMMARY

(Erase heading not required.)

11th Division "G".

SPETEMBER 1916.

Place	Date	Hour	Summary of Events and Information	Remarks and references to Appendices
CAMOUFLAGE SENLIS.	13th.		Corps and Divisional Artillery continued to bombard THIEPVAL and enemy defences to be attacked on the 14th inst. at intervals during the day and night. The enemy shelled our trenches intermittently throughout the day otherwise the situation all day was quiet. Fine day. Wind North West.	
do	14th	5am 11am 6-30pm	Situation normal. Our trenches were shelled intermittently between 1 a.m. and 3 a.m. SKYLINR TRENCH was shelled by 5.9 between 8 a.m. and 9 a.m. otherwise situation quiet. The 32nd Brigade. (8th West Riding and 9th West Yorkshires) attacked and captured the line R.31.d.79 - R.31.b.60 - 51 - WONDER WORK - 23 - 03 - a.91 - 76 - 45, S.W. of THIEPVAL also trench from a.91 to about 6.1 with advanced posts at 31.c.46 and 58 and 68, having reached this objective by about 6-50 p.m. Fierce bombing continued for some time on left flank, where the support Battalion, 6th Yorkshires became engaged as eventually did the 6th York and Lancs. who were in Brigade Reserve. As a result of this operation about 1000 yards of German trenches were taken, including the WONDER WORK Redoubt, 100 prisoners mostly of the 209th Regt. & 3 Machine Guns. Bombing counter attacks were successfully repulsed. The artillery barrage supporting the attack was very accurate and well timed. Simultaneously with above, the 33rd Inf. Bde. (6th Border Regt) occupied without opposition the line R.32.d.23 - 25 - 03 - c.56 - 33 with advanced posts at d.26, 34, 57 and 67. 6th Lincolns also pushed out post to R.32.d.8.6. About mid-night, bombing counter attack on the 6th Border Regt. were repulsed, our Artillery being very effective.	APPX. "G". O.O. 22. //14/9/16.

CASUALTIES.

	Officers.			Other Ranks.		
	Killed.	Wounded.	Missing.	Killed.	Wounded.	Missing.
9th West Yorks.	8	4	—	33	240	33
6th Yorkshires.	2*	1	1	23	103	14 *Lt.Col. Forsyth killed.
8th West Riding.	3	5	—	20	209	21
6th York & Lancs.	—	5	—	—	31	2
32nd Bde. M.G.Coy.) " T.M.Btty)	—	1	—	—	7	1
	13	15	1	56	590	71

Army Form C. 2118.

WAR DIARY
or
INTELLIGENCE SUMMARY

(Erase heading not required.)

11th Division "G".

SEPTEMBER 1916.

Instructions regarding War Diaries and Intelligence Summaries are contained in F.S. Regs., Part II. and the Staff Manual respectively. Title Pages will be prepared in manuscript.

Place	Date	Hour	Summary of Events and Information	Remarks and references to Appendices
CAMOUFLAGE SENLIS. V.16.d.	15th		During the night 14th/15th and on the 15th. all the gains made yesterday were maintained and good progress was made in the work of consolidation. New trenches were dug from 32.c.63 - 65, 31.d.07 - 19.a.91 and from d.64 - 66. The two latter were joined up to WONDER WORK and HOHENZOLLERN TRENCH.	
			The 33rd Bde. during the night bombed up CONSTANCE TRENCH and consolidated it as far as point R.23.d.64.	
			During the day the enemy Artillery was active against both sectors of our front, particularly the area behind the WONDER WORK and the remains of the C.T's leading to it.	APPX. "D". D.O. 23.
		10p.m.	During the relief of the 32nd Inf. Bde. in left sector by the 147th Bde. 49th Division, the enemy made a strong bombing attack against our post at R.31.c.68 and rushed it. The 6th Yorkshires at once attacked and recaptured the post. Two of our Lewis guns were put out of action by enemy rifle grenades.	APPX. "E". O.O.24.
			During the night one prisoner of the 213th Res. Inf. Regt. was captured.	
			Fine day with N.E. wind.	
do	16th.		Enemy artillery was active during the day and night against both sectors of Divisional front.	
			During the night 15th/16th the 32nd Inf. Bde. was relieved in the left sector (WONDER WORK) by the 149th Inf. Bde. (W.R.) Division.	APPX. "F". D.O.25.
		9-30pm.	The 33rd Inf. Bde. captured DANUBE TRENCH up to Point R.32.b.62 after a bombing attack. They also occupied CONSTANCE TRENCH up to Point R.33.a.54.	
			During the night 16th/17th the 34th Inf. Bde. relieved the 8th Canadian Brigade on line R.33.a.54- MOUQUET FARM-R.28.b.57, suffering very few casualties. 3rd Canadian Division on our right. 149th (W.R.) Division on our left.	
			Fine day with cold North Wind.	
do	17th.		Enemy artillery showed a good deal of activity, several trenches being badly damaged. At about 7 p.m. enemy artillery opened fire on CONSTANCE TRENCH under cover of which a bombing party forced an entrance into our trench at R.33.a.5.4. The enemy were immediately counter-attacked and ejected by the 6th Lincoln Regt. who suffered several casualties. DANUBE & PEAR TRENCHES were heavily shelled about the same time.	
			During the night two prisoners of the 212th and 213th Res. Inf. Regts. were captured by 34th I.B.	
			Fine day. N.W. wind.	

Army Form C. 2118.

WAR DIARY
or
INTELLIGENCE SUMMARY

(Erase heading not required.)

11th Division "G"

SEPTEMBER 1916.

Instructions regarding War Diaries and Intelligence Summaries are contained in F. S. Regs., Part II. and the Staff Manual respectively. Title Pages will be prepared in manuscript.

Place	Date	Hour	Summary of Events and Information	Remarks and references to Appendices
CAMOUFLAGE. SENLIS. V.16.d.	18th.		Very wet day with strong wind, consequently the Artillery of both sides were inactive as observation was impossible. No operations were possible on account of the weather. During the night 18th/19th the right Battalion of the 34th Inf. Bde. suffered about 50 casualties from shell fire. Wind. S.W.	
do	19th.		Enemy's artillery activity was normal. CONSTANCE & DANUBE TRENCHES were shelled with H.E. and shrapnel which did little damage. Our patrols were active at night but encountered no enemy patrols. The weather continued wet and proposed operations had to be postponed. During the night 18th/19th the right Battalion of the 34th Inf. Bde. was relieved by a Battalion of the 9th Canadian Brigade. The front now held by the 34th Inf. Bde. runs from R.28.c.21 - MOUQUET FARM - R.33.a.77. The 33rd Inf. Bde. continues line from R.33.a.5.4 - CONSTANCE TRENCH - 82 - 21 - DANUBE TRENCH - R.32.c.27 - 38. The 3rd Canadian Division is on our right and the 49th Division on our left.	
do	20th.		The weather still continued wet and the proposed attack by the 33rd Inf. Bde. on JOSEPH TRENCH had to be again postponed. Vigorous efforts to consolidate our new line were continued, but progress was retarded by the weather. In each Brigade Sector, support and reserve lines are being constructed and two main C.T's to afford secure communication from front to rear. Situation on our front was normal during the day and night. The 3rd Canadian Division on our right attacked GRABEN TRENCH & HOHENZOLLERN REDOUBT at 5-30 a.m. They gained their objectives but were driven back in the afternoon by a powerful counter attack.	APPX. "G". D.O.26.
do	21st.		During the night 20th/21st: 8 men of the 11th Company, 93rd Inf. Regt. 8th Division surrendered to the 34th Inf. Bde. at MOUQUET FARM. This Regt. was in front of this Division S.E. of ARRAS in August last. During the day and night enemy's Artillery activity was normal, CONSTANCE & DANUBE TRENCHES and the area about the QUARRY being the most heavily shelled. Our Artillery fired intermittently throughout the day and night on enemy trenches and approaches thereto. Continued.	

Army Form C. 2118.

WAR DIARY
or
INTELLIGENCE SUMMARY

(Erase heading not required.)

11th Division "G".

SEPTEMBER 1916.

Instructions regarding War Diaries and Intelligence Summaries are contained in F.S. Regs., Part II. and the Staff Manual respectively. Title Pages will be prepared in manuscript.

Place	Date	Hour	Summary of Events and Information	Remarks and references to Appendices
CAMOUFLAGE. V.16.d.	21st Contd.		The work of consolidating our new trenches continued in spite of bad weather. Enemy working parties were also busy opposite our front although interferred with by our Artillery and Machine Guns. Showery day. Wind West.	
do.	22nd.		Hostile artillery did not show any marked activity during the day. CONSTANCE TRENCH was heavily shelled.	
		7 pm.	The area round MOUQUET FARM was heavily shelled, especially the QUARRY R.33.b.	
		7-9pm.	The S.O.S. signal (red-blue-red rockets) was sent up from R.33.a. by the 9th Sherwood Foresters who reported that the enemy had attacked and gained a footing in CONSTANCE TRENCH at Point R.33.a.5.4. The 9th Sherwood Foresters immediately counter-attacked and drove out the enemy.	
		7-40pm.	The Artillery barraged the enemy trenches directly the S.O.S. was seen.	APPENDIX H O.O. No.27 d/21/9/16.
			On the night of the 22/23rd the 32nd Inf. Bde. relieved the 33rd and 34th Inf. Bdes. in the right sectors of Divisional front. On relief the 33rd Inf. Bde. moved to shelters about MAILLY MAILLET less one Battalion to DONNET POST and the 34th Bde. to shelters about ENGLEBELMER less one battalion to CRUCIFIX CORNER. The detached battalions were placed under the orders of the 32nd Inf. Bde. for tactical purposes. Fine day. Wind West.	
do	23rd.		The enemy artillery was generally inactive during the day but was active during the night on our front and support lines and O.T's. Some damage was done to DANUBE TRENCH, POLE STREET and PEAR STREET.	
		11pm.	A reconnaissance made of MOUQUET FARM proved that the N.E. and N.W. sides of the FARM were strongly held by Infantry and Machine Guns. On our right the 1st Canadian Division relieved the 3rd Canadian Division. Fine day. N.W. Wind.	

Army Form C. 2118.

WAR DIARY
or
INTELLIGENCE SUMMARY

(Erase heading not required.)

11th. DIVISION "G".

SEPTEMBER 1916.

Instructions regarding War Diaries and Intelligence Summaries are contained in F.S. Regs., Part II. and the Staff Manual respectively. Title Pages will be prepared in manuscript.

Place	Date	Hour	Summary of Events and Information	Remarks and references to Appendices
CAMOU-FLAGE. V.16.d.	24th.	5 pm.	A quiet morning with normal enemy artillery activity. Our Heavy Artillery(15" Howitzer, 12" and 9.2" howitzers) bombarded MOUQUET FARM until 6 pm.	
		6.58 pm. to 7 pm.	At 6.58 p.m. the Divisional Artillery put a shrapnel barrage on MOUQUET FARM, HIGHT TRENCH and all known enemy machine gun emplacements which could fire into the Farm area.	
		7 pm.	One company of the 32nd. Inf.Bde. attacked the Farm and after four attempts succeeded in gaining a footing in the N.W. end of the Farm. The Farm was strongly held by the enemy who succeeded in forcing our men back to our own lines by a strong bombing attack supported by machine gun fire. We had about 30 casualties, ostly wounded.	APPENDIX I
	25th.		Fine day with mist in the morning. Wind N.W. A quiet morning. Enemy artillery generally less active. On the night 25th/26th. the 32nd. Inf. Bde. was relieved in the front line by the 33rd. and 34th Inf. Bdes. The 34th. Inf. Bde. taking over the Right Sector from R.28.c.21 to R.33.a.54., the 33rd. Inf. Bde. taking over the Left Sector from R.33.a.54 to the WELL about R.32.c.7.3. The 4 Battalions of the 32nd. Inf. Bde. moved to shelters in W.8 Central. On completion of relief Brigade Headquarters were all situated in dug-outs in and around OVILLERS as follows - 32nd. Inf. Bde. at X.8.b.7.5. 33rd. " " at X.8.a.8.9. 34th. " " at X.8.b.16 - 24.	O.O.28. d/24/9/16.
do	26th.	9.30 a.m.	Weather fine. Advanced Divisional Headquarters opened at DONNETS POST. (W.12.d.9.2). During the morning the attacking troops of the 33rd. and 34th. Inf.Bdes. moved into their"form-ing up"places.	
do		12.35 pm.	The Division, in conjunction with the 1st. Canadian Division on its right and 18th.Division on its left, attacked, its final objective being the High ground running through the following line:- R.21.d.99. - along HESSIAN TRENCH - STUFF REDOUBT - R.20.d.1.0. The 34th. Inf.Bde. attacked on the right, the 33rd. Inf. Bde. on the left, the 32nd. Inf. Bde. being in Reserve. The artillery was allotted the task of covering the attack and destroying the enemy's defences both prior to and during the infantry assault and was composed as follows :- (a) Part of 2nd. Corps H.A. (b) 11th.Divn.Artillery. (c) Part of 25th.Divn.Artillery.(d) 48th.Divn.Artillery.	APPENDIX J O.O.29. d/25/9/16.

Army Form C. 2118.

WAR DIARY or INTELLIGENCE SUMMARY

(Erase heading not required.)

11th. DIVISION "G".

SEPTEMBER 1916.

Instructions regarding War Diaries and Intelligence Summaries are contained in F. S. Regs., Part II. and the Staff Manual respectively. Title Pages will be prepared in manuscript.

Place	Date	Hour	Summary of Events and Information	Remarks and references to Appendices
DONNET POST. W.12.d. 9.2.	26th contd.	1.10 pm.	33rd. Inf. Bde. reported that at 12.56 p.m. flags and flares were seen in 1st. Objective, little opposition had been met, large number of prisoners surrendering. 34th.Inf.Bde. report that at 12.40 p.m. three waves had passed MOUQUET FARM. Two battalions of 32nd.Inf.Bde. moved forward from W.8 central to CRUCIFIX CORNER East of the ANCRE Valley; at the same time the two Brigade Reserve Battalions of the 33rd. and 34th.Inf.Bdes moved forward.	
		1.35 pm.	34th.Inf.Bde. report they have reached their first objective.	
		2.24 pm.	Telephone message received from 34th.Inf.Bde. that some of their troops have reached 2nd.objective, but situation at MOUQUET FARM not yet cleared up.	
		2.49 pm.	Message received from 33rd.Inf.Bde that they have reached their 2nd. Objective.	
		3 pm.	Situation believed to be as follows, that whole of 2nd. objective has been gained, and fighting now going on for 3rd. objective. 33rd. Inf. Bde. have already sent down 15 officers, and 350 other prisoners, belonging to 153rd. 165th. and 93rd. Regts. also one belonging to 213th. Regt. 34th.Inf.Bde. believe they have men in STUFF REDOUBT and HESSIAN TRENCH, but this is doubtful as Canadians report they are troubled by Machine Gun fire from STUFF REDOUBT, and that they cannot get touch with 34th.Inf.Bde. Whole of 32nd.Inf.Bde. now concentrated East of River ANCRE.	
		4 pm.		
		7 pm.	Situation now as follows - Right Brigade. 1st. Objective captured and consolidated, MOUQUET FARM having been finally cleared at 6.30 p.m., 1 officer and 55 other prisoners being taken out of the cellars there. Part of 2nd. objective also taken, but parties of Germans still holding out in ZOLLERN REDOUBT. 34th.Inf.Bde. believe they have men in parts of 3rd.Objective but this is doubtful. Left Brigade. have gained their 1st. and 2nd. Objectives and hold the 3rd Objective from R.20.d.1.0 to 5.0.	
		11 pm.	Situation at this time as follows :- Right Brigade. 9th. Lancs.Fusiliers and 8th.Northd.Fusiliers reported to be in STUFF REDOUBT and HESSIAN TRENCH but they were out of touch with Brigade Headquarters. 5th.Dorset Regt. are in parts of 2nd. Objective, but enemy still holding out in ZOLLERN REDOUBT. 11th. Manchester Regt. in vicinity of MOUQUET FARM and out old front line. Casualties in 3 first named battalion feared heavy. Left Brigade. 9th. Sherwood Foresters in HESSIAN TRENCH. 6th. Border Regt. 1 Coy. in ZOLLERN TRENCH remainder in SCHWABEN & JOSEPH TRENCHES.	

Army Form C. 2118.

WAR DIARY
or
INTELLIGENCE SUMMARY

(Erase heading not required.)

11th. DIVISION "G"

SEPTEMBER 1916.

Instructions regarding War Diaries and Intelligence Summaries are contained in F. S. Regs., Part II. and the Staff Manual respectively. Title Pages will be prepared in manuscript.

Place	Date	Hour	Summary of Events and Information	Remarks and references to Appendices
DONNET POST W.12.d. 9.2.	26th. contd.		Left Brigade.(contd) 7th. S.Staffs. in ZOLLERN TRENCH with some men in MIDWAY LINE. 6th.Lincoln Regt. in our original front line.	
	27th.	2.15 am.	34th. and 33rd. Inf. Bdes. ordered to clear up situation generally, establish touch with each other and with flanking Divisions.	APPENDIX "K". O.O.30 d/27/9/16
		8 am.	Situation not clear. No touch with flanking Divisions yet obtained. 32nd. Inf. Bde. ordered to be ready to move at half-hour's notice.	
		10 am	Two battalions of 32nd. Inf. Bde. were ordered forward to occupy trenches in front of and around MOUQUET FARM.	
		3 pm.	These two battalions of 32nd. Inf. Bde. (9th.W.Yorks and 6th.Yorks Regts) on the right and the 33rd. Inf. Bde. on the left, attacked with the object of making good the line R.21.d.99 - STUFF REDOUBT - R.20.d.1.0.	APPX. "L" O.O.31. d/27/9/16
		3.15 pm.	33rd. Inf. Bde. report that their Headquarters moved forward to X.2.b.0.4.	
		6 pm.	Result of attack by 32nd. Inf.Bde. on right not clear, but STUFF REDOUBT reported taken at 3.30 pm. Touch with Canadians established at R.28.a.36. Attack by 33rd. Inf.Bde. on left successful. Their line now runs R.20.d.91 - R.20.d.10, and touch established with left of 32nd.Inf.Bde. but not with 18th.Division.	
		8.55 pm.	33rd. Inf. Bde. report they are in touch with 53rd.Inf.Bde. (18th.Divn) in ZOLLERN TRENCH at R.26.a.8.2.	
		10pm.	Command of Right Sector passed to G.O.C. 32nd. Inf. Bde. with Headquarters at POZIERES CEMETERY.	APPX "M" O.O. 32. d/27/9/16
		11.20 pm.	Orders issued to Brigades to clear up situation and establish touch with Divisions on right and left, also for 34th. Inf.Bde. (less 11th.Manchester Regt). to be withdrawn to OVILLERS tomorrow, being replaced by 32nd. Inf.Bde.	
do	28th.	5.20 am.	Situation not clear in STUBB REDOUBT and HESSIAN TRENCH East, though touch with Canadians gained at about R.21.d.7.8. Situation with left Brigade unchanged.	
		10am.	Command of Division on our right passed from G.O.C. 1st. Canadian Division to G.O.C. 3rd. Canadian Division.	

Army Form C. 2118.

Instructions regarding War Diaries and Intelligence
Summaries are contained in F.S. Regs., Part II.
and the Staff Manual respectively. Title Pages
will be prepared in manuscript.

WAR DIARY
or
INTELLIGENCE SUMMARY
(Erase heading not required.)

11th. DIVISION "G"

SEPTEMBER 1916.

Place	Date	Hour	Summary of Events and Information	Remarks and references to Appendices
DONNET POST. W.12.d.9.2	28th. (contd).	12.30 pm.	32nd. Inf. Bde. report they do not hold HESSIAN TRENCH East of point R.21.c.87; from this point to R.21.d.99 is in hands of the enemy. During attack yesterday 9th.W.Yorks Regt. lost direction and congregated in South East end of STUFF REDOUBT.	
		9.15 pm.	Orders received from II Corps for (inter alia) (a) 11th.Division to carry through tomorrow an attack on HESSIAN TRENCH East (b) 25th.Division to relieve 11th.Division as early as possible.	APPX. "N". O.O.33. d/28/9/16.
		9.20 pm.	Precautionary orders issued in case of hostile counter attack.	
			During night 34th. Inf. Bde. (less 11th. Manchesters) attached to 32nd.Inf.Bde) withdrawn to OVILLERS.	
	29th.	12 noon	Under cover of a heavy artillery barrage, the 32nd. Inf.Bde. attacked HESSIAN TRENCH from R.21.d 99 to R.21.c.97 and the Northern face of STUFF REDOUBT R.21.c.87 - 58 - 38 - 18 with 3 companies of 6th.Work and Lancs.Regt. and half the then present garrison of the Southern and Western sides of STUFF REDOUBT.	
		4.30 pm.	Reports received that the objectives were reached but strong counter-attack by the enemy at 1.30 pm. drove our troops out of some of the positions won. Touch with Canadians definitely established at R.21.d99.	
		5.30 pm.	7th.S.Staffords placed at the disposal of 32nd.Inf.Bde.	
		5.54 pm.	Decided that it was too late for another attack on STUFF REDOUBT to take place tonight.	
		11.20 pm.	Situation now as follows :- We hold HESSIAN TRENCH from R.21.d.99 to R.21.d.38. From here to R.21.c.87 to R.21.c.58 to 37 is in enemy's hands. From R.21.c.87 - 55 - 45 - 18, and from R.21.c.45 to R.20.d.10 is in our hands. Enemy also hold from R.21.d.13 through R.21.c.97 Northwards.	
		11.30 pm.	Preliminary Orders issued for relief of Division by 25th.Division.	APPX. "O". O.O.34. d/29/9/16.
do.	30th.	9.10 am.	H.Q. 34th. Inf.Bde . moving to ACHEUX. From 10.30 a.m. onwards our artillery fired on the enemy's positions in STUFF REDOUBT and HESSIAN TRENCH.	
		4 pm.	Three bombing attacks were launched by 32nd. Inf.Bde. all working towards point R.21.c97., one party along HESSIAN TRENCH onwards Westwards from R.21.d.38, another party eastwards from R.21.c. 55. and a third party Northwards from R.21.d.13.	

Army Form C. 2118.

WAR DIARY
or
INTELLIGENCE SUMMARY

(Erase heading not required.)

11th. DIVISION "G"

SEPTEMBER 1916.

Instructions regarding War Diaries and Intelligence Summaries are contained in F. S. Regs., Part II. and the Staff Manual respectively. Title Pages will be prepared in manuscript.

Place	Date	Hour	Summary of Events and Information	Remarks and references to Appendices
DONNET POST. W.12.d. 9.2	30th. (contd)	8 pm.	Reports received that these operations had been successful and that our line now runs R.21.d.99 - R.21.c.97 - 87 - 55 - 45 - 18 and from R.21.c.45 to R.20.d.1.0. During the afternoon the 33rd. Inf.Bde. (less 7th.S.Staffords Regt) was relieved by the 7th. Inf.Bde. in the left sector, the relief being completed at 8 p.m. The 33rd. Inf. Bde. moved to HEDAUVILLE. During the night the relief of the 32nd.Inf. Bde. by 75th.Inf.Bde. was commenced, but was not completed until 7 a.m. on 1st. October, the 32nd.Inf.Bde. moving to ACHEUX and VARENNES on relief. Winter time came into force at 12 midnight.	APPX. "P" 0.0.35 d/30/9/16.

C.W.Wathanield
Lieut.General,
Commanding 11th. Division.

2449 Wt. W14957/Mg0 750,000 1/16 J.B.C. & A. Forms/C.2118/12.

Appendix B.

SECRET.

Copy No. 21

11th Division Order No. 21.

Ref: 1/5,000 Trench Map. THIEPVAL.
1/20,000 57.d.S.E. Edn.2d.

12/9/16.

INTENTION. 1. The 11th Division will capture the line R.31.d.98 - WONDER WORK - b.23 - b.03 - b.91 - c.76, (the portion b.03 - b.91 - c.70 being organised as a defensive flank and a block formed on the right about R.32.c.08) on the afternoon of the 14th. September.

DISPOSITIONS. 2. 'A'. The 32nd Inf. Bde. is detailed for this task.
'B'. The 33rd Inf. Bde. will bring machine gun fire to bear on approaches likely to be utilized by the enemy for reinforcing his troops South of THIEPVAL, especial attention being paid to communication trench R.32.a.26 - 28 - R.32.a.09, trench running along the hedge running Northwards from R.32.a.77 to about R.26.c.74.
Trenches R.32.c.39 - 31.b.91 and 31.b.82 to b.23 should be fired on up to ZERO + 7 minutes.
'C'. The 34th Inf. Bde. will be in Divisional Reserve and disposed as under :-
(1) 1 Battalion will be moved to dug-outs at CRUCIFIX CORNER and SOUTH BLUFF near BLACK HORSE BRIDGE by 12 noon on the 14th.

(2) 34th Inf. Bde. less 1 Battalion, will remain at BOUZINCOURT ready to move if required.

ARTILLERY. 3. The following artillery will cover the attack and destroy enemy's defences :-

(a) Part of 11 Corps Heavy Artillery.
(b) Three French 75 mm Batteries.
(c) 11th Divisional Artillery.
(d) Part of 25th Divisional Artillery.
(e) Part of 48th Divisional Artillery.

At ZERO an intense bombardment will be placed on the whole front to be attacked.
At ZERO + 3 minutes fire will be raised from TURK STREET and the batteries hitherto firing on that target will be lifted on to the objective.
At ZERO + 7 minutes fire will be lifted from the front to be attacked, and until ZERO + 33 minutes will engage objectives as laid down in the attached table and Map (Appendix 1).
Prior to the attack the artillery detailed above will destroy the enemy's defences and, to deceive him, will carry out bombardments similar to the one to be carried out on the 14th., at irregular intervals.
Prior to and during the attack the 11th. Divisional Trench Mortar Batteries will engage the salient occupied by the enemy about R.31.c.48, 68 and 58.

ACTION BY 32nd. INF. BRIGADE. 4. (a) The waves of the assaulting infantry will follow the artillery barrage closely, until the objective is reached.
There will be no halt at TURK TRENCH which will be dealt with by especially detailed clearing up parties.
(b) Attention is drawn to 11th. Divisional Standing Orders, especially to paras 15, 16.

HOUR OF ZERO.

5. ZERO will be at 6.30 p.m.

CONSOLIDATION.

6. After capturing its objective the 32nd. Inf. Brigade will consolidate the positions gained, paying special attention to the following points :- R.31.d.98, R.31.b.61, R.31.b.23, R.31.b.03, R.31.a.91 and open up communications from our present front line to the conquered positions.

The C.R.E. will detail R.E. and Pioneers to assist in the construction of these posts and communication trenches Vide Appendix II.

R.E. and Pioneers not employed as above will be at the disposal of the C.R.E. ready to move as ordered

The C.R.E. will arrange with the 32nd. Inf. Bde. as to where R.E. stores will be located and will detail carrying parties.

LOCATION OF POSITION.

7. The Infantry will light flares at ZERO + 10 minutes and at regular intervals of 10 minutes after that hour to show their position to aeroplanes. Should parties be without flares men should wave their trench helmets whenever an aeroplane passes over them during the hours of daylight.

LIAISON.

8. Liaison officers will be detailed as under :-
From 11th. Division to:-

3rd. Canadian Division.	A Captain to be detailed by G.O.C. 34th. Inf. Brigade
32nd. Inf. Bde.	Captain E.L.WRIGHT.G.S.O. 3.

From 32nd. Inf. Bde. to :-

33rd. Inf. Bde.	1 Officer.
148th. Inf. Bde.	1 Officer.

From 33rd. Inf. Bde. to :-

Canadian Bde.	1 Officer.
32nd. Inf. Bde.	1 Officer.

From Battalion of 34th. Inf. Bde. at CRUCIFIX CORNER to :-

32nd. Inf. Bde.	1 Officer.

9. Medical arrangements will be as under :-

Main Dressing Stations (1) VARENNES -(for serious cases).
(2) EAST CLAIRFAYE - (for light cases)
Divisional Collecting Stations for walking cases - BOUZINCOURT.

Advanced Dressing Stations (1) BLACK HORSE BRIDGE.
(2) AVELUY CHATEAU.

Para 9 contd.

Lines of evacuation :-
(a) From Advanced Dressing Stations at BLACK HORSE BRIDGE :- Across BLACK HORSE BRIDGE through MARTINSART WOOD to BOUZINCOURT.

(b) From Advanced Dressing Station AVELUY CHATEAU :- Through AVELUY and MARTINSART WOOD to BOUZINCOURT.
At BOUZINCOURT, all wounded will be directed to VARENNES or to EAST CLAIRFAYE as considered necessary.

ADMINISTRATIVE ARRANGEMENTS

10. For Administrative arrangements, less Medical, see Appendix 3 attached.

WATCHES.

11. Watches will be synchronised at 4 p.m., 5 p.m., and 6 p.m. on 14th.

REPORTS.

12. Reports to 11th. Divisional Headquarters.

Issued at 8-15/pm

J. D. Coleridge Lieut. Col.
General Staff, 11th. Division.

Copy No. 1   A.D.C. for G.O.C.
      2-3   C.R.A.
      4   C.R.E.
      5   32nd. Inf. Bde.
      6   33rd.   "   "
      7   34th.   "   "
      8   6th. E. Yorks.
      9   Signal Co.
      10   A.A. & Q.M.G.
      11   A.D.M.S.
      12   A.P.M.
      13   11th. Divnl. Train.
      14   Captain E.L.Wright.
  15-16   Liaison Officer detailed by 34th. Inf. Bde.
  17-18   2nd. Corps.
      19   49th. Division.
      20   3rd. Canadian Divn.
  21-22   Diary.
  23-24   File.
      25   4th. Squadron, R.F.C.

APPENDIX 1.　　SECRET.

Proposed Artillery Programme for "X" Day

PHASE I (shewn ———).

Guns Required.		French.		Rate of fire of 18 pr. guns in number of rds per gun per min.	Time.	Infantry action.	Remarks.
18-Pdr.Btys.	4.5" Btys.	7.5 Btys.	6" How.				
16 of 11th.D.A. 9 of 25th.D.A. 9 of 48th.D.A.	4 of 11th.D.A. 3 of 25th.D.A. 3 of 48th.D.A.	3	1	3	Zero to + 3 minutes.	Infantry will be clear of their trenches at ZERO + 2.	Other guns at corresponding rates of fire. LEFT Flank during all Phases will be covered by the fire of 2 Heavy T.Ms. 12 Medium T.Ms also Stokes Mortars.
Total batteries) 34.	10 batteries.	3 Btys.	1 Bty.				
Total guns.) 136	40 guns.	12 guns.	4 guns.				
Grand Total of 192 Guns and Hows.							

PHASE II (Shewn ———).

| | | | | 3 | + 3 to + 7 min. | Reach TURK ST. line at + 3 min.30 sec. Approach final objective and assault when artillery lifts at + 7 min. | |

Contd.　　　　　　　　　　　　　　　　　　　　　APPENDIX 1.

Guns Required.		FRENCH.		Rate of fire of 18-pdr.guns in number of rds per gun per min.	Time.	Infantry action.	Remarks.
18-pdr.Btys.	4.5" Btys.	7.5 Btys.	6"How.				

PHASE III (shewn ———).

| | | | | 3 | + 7 min. to + 11 ? | Clearing enemy trenches and con- solidating. | |

PHASE IV. (shewn ———)

| | | | | 2 | + 11 min to + 18 min. | Consolid- ating. | |

PHASE V.

| | | | | 1 | + 18 min to + 33 min. | Pushing out patrols. | |

APPENDIX II.

The detail for R.E. Companies and Pioneers will be as under :-

1.	Section 86th. Field Coy.	To assist to consolidate and make strong point at R.31.a.91.
1.	Section 67th. Field Coy.	To assist to consolidate points R.30.d.98 and R.31.b.61.
1.	Section 67th. Field Coy.	To assist to consolidate points R.31.b.23. and 03.
1	Section 67th. Field Coy. with 1 Coy. 6th. E.Yorks (Pioneers).	To construct communication trenches - (a) from R.31.d.07 to centre of WONDER WORK. (b) from R.31.d.64 to R.31.d.79.
1	Section 67th. Field Coy. and 1 Coy 6th. E. Yorks (Pioneers).	To be in reserve in dug-outs at CRUCIFIX CORNER.
	86th. Field Coy (less 1 Section).	To be in reserve in dug-outs at the BLUFF E. end of BLACK HORSE BRIDGE.

The 68th. Field Company and 2 companies of Pioneers will remain at the disposal of G.O.C. 3rd. Infantry Brigade.

APPENDIX III.

ADMINISTRATIVE INSTRUCTIONS.

Divisional Stragglers Posts.

1. OVILLERS.   X.8. C.4.8
2. CRUCIFIX CORNER.   W.11. D.0.1
3. BROOKERS PASS.   W.11. C. D
4. POPLAR BRIDGE.   W.11. A. B
5. COLLECTING STATION W.16. B.8.5.

2. Prisoners of War.

Any prisoners taken will be marched down to CRUCIFIX CORNER under escort which will be kept as small as possible and be handed over at that point to the A.P.M., or representative.

3. RATIONS. Troops will carry on the person the un-expended portion of the days' ration and the Iron Ration.

In addition, 1 days ration of preserved meat, Biscuit and Grocery Ration, packed in sand-bags (8 rations in a bag) will be dumped under Brigade arrangements, as far forward as is deemed advisable. These bags will be placed packed under Divisional arrangements and sent to the Brigade Dump in BLIGHTY VALLEY. The bags will have a strip of white material tied to them to identify them.

4. HOT MEAL. M. & V. rations at the rate of 1 tin to two men will be issued to provide a hot meal before the attack begins.

5. WATER. Water bottles will be carried filled.
In addition, Petrol tins will be provided and w water stored in them under Brigade arrangements and dumped at the same place as the bags of rations. (One petrol contains water rations for 8 men).

6. RUM. An issue of rum will be drawn and will be stored under Brigade arrangements.
It will be issued to troops under orders of the Brigade Commander .

7. AMMUNITION. All S.A.A., Grenades, Stokes Bombs, Rockets, Flares etc., required, can be drawn under Brigade arrangements from Advanced Divisional Dump. (W 11 d 9.2)
All Mills No. 5 Grenades will be issued fuzed.

W. J. Gordon.
Lieut.Colonel
A.A. & Q.M.G.   11th. Division.

SECRET.

To:-...............

The following amendments are to be made to 11th. Division Order No. 21 dated 12th. September 1916. -

Para 2 'Q'.

1. The 34th. Infantry Brigade will remain concentrated at BOUZINCOURT ready to move at 2 hours notice.

2. One Battalion 33rd. Infantry Brigade will move from BOUZINCOURT to dug-outs at CRUCIFIX CORNER and SOUTH BLUFF, East of BLACK HORSE BRIDGE by 4 p.m. on 14th.
Details of move to be arranged by B.G.s C. 32nd. and 34th. Infantry Brigades.

Para 3. ARTILLERY.

From line 13 onwards paragraph will now read as follows :-

At ZERO + 6 minutes fire will be lifted from the front to be attacked and targets will be engaged with a view to preventing the enemy reinforcing the front attacked.

Para 7. LOCATION OF POSITION.

The Infantry will light flares at 6.40 p.m., 6.50 p.m 7. p.m. and 7.10 p.m. to show their positions to aeroplanes.
About 6.45 a.m. on the 15th. September, the contact aeroplane will fire off one ordinary Very Light; when this signal is seen, the Infantry will light more red flares. Should parties be without flares the men will wave their helmets round their heads.

Para 11

Watches will be synchronised at 3 p.m., 4 p.m., and 5 p.m.

13th. September 1916.

J. D. Coleridge, Lieut. Colonel,
General Staff, 11th. Division.

SECRET.

To:-..............

The following amendments are to be made to 11th. Division Order No. 21 dated 12th. September 1916. -

Para 2 'O'.

1. The 34th. Infantry Brigade will remain concentrated at BOUZINCOURT ready to move at 2 hours notice.

2. One Battalion 33rd. Infantry Brigade will move from BOUZINCOURT to dug-outs at CRUCIFIX CORNER and SOUTH BLUFF, East of BLACK HORSE BRIDGE by 4 p.m. on 14th.
Details of move to be arranged by B.G.s C. 32nd. and 34th. Infantry Brigades.

Para 3. ARTILLERY.

From line 13 onwards paragraph will now read as follows :-

At ZERO + 6 minutes fire will be lifted from the front to be attacked and targets will be engaged with a view to preventing the enemy reinforcing the front attacked.

Para 7. LOCATION OF POSITION.

The Infantry will light flares at 6.40 p.m., 6.50 p.m 7. p.m. and 7.10 p.m. to show their positions to aeroplanes.
About 6.45 a.m. on the 15th. September, the contact aeroplane will fire off one ordinary Very Light; when this signal is seen, the Infantry will light more red flares. Should parties be without flares the men will wave their helmets round their heads.

Para 11

Watches will be synchronised at 3 p.m., 4 p.m., and 5 p.m.

13th. September 1916.

J. D. Coleridge Lieut. Colonel,

General Staff, 11th. Division.

Appendix C.

SECRET.

11th. Division Order No. 22.   Copy No...........

Ref Map 1/5000 57D.S.E. and 57C.S.W. THIEPVAL.   14th. Septbr.1916.

1. Operations on a large scale will be carried out by the 4th. Army and the French on the morning of the 15th. inst.

2. The Reserve Army will co-operate as follows :-

   i. The Canadian Corps will attack line M.31.b.74 - COURCELETTE SUB RERIE - R.36.a - R.29.d.91 - along German trench to point R.34.b.34.
   ii. The 5th. Corps will carry out raids and discharge smoke.
   iii. Artillery of 2nd. and 5th. Corps will make feints under orders already issued.
   iv. The troops of the 2nd. Corps will act as under :-

   (a) 49th. Division will discharge smoke and throw gas into THIEPVAL between ZERO and + 30 minutes on a front to be selected by G.O.C. 49th. Division.

   (b) 18th. Division will be ready to move off at 6 hours notice.

   (c) 2nd. Corps Mounted Troops (1/1st. Yorkshire Dragoons, 2nd. Cyclist Battalion and No.4 Machine Gun Company) and 2 R.F.A. Brigades (to be detailed by G.O.C., R.A.) will be ready to move off at ½ hours notice.

   (d) The 11th. Division will be prepared to take advantage of any success gained on the previous afternoon.

3. (a) The 32nd. Infantry Brigade will improve the positions gained and prolong their left flank to the line R.31.a.93 - 94 - 55.

   (b) The 33rd. Infantry Brigade during the night 14th/15th. will :
   (1) Capture points R.32.d.23 - 25 - 14 and establish a bombing post about R.32.d.57 in CONSTANCE TRENCH.
   (2) Capture the POLE TRENCH R.32.d.03 to R.32.c.56; establish bombing posts towards R.32.c.58 and 68, and eventually link up towards 32nd. Inf. Bde. about R.32.c.27. Artillery fire will be kept off these points after 7 p.m. on the 14th.

   (c) The 34th. Infantry Brigade will be held in readiness to move at ½ hours notice. Staff and selected officers will reconnoittre the ground and roads about POZIERES.
   (d) Administrative arrangements will be detailed later.

4. ZERO hour will be detailed later.

Issued at 11-30 a.m.

J. D. Coleridge
Lieut. Col.
General Staff, 11th. Division.

Copy No. 1. A.D.C. for G.O.C.
2-3 C.R.A.   Copy. No. 12. A.P.M.
4   C.R.E.   13. 11th. Divl. Train.
5   32nd. Inf. Bde.   14. Capt. E. L. Wright.
6   33rd.   "   "   15-16   Liaison Officer.
7   34th.   "   "   17-18   2nd. Corps.
8   6th. E. Yorks.   19. 49th. Divn.
9   Signal Co.   20. 3rd. Can. Divn.
10   A.A. & Q.M.G.   21-22   Diary.
11   A.D.M.S.   23-24   File.
                                         25. R.F.C.

Appendix D.
SECRET.

Copy No. 18

11th Division Order No. 23.

15th September 19[..]

Reading 1/70,000 Sheet 57.d.S.E.

1. The 32nd Inf. Bde. (less Machine Gun Coy. and Light Trench Mortar Battery) will be relieved in the Left Sector to-night by the 147th Inf. Bde. 49th Division (less M.G. Coy. and L.T.M. Batty).

   All details of relief will be arranged direct between B.G.C. Brigades. Relief will be completed by 6 a.m. 16th inst.

   The command of the Sector will be taken over on completion of the relief.

2. After relief the 32nd Inf. Bde. will take over the billets vacated by the 147th Inf. Bde. at HEDAUVILLE.

3. The 32nd Machine Gun Coy. and Light Trench Mortar Battery will be relieved by similar Units of the 147th Inf. Bde. on the 16th inst. Relief to be completed by 6 a.m. on the 17th Sept.

4. The 7th South Staffords will move from SOUTH BLUFF and CRUCIFIX CORNER to BOUZINCOURT as soon as possible after 7 p.m. to-day.

5. Completion of reliefs will be reported to D.H.Q.

Issued at _____

T. D. Coleridge Lieut-Colonel.
Gen. Staff. 11th Division.

Copy No. 1.   A.D.C. for G.O.C.
        2.   C.R.A.
        3.   C.R.E.
        4.   32nd Inf. Bde.
        5.   33rd Inf. Bde.
        6.   34th Inf. Bde.
        7.   6th E. Yorks R.
        8.   Signals.
        9.   A.A. & Q.M.G.
       10.   A.D.M.S.
       11.   A.P.M.
       12.   Divl. Train.
       13.   D.A.D.O.S.
       14.   2nd Corps.
       15.   49th Div.
       17.   3rd Canadian Div.
  18 & 20.   File.
  18 & 19.   Diary.

Appendix F.

SECRET.

Copy No. 18

11th Division Operation Order 24.

15th Sept. 1916.

Ref: Map. 1/5000 THIEPVAL
57.D.S.E. & 57.d.S.W.

1. The following operations will be carried out by the 33rd Inf. Brigade as soon as the necessary artillery and other preparations can be completed :—

    (a) Clear enemy out of the nest of trenches and dug-outs about R.32.c.68 – 58 – 38 and connect up with Left Brigade in WONDER WORKS trench.

    (b)(i) Occupy CONSTANCE TRENCH on night 15/16th as far as possible North East of point R.32.b.70 and make an endeavour to establish connection with the Left of the Canadians about R.33.a.77.

    (ii) From reports it seems likely that the chief opposition would be from the enemy's strong point about R.33.a.54.

    (iii) If arrangements can be made in time for the temporary withdrawal of the Canadian Post at YY this strong point will be dealt with this afternoon by 9.2 Howitzers.

    (iv) The C.R.A. has been warned and the 11th Divisional and attached Artillery will be ready to co-operate if called on by G.O.C. 33rd Inf. Bde.

    (v) To assist this operation the Corps H.A. have been ordered to bombard this afternoon, the nest of trenches at the top of the valley in R.32.b. and R.33.a.

    (vi) Any further assistance required from the H.A. should be applied for.

    (vii) Operations to commence 11 p.m. to-night.

    (c) Connect the trench ordered in 11 Corps Operation Order No. 21, para: 3 (c) from about R.33.c.14 with CONSTANCE TRENCH.

    (d) Continue this connection Westwards from about its junction with CONSTANCE TRENCH to vicinity of R.32.c.6 so as to have a new trench facing North, not subject to enfilade.

2. Report when operations a, c, d, are likely to be carried through.

Issued at 4.30 p.m.

T. D. Coleridge
Lieut-Colonel.
Gen. Staff. 11th Div.

Copy No. 1. A.D.C. for G.O.C.
2   C.R.A.
3   C.R.E.
4   32nd. Inf. Bde.
5   33rd. " "
6   34th. " "
7   6th. E. Yorks.Regt.
8. Signals.
9   A.A. & Q.M.G.
10 A.D.M.S.
11 A.P.M.
12 Divnl.Train.
13 D.A.D.O.S.
14 II Corps.
15 49th. Divn.
16 3rd. Canadian Div.
17 File.
18– AC Diary.

TABLE OF MOVES
on
6th SEPTEMBER 1916.

Additional Transport	Unit.	Location.	Destination.	Time to pass Starting Point.	Route.	Remarks.
2 Lorries	9th Bn W. Yorks.	ARQUEVES	SENLIS	7.50 a.m.	LEALVILLERS – VAREBBES – Point 140 Tail of Column to be clear of X roads in P.32 central by 10 a.m.	(1) Starting Point P.8.d.7.3. (2) Times past the Starting point allow for a 3 minutes gap between units. (3) Billeting parties will report to Staff Captain at SENLIS Church at 9 a.m. (4) 1st Line Transport will march with the units. (5) Baggage wagons of the Infantry Battalions will join them on the evening of the 5th. (6) Motor lorries will report at Bde. H.Qrs at 7 a.m. Guides from units will meet them there.
2 Lorries	8th Bn Duke of Wellingtons	Do.	Do	8.01 a.m.		
1 Lorry	32nd M.G.Co.	RAINCHEVAL	do	8.1½ a.m.		
1 Lorry	32nd Bde L.T.M.Bty.	ARQUEVES	do	8.1½ a.m.		

Appendix F

SECRET.

11th Division Order No. 25.   Copy No. 18

Ref: Map 1/5000 THIEPVAL,
     1/5000 FERME DU MOUQUET.   16th Sept. 1916.

1. ~~Fourth Army continue~~ the attack to-day at 9-30 a.m.

   Canadian Corps will ~~attack ZOLLERN REDOUBT and~~ ZOLLERN GRABEN from South East this afternoon.

   ~~V~~ Corps patrols and raids.

2. The attack ordered to be carried out by 11th Division in 11 Corps Operation No. 25 is temporarily postponed. Preparations to continue and plan to be submitted to D.H.Q. by 33rd Inf. Bde.

3. The 34th Inf. Bde. will relieve the 8th Canadian Brigade 3rd Canadian Division in the line held by that Brigade to-night under arrangements to be made direct between Brigadiers concerned.

   As the frontage held by the 8th Canadian Brigade is liable to change the 34th Inf. Bde. in taking over this frontage will make certain of occupying all points held by the 8th Canadian Brigade at time of relief.

4. The area of any newly captured trenches taken over by 34th Inf. Bde. will be held on the lines laid down in 11 Corps G.1106.

5. The boundary between the 11th Division and 3rd Canadian Division will be notified later.

6. Arrangements for medical reliefs in Sector taken over from 8th Canadian Brigade will be made by Administrative staff.

7. Command of the frontage taken over from 8th Canadian Brigade will be assumed by B.G.C. 34th Inf. Bde. from the time of relief which will be ~~notified~~ reported to D.H.Q.

   Command of this frontage will pass from 3rd Canadian Division to 11th Division at the same hour.

8. ACKNOWLEDGE.

Issued at 12 noon.

J. D. Coleridge
Lieut-Colonel.
Gen. Staff. 11th Division.

Copy No. 1. A.D.G. for G.O.C.
         2 C.R.A.
         3 C.R.E.
         4 32nd Inf.Bde.
         5 33rd   "   "
         6 34th   "   "
         7 6th E. Yorks.
         8 Signals.
         9 A.A.& Q.M.G.
        10 A.D.M.S.
        11 A.P.M.
        12 Divl. Train.
        13 D.A.D.O.S.
        14 11 Corps.
        15 49th Div.
        16 3rd Canadian Div.
        17 File.
    18 & 19 Diary.

Appendix G.

SECRET.
Copy No......19.

11th. Division Order No.26.
20th. Sept.1916.

Ref. 1/20,000 57 D.S.E.

1. Pending further orders the 11th. Division will be disposed as under –

   (a) 32nd.Inf.Bde. (i) 3 Battns. In Billets MAILLY MAILLET.
                     (ii) 1 Battn. In shelters near MAILLY)
                                               MAILLET.)
   (b) 33rd. Inf.Bde. (i) 2 Battns. In the line and in dugouts in support.
                     (ii) ½ Battn. DORNET POST & RIBBLE STREET.
                     (iii) ½ " CRUCIFIX CORNER.
                     (iv) 1 " In billets in ENGLEBELMER.
   (c) 34th.Inf.Bde. (i) 2 Battns. In the line and in dugouts in support.
                     (ii) 1 Battn. In shelters South of CRUCIFIX CORNER.
                     (iii) 1 " In billets in ENGLEBELMER.
   (d) R.E.. 3 Field Coys. AVELUY.
   (e) Pioneers. 6th.E.Yorks Regt. AVELUY.

2. (a) The 32nd. Inf. Bde. will move to their new locations tomorrow and will be clear of BOUZINCOURT by 11 a.m.
   Material for shelters for 1 Battalion will be dumped at CampCommandant's Office, MAILLY WOOD, by 12 noon tomorrow, and will be erected by the 32nd.Inf.Bde. A Staff Officer 11th. Division will meet a Staff Officer 32nd.Inf.Bde. at BOUZINCOURT at 9.30 a.m. tomorrow and will show him the camp site.
   (b) The 33rd. Inf.Bde. will assume its new dispositions by 12 noon tomorrow. 147th.Bde. (49th.Divn.) are arranging to vacate Southern half of CRUCIFIX CORNER Dugouts by 9 a.m.
   (c) (i) The battalion of the 34th. Inf. Bde. now in LA BOISSELLE will move into shelters South of CRUCIFIX CORNER by 5 p.m. 22nd. inst. The shelters will be dumped at CRUCIFIX CORNER by 12 noon tomorrow and will be erected by the 34th. Inf. Bde.
   A Staff Officer of the 11th. Division will meet a Staff Officer of the 34th. Inf.Bde. at CRUCIFIX CORNER at 10 a.m. tomorrow and will show him the camp site.
   (ii) The battalion of the 34th.Inf.Bde now at BOUZINCOURT will move to OVILLERS tomorrow and will be clear of BOUZINCOURT by 11.30 a.m., this battalion will march via MARTINSART WOOD.
   (d) The battalion of the 34th. Inf. Bde. now at ALBERT will move to ENGLEBELMER tomorrow; battalion to be clear of BOUZINCOURT by 12 noon.

3. Divisional Headquarters will remain as at present. Major
   (V.16.d.)
   Issued at .....10.30 p.m.
                                              for Lt.Colonel,
                                     General Staff,11th.Division.

Copy No.1. A.D.C. for G.O.C.
       2 –3 C.R.A.   12. A.P.M.
         4 C.R.E.   13 11th.Divnl.Train.
         5 32nd.Inf.Bde.   14–15 2nd.Corps.
         6 33rd. " "   16 49th.Divn.
         7 34th. " "   17 3rd.Can.Divn.
         8 6th.E.Yorks.   18 2 .Divnl.Arty.
         9 Signal Coy.   19–20 D..ry.
        10 A.A. & Q.M.G. 21–22 File.
        11 A.D.M.S.

Appendix J.

SECRET

11th Division Order No. 29.

Copy No. 28
24th Sept. 1916.

Ref: Maps.- 1. GRANDCOURT.   Edn: 2.)
           2. ST. PIERRE DIVION   "   1.)
           3. COURCELETTE.   "   3.)
           4. FERME DU MOUQUET.   "   5.) 1/5,000.
           5. THIEPVAL.   "   4.)
           6. OVILLERS.   "   1.)

           BEAUMONT.   "   2.D)
           LE SARS.   "   2.E) 1/10,000.
           OVILLERS.   "   2.C)

GENERAL. 1. (a) The 2nd Corps and the Canadian Corps will take part in offensive operations on a large scale on a date to be detailed later, for the purpose of capturing the high ground from COURCELETTE Westwards to the ANCRE through STUFF and SCHWABEN REDOUBTS.

(b) The final objectives allotted to Divisions will be as under :-

1st Canadian Division. from M.19.d.35 to R.22.a.40 inclusive.

11th Division. from R.22.a.10 exclusive along HESSIAN TRENCH - STUFF REDOUBT - R.20.d.10 inclusive.

18th Division. from R.20.d.10 exclusive along the HESSIAN TRENCH - SCHWABEN REDOUBT - R.19.d.00 inclusive.

(c) Boundaries between Divisions will be as under:-
Between 1st Canadian and 11th Divisions:
Road R.28.c.21 - 39 - a.64. to R.22.a.10 inclusive to the 1st Canadian Division.

Between 11th and 18th Divisions:
From WELL 32.c.78 along hedge through R.32.a.77 - 26.c.73 - R.26.a.80 - R.20.d.10 inclusive to the 11th Division.

OBJECTIVES. 2. The objectives allotted to the 11th Division are
11th Division. as under :-

1st Objective. R.28.a.31 to R.26.c.93.

2nd Objective. R.21.d.99 along ZOLLERN TRENCH to R.26.a.82.

3rd Objective. R.21.d.99 along HESSIAN TRENCH - STUFF REDOUBT - R.20.d.10 inclusive.

DISPOSITIONS. 3. (a) **Right Attack. 34th Inf. Bde.** =

Forming Up Places. Firing Line, Support and Reserve Trenches in Right Sector.

1st Objective. R.28.a.36 inclusive to R.27.c.54 inclusive.

2nd Objective. R.21.d.48 inclusive, ZOLLERN REDOUBT to and along ZOLLERN TRENCH to R.26.b.86 ~~inclusive.~~ *exclusive.*

3rd Objective. R.21.d.99 inclusive along HESSIAN TRENCH, STUFF REDOUBT to R.20.d.91 exclusive.

-2-

The G.O.C. 34th Inf. Bde. will give particular attention to the following points :-

(i) Detail a party to proceed along the boundary road and keep touch with the 1st Canadian Division.

(ii) Detail a party to block the Northern exits from MOUQUET FARM, provided that place is not in our hands on the day of the attack.

(iii) Clearance of Points R.27.c.54 and 38.

(b) **Left Attack. 33rd Inf. Bde.**

Forming Up Places. CONSTANCE TRENCH, DANUBE TRENCH and DANUBE VALLEY.

1st Objective.   R.27.c.54 exclusive - R.32.b.79 along SCHWABEN TRENCH to R.26.c.93 inclusive.

2nd Objective.   R.26.b.86 inclusive along ZOLLERN TRENCH to R.26.a.82 inclusive.

3rd Objective.   R.21.d.91 inclusive along HESSIAN TRENCH to R.20.d.10 inclusive.

The G.O.C. 33rd Inf. Bde. will give particular attention to the following points :-

(i) Clearance of MIDWAY LINE.

(ii) Formation of Strong Point to guard Left Flank of 11th Division and connect with right of 18th Division about R.26.c.93.

(c) **Reserve. 32nd Inf. Bde.** will be located as under:-

1 Battalion.   Shelters South of CRUCIFIX CORNER.

1 Battalion.   South portion of CRUCIFIX CORNER and RIBBLE STREET.

1 Battalion.   Shelters in W.8. Central.

1 Battalion.   VARENNES.

All to be ready to move at 1/2 hours notice.

(d) **Brigade Head Quarters.**

32nd Inf. Bde.   X.8.b.75.

33rd Inf. Bde.   X.8.a.88.

34th Inf. Bde.   X.8.b.16.

ACTION TO BE TAKEN BY ASSAULTING INFANTRY. 4. (a) Troops detailed for the various objectives will follow one another closely under cover of the artillery barrages.
On the 1st Objective being gained there will be a pause of   minutes in the advance when all men not actually occupying the 1st Objective will lie down.
At ZERO +   minutes the troops will advance in successive waves to attack the 2nd Objective.
On the 2nd Objective being gained there will be a pause of   minutes in the advance when all men not actually occupying the 2nd Objective will lie down.

Times will be detailed later.

At ZERO + minutes the troops will advance in successive waves to attack the 3rd Objective.

As the troops detailed for the capture of the various objectives advance and vacate our forward trenches, Brigade Reserves will advance so as to be ready to press forward to support the assaulting troops.

The enemy's positions must be assaulted by wave after wave until all opposition is broken down.

Especial clearing up parties will be detailed to deal with any enemy left in the 1st and 2nd Objectives.

(b) The instructions contained in 11th Divl. Standing Battle Orders will be adhered to in all respects.

Especial attention is drawn to paras 15 and 16.

ARTILLERY. 5. The following artillery will cover the attack and destroy enemy's defences both prior to and during the attack.

(a) Part of the 2nd Corps Heavy Artillery.
(b) 11th Divisional Artillery.
(c) Part of the 25th Divl. Artillery.
(d) 48th Divisional Artillery.

Times will be detailed later

At ZERO a heavy bombardment will be placed on the 1st Objective and ZOLLERN REDOUBT.

At ZERO + A minutes fire will be transferred from the 1st Objective and gradually from ZOLLERN REDOUBT on to the 2nd Objective.

At ZERO + A + B minutes fire will be transferred from the 2nd Objective on to the 3rd Objective.

At ZERO + A + B + C minutes fire will be lifted from the 3rd Objective on to hostile lines of approach.

After the initial barrages one battery will be placed at direct disposal of each Infantry Brigadier.

In event of a general rebombardment becoming necessary arrangements will be made by Divisional Head Quarters.

ZERO HOUR. 6. ZERO will be at an hour to be notified later.

CONSOLIDATION. 7. (a) The 3rd Objective after capture will be consolidated without delay.

(b) Posts will be established forward of the 3rd Objective ~~as shown in Map~~ (Details follow)

(c) Strong Points will be organized as under :-

(1) R.21.d.99.
(2) Northern Side of ZOLLERN REDOUBT.
(3) Northern Side of STUFF REDOUBT.
(4) R.20.d.12.

(d) MIDWAY line and the Western face of ZOLLERN REDOUBT from about R.27.d.91 - 50 - b.51 - 03 - 21.d.01 - c.55 to be repaired to form communication trenches from our present line to the captured positions.

(e) After intermediate objectives have been gained the valley running North from R.32.a.30 may be used for communication purposes by the 11th Division.

(f) The C.R.E. will detail R.E. and Pioneers to assist in the construction of the posts and communications detailed in sub-paras (b), (c), and (d). (vide APPENDIX 1.).

(g) The C.R.E. will arrange with the 33rd and 34th Infantry Brigades as to where R.E. stores will be located and will detail carrying parties.

(h) The C.R.E. will reconnoitre tracks likely to be easily repairable with a view to opening them up for wheeled traffic Northwards after the attack.

(i) R.E. and Pioneers not employed as detailed in sub-para (f) above will be at the disposal of the C.R.E. ready to move as ordered.

(j) A working party of 4 Officers and 200 men from the 32nd Inf. Bde. will be detailed to be ready to improve the POZIERES - THIEPVAL track from R.34.c.18 to R.33.a.54, should circumstances permit, for the use of Artillery

LOCATION OF POSITION.   8.   The Infantry will light flares and wave red flags on their arrival at each objective to show their position to aeroplanes.
Should parties be without flares men should wave their trench helmets whenever an aeroplane passes over them during the hours of daylight.

MEASURES FOR KEEPING DIRECTION.   9.   Officers and N.C.O's detailed to take part in the assault must study the ground beforehand and impress land marks on their memory. Compass bearings will be taken before-hand.
The left Battalion of the 34th Inf. Bde. will direct and will march with its right on Trench R.27.d.91 - 59 - b.51 - 08 - 21.d.01 - c.55. It must be remembered that the 34th Bde. will have a road on its right and that the 33rd Inf. Bde. will have a distinct valley on its left.

LIAISON.   10.   Liaison Officers will be detailed as under :-

From 11th Division to :-

18th Division.	A Captain to be detailed by 33 Inf.Bde
1st Canadian Division.	Capt. POWELL, 8th North'd Fus
33rd Inf. Bde.	Capt. THOMSON. (G.S.) Scots Gds.
34th Inf. Bde.	Capt. GATTIE, Monmouth Regt.

From 33rd Inf. Bde. to :-

34th Inf. Bde.	1 Officer.
53rd Inf. Bde.	1 Officer.

From 34th Inf. Bde. to :-

33rd Inf. Bde.	1 Officer.
2nd Canadian Inf. Bde.	1 Officer.

From 32nd Inf. Bde. to :-

H.Q. 33rd and 34th Inf. Bde. 2 Officers at X.8.a.88 and X.8.b.16.

ADVANCED H.Q. 11th Division.

MEDICAL 11. (1) Main Dressing Stations.
ARRANGE-   (i) VARENNES (for serious cases)
MENTS.   (ii) EAST CLAIRFAYE. (for slightly wounded cases)

            (2) Divisional Collecting Station for walking cases.
                AVELUY CHATEAU.

            (3) Advanced Dressing Stations.
                (i) X.2.b.7.4.
               (ii) AVELUY CHATEAU.

            (4) Line of evacuation:- AVELUY, MARTINSART WOOD
                               and LOUZINCOURT.

ADMINISTRAT- 12. For Administrative arrangements less Medical
IVE ARRANGE-   see APPENDIX 2 attached.
MENTS.

WATCHES.   13. Watches will be synchronized at 6 a.m. 8 a.m.
                10 a.m. on day of attack.

MACHINE GUNS.14. Machine Guns will act on a plan drawn up by the
                2nd Corps. Details follow.
                Machine Guns will remain under Brigadiers. The
                only object of using them in combination is to
                ensure full co-operation and liaison between
                M.G. Coys. of the Corps.

TANKS.   15. Two Tanks are allotted to the 11th Division.
                They will operate on the Right Flank in con-
                junction with the 34th Inf. Bde.
                They will be moved into concealed positions
                during ------ and will follow the assaulting
                troops. They will move from these positions
                at ZERO.
                Special orders are under issue to O.C. Heavy
                M.G. Section.

REPORTS.   16. Reports to Advanced Divisional Headquarters at
                BONNET'S POST (Ref: W.12.d.9.2). after 7 a.m.
                on the day of the attack.

                                          T. D. Coleridge
                                          Lieut Colonel.
Issued at. 5 a.m.   Gen. Staff. 11th Division.

Copy No. 1. A.D.C. for G.O.C.
      2-3. C.R.A.
        4. C.R.E.
        5. 32nd Inf. Bde.
        6. 33rd Inf. Bde.
        7. 34th Inf. Bde.
        8. 6th E. Yorks Regt.   17. 1st Can. Div.
        9. Signal Coy.   18. 25th Div. Arty.
     10. A.A. & Q.M.G.   19-20. Diary.
     11. A.D.M.S.   21-22. File.
     12. A.P.M.   23. 18th Div.
     13. 11th Div. Train.   24. 4th Squad. R.F.C.
     14. & 15 2nd Corps.   25. O.C. Heavy M.G. Section.
     16. 49th Div.   26 to 29. Liaison Officers.

APPENDIX I

STRONG POINTS.
The following will be detailed to assist in the consolidation of Strong Points.
1. One section 86th Field Coy. for point about R.21.d.99.
2. One section 86th Field Coy. for point Northern side of ZOLLERN REDOUBT about R.21.d.01.
3. One section 86th Field Coy. for point Northern side of STUFF REDOUBT about R.21.c.58.
4. One section 68th Field Coy. for point about R.20.d.12.

COMMUNICATION TRENCHES.
The O.C. 6th E. Yorks. Pioneers will detail 1 Coy. to clear a Line of Communication Trench forward approx R.28.c.01 through ZOLLERN REDOUBT to R.21.c.97.
1. Coy. to clear a line of communication trench from approx R.33.a.77 - R.27.c.54. and up MIDWAY LINE - R.20.d.10.

RESERVES.
R.E. and Pioneers in reserve will be posted as under:-
67th Field Coy.   AVELUY.
68th Field Coy. less 2 sections) in dugouts near 3rd Street
86th Field Coy. less 3 sections) S. of the road in OVILLERS.
1 Section 68th Field Coy. AVELUY.
6th E. Yorks. Pioneers less 2 Coys. AVELUY.

ROADS.
1 Section 68th Field Coy, 1 Section 86th Field Coy, and 2 Coys of Pioneers in reserve will be prepared to make roads available for wheeled traffic on receipt of orders from C.R.E. as under:-
Right Road.
1 Section 86th Field Coy. and 1 Coy. Pioneers.
POZIERES-POZIERES CEMETERY R.34.c.50-R.34.c.27-48-R.28.c.21-39.

Left Road.
1 Section 68th Field Coy. and 1 Coy. Pioneers.
From CRUCIFIX CORNER - W.12.d.83 - X.1.b.90 - X.2.a.22 - 79 -
R.32.d.25 - b.62 - 96 - 88 thence N.W. to
R.26.c.83. thence N.E. to R.26.c.93 - d.97.

RUNNERS.
O.C's Field Coys and O.C. 6th E. Yorks will each detail 2 bicycle orderlies to report to Adjutant R.E. at Advanced D.H.Q. DONNETS POST at 1 hour before ZERO.

ADVANCED DUMP.
An advanced Divisional R.E. Dump has been made at X.9.a.15.

C.R.E. WILL BE AT ADVANCED D.H.Q.

Sections for consolidation of strong points not to exceed 1 Officer and 20 N.C.O's and men.
Carrying parties to be detailed by O.C.'s Field Coys from the Infantry parties at their disposal.
Officers in charge of Sections must keep in touch with Battalion Commanders, they will not take their sections forward until notified by the Battalion Commander that the objective is gained.
Actual points for consolidation as strong points can only be decided on the ground as they should include existing dugouts for the accommodation of the garrison.
O.C's Pioneer Companies detailed for Communication trenches must decide for themselves when the enemy barrage fire has ceased sufficiently for them to do effective work.
All officers in charge of parties should carefully observe ground where they are to be employed and lines for advance from commanding positions in our line.
O.C's 68th and 86th Field Coys to keep in touch with G.O.C's 33rd and 34th Brigades respectively.

APPENDIX B

ADMINISTRATIVE INSTRUCTIONS.

Divisional Stragglers' Posts.

1. OVILLERS.   X.8.c.4.8.
2. CRUCIFIX CORNER. W.11.d.0.1.
3. POND BRIDGE.   W.23.a.5.9.
4. BROOKERS PASS.   W.11.d.3.5.
5. COLLECTING STATION. W.18.a.8.9.

Brigade Stragglers Posts will be established under Brigade arrangements.

2. PRISONERS OF WAR.
Any prisoners taken will be marched down to CRUCIFIX CORNER under escort, which will be kept as small as possible, and be handed over at that point to the A.P.M. or representative.

3. RATIONS.
Troops will carry on the person the unexpired portion of the day's ration and the Iron Ration.

In addition for attacking Brigades, one day's ration of preserved meat, biscuit and grocery ration, packed in sand bags (8 rations in a bag) will be dumped under Brigade arrangements as far forward as is deemed advisable. These bags will be packed under Divisional arrangements and handed over to Brigades. The bags will have a strip of white material tied to them to identify them.

4. HOT MEAL.
G.Os.C. Brigades will arrange that troops are provided with a hot meal before the attack begins.

5. WATER.
Water bottles will be carried filled.

In addition, petrol tins will be provided and water stored in them under Brigade arrangements and dumped at the same place as the bags of rations. (1 petrol tin contains water rations for 8 men).

6. RUM.
An issue of rum will be drawn and will be stored under Brigade arrangements.

It will be issued to troops under orders of the Brigade Commander.

7. AMMUNITION.
All S.A.A., grenades, Stokes' bombs, rockets, flares etc., required can be drawn under Brigade arrangements from advanced Divisional Dump. (W.11.d.C.2).

Four G.S. wagons containing grenades and S.A.A. will be posted at X.2.d.9.5. to provide an Advanced Divisional Dump during operations.

Brigade dumps will be drawn upon before application is made to Divisional Dump.

All Mills No.5. grenades will be issued fuzed.

All advanced or battalion dumps must be protected from shell fire by digging in.

Ammunition dumps will not be utilized for the storage of rations and water.

8. **DUMPS.**

It is notified for the information of all troops taking part in the operations that dumps are situated as follows, and these dumps are available for all, though, in accordance with their locality they are allotted to individual Brigades:-

AMMUNITION DUMPS.

Divisional.	1.	X.3.a.4.5.	In small dugouts on side of OVILLERS-COURCELETTE road.
	2.	X.3.c.0.5.	In G.S. wagons on side of road.
	3.	W.11.d.0.2.	At CRUCIFIX CORNER QUARRY.
34th Brigade.	1.	R.33.c.9.2.	Ration Trench.
	2.	R.34.c.2.2.	KAY dump.
33rd Brigade.	1.	X.2.a.2.8.	
	2.	X.2.a.6.8.	
	3.	X.2.a.2.1.	
	4.	X.2.d.5.6.	

RATION DUMPS.

In addition to the day's ration in labelled sandbags with the troops, a reserve dump is established at W.18.a.3.8.

WATER DUMPS.

Will be made under Brigade arrangements with a view to establishing forward water and ration dumps in the vicinity of MOUQUET FARM as soon as the operations admit of this.

PACK TRANSPORT.

Brigade pack transport should be employed in carrying forward supplies (Rations and water) to the advanced troops as far as circumstances permit.

32nd Brigade pack transport will be placed at the disposal of Divisional Headquarters to rendezvous at 11 a.m. 26th at W.17.b.9.5.

It is intended to establish a forward dump for all necessaries on the line MOUQUET FARM - R.33.a. Central - as soon as ever operations will permit of this being done. Brigades will co-operate to attain this.

SECRET

Amendments to 11th Division Order No.29.

Page 2. line 16. for R.21.d.91 read R.20.d.91.

Page 2. Para 4. (a) First 5 sentences amend to read as follows:-

4.(a) Troops detailed for the various objectives will follow one another closely under cover of the artillery barrages.

On the 1st Objective being gained there will be a pause in the advance when all men not actually occupying the 1st Objective will lie down.

At ZERO + 24 minutes the troops will advance in successive waves to attack the 2nd Objective.

On the 2nd Objective being gained there will be a pause of 60 minutes in the advance when all men not actually occupying the 2nd Objective will lie down.

At ZERO + 98 minutes the troops will advance in successive waves to attack the 3rd Objective.

Page 3. Para 5. will read as under:-

5. The following artillery will cover the attack and destroy enemy's defences both prior to and during the attack.

(a) Part of the 2nd Corps Heavy Artillery.
(b) 11th Divisional Artillery.
(c) Part of the 25th Divl. Artillery.
(d) 48th Divisional Artillery.

At ZERO a heavy bombardment will be placed on and in front of the 1st Objective and ZOLLERN REDOUBT. Between ZERO + 7 and + 14 minutes the barrage will lift from the 1st Objective on to a line about 150 yards beyond and roughly parallel to it where it remains until ZERO + 25 minutes.

At ZERO + 25 minutes the barrage will lift at the rate of 100 yards per minute reaching the 2nd Objective at ZERO + 33 minutes and remaining there until ZERO + 38 minutes, when it will lift on to the final objective remaining there until ZERO + 104 minutes.

At ZERO + 104 minutes, the barrage lifts from the final objective to a line roughly 200 yards beyond and parallel to it.

The Howitzers will operate beyond the 18 pounder barrage in each phase engaging special targets.

After the initial barrages one battery will be placed at direct disposal of each Infantry Brigadier.

In event of a general rebombardment becoming necessary arrangements will be made by Divisional Head Quarters.

Page 4. Para 8. For "red flags" read "yellow flags"
After "aeroplanes" in line 3 add:-
Infantry will also light flares when the contact aeroplanes fire one Very White Light.

Para 10. Strike out last line. "ADVANCED H.Q. 11th Div."

Appendix 1. Line 46. after touch with add "Brigade and"

25/9/16

T.S. Coleridge Lieut Colonel.

Diary

SECRET

Addendum to 11th Division Order No. 29.

Copy No.

Page 3.

At the end of Para 4. (a) add

"When the line has been established on the final objectives strong patrols with Lewis Guns will be pushed forward to the Regina Trench. (which runs due East from R.21.a.7.5), and STUFF TRENCH (which runs West from R.21.a.6.7 to SCHWABEN REDOUBT in R.19.d.); <u>the important point</u> being to secure for ourselves observation over the GRANDCOURT valley and to deny to the enemy all observation South of the Main Crest line."

Page 4. Para 8. add

"The front line Infantry will also show flares at ZERO + 1 hour 45 minutes and again at + 2 hours 15 minutes, or at any time on demand being made from Contact Aeroplanes sounding Klaxon horns or dropping White Lights".

H.Q. 11th Division.
25th Sept. 1916.

J.D. Coleridge
Major.
Gen.Staff. 11th Div.

Appendix K.

Copy No. ...
24th Sep. 1916

11th Division Order No. 30

1. 11th Division will on night of 26th/27th clear up the situation generally, consolidate their gains & establish direct touch (a) with the Canadians about points R.28.a.3.6 and R.21.d.9.9. (b) With the 18th Division about R.20.d.10 (believed to be already held) and R.26.b.0.3.

2. If the situation permits an intention is to push on again to-day, Canadians to REGINA Trench, 11th Division on GRANDCOURT, 18th Division to SCHWABEN REDOUBT. Proposed approximate hour for ZERO is 10 A.M.

3. (a) The 34th Infantry Brigade will:—
   1. Clear ZOLLERN REDOUBT.
   2. Get touch with 1st Canadian Division at R.28.a.36
   3. Occupy ZOLLERN trench & get in touch with 33rd Infy. Bde. about 26.b.86.
   4. Be prepared to support & reinforce elements of 11.16 and L.Fs in 3rd Objective.
   5. Get touch with 1st Canadian Divn east of R.21.d.99
   6. Consolidate positions gained.

   (b) The 33rd Infantry Brigade will:—
   1. Work eastwards along ZOLLERN trench from R.26.b.86 and get touch with 34th Infy. Bde.
   2. Support & reinforce elements of 4th Sherwood Foresters in HESSIAN trench about R.20.d.30-10
   3. Work eastwards along HESSIAN trench towards STUFF REDOUBT and get touch with 34th Infantry Brigade.
   4. Get touch with 18th Division west of R.26.a.8. and R.20.d.10.
   5. Consolidate positions gained

   (c) The 32nd Infantry Brigade will remain in reserve and will be ready to move at ½ hour's notice.

4. Divisional Artillery will be ready to support and protect any forward movements and to crush any counter-attacks.

5. The Light T.M. Batteries of 32nd and 34th Infantry Brigades will support 34th. Infty. Bde. in the clearance of ZOLLERN REDOUBT.

6. The Tanks, if available, will support 34th Infy. Bde.

T. Coleridge
Lieut. Colonel
Gen. Staff, 11th Division.

Issued at 2.15 a.m.

Copy 1 to A.A. & Q.M.G.   12. A.P.M.   25. O.C. Heavy Mch Guns
  2-3   G.H.Q.   13. 11th Divl. Train   26/29 Division Officers
   4   C.R.A.   14 & 15. Small arms
   5   32nd I. Bde.   16. 4 Gun. Divn.
   6   33rd -"-   17. 1st Canadian Div.
   7   34th -"-   18. 25th Divl. Arty.
   8   6/E Yorks Regt   19-20. Diary
   9   Signal Coy   21-22. File
  10   A.A. & T.M.G.   23. 18th Divn.
  11   A.D.M.S.   24. 4th Sqdn. R.F.C.

Appendix I.

Secret.
Copy No..........
27.9.16.

11th Division Order No. 31.

The 2nd Corps will resume the offensive to-day in co-operation with the Canadian Corps on the right.

2. As a preliminary to other operations the 11th. Division will make good the line R.21 d 99 - STUFF REDOUBT - R.31 d 10 inclusive and will regain touch with the 1st Canadian Division on the right and the 18th. Division on the left.

3. <u>Right attack</u>. Objective R. 21 d 99 inclusive - STUFF REDOUBT - to R 20 d 91 (exclusive). The attack will be carried out by the 32nd Infantry Brigade, less 2 Battalions.

<u>Left attack</u>. Objective R. 20 d 91 (inclusive) to R. 20 d 10 (inclusive). The attack will be carried out by 33rd. Infy. Bde.

4. The 34th. Infantry Brigade will support the Right attack.

5. Two Battalions, 32nd Infantry Brigade, will be in Divisional Reserve at OVILLERS at a site to be selected and pointed out by 34th Infantry Brigade.

6. Special mopping up parties will be detailed by all attacking troops.

7. ZERO hour will be 3 p.m. By 2.45 p.m. attacking troops will be formed up as under ready to advance.

<u>Right attack</u>. ZOLLERN TRENCH from R.21 d 43 to R. 26 b 86.

<u>Left attack</u>. ZOLLERN TRENCH, R.26 b 86 to R 26 a 82.

<u>Artillery Barrage</u>. The Artillery covering the Divisional front will open fire at a steady rate on the objectives at 2.45 p.m.

At ZERO the barrage will become intensive.

At ZERO + 8 the barrage will lift on approaches to the objectives and all known machine emplacements and enemy posts.

J. D. Coleridge
Lieut. Colonel,
General Staff, 11th. Divn.

Issued at 2 p.m.

Copy 1 to A.A. for Col.
2. C. R.A.
3. " "
4. C.R.E.
5. 32nd. I. Bde
6. 33rd. " "
7. 34th. " "
8. 6/C. York Regt.
9. Signal Coy.
10. A.A. Dmk.
11. A.D.M.S.
12. A.P.M.
13. 11th. Div. Train
14 + 15. 2nd Corps
16. 49th Divn.
17. 1st Canadian Divn
18. 25th. Div. Arty.
19 + 20. Diary
21 + 22. File
23. 18th. Divn.
24. 4th. Sqdn. R.F.C.
25. A.C. Heavy M.G. Sectn.
26-29. Liaison Officers.

SECRET.

To:-...............

Reference Operation Order No.27.

Para 1 is to be committed to memory and then destroyed.

The date is not to be mentioned outside H.Q. of units addressed.

21st September 1916.

J. D. Coleridge
Lieut.Colonel
G.S. 11th.Divn.

SECRET.

Ammendment to 11th Division Order No. 27.

Para 4 is ammended to read as under :-

33rd Inf. Bde.	In shelters near	MAILLY MAILLET.	3 Battalions.
	" " "	BONNET POST &) RIBBLE STREET.)	1 Battalion.
34th Inf. Bde.	In shelters near	ENGLEBELMER	2 Battalions.
	" " "	MAILLEY MAILLET.	1 Battalion.
	" " S.of	CRUCIFIX CORNER.	1 Battalion.

21st Sept

Major.

Appendix H.

SECRET.

11th Division Order No. 27.   Copy No. 19

Ref: 1/20,000. 57.D.S.E.   21st Sept. 1916.

1. A large general operation will be carried out about the 26th Sept. by the <u>II</u> Corps in co-operation with the Divisions on our flanks.

2. The <u>18th Division</u> will carry out the attack on the left, THIEPVAL SPUR, relieving the right Brigade of the <u>49th Division</u> probably on the 24th inst. Left Brigade of <u>49th Division</u> will continue to hold the line.

3. The following preliminary moves will take place :-

    (a) The 32nd Inf. Bde. will relieve the 34th Inf. Bde. in the front line of the right sector on the night of the 22nd/23rd.
    (b) The 32nd Inf. Bde. will relieve the 33rd Inf. Bde. in the front line of the left sector on the night of the 22nd/23rd.
    (c) All reliefs will be under arrangements to be made direct between Brigadiers concerned.

    Relief (a) will be completed by midnight 22nd/23rd.
    "   (b) will not commence before midnight 22nd/23rd.

4. By 6 a.m. on the 23rd inst., Brigades will be disposed as under:-

32nd Inf. Bde.	Front Line trenches and Support.	4 Battalions.
33rd Inf. Bde.	Billets, MAILLY MAILLET.	3 Battalions.
	In shelters near DONNET POST & RIBBLE STREET	1 Battalion.
34th Inf. Bde.	Billets in ENGLEBELMER.	3 Battalions.
	Shelters S. of CRUCIFIX CORNER.	1 Battalion.

5. The battalions of 33rd and 34th Inf. Bdes. East of the ANCRE are placed at the disposal of 32nd Inf. Bde. for tactical & working purposes.

6. The 3 Field Coys. R.E. and Pioneer Battn. will remain at AVELUY.

7. The 32nd Inf. Bde. will hold the line in the manner laid down in II Corps G.1106 (11th Divn. G.125. dated 7/9/16). The plans now in hand for the preparation of good starting places for attacks, for consolidation of Brigade Sectors and for the construction of good communications will be handed over by the B.G.C's 33rd. and 34th Bdes. to the B.G.C. 32nd Bde. who will continue the work vigorously.

    The troops mentioned in para 5 will be at the disposal of the 32nd Inf. Bde. and further assistance will be supplied by the C.R.E.

8. Completion of all reliefs will be reported to D.H.Q.

                                        T.D. Colender
                                        Lieut-Colonel.
Issued at 4 p.m.   G. Staff. 11th Division.

Copy No. 1.   A.D.C. for G.O.C.
     2 – 3.   C.R.A.
         4.   C.R.E.   12.   A.P.M.
         5.   32nd Inf.Bde.   13.   11th Div.Train.
         6.   33rd Inf.Bde.   14 – 15.   II Corps.
         7.   34th Inf.Bde.   16.   49th Div.
         8.   6th E. Yorks.   17.   3rd Canadian Div.
         9.   Signal Coy   18.   25th Div. Arty.
        10.   A.A. & Q.M.G.   19 – 20.   Diary
        11.   A.D.M.S.   21 – 22.   File.
                                    23.   18th Divn.

Bde.	Units.	From.	Destination on night.	Destination at ZERO.	REMARKS.
54th.	2 Bns.	ENGELBELMER Shelters.	Right Sector, Firing & Support Lines.	Moving to the attack.	(×)(a) March to be carried out in easy stages, men to have meals en route.
	1 Bn.	do	Dugouts North East of OVILLERS.	Ready to move to Right Sector) Reserve Line)	(b) Men's packs to be carried in lorries as far as AVELUY.
	1 Bn.	Shelters South of CRUCIFIX CORNER.	Stand Fast.		(c) Relief to be completed by midnight on _____
					(d) Exact dispositions to be sent to D.H.Q. as early as possible.
33rd.	1/2 Bn.	MAILLY MAILLET Shelters.	CONSTANCE TRENCH.	Moving to the attack.	(×)(a) March to be carried out in easy stages, men to have meals en route.
	1/2 Bn.	do	DANUBE TRENCH.	do	(b) Men's packs to be carried in lorries as far as AVELUY.
	1/2 Bn.	do	STAFFORD & POLE TRENCH Area.	Moving into CONSTANCE TRENCH.	(c) Relief to be completed by 5 a.m.
	1/2 Bn.	do	Dugouts in 2nd & 3rd Street.	Ready to move do	(d) Exact dispositions to be sent to D.H.Q. as early as possible.
	1 Bn.	do	Dugouts in 1st Street.		
	1 Bn.	RIBBLE STREET & South End CRUCIFIX CORNER.	Stand Fast.	Ready to move to OVILLERS.	
32nd.	1 Bn.	Right Sector Trenches.	W.2.d.} W.9.d.} Bivouac.	VARENNES.	Busses will be provided by 2nd. Corps. Details later.
	1 Bn.	OVILLERS.	do	(Ready to move (to Shelters (South of CRUCIFIX (CORNER.	
	1 Bn.	Left Sector.	do	Shelters W.9.d.	91 shelters will be dumpted at selected Camp site by 5 P.m.
	1 Bn.	Left Sector.	do	(Ready to move to (RIBBLE STREET & (South End CRUCIFIX (CORNER.	

× Men should march in small bodies & start in the morning, dinners & teas & & taken en route

Appendix I.

SECRET.

Copy No. 20

11th Division Order No.28. (Preliminary).

Ref: GRANDCOURT
    ST. PIERRE DIVION
    COURCELETTE } 1/5,000.
    FERME DU MOUQUET
    THIEPVAL
    OVILLERS

    BEAUMONT
    LE SARS } 1/10,000.
    OVILLERS

24th Sept. 1916.

GENERAL.
1. In continuation of 11th Division Order No.27. The objective of the Canadian Corps is the German System of trenches from R.19.d.3.5 through KENORA and REGINA trenches to R.22.a.48 inclusive.

    The objective of the 2nd Corps is from the road running North through R.28.c.22 exclusive, which id the boundary between the two Corps, HESSIAN TRENCH, STUFF REDOUBT, THIEPVAL and SCHWABEN REDOUBT.

    The objective of the 11th Division is from R.21.d.99 inclusive, STUFF REDOUBT - HESSIAN TRENCH - R.20.d.10 inclusive, whence the 18th Division will prolong the line along HESSIAN TRENCH to SCHWABEN REDOUBT.

OBJECTIVES.
2. The 34th Inf. Bde. will attack on the Right. The 33rd Inf. Bde. will attack on the Left.

    Final Objective 34th Inf. Bde.

    R.21.d.99 inclusive - STUFF REDOUBT - HESSIAN TRENCH to R.20.d.91 exclusive.

    Final Objective 33rd Inf. Bde.

    R.20.d.91 inclusive - R.20.d.10 inclusive.

    Details regarding capture of intermediate objectives follow.

    The boundary between the 2 Brigades is the line R.33.a.54 - R.27.c.29 - R.20.d.91. all inclusive to the 33rd Inf. Bde.

RELIEFS.
3. As a preliminary to the above operations the 34th and 33rd Inf. Bdes. will relieve the 32nd Inf. Bde. on the night (date to be communicated secretly later) in accordance with the attached table.

WORK.
4. The 32nd Inf. Bde., R.E., 6th E. Yorks, and the attached troops will press on with the construction and improvement of forming up places and communications, of which details have been handed to G.O.C. in 32nd Inf. Bde.

- 2 -

<u>Marking of Forming Up Places.</u> 5. The G.O.C's 34th: and 33rd: Inf. Bdes. will have direction boards erected, and the forming up places marked with the names of the units by whom they will be occupied prior to the attack. Further instructions on this subject will be issued later.

<u>Bde.H.Q.</u> 6. Brigade H.Q. will be as under after the relief:-

    32nd Inf. Bde: X.8.b.75. With telephone wires to battalion Hd.Qrs.

    33rd Inf. Bde: X.8.a.88.

    34th Inf. Bde: X.8.b.16-24.

<u>BRIGADE DUMPS.</u> 7. Instructions have been issued by the A.A. & Q.M.G. regarding dumps. The actual sites of the dumps will be reported to D.H.Q.

<u>PLANS.</u> 8. The B.G.C's 33rd and 34th Brigades will submit detailed plans regarding how they propose to carry out the operations to D.H.Q. as soon as possible.

                                  J. D. Coleridge
                                          Lieut-Colonel.
                               Gen.Staff, 11th Division.

Issued at <u>6 p.m.</u>

Copy No. 1.   A.D.C. for G.O.C.
    2 & 3.   C.R.A.
       4.   C.R.E.
       5.   32nd Inf.Bde.
       6.   33rd Inf.Bde.
       7.   34th Inf.Bde.
       8.   6th E. Yorks.
       9.   Signal Coy.
      10.   A.A. & Q.M.G.
      11.   A.D.M.S.
      12.   A.P.M.
      13.   11th Div. Train.
  14 & 15.   2nd Corps.
      16.   49th Div.
      17.   1st Canadian Div.
      18.   25th Div.Arty.
  19 & 20.   Diary.
  21 & 22.   File.
      23.   18th. Divn.

Bde.	Units.	From.	Destination on night.	Destination at ZERO.	REMARKS.
34th.	2 Bns.	ENGELBELMER Shelters.	Right Sector, Firing & Support Lines.	Moving to the attack.	✗(a) March to be carried out in easy stages, men to have meals en route.
	1 Bn.	do	Dugouts North East of OVILLERS.	Ready to move to Right Sector Reserve Line	(b) Men's packs to be carried in lorries as far as AVELUY.
	1 Bn.	Shelters South of CRUCIFIX CORNER.	Stand Fast.	Moving to dug-outs North East of OVILLERS.	(c) Relief to be completed by midnight on _____
					(d) Exact dispositions to be sent to D.H.Q. as early as possible.
33rd.	1/2 Bn.	MAILLY MAILLET Shelters.	CONSTANCE TRENCH.	Moving to the attack.	✗(a) March to be carried out in easy stages, men to have meals en route.
	1/2 Bn.	do	DANUBE TRENCH.	do	(b) Men's packs to be carried in lorries as far as AVELUY.
	1/2 Bn.	do	STAFFORD & POLE TRENCH Area.	Moving into CONSTANCE TRENCH	(c) Relief to be completed by 5 a.m.
	1/2 Bn.	do	Dugouts in 2nd & 3rd Street.	Ready to move	(d) Exact dispositions to be sent to D.H.Q. as early as possible.
	1 Bn.	do	Dugouts in 1st Street.	do	
	1 Bn.	RIBBLE STREET & South End CRUCIFIX CORNER.	Stand Fast.	Ready to move to OVILLERS.	
32nd.	1 Bn.	Right Sector Trenches. OVILLERS.	W.2.d.) Bivouacs.	VARENNES.	Busses will be provided by 2nd. Corps. Details later.
	1 Bn.	do	W.9.d.) do	(Ready to move to Shelters South of CRUCIFIX CORNER.	
	1 Bn.	Left Sector.	do	Shelters W.9.d.	91 shelters will be dumped at selected Camp site by 5 p.m.
	1 Bn.	Left Sector.	do	(Ready to move to RIBBLE STREET & South End CRUCIFIX CORNER.	

✗ Men should march in small bodies & start in the morning, dinners + teas to be taken en route.

Appendix M.

Secret.
Copy No. ...
27.9.16.

11th Division Order No. 32

1. (a) The Division will to-night and to-morrow consolidate thoroughly all ground gained; establish permanent touch with Canadians on their right and 18th Division on their left; develop communications; establish new Brigade Headquarters in new positions; reorganise and settle into new battle field.

(b) Posts and observation posts to be established at points whence observation can be obtained down the northern slopes of the Main ridge towards the GRANDCOURT valley.

(c) Eventually, any points remaining in the enemy's hands whence his sight of ruin to our observation north of the main ridge will be shelled and observed.

(d) Every endeavour should be made by active patrolling to ascertain the state of the enemy's defences and his new dispositions.

2. 18th Division will resume every branch the attack upon the SCHWABEN … with details as originally ordered in their Corps Operation Order No. 31. ZERO will be … fixed by the Divisional Commander and communicated … in advance.

3. Corps … will have sufficient guns allocated to protect the front of the 11th Division and employ remainder for support of the attack of the 18th Division.

The orders above :—

Para. 1 (a) (1) Every effort to be made to gain touch with Divisions on our flanks to-night.
With the Canadian Division on R.27.a.20
With 18th Division at R.20.d.0.
A report to be rendered when this is done.

(2) The R.E. will press on with communications giving particular attention to road construction.

(3) Brigades will report locations of new Brigade H.Q. by 11 a.m. to-morrow.

(4) The 34th Infy. Bde. will be withdrawn from the line to billets at OVILLERS, less 2 Battns. in Mouquet area and Fifth Reserve.

(5) The 32nd Infy Bde. will relieve the 33rd Infy Bde in the right sector, details of relief to be arranged by Brigadiers concerned.
Command of the right sector to pass at 10 p.m. to-night.

(6) The enemy on the latter front will be vigorously … on under orders of the G.O.C. 7th Bde.

Paras. 1 (b), 1 (c) & 1 (d)
Have formed subject of orders No. 12
and 25/9/16 which is to be used on all commands.

Guy Mir---
for Lieut-Colonel.
General Staff, 11th Div.

Issued at 1 p.m.

1) G.O.C.   12 …   24 C.R.A. 2nd R.Bde.
2) C.R.E.   13 1st … Bde Res. 25 C.O. Heavy … Art.
3) H.Q.   14 & 15 Brigades   26) Liaison Officers
4) Signal Bde.   17 Canadian Div.   27)
5) Major ...   18 18th Div. Corps
6) W.E.L. …   19 & 20 …
7) A/Q and Corps   21 & 22 …
10) R.A. Corps   23 11th Div.
11) A.D.M.S.

Appendix N.

SECRET.

11th. Division Order No. 33.　　　Copy No. 6.
　　　　　　　　　　　　　　　　　28th. Sept. 1916.

1.　　　The enemy are reported to be still holding the North of STUFF REDOUBT and HESSIAN TRENCH from R.21.d.99 to R.21.c.87.

2.　　　The enemy is also reported to be massing North of HESSIAN TRENCH in R.21.b.

3.　　　It is possible that he may counter-attack during the night 28th/29th.

4.　　　The artillery will maintain a defensive barrage along the whole front held by the 11th. Division, paying especial attention to the supposed threatened area.

5.　　　The 32nd. Infantry Brigade and the 11th. Manchester Regt. will hold the Right Sector. Support and Reserve Troops will be moved forward ready to counter-attack should the enemy enter our lines.

6.　　　The 33rd. Infantry Brigade will hold the Left Sector and will hold two battalions ready to support the 32nd. Infantry Brigade.

7.　　　The 34th. Infantry Brigade, less 1 Battalion will be collected in OVILLERS and form the Divisional Reserve.

8.　　　ACKNOWLEDGE.

Issued at 9.20 p.m.　　　　　　　　　　(Sd) J.D.COLERIDGE. Lt.Col.
　　　　　　　　　　　　　　　　　　General Staff, 11th.Division.

Copy No. 1　32nd. Inf.Bde.
　　　　2.　33rd.　"　　"
　　　　3.　34th.　"　　"
　　　　4.　C.R.A.
　　　　5.　File.
　　　　6.　Diary.
　　7 - 8　II Corps.

Appendix O.

SECRET.
29th Sept.1916.
Copy No. 9.

11th. DIVISION.

Preliminary Order No.34.

1. The 11th. Division will be relieved by the 25th. Division in the line on the night of the 30th.Sept/1st.October.

2. Units will move in accordance with attached Table of Moves.

3. R.E. Companies and Pioneers will be relieved by similar units of the 25th.Division under arrangements to be made by C.R.Es concerned.

4. Command of the line will pass from 11th.Division to 25th.Division at 9 a.m. on the 1st.October.

Issued at 11.30 p.m.

(Sd) J.D.COLERIDGE, Lt.Col.
General Staff, 11th. Division.

Copy No. 1. C.R.A.
        2. C.R.E.
        3. 32nd.Inf.Bde.
        4. 33rd. " "
        5. 34th. " "
        6. Signal Co.
        7. A.A. & Q.M.G.
        8. File.
        9. Diary.

TABLE OF MOVES.

Date.	Unit.	From.	To.	Route.	Remarks.
30-9-16. bb	54th.Inf.Bde. (less 11th.Manctrs.)	OVILLERS.	ACHEUX & VARENNES.	Via HEDAUVILLE.	To be clear of CRUCIFIX CORNER by 10 a.m.
Night 30-9-16 1-10-16.	32nd.Inf.Bde. & 11th.Manchesters.	Line.	W.8 Central.		Relief to be carried out during night 30-9-16/1/10/16.
	33rd. Inf.Bde.	Line.	HEDAUVILLE.		—do—
1-10-16.	11th.D.H.Q.	CAMOUFLAGE. V.16.d.	ACHEUX.		
	(a) 32nd.Inf.Bde. * (b) 33rd.Inf.Bde. *	W.8 Central. HEDAUVILLE.	ACHEUX,VARENNES. ACHEUX,LEALVILLERS.	Via HEDAUVILLE (a) To be clear of HEDAUVILLE by 11 am. (b) To be clear of HEDAUVILLE by 10 am.	To be completed at times which will be notified later.
	34th.Inf.Bde. *	ACHEUX.VARENNES.	"A" Area.		Dismounted personnel will be conveyed by rail, either on 1st. or 2nd.October to :A" Area; remainder moving by road to this area under arrangements to be notified later. Move to be completed by evening of 2nd. October.
	* Dismounted personnel.				

Appendix P.

11th. Division Order No.35.   SECRET

Copy No....

Ref.Maps. 1/40,000   30-9-16..
Sheet 57D.

1. The 11th. Division will be relieved in the line tonight in accordance with the attached Table.

   All details of Infantry Reliefs will be arranged by G.O's C. Infantry Brigades concerned.

2. R.E. and Pioneer reliefs will be arranged direct by respective C.R.E's of Divisions.

   Medical reliefs will be arranged by the A.D.M.S. in conjunction with the A.D.M.S. 25th. Division.

3. The G.O.C. 25th. Division will assume command of the line at 9 a.m. on 1st. October, at which hour Divisional Headquarters will close at DONNETS POST and re-open at ACHEUX.

4. Completion of all reliefs will be reported to D.H.Q.

5. ACKNOWLEDGE.

Issued at 11.20 a.m.

J. D. Colenso
Lieut.Colonel,
General Staff, 11th.Division.

```
Copy No. 1  to A.D.C. for B.O.C.
        2- 3   C.R.A.              14-15   2nd. Corps.
           4   C.R.E.                 16   3rd.Canadian Divn.
           5   32nd. Inf.Bde.         17   25th.Divnl.Arty.
           6   33rd.  "   "           18   18th.Division.
           7   34th.  "   "           19   4th.Sqd.R.F.C.
           8   6th.E.Yorks Regt.      20   O.C. Hvy.M.G.Section.
           9   Signal Coy.         21-24   Liaison Officers.
          10   A.A. & Q.M.G.       25-26   Diary.
          11.  A.D.M.S.            27-28   File.
          12   A.P.M.                 29   25th.Division.
          13   11th. Divnl.Train.
```

11th. Division Order No.35.   30/9/16.

TABLE OF MOVES.

Date.	Unit.	From.	To.	Route.	Remarks.
30-9-16.	34th.Inf.Bde; (less 11th.Manchtrs.	OVILLERS.	ACHEUX and VARENNES.	via HEDAUVILLE.	To be clear of CRUCIFIX CORNER by 10 a.m.
Night 30-9-16 — 1-10-16	32nd.Inf.Bde. & 11th.Manchesters.	Line.	W.S. Central.		Relief to be carried out during night 30-9-16/1-10-16.
	33rd. Inf. Bde.	Line.	HEDAUVILLE.		—do—
1-10-16.	11th. D.H.Q.	CAMOUFLAGE. V.16.d.	ACHEUX.		
	(a) 32nd.Inf.Bde. * (b) 33rd. Inf.Bde.*	W.S. Central. HEDAUVILLE.	ACHEUX, VARENNES. ACHEUX, LEALVILLERS.	Via HEDAUVILLE. (a) To be clear of HEDAUVILLE by 11 a.m. (b) To be clear of HEDAUVILLE by 10 a.m.	To be completed at times which will be notified later.
	34th.Inf.Bde. *	ACHEUX, VARENNES.	"A" Area.		Dismounted personnel will be conveyed by rail, either on 1st. or 2nd.October to "A" Area; remainder moving by road to this area under arrangements to be notified later. Move to be completed by evening of 2nd.October
	* Dismounted personnel.				

SECRET

PLAN FOR MINOR OPERATION TO BE CARRIED OUT ON 30th.inst.

The enemy still retains a "wedge" driven into our line at R.21.c.97 then South along trench to about d.13. This "wedge" is strongly held. It prevents our front line being a continuous one and is a source of danger to reliefs and carrying parties. On right we hold HESSIAN TRENCH to about R.21.d.93 and on left we hold 87.

1. **OBJECTIVE.**
   (a) To drive the enemy out of this "wedge" and to construct a strong post or bombing block N. of XXXXXXXXX 87- 97 so as to deny the use of SUNKEN ROAD to the enemy.

   (b) To join our line across from 87 - 97 so as to hand over a continuous front line on relief.

2. **ARTILLERY ACTION.**
   (a) From 10 a.m. onwards until 3.30 p.m. the 4.5" Howitzers will keep up a slow rate of fire with H.E. on trenches 21.d.05 - 21.c.97 up to 21.a.80.

   (b) (i) From 3.30 p.m. to 4 p.m.
       4 18 pr. batteries will barrage trenches R.21.d.05 - 21.a.80 - 87 - 97 and for 200 yards along HESSIAN TRENCH East from 97, also from c.87 - 89 to a.80.
       (ii) 4.5" Howitzers will block -
       2 trenches running N.W. from STUFF REDOUBT from Pts. 98 and 38.
       Trench running from 88 N.E. to a.80.

   (c) At ZERO hour artillery fire will lift on to the line 21.c.69 - 89.

3. **INFANTRY ACTION.**
   At ZERO 3 specially organised bombing parties supported if possible by Stokes Mortars will advance as under towards C.97.
   (a) Party from S.Staffords from D.13.
   (b) Party of 6th. Yorks and W.Yorks from 58 - 87.
   (c) Party of York & Lancs. from 18 - 58.

4. ZERO hour will be at 4 p.m.

5. The M.Gs. of flanking Brigades should co-operate wherever possible under arrangements to be made by B.G.C. 32nd. Inf. Bde.

30th.September 1916.   Lieut.Colonel,

                                                General Staff, 11th. Divn.
Issued over 'phone to 32nd.I.B. at 10 a.m.

C.R.A.
32nd. Inf.Bde.
33rd. "   "
2nd. Corps.
18th. Divn.
3rd. Canadian Divn.

Mouquet Farm –

Operations against –

34th. Inf. Bde.   SECRET.
----

              tonight
        The G.O.C. wishes you to clear up the situation at MOUQUET FARM. The present enemy garrison should be captured or driven out and steps taken to prevent the enemy again reoccupying any portion of the Farm.

2.   Please forward a brief report of the action you propose to take in the matter tonight for the information of the G.O.C.

21st September 1916.   Major,

                                        General Staff, 11th. Divn.

Copy No. 7.

32nd INFANTRY BRIGADE ORDER NO. 23.

Intention. 1. The 6th Bn York & Lancaster Regiment will clear the enemy out of MOUQUET FARM and occupy and consolidate the trench running on the N.W. side of the farm, this evening.

Artillery arrangements 2. The heavy artillery will bombard MOUQUET FARM and HIGH TRENCH from 5 p.m. to 6 p.m.

All troops within a radius of 500 yards of MOUQUET FARM will be cleared by 5 p.m.

At 6.58 p.m. a barrage will be placed on HIGH TRENCH from R.27.d.50.25 to R.27.d.1.2.

At 7 p.m. the barrage will lift on to the communication trenches from R.27.d.4.2;5.0--R.27.d.1.2 to R.27.c.2.6 and on all known M.G. emplacements.

The Assault. 3. The assault will be carried out by 2 platoons in 2 waves.

The first wave will rush and occupy the trench reported on the N.W. side of the farm, or if this trench cannot be found a line of shell holes covering the farm will be consolidated.

The 2nd. wave will seize the entrances to the cellars and dug-outs of the farm and clear them up. If necessary fumite bombs will be thrown into the dug-outs and block the entrances.

A 3rd. platoon will be held in readiness to reinforce if necessary.

A carrying party for material for consolidation, bombs, water, etc. will be detailed from a 4th platoon.

Times: At 6 p.m. the assaulting troops will start moving forward to re-occupy the front line. Troops to be in position by 6.30 p.m.

The troops normally occupying the front line will at the same time re-occupy the support trench.

At 7 p.m. the assault will be made.

Watches: Watches will be synchronised by telephone at 4 p.m., 5 p.m., and 6 p.m.

V.B.Middleton for Captain,
Brigade Major.

24th September 1916.

Issued at 4 p.m.

Copies to:-
No 1. 9th West Yorkshire Regt.
2. 6th Yorkshire Regt.
3. 8th Duke of Wellingtons Regt.
4. 6th York and Lancaster Regt.
5. 32nd M.G.Coy.
6. 32nd. L.T.M.Bty.
7. 11th Division.
8)
9) War Diary.

32. Brigade.

Report on Situation.

The attack on Mouquet Farm was carried out by one company, the enemy was met with in strong force preceded by a heavy bombing attack.

My attack reached the Northern mound but owing to the artillery barrage being ineffective, the german works were untouched. The enemy were thoroughly prepared. The company attacked 4 times. The telephone was cut about 7.30 pm & I received no news till 8.25 p.m. I then phoned to 32 Bde for further barrage

Major Ford in charge of operations at Quarry reports without a strong barrage no result can be expected.

G.H.M.d.g Wood Lt Col
6 York & Lancaster Regt

2 Aug. 16
10.55 pm

R.B.

The attack on MOUQUET FARM has failed A.A.A. At 8.30 P.M. a report was received that we held the North West end of MOUQUET FARM and that further artillery support was required, the C.R.A. 11th Division to 'C' 59 & 60th Battys were called on for support, which was given. A.A.A. At 9.25 p.m. it was reported that parties with material for consolidation had had great difficulty in getting up material owing to enemy's barrage & one of the party being buried a further party was being sent up the material being drawn from the Canadian Dump & that this material was being sent up as quickly as possible A.A.A. At 10.25 information was received that the party holding the N.W. end of MOUQUET FARM had been compelled to withdraw & that all our troops had fallen back on our original front line. It appears that the Coy which made the attack, attacked from Kemis & only held the N.W. of the farm for a short time owing to heavy M.G. fire & a strong bombing attack. The failure of the attack was due to our barrage not being placed close on to the enemy's front line the consequence being that when our infantry attacked it was met by heavy rifle fire & bombs. The distance between the lines is only about 250 yards. During the heavy howitzer bombardment about 75 per cent of the shells fired failed to explode.

B.M. 331.

11th Division.

Herewith report from O.C. 6th Y&L.
A report for further operations
will be submitted as soon as possible.

N.T. Price Brig Genl
32nd Inf Bde.

24.9.16.

Enderby Ground had not been reconnoitred
before hand   ADW

52 Brigade

Report on Reconnaissance on MOUKE FARM
on night of 23/24 Sept 1916.

(1) At 11.30 pm
2 Lt Measures with 1 NCO & 1 man left the
front line trench at 33 b 49 & proceeded
to 27 d 31.
From there he saw a trench running at
right angles to my front line from NE
corner of farm, the enemy were in this
& sending up flares, he was 15 yds
from them, he also saw another trench
about 50 yds behind this running
parallel to it & by the number of flares
this was strongly held as the flares
were 3 or 4 yds apart.
He was fired at from both these
trenches. He returned at 12.20 am
24.9.16.

(2).
2 Lt Hanson started at 11.30 pm from
pt 33 b 28 with a similar party towards
W portion of Farm; on leaving the
trench he was immediately sniped
at from the Farm. He crawled up to
pt 33 b 29 15 yds to the left of the
farm & lay in a shell hole.

& observed. By the flare lights he observed a C.T. directly in front of him, it curved round behind the farm running parallel to our front line. Flares were sent up often from C.T. & curved trench & therefore he thought trenches strongly held. The top of the rubble heap was occupied by snipers.

At the back of the farm nearest him he noticed a place that looked like an emplacement.

He returned about 1.am, 24.9.16.
A Lewis gun from my trench each side of the farm played a cross fire behind the farm.

On receiving these reports at 2.15 am & 2.30 am respectively I decided to abandon the attempt as per Scheme, till I could re-organise it on a more prepared scale.

G H Wedgwood Lt Col
com 6 York & Lancaster Regt

24. 9. 16
3. am

SECRET.   URGENT.

32nd Inf. Bde.

C.R.A. for information.

The situation at MOUQUET FARM is to be cleared up without delay either to-day or to-night.

The following methods are suggested :-

(a) Withdraw garrison and use heavy howitzer to destroy entrances and enemy sniper posts covering entrances.
Then at a given hour to rush the place with 10 or 12 determined men under a 18 pounder shrapnel barrage directed on all known Machine Gun positions and posts held by the enemy.

(b) Employment "Special Section R.E." with poisonous gas or lachrymatory bombs.

(c) Surprise attack by bayonet men covered by Stokes and Machine Gun barrage.

(d) A Tank.

(e) A borer.

Any other alternative, but the matter is urgent and you will take early action, submitting your proposals here at once in order that arrangements may be made with the Artillery.

H.Q. 11th Division.   Major.
24th September 1916.   Gen.Staff.11th Division.

Orders for Clearing up of MOUQUET FARM.

21/9/16.

1. The situation must be cleared up tonight and all Germans in the farm killed or taken.

2. The procedure will be as follows :-
A party consisting of 4 bombers and 4 bayonet men under a reliable N.C.O. will leave our trench just West of the Farm and will creep round to the North West entrance to the galleries.

3. They will rush the sentries at the top of the stairs and throw in smoke bombs; after this has been done the entrance will be blocked. To assist in that a N.C.O. and 4 men with tools will follow the fighting party.
At the same time the remainder of the platoon will leave our trench on the Eastern side and work their way up to the N.E. entrance to the gallery.
On reaching the entrance they will be ready to deal with any Germans who attempt to come out that way.

4. The platoon will be under the command of 2/Lt. Hall who will detail their duties.

5. Both parties will leave our trenches simultaneously at 11.30 p.m. Watches to be compared beforehand.

6. O.C. Q Coy. will have 2 Lewis Guns from the Quarry placed in our front trench by 11.30 p.m. As soon as 2/Lt. Hall's party is heard at work these guns will be moved out and will be placed on the rubble mound in front of our trench to deal with a relief, which may be expected between 1 and 2 a.m.

7. Prisoners will be passed back to O.C. Q Coy. who will send them to the Quarry where they will be handed over to an Officer detailed by O.C. R Coy. who will have with him a conducting party of 10 men.

8. 2/Lt. Hall will make sure that all entrances to the galleries are stopped before bringing his men back.

9. O.C. Q Coy. will make sure a sniping post is established on the forward mound before his Lewis Guns are relieved.
Snipers to have food and water.

10. O.C. Q Coy. will detail a sentry group to remain in the communication trench running from our trench to N.E. corner of Farm until the operation is complete.

11. The garrison of the Farm is said to be two platoons.

12. At 11.30 p.m. 1 N.C.O. and 3 men, Q Coy. will scout for the suspected half blocked entrance at S.E. corner of Farm, inside our lines to prevent a German escaping this way.

(Sd) B.A. Wright,
Commanding 11th. Man. Regt.

The Adjutant,
    11th. Manchester Regt.   22/9/16.

Sir,

I wish to report the various reasons of the failure of the work that was to be done by myself and party last night.

It was 9.45 p.m. when I received my final instructions from H.Q.. I at once proceeded to KAY Dump and ordered a box of 'P' bombs and 2 boxes of Mill's Grenades to be sent to my dugout at once. I then went up trench and warned the N.C.Os of Nos 12 and 11 platoons to furnish me with 2 effective N.C.Os and 15 men each to be paraded outside my dugout at 10.30 p.m. I next warned Cpl.Shepley to find 8 picked men and parade as before. I next saw the C.S.M., told him what I had done and asked him to see that my orders were carried out, also to find 1 L/Cpl and 4 men with shovels. Next I reported to my Coy. Commander, gave him orders to read over and after a short consultation with him got the N.C.Os together in my own dugout and explained what we were ~~going~~ going to do. The parties were fallen in already to move off at 10.45 when I found the smoke bombs were not detonated as I had ordered which delayed the start until 10.55 I proceeded at the utmost pace along the trench urging the men forward, but it was not until 12.5 a.m. I reported to Major Oliver at the Quarry. He provided me with guide and we at once proceeded to front line which we reached at 1.15 a.m. I posted the men under their N.C.Os at Right of Farm and then proceeded to left with Cpl. Shepley and his party. When pointing out to him the nature of his task I noticed what I took to be signals to the enemy front line which consisted of 2 rifle shots causing little noise but showing a shower of sparks. I thought it best to investigate, so we left trench and proceeded from shell hole to shell hole until we reached a point about 10 yards from what was had been the original N.W. corner of Farm.

At 1.35 we heard a challenge and the relieving party came into view. I knew there was no use trying to carry out my pre-arranged plan then, so I decided to wait until everything was quiet again. The releif took about 30 minutes to complete, one party filing in by one entrance and the other leaving by the second. I estimate the strength of garrison at 50 though I couldn't make an accurate count.

The few sentries at each entrance seemed to be very alert and fired lights at about 3 minutes intervals.

By this time the moon had risen and was flooding the ground with light making the success of the operation most uncertain, for objects were easily picked out at 20 yards distance and the movements of parties of 17 men each were sure to have been seen. I then returned to trench and waited until 2.45 a.m. and as the moon showed no signs of being obscured decided to abondon the work for the night.

I hope to be allowed another chance of carrying out the work tomorrow night at say 7.30 p.m.

                                (Sd).   J. Norman Hall,
                                                    2/Lieut.
                                            11th.Manchester Regiment.

Orders for Clearing up of MOUQUET FARM.

21/9/16.

1. The situation must be cleared up tonight and all Germans in the farm killed or taken.

2. The procedure will be as follows :-
    A party consisting of 4 bombers and 4 bayonet men under a reliable N.C.O. will leave our trench just West of the Farm and will creep round to the North West entrance to the galleries.

3. They will rush the sentries at the top of the stairs and throw in smoke bombs; after this has been done the entrance will be blocked. To assist in that a N.C.O. and 4 men with tools will follow the fighting party.
    At the same time the remainder of the platoon will leave our trench on the Eastern side and work their way up to the N.E. entrance to the gallery.
    On reaching the entrance they will be ready to deal with any Germans who attempt to come out that way.

4. The platoon will be under the command of 2/Lt. Hall who will detail their duties.

5. Both parties will leave our trenches simultaneously at 11.30 p.m. Watches to be compared beforehand.

6. O.C. Q Coy. will have 2 Lewis Guns from the Quarry placed in our front trench by 11.30 p.m. As soon as 2/Lt. Hall's party is heard at work these guns will be moved out and will be placed on the rubble mound in front of our trench to deal with a relief, which may be expected between 1 and 2 a.m.

7. Prisoners will be passed back to O.C. Q Coy. who will send them to the Quarry where they will be handed over to an Officer detailed by O.C. R Coy. who will have with him a conducting party of 10 men.

8. 2/Lt. Hall will make sure that all entrances to the galleries are stopped before bringing his men back.

9. O.C. Q Coy. will make sure a sniping post is established on the forward mound before his Lewis Guns are relieved.
    Snipers to have food and water.

10. O.C. Q Coy. will detail a sentry group to remain in the communication trench running from our trench to N.E. corner of Farm until the operation is complete.

11. The garrison of the Farm is said to be two platoons.

12. At 11.30 p.m. 1 N.C.O. and 3 men, Q Coy. will scout for the suspected half blocked entrance at S.E. corner of Farm, inside our lines to prevent a German escaping this way.

(Sd) B.A. Wright,
Lieut.
Commanding 11th.Man.Regt.

WAR DIARY

of

"G" Branch, 11th.Division.

for October 1916.

Army Form C. 2118

WAR DIARY
or
INTELLIGENCE SUMMARY
(Erase heading not required.)

11th Division. "G".

OCTOBER 1916.

Instructions regarding War Diaries and Intelligence Summaries are contained in F. S. Regs., Part II. and the Staff Manual respectively. Title Pages will be prepared in manuscript.

Place	Date	Hour	Summary of Events and Information	Remarks and references to Appendices
DONNET POST W.12.d.9.2.	1st.	7-42am. 9 am.	Relief of 32nd Inf. Bde. by 75th Inf. Bde. reported complete. Relief of Division less Artillery by 25th Division complete and command of the line passed to G.O.C. 25th Division at 9 a.m. Line actually handed over is as stated in Diary for 30th September. In close touch with 3rd Canadian Division on our right and by patrols with 18th Division on our left.	vide. O.O.35. d/30/9/16.
ACHEUX.	"	9 am.	Divisional H.Q. opened at ACHEUX. Following moves took place to-day:- 1. (a) 34th Inf.Bde. moved to PROUVILLE, BERNAVILLE, BERNEUIL & RIBEAUCOURT with Headquarters at RIBEAUCOURT. (b) 6th E. Yorks Regt. to BERNAVILLE. (c) 3 Field Companies to OUTREBOIS and OCCOCHES. Dismounted personnel moving by train from ACHEUX VARENNES to CANDAS. 2. 32nd Inf. Bde. moved to ACHEUX and VARENNES with H.Q. at VARENNES. 3. 33rd Inf. Bde. moved to ACHEUX and LEALVILLERS with H.Q. at LEALVILLERS. Weather fine.	
BERNAVILLE.	2nd.		Divl. Hd. Qrs. moved to BERNAVILLE midday. 33rd Inf. Bde. moved by bus and train to BOISBERGUES Area. 32nd Inf. Bde. " " " " " BEAUMETZ Area with H.Q. at BEAUMETZ. Weather: Heavy rain from 11 a.m. onwards.	
do	3rd		33rd Inf. Bde. moved by route march to CRAMONT Area with H.Q. at CRAMONT. 34th Inf. Bde. " " " " " FRANSU Area " " " FRANSU. Weather wet, clearing in afternoon.	

Army Form C. 2118

WAR DIARY
or
INTELLIGENCE SUMMARY

(Erase heading not required.)

11th Division. "G"

OCTOBER 1916.

Instructions regarding War Diaries and Intelligence Summaries are contained in F.S. Regs., Part II. and the Staff Manual respectively. Title Pages will be prepared in manuscript.

Place	Date	Hour	Summary of Events and Information	Remarks and references to Appendices
DOMART-en-PONTHIEU.	4th.		Divl. Headquarters moved to DOMART-en-PONTHIEU midday. Division reorganising, re-equipping and training. Weather fine but dull.	
do	5th.		Units re-equipping and training. Location of units attached. Weather fine.	Location Return. Appendix "A"
do	6th.		ditto. Weather fine during day. Heavy rain during night.	
do	7th.		ditto. 33rd & 34th Inf. Bdes. inspected by Lt.Gen. C.W. JACOB, C.B., Commander 2nd Corps. Report on Operations 24/9/16 to 1/10/16 attached. Weather fine during morning. Rain in afternoon.	Report on Operations 24/9/16 to 1/10/16. Appendix "B".
do	8th.		The 6th E. Yorks Regt. (Pioneers) moved by route march to 2nd Corps Area and passed under the Command of that Corps. No other changes in the dispositions of Units of the Division which continued refitting and training. Wet day.	
do	9th		Training continued. Weather dull but fine.	
do	10th.		ditto. Weather fine.	

1875 Wt. W593/826 1,000,000 4/15 J.B.C. & A. A.D.S.S./Forms/C. 2118.

Army Form C. 2118

WAR DIARY
or
INTELLIGENCE SUMMARY
(Erase heading not required.)

Instructions regarding War Diaries and Intelligence
Summaries are contained in F.S. Regs., Part II.
and the Staff Manual respectively. Title Pages
will be prepared in manuscript.

11th Division "G".

OCTOBER 1916.

Place	Date	Hour	Summary of Events and Information	Remarks and references to Appendices
DOMART-en-PONTHIEU.	11th.		Training continued. The Commander-in-Chief arrived at D.H.Q. at 2 p.m. and rode round and inspected several Units of the Division at Training. The C-in-C expressed his satisfaction at what he had seen.	
do	12th.		Training continued. Weather showery.	
do	13th.		ditto. Weather dull and showery.	
do	14th.) 15th.) 16th.) 17th.)		No change in the disposition of the Division. In each Brigade area a trench system consisting of a front line joined to support lines by several C.T's was dug and each battalion practised the attack on these trenches. The training od specialists continued under their own officers. Weather generally fine.	
ST OUEN.	18th.		Training continued. D.H.Q. moved from DOMART to ST OUEN. The Three Field Companies R.E. and 3 Machine Gun Companies moved by route march to 2nd Corps area and passed under the orders of that Corps.	
do	19th.		Training continued. Weather wet.	

1875   Wt. W593/826   1,000,000   4/15   J.B.C. & A.   A.D.S.S./Forms/C. 2118.

Army Form C. 2118

WAR DIARY
or
INTELLIGENCE SUMMARY

(Erase heading not required.)

11th Division "G".

OCTOBER 1916.

Instructions regarding War Diaries and Intelligence Summaries are contained in F. S. Regs., Part II. and the Staff Manual respectively. Title Pages will be prepared in manuscript.

Place	Date	Hour	Summary of Events and Information	Remarks and references to Appendices
ST OUEN.	20th.		Training continued. Weather fine but cold. The 4th Corps took over the administration of "B" area from Reserve Army.	
do	21st.		ditto. Weather fine but cold. Orders were received from 4th Corps that the Division less detached Units was to move to "R" area on the 24th instant.	
do	22nd.		Training continued. Weather wet.	Appendix "C" O.O.No.36.
do	23rd.		ditto. Reserve Army postponed move to "R" area until the 25th instant. Weather wet.	
do	24th.		Training continued. Move to "R" area postponed until the 27th instant.	
do	25th.		Training continued but the weather was wet and cold. Move of Division to "R" area was postponed until the 29th inst.	
do	26th.		Training continued. Weather showery and cold.	
do	27th.		ditto. ditto.	

1875 Wt. W⁵593/826 1,000,000 4/15 J.B.C.& A. A.D.S.S./Forms/C. 2118.

Army Form C. 2118

WAR DIARY
or
INTELLIGENCE SUMMARY

(Erase heading not required.)

11th Division "G".

OCTOBER 1916.

Instructions regarding War Diaries and Intelligence Summaries are contained in F.S. Regs., Part II. and the Staff Manual respectively. Title Pages will be prepared in manuscript.

Place	Date	Hour	Summary of Events and Information	Remarks and references to Appendices
ST OUEN.	28th.		Training continued, special attention being paid to the training of specialists. Move of Division was again postponed to the 31st inst. Cold and wet.	
do.	29th.		Church parades. Cold and wet morning, cleared later.	
do	30th.		Training continued. Wet and windy. Move to "B" area postponed until 4th November.	
do	31st.		Training continued. Weather showery. Table shewing location of units on this date is attached.	APPENDIX D. Location Return.
			SUMMARY FOR OCTOBER 1916. The Division (less artillery) was withdrawn from the line on the 1st.October and moved back to Reserve Army "B" area, West of DOMART EN PONTHIEU. On the 8th.October, the 6th.E.Yorks Regt.(Pioneers) moved back to 2nd. Corps Area and passed under the Command of that Corps. On the 18th.inst. the 3 Field Coys. R.E. and 3 Machine Gun Companies also moved back to 2nd. Corps and passed under the orders of that Corps. The rest of the Division remained in "B" area for the whole month for refitting and training. The following appendices are attached :- Appendix "A". Location of Units on 5th.October. " "B" Report on Active Operations from 24th.Sept. to 1st.October. " "C" O.O. No.36. Move to "R" area, Reserve Army, (this was postponed). " "D" Location of units on 31st.October.	

J.D. Crosby Lt. Col.
for Lieut.General,
Commanding 11th.Division.

APPENDIX "A".

5th. October 1916.

LOCATION TABLE showing position of units of
11th. Division at 6 a.m. day after date
return is rendered.

11th. Division.	H.Q.	DOMART – en – PONTHIEU.	
32nd. Infantry Brigade.	H.Q.	BEAUMETZ.	
9th. W. Yorkshire Regt.	H.Q.	BEAUMETZ.	Bn. BEAUMETZ.
6th. Yorkshire Regt.	H.Q.	do	Bn. do
8th. W. Ridings Regt.	H.Q.	DOMLEGER.	Bn. DOMLEGER.
6th. York & Lancs. Regt.	H.Q.	AGENVILLE.	Bn. AGENVILLE.
32nd. M.G. Co. & T.M. Battery.		DOMLEGER.	
33rd. Infantry Brigade.	H.Q.	CRAMONT.	
6th. Lincoln Regt.	H.Q.	CRAMONT.	Bn. CRAMONT.
6th. Border Regt.	H.Q.	do	Bn. do
7th. S. Stafford Regt.	H.Q.	MAISON ROLLAND.	Bn. MAISON ROLLAND.
9th. S. Foresters	H.Q.	MESNIL DOMQUEUR.	Bn. MESNIL DOMQUEUR.
33rd. M.G. Co. & T.M. Battery.		CRAMONT.	
34th. Infantry Brigade.	H.Q.	FRANSU.	
8th. Northd. Fusiliers.	H.Q.	DOMQUEUR.	Bn. DOMQUEUR.
9th. Lancs. Fusiliers.	H.Q.	HOUDENCOURT.	Bn. FRANQUEVILLE.
5th. Dorset Regt.	H.Q.	FRANQUEVILLE.	Bn. FRANQUEVILLE.
11th. Manchester Regt.	H.Q.	FRANSU.	Bn. FRANSU.
34th. M.G. Co. & T.M. Battery.		SURCHAMPS.	

Pioneer Battalion.

6th. E. Yorks Regt.	H.Q.	ST. OUEN.	Bn. ST. OUEN.
C.R.E. 11th. Division.	H.Q.	DOMART – en – PONTHIEU.	
67th. Field Co. R.E.)			
68th. " " ")		ST. OUEN.	
86th. " " ")			
A.D.M.S., 11th. Division.	H.Q.	DOMART – en – PONTHIEU.	
33rd. Field Ambulance.		MAISON ROLLAND.	
34th. " "		REDERIE FARM.	
35th. " "		LONGVILLERS.	
21st. Sanitary Section.		DOMART – en – PONTHIEU.	
A.D.V.S., 11th. Division.	H.Q.	DOMART – en – PONTHIEU.	
22nd. Mobile Vet Section.		DOMQUEUR.	
Divisional R.A.	H.Q.	BOUZINCOURT. (attached 25th. Divn).	
11th. Divisional Train.	H.Q.	DOMQUEUR.	
No.1 Company.		SENLIS.	
No.2 "		DOMQUEUR	
No.3 "		CRAMONT MILL.	
No.4 "		LAHAIE FARM.	
11th. Divisional Supply Column.		LE PLOUY, DOMQUEUR.	

APPENDIX "C"

SECRET.

Copy No. 18.

11th Division Order No. 36.

Ref. Map 1/100,000
Sheet LENS.

23rd October 1916.

The 11th Division (less detached Units) will move tomorrow from "B" Area to "R" Area.

Moves will take place as ordered in attached March Table.

2. Units not mentioned in this order will move under orders to be issued by the A.A. & Q.M.G..

3. Divl. Hd. Qrs. will close at ST OUEN at 10 a.m. on the 24th October and will reopen at CANAPLES at the same hour.

4. ACKNOWLEDGE.

R.F. Guy Major,
for Lieut-Colonel.
Gen.Staff. 11th Division.

Issued at 12 noon.

Copy No. 1. A.D.C. for G.O.C.
2. C.R.A.
3. C.R.E.
4. 32nd Inf. Bde.
5. 33rd Inf. Bde.
6. 34th Inf. Bde.
7. 6th E. Yorks R.
8. Signal Coy.
9. A.A. & Q.M.G.
10. A.D.M.S.
11. A.P.M.
12. 11th Div. Train.
13. B.A.D.O.S.
14. Camp. Comdt.
15. 4th Corps.
16. 2nd Corps.
17 & 18. War Diary.
19 & 20. File.
21. 1st Cav DIV.

MARCH TABLE to accompany 11th Division Order No. 36.

Date.	Unit.	Starting Point.	Route.	Destination.	Remarks.
24th Oct.	34th Inf.Bde. 34th Fd.Amb.	Tail of Column to be South of DOMART by 10 a.m.	DOMART ST LEGER les DOMART. PERNOIS. HALLOY.	PERNOIS. HALLOY. LA VICOGNE VALHEUREUX.	Extra accommodation is available at HAVERNAS if required. Bde.Hd.Qrs. at PERNOIS.
do.	32nd Inf.Bde. 35th Fd.Amb.	Tail of Column to clear BEAUMETZ by 9-30 a.m. (?). Head of Column not to reach DOMART before 10-30 a.m.	BEAUMETZ. DOMART. ST LEGER les DOMART.	BERTEAUCOURT. ST LEGER les DOMART.	Bde. Hd.Qrs. at BERTEAUCOURT.
do	33rd Inf.Bde. 33th Fd.Amb.	Head of Column not to reach BEAUMETZ before 9-30 a.m.	BERNAVILLE Main road E. of GORGES & BERNEUIL MONTRELET BONNEVILLE.	BONNEVILLE MONTRELET FIEFFES.	Bde HD.Qrs. at BONNEVILLE.

APPENDIX "D".

S E C R E T.

31st October 1916.

LOCATION TABLE showing position of units of 11th. Division at 6 a.m. day after date return is rendered.

11th. Division.	H.Q.	ST. OUEN.

32nd. Infantry Brigade   H.Q.   BEAUMETZ.

9th. W. Yorkshire Regt.	H.Q.	BEAUMETZ.	Bn. BEAUMETZ.
6th. Yorkshire Regt.	H.Q.	do	Bn. do
8th. W. Riding Regt.	H.Q.	DOMLEGER.	Bn. DOMLEGER.
6th. York & Lancs. Regt.	H.Q.	AGENVILLE.	Bn. AGENVILLE.
32nd. Machine Gun Company.		attached 18th. Division.	
32nd. L.T.M. Battery.		DOMLEGER.	

33rd. Infantry Brigade.   H.Q.   CRAMONT.

6th. Lincoln Regt.	H.Q.	CRAMONT.	Bn. CRAMONT.
6th. Border Regt.	H.Q.	CRAMONT.	Bn. CRAMONT.
7th. S. Stafford Regt.	H.Q.	MAISON ROLLAND.	Bn. MAISON ROLLAND.
9th. S. Foresters.	H.Q.	MESNIL DOMQUEUR.	Bn. MESNIL DOMQUEUR.
33rd. Machine Gun Company.		attached 19th. Division.	
33rd. L.T.M. Battery.		CRAMONT.	

34th. Infantry Brigade.   H.Q.   FRANSU.

8th. North'd. Fusiliers.	H.Q.	DOMQUEUR.	Bn. DOMQUEUR.
9th. Lancs. Fusiliers.	H.Q.	HOUDENCOURT.	Bn. FRANQUEVILLE.
5th. Dorset Regt.	H.Q.	DOMQUEUR.	Bn. DOMQUEUR.
11th. Manchester Regt.	H.Q.	FRANSU.	Bn. FRANSU.
34th. Machine Gun Company.		attached 39th. Division	
34th. L.T.M. Battery.		SURCAMPS.	

Pioneer Battalion.

   6th. E. Yorks Regt.   H.Q. & Battn. W.9.d.5.4. Sheet 57D. S.E.

C.R.E. 11th. Division.   H.Q.   ST. OUEN.

67th. Field Co. R.E.	X.17.a.3.0.)	
68th. " " "	W.12.d.8.2.)	attached 18th. Div:
86th. " " "	W.17.a. AVELUY.	attached 19th. "

A.D.M.S., 11th. Division.   H.Q.   ST. OUEN.

33rd. Field Ambulance.	MAISON ROLLAND.
34th. " "	REDERIE FARM.
35th. " "	LONGVILLERS.
21st. Sanitary Section.	ST. OUEN.

A.D.V.S., 11th. Division.   H.Q.   ST. OUEN.

   22nd. Mobile Vet. Section.   DOMQUEUR.

Divisional R.A.   H.Q.   TARA HILL. W.30.a.

11th. Divisional Train.   H.Q.   DOMQUEUR.

No. 1 Company.	SENLIS.
No. 2 Company.	DOMQUEUR.
No. 3 Company.	CRAMONT HILL.
No. 4 Company.	LAHAIE FARM.

11th. Divisional Supply Column.   LE PLOUY, DOMQUEUR.

WAR DIARY

"G" Branch 11th Div.

WAR DIARY

GENERAL STAFF.

11th Division.

November
1916.

Army Form C. 2118

WAR DIARY
or
INTELLIGENCE SUMMARY

11th. Division. "G".

November 1916.

(Erase heading not required.)

Instructions regarding War Diaries and Intelligence Summaries are contained in F.S. Regs., Part II. and the Staff Manual respectively. Title Pages will be prepared in manuscript.

Place	Date	Hour	Summary of Events and Information	Remarks and references to Appendices
ST.OUEN.	1st.		Training continued. Weather showery.	
do	2nd.		do do Weather fine.	
do	3rd.		do do Move of Division to "R" Area postponed indefinitely. Weather fine.	
do	4th.		do do Weather fine.	
do	5th.		Church parades. Weather stormy.	
do	6th.		Training continued. Weather wet.	
do	7th.		do do Weather very wet.	
do	8th.		do do Weather wet.	
do	9th.		do do Weather wet.	
do	10th.		do do Weather fine and cold. D.O. 37 issued cancelling D.O. 36 and ordering move of Division into YVRENCH Area.	Appx. "A" D.O.No.37.
YVRENCH.	11th.		Division moved into YVRENCH Area. Div.Hd.Qrs. established at YVRENCH. Training continued by those units which did not move. Weather dull and misty.	
do	12th.		Church parades. At midday orders were received from 4th.Corps for Division to move to CANAPLES Area tomorrow 13th. Divisional Order No.38 issued accordingly. At 6 p.m. orders for the move were cancelled. Weather dull.	Appx. B. D.O. No.38. Appx. C. Location Return.
do	13th.		Orders again received from 4th.Corps for Division to move to CANAPLES Area, tomorrow 14th. Divisional Order No.39 issued accordingly. Weather very misty. In early morning 2nd. and 5th. Corps attacked North and South of the River ANCRE.	Appx D. D.O.39.

1875 Wt. W593/826 1,000,000 4/15 J.B.C. & A., A.D.S.S./Forms/C. 2118.

Army Form C. 2118.

WAR DIARY
or
INTELLIGENCE SUMMARY

(Erase heading not required.)

11th. Division. "G".

November 1916.

Instructions regarding War Diaries and Intelligence Summaries are contained in F. S. Regs., Part II. and the Staff Manual respectively. Title Pages will be prepared in manuscript.

Place	Date	Hour	Summary of Events and Information	Remarks and references to Appendices
CANAPLES.	14th.		Division moved into CANAPLES Area. Divisional Headquarters established at CANAPLES. Location return of units attached. Divisional Order 40 issued for move of Division into 2nd.Corps Area.	Appx. E. D.O. 40 Appx. F Location Return.
do	15th.		Brigade Groups moved in accordance with D.O.40. G.O.Cs 32nd. and 33rd. Bdes. went forward to reconnoitre probable eventual dispositions of their Brigades in 2nd.Corps Area. Orders were received in the afternoon for Divnl.Hd.Qrs. to move to huts North of BOUZINCOURT tomorrow. Signal Company (less detachment) and Divnl.Hd.Qrs. details marched to CONTAY and RUBEMPRE respectively in the evening. At midnight the Division passed under the orders of 2nd.Corps. Weather fine.	Appx. G. Location Return.
CONTAY.	16th.		In early morning orders were received cancelling the moves of 32nd. and 33rd. Bde Groups as laid down in D.O.40 and also the move of Divisional Headquarters to BOUZINCOURT. 32nd.Bde.Group marched to LEALVILLERS and ACHEUX., 33rd.Bde.Group to HEDAUVILLE and VARENNES., 34th.Bde. Group to CONTAY-VADENCOURT-HARPONVILLE. Divisional Headquarters to CONTAY. The Division passed under the orders of 5th.Corps at 12 noon today. Weather fine and frosty.	
HEDAUVILLE.	17th.		34th.Brigade Group marched to PUCHEVILLERS. and RAINCHEVAL. Divisional Headquarters moved to HEDAUVILLE. 6th.E.Yorks Regt. 3 Field Companies R.E. and Three Machine Gun Companies rejoined the Division from 2nd.Corps. Weather fine dry, very cold wind.	Appx M. Location Return.
do	18th.		At 6.10 a.m. the 5th.Corps attacked North of the River ANCRE in conjunction with the 2nd.Corps on the South of the River. 33rd.Brigade less two battalions moved in morning to bivouacs at Q.31.b South of ENGLEBELMER. In evening 33rd.Bde.Hd.Qrs. moved back to HEDAUVILLE. Troops of 34th.Bde.Group at RAINCHEVAL move to PUCHEVILLERS midday. Snow and sleet in early morning turning to rain during the day.	Appx. L Location Return.

Army Form C. 2118.

WAR DIARY
or
INTELLIGENCE SUMMARY
(Erase heading not required.)

11th. Division. "G".

November 1916.

Instructions regarding War Diaries and Intelligence Summaries are contained in F.S. Regs., Part II and the Staff Manual respectively. Title Pages will be prepared in manuscript.

Place	Date	Hour	Summary of Events and Information	Remarks and references to Appendices
HEDAUVILLE.	19th.		2 Battalions of 33rd.Bde.returned to HEDAUVILLE. M.G.Coy. and Light T.M. Battery to VARENNES. D.O. 41 issued for move of 32nd.Inf.Bde.(less 1 battn) from LEALVILLERS and ACHEUX, to PUCHEVILLERS and of 34th.Bde. from PUCHEVILLERS to LEALVILLERS and ACHEUX.	Appx. J D.O. 41 dated 19/11/16.
do	20th.		Moves of 32nd.Bde. (less 1 battn) and 34th.Bde. carried out in accordance with D.O. No.41. One battalion 32nd.Bde. and 67th.Fd.Coy.R.E. former to W.9.b.9.8, latter to AVELUY for work under CRE. II Corps. 33rd.Bde. moved up to relieve 63rd.Bde. 37th.Divn. in the line from R.ANCRE at about R.8.c.4.6 as far North as a line drawn from R.1.c.7.0 to Q.22. central. One battalion 33rd.Bde. (9th.S.Foresters) moved to N.BLUFFS area near AUTHUILLE.	Appx. K D.O. 42 dated 20-11-16. Appx. L D.O.43. d/20/11/16
do	21st.	1 am 6 a.m	Relief of 63rd.Bde. by 33rd.Bde. reported complete. G.O.C. 11th.Division assumed command of this portion of the line at which hour Divn. passed under the orders of 2nd.Corps. The Division commenced to take over the new line held by 19th.Divn.from R.21.a.6.8 to R.8.c.4.6. 34th.Bde. moved up in accordance with D.O. 43 to relieved 56th. and 58th.Bdes. (19th.Divn). Bde.Hd.Qrs. established at ST.PIERRE DIVION. 9th.Sherwood Foresters placed under orders of 34th.Bde. at night took over front line held by 56th.Bde. (19th.Divn.) from R.14. central to R.8.c.4.6. 32nd.Bde. moved to HEDAUVILLE and VARENNES. German belonging to 25th.I.R. gave himself up to 7th.S.Stafford Regt. at R.8.a.9.8. A German 77 m.m. gun was brought in from R.1.c.3.5 by 6th.Border Regt. Hostile artillery normal.	
do	22nd.		32nd.Bde. moved to MARTINSART and huts in that vicinity. 34th.Bde. continued their move forward into forward area and at night took over the remainder of front from 19th.Divn. Relief being completed at 10.45 p.m. 6th.E.Yorks move to vicinity of MARTINSART. 7th.Cav.Pioneer battalion arrived to be attached to Divn. for work on roads in forward area.	

Army Form C. 2118.

WAR DIARY
or
INTELLIGENCE SUMMARY

11th. Division. "G".

November 1916.

(Erase heading not required.)

Instructions regarding War Diaries and Intelligence Summaries are contained in F. S. Regs., Part II. and the Staff Manual respectively. Title Pages will be prepared in manuscript.

Place	Date	Hour	Summary of Events and Information	Remarks and references to Appendices
HEDAUVILLE.	22nd (contd).		5th.S.Wales Borderers and 81st. and 94th.Field Coys. R.E. 19th.Divn). also attached to this Divn. for work. Enemy shelled HAMEL BEAUCOURT and BEAUCOURT ROAD, otherwise situation normal. During the night 9th.S.Foresters were relieved in the front line by a Battalion of 34th.Bde. and at 8 a.m. repassed under orders of G.O.C. 33rd.Bde.	
do.	23rd.		At 6 a.m G.O.C. 11th. Divn. assumed command of the line covered by 18th. and 19th.Divl.Artilleries under command of C.R.A. 19th.Divn. 61st.Division on our right 37th.Divn. on our left. On South of River front line consists of a newly dug trench not entirely joined up, needing a great deal of work. North of River front line consists of a newly-dug posts only, each post consisting of about 1 N.C.O. and 8 men with no means of communication by day - with no proper cover from shell fires. The enemy shelled our front line trenches in neighbourhood of R.14.a.8.9 from 4. to 5.30 p.m. with 5.9 H.E. gas and tear shells. About the same time the enemy put up a shrapnel barrage over BEAUCOURT.	Appx. M D.O.44 d/25/11/16 and Map.
do	24th.		A wounded man of 117th. Ersatz Musketen Battalion gave himself up at R.1.d. and an unwounded man of 25th. I.R. gave himself up at R.7.b.2.9. Hostile artillery was active at night North and South of the River.	
do	25th.		In the early morning patrols from 33rd.Bde. were active; they encountered the enemy in considerable force and inflicted heavy casualties. Two new posts were established at R.2.c. without opposition. D.O. 44 issued with reference to new Divnl.Area. German of 117th. Erstaz Musketen Battalion gave himself up in R.7.b. in the morning. Hostile artillery again active at night edpecially North of the River. G.O.C. 7th.Division assumed command of line on our left.	
do and Q.26.c.0.4.	26th.		Advanced Divnl.Hd.Qrs. consisting of G.O.C., allG Staff and A.A. & Q.M.G. opened at Q.26.c.0.4. Q Branch remaining at HEDAUVILLE. 32nd.Bde. moved from MARTINSART to ENGLEBELMER. New posts were established by 33rd.Bde. at R.2.c.6.2 and 5.4. The enemy shelled the area round MESNIL between 4 and 6 p.m. At night 6 Germans of 25th.I.R. were taken prisoners by 9th.S.Foresters. One prisoner was wounded.	

2449 Wt. W14957/M90 750,000 1/16 J.B.C. & A. Forms/C.2118/12.

Army Form C. 2118.

WAR DIARY
or
INTELLIGENCE SUMMARY

11th. Division. "G". November 1916.

(*Erase heading not required.*)

Instructions regarding War Diaries and Intelligence Summaries are contained in F.S. Regs., Part II and the Staff Manual respectively. Title Pages will be prepared in manuscript.

Place	Date	Hour	Summary of Events and Information	Remarks and references to Appendices
Q.26.c.0.4	27th.		Hostile artillery active both N. and S. of the river causing some casualties. Some gas shells were used. Digging of new trenches and improvement of existing trenches continued. Move of 2 battalions of 32nd.Bde. to FORCEVILLE as ordered in D.O.44 cancelled. D.O. 45 issued for relief of 33rd.Bde. by 32nd.Bde. "Q" Branch moved from HEDAUVILLE to FORCEVILLE.	Appx. N D.O.45 d/27/11/16
do	28th.		Relief of 33rd.Bde. by 32nd.Bde. commenced in accordance with D.O.45. Scheme for capture of trenches R.1.d.5.3 - R.1.c.7.9 and neighbouring defences submitted to 2nd.Corps attached. Enemy's artillery quiet during the day, though some gas shells were fired into BEAUCOURT in the afternoon. Relief of 11th.Divnl.Artillery by 61st.Divisional Artillery being completed., today the artillery again came under the orders of the G.O.C. 11th.Division.	Appx. O.
do	29th.		Situation unchanged. Hostile artillery activity normal until 4.45 p.m. when heavy bombardment of our front line North of the ANCRE commenced. This died down after an hour, having done very little damage. Relief of 33rd.Bde. by 32nd.Bde. being completed at night. Weather fine but misty. Frost at night.	
do	30th.		Situation unchanged. Intermittent shelling of ST. PIERRE DIVION throughout the day. BOIS D'HOLLANDE shelled with Heavy H.E. from 10 to 11 a.m. BEAUCOURT TRENCH heavily shelled from 3.30 p.m. to 4.30 p.m. with 4.2 and gas shells. Two prisoners of 230th. R.I.R. taken by 32nd.Bde. about R.8.b.1.6 south of BOIS D'HOLLANDE.	

Major General,

Commanding 11th. Division.

Army Form C. 2118.

WAR DIARY
or
INTELLIGENCE SUMMARY

(Erase heading not required.)

Instructions regarding War Diaries and Intelligence Summaries are contained in F. S. Regs., Part II. and the Staff Manual respectively. Title Pages will be prepared in manuscript.

Place	Date	Hour	Summary of Events and Information	Remarks and references to Appendices
			SUMMARY.	

From 1st. to 10th. Division was in Fifth Army "B" Area. During this period, training was continued as far as the weather allowed.
On the 11th.inst. the Division moved to YVRENCH area, a move which only affected very few units of the Division.

On the 12th.inst and order was received to move the following day to CANAPLES Area. This move was cancelled but took place on 14th.
At midnight 15th/16th the Division passed under orders of 2nd.Corps and at noon 16th. under orders of 5th.Corps.
Moves continued on 15th., 16th., 17th., 18th., and 19th. On the 20th. the Division was located in the neighbourhood of HEDAUVILLE, VARENNES, PUCHEVILLERS, LEALVILLERS, ACHEUX and BOUZINCOURT.
On the night 20th/21st. the 33rd.Inf.Bde. took over the line North of the ANCRE from 63rd.Bde. (37th.Division.).
At 6 a.m. 21st. the Division passed under the orders of 2nd.Corps.
On night 21st/22nd. and 22nd/23rd. the 34th.Bde. took over the line held by 19th.Division (S.of ANCRE).
The front line trenches and communication trenches required a great deal of labour. The line to the North of the River being held weakly by a series of posts. To assist in this work 2 Field Companies and 2 Pioneer Battalions were attached to the Division and placed under the orders of the C.R.E. 11th.Division.
On night 28th/29th. and 29th/30th. the 32nd.Inf.Bde. relieved the 33rd.Inf.Bde.
During the period in the trenches hostile artillery has been active, at intervals and has on several occasions used gas shells. 10 unwounded. 2 wounded.
Number of prisoners captured.

CASUALTIES.
	OFFRS.	O.R.
Killed.	3	93
Wounded.	15	335
Missing.	-	5

J.D. Crewe M. Colonel
for Major General,
Commanding 11th.Division.

APPENDIX "A"

SECRET.

11th Division Order No. 37.

Copy No. 19.

Ref. Map. 1/100,000.
Sheets LENS and ABBEVILLE.

10th November 1916.

1. 11th Division Order No. 36 is cancelled.

2. The Division (less units at present detached) will move into YVRENCH Area tomorrow the 11th instant in accordance with instructions already issued by the A.A. & Q.M.G. (vide 11th Division No. 74/A.B./53 dated 7th and 9th November respectively).

3. All moves will be completed by 6 p.m. tomorrow the 11th instant, but the villages of COULONVILLERS, YVRENCH, YVRENCHEUX and RIBEAUCOURT will not be available for troops of this Division until after 12 noon tomorrow. Completion of all moves to be reported to D.H.Q.

4. Divl. Hd. Qrs. will close at ST OUEN at 2 p.m. tomorrow 11th instant and reopen at YVRENCH at the same hour.

5. ACKNOWLEDGE.

Issued at 11 am.

E.Wright Capt
for Lieut-Colonel,
Gen. Staff. 11th Division.

Copy No. 1. A.D.C. for G.O.C.
2. C.R.A.
3. C.R.E.
4. 32nd Inf. Bde.
5. 33rd Inf. Bde.
6. 34th Inf. Bde.
7. 6th E. Yorks Regt.
8. Signal Coy.
9. A.A. & Q.M.G.
10. A.D.M.S.
11. A.P.M.
12. 11th Divl. Train.
13. D.A.D.O.S.
14. Camp Commandant.
15. 46th Division.
16 & 17. War Diary.
18 & 19. File.

"A" Form.
MESSAGES AND SIGNALS.
Army Form C.2121 (in pads of 100).

| Prefix | Code | m. | Words | Charge | This message is on a/c of: | Recd. at | m. |

Office of Origin and Service Instructions.

Sent At......m.
PRIORITY. To
By

Service.
(Signature of "Franking Officer.")

Date..........
From..........
By..........

TO {
C.R.E.   54th Bde.   A.D.M.S.   D.A.D.O.S.
32nd Bde.   Signals.   A.P.M.   Camp Comdt.
33rd Bde.   11th Div. Train.
}

Sender's Number: G.114. Day of Month: 14th. In reply to Number: AAA

Following moves will take place tomorrow 15th aaa Divl. Hd. Qrs. to CANAPLES aaa 32nd Bde. Group to BERTEAUCOURT PERNOIS HALLOY with Bde. Hd. Qrs. at BERTEAUCOURT aaa 33rd Bde Group to BONNEVILLE MONTRELET PIERRES with Bde. Hd. Qrs. at BONNEVILLE aaa 34th Bde. Group ST OUEN ST LEGER REBERIE FARM SURCHAMPS LANIE FARM FRANQUEVILLE HOUDENCOURT BARLETTE LANCHES with Bde. Hd. Qrs. ST OUEN aaa Written orders follow aaa Addressed all concerned.

PRIORITY

From 11th Division.
Place
Time 12-45 h

Captain,
for G.S.O. 1.
11th Div.

APPENDIX "B"

A.M.O.R.S.

Copy No. 17

11th. Division Order No. 38.

Ref. Map.1/100,000.
Sheet LENS.

12th. November 1916.

1. The 11th.Division (less detached Units) will move tomorrow from YVRENCH Area to CANAPLES Area.

2. Moves will take place in accordance with attached March Table.

3. Units not mentioned in this order will move under orders to be issued by the A.A. & Q.M.G.

4. Divisional Headquarters will close at YVRENCH at 12 noon on the 13th. inst. and will reopen at CANAPLES at the same hour.

Issued at 3/pm

Ed.Wright
Captain,
for Lieut.Colonel,
Gen. Staff, 11th.Division.

Copy No. 1. A.D.C. for G.O.C.
2. C.R.A.
3. C.R.E.
4. 32nd Inf. Bde.
5. 33rd Inf. Bde.
6. 34th Inf. Bde.
7. 6th E. Yorks Regt.
8. Signals.
9. A.A. & Q.M.G.
10. A.D.M.S.
11. A.P.M.
12. 11th Div. Train.
13. D.A.D.O.S.
14. Camp Comdt.
15. 4th Corps.
16. 2nd Corps.
17 & 18. War Diary.
19 & 20. File.

MARCH TABLE TO ACCOMPANY 11th.Division Order No. 38.

DATE.	Unit.	DESTINATION.	ROUTE.	REMARKS.
12th Nov Octr.	32nd Inf.Bde.(less Machine Gun Coy). 35th Field Ambulance. No 2 Coy. Train. under orders of G.O.C. 32nd Inf.Bde.	BERTEAUCOURT PERNOIS HALLOY With Bde.H.Q. at BERTEAUCOURT.	BEAUMETZ – DOMART – ST LEGER.	Tail of column to clear (a) BEAUMETZ by 9-30 a.m (b) RIBEAUCOURT by 11 a.m
13th Nov Octr.	33rd Inf.Bde.(less Machine Gun Coy). 33rd Field Ambulance. No.3 Coy. Train. under orders of G.O.C. 33rd Inf.Bde.	BONNEVILLE – MONTRELET FIEFFES With Bde.H.Q. at BONNEVILLE.	BEAUMETZ-BERNAVILLE- Main road E. of GORGES and BERNEUIL-MONTRELET.	Head of column not to reach BEAUMETZ before 9-30 a.m.
13th Nov Octr.	34th Inf. Bde.(less Machine Gun Coy). 34th Field Ambulance. No. 4 Coy. Train. Under orders of G.O.C. 34th Inf.Bde.	ST OUEN ST LEGER SURCAMPS LA HAIE FARM FRANQUEVILLE HOUDENCOURT BARLETTE. LANCHES with Bde. H.Q. at ST OUEN.	any route.	No move to take place before 11 a.m.

APPENDIX "C".

SECRET.

12th. November 1916.

LOCATION TABLE shewing position of Units
of 11th. Division at 6 a.m. day afterdate
return is rendered.

* * * * * * * * * *

11th. Division.	H.Q.	YVRENCH.	
32nd. Infantry Brigade.	H.Q.	BEAUMETZ.	
9th. W. Yorks Regt.	H.Q.	BEAUMETZ.	Bn. BEAUMETZ.
6th. Yorks Regt.	H.Q.	do	Bn. do
8th. W. Ridings Regt.	H.Q.	DOMLEGER.	Bn. DOMLEGER.
6th. York & Lancs. Regt.	H.Q.	AGENVILLE.	Bn. AGENVILLE.
32nd. Machine Gun Company.		attached to 18th. Division.	
32nd. L.T.M. Battery.		DOMLEGER.	
33rd. Infantry Brigade	H.Q.	CRAMONT.	
6th. Lincoln Regt.	H.Q.	CRAMONT.	Bn. CRAMONT.
6th. Border Regt.	H.Q.	do	Bn. do
7th. S. Stafford Regt.	H.Q.	MAISON ROLLAND.	Bn. MAISON ROLLAND.
9th. S. Foresters	H.Q.	COULONVILLERS.	Bn. COULONVILLERS.
33rd. Machine Gun Company.		attached 19th. Division.	
33rd. L.T.M. Battery.		CRAMONT.	
34th. Infantry Brigade.	H.Q.	FRANSU.	
8th. Northd. Fusiliers.	H.Q.	DOMQUEUR.	Bn. DOMQUEUR.
9th. Lancs. Fusiliers.	H.Q.	RIBEAUCOURT.	Bn. RIBEAUCOURT.
5th. Dorset Regt.	H.Q.	DOMQUEUR.	Bn. DOMQUEUR.
11th. Manchester Regt.	H.Q.	FRANSU.	Bn. FRANSU.
34th. Machine Gun Company.		attached 39th. Division.	
34th. L.T.M. Battery.		MESNIL DOMQUEUR.	

Pioneer Battalion.

   6th. E. Yorks Regt.   H.Q. and Battalion. W.9.d.5.4. Sheet 57D.S.E.

C.R.E., 11th. Division.   H.Q.   YVRENCH.

67th. Field Co. R.E.	X.17.a.3.0)	
68th. " " "	W.12.d.8.2.)	attached 18th. Div.
86th. " " "	W.17.a. AVELUY.	attached 19th. Div.

A.D.M.S., 11th. Division.   H.Q.   YVRENCH

   33rd. Field Ambulance.   MAISON ROLLAND.
   34th.   "   "   MESNIL DOMQUEUR.
   35th.   "   "   LONGVILLERS.
   21st. Sanitary Section.   YVRENCH.

A.D.V.S., 11th. Division.   H..Q   YVRENCH.

   22nd. Mobile Vet. Section.   DOMQUEUR.

Divisional R.A.   H.Q.   TARA HILL. W.30.a.

11th. Divisional Train.   H.Q.   DOMQUEUR.

   No. 1 Co.   SENLIS.
   No. 2 "   MONTIGNY.
   No. 3. "   CRAMONT MILL.
   No. 4 "   LE PLOUY.

11th. Divisional Supply Column.   LE PLOUY, DOMQUEUR.

APPENDIX "D".

SECRET.

Copy No. 18

11th. Division Order No. 39.   13th. Novr. 1916.

Ref. Map 1/100,000
Sheet LENS.

1. The 11th. Division (less detached Units) will move tomorrow from YVRENCH Area to CANAPLES Area.

2. Moves will take place in accordance with attached March Table.

3. Units not mentioned in this Order will move under orders to be issued by the A.A. & Q.M.G.

4. Divisional Headquarters will close at YVRENCH at 12 noon on the 14th. inst and will reopen at CANAPLES at the same hour.

5. Orders for further move will be issued later.

6. Acknowledge.

Issued at 6.30 p.m.

J. D. Coleridge
Lieut. Colonel,
Gen. Staff, 11th. Division.

Copy No. 1 A.D.C for G.O.C.
        2. C.R.A.
        3. C.R.E.
        4. 32nd. Inf. Bde.
        5. 33rd. "   "
        6. 34th. "   "
        7. 6th. E. Yorks Regt.
        8. Signal Co.
        9. A.A. & Q.M.G.
       10. A.D.M.S.
       11. A.P.M.
       12. 11th Div. Train.
       13. D.A.D.V.S.
       14. Camp Commdt.
       15. 4th Corps.
       16. 2nd Corps.
17 & 18 War Diary ✓
19 & 20. File.

MARCH TABLE TO ACCOMPANY 11th.Division Order No. 39.

Date.	Unit.	Destination.	Route.	Remarks.
14th.Novr.	32nd.Inf.Bde.(less Machine Gun Coy). 35th. Field Ambulance. No. 2 Company Train. under orders of G.O.C. 32nd.Inf.Bde.	BERTEAUCOURT. PERNOIS. HALLOY. With Bde. H.Q. at BERTEAUCOURT.	BEAUMETZ- DOMART - ST. LEGER.	Tail of column to clear (a) BEAUMETZ by 9.30 a.m. (b) RIBEAUCOURT by 11 a⌐
14th.Novr.	33rd.Inf.Bde.(less Machine Gun Coy.) 33rd. Field Ambulance. No.3 Coy. Train. under Orders of G.O.C. 33rd.Inf.Bde.	BONNEVILLE - MONTRELET. FIEFFES. With Bde. H.Q. at BONNEVILLE.	BEAUMETZ - BERNAVILLE- Main road E. of GORGES and BERNEUIL-MONTRELET.	Head of column not to reach BEAUMETZ before 9.30 a.m.
14th.Novr.	34th.Inf.Bde. (less Machine Gun Coy). 34th.Field Ambulance. No.4 Coy. Train. Under orders of G.O.C. 34th.Inf.Bde.	ST. OUEN. ST. LEGER. SURCAMPS LA HAIE FARM FRANQUEVILLE HOUDENCOURT BARLETTE LANCHES with Bde. H.Q. at ST. OUEN.	any route.	No move to take place before 11 a.m.

SECRET.

```
C.R.A.           11th.Div.Train.
C.R.E.           D.A.D.O.S.
32nd.Inf.Bde.    Camp Commdt.
33rd.  "    "    4th.Corps.
34th.  "    "    2nd.Corps.
6th.E.Yorks      War Diary.
Signals.         File.
A.A. & Q.M.G.
A.D.M.S.
A.P.M.
```

Reference Divisional Order No. 40.

Brigade Hd.Qrs. will be established tomorrow 15th. as follows :-

32nd. Bde. - HERISSART.

33rd. Bde. - CONTAY.

34th. Bde. - BERTEAUCOURT.

14th.November 1916.

EhWright
Captain,
for Lieut.Colonel,
Gen.Staff,11th Division.

APPENDIX "E"

SECRET

Copy No. 17

11th Division Order No. 40.

14th November 1918.

Ref. Maps.1/100,000 LENS, Sheet 11.
1/40,000 Sheet 57.D.

1. The 11th Division (less detached units) will move into 11 Corps Area on the 15th, 16th, and 17th instants.

2. Moves will take place in accordance with the attached March Table.

3. Units not mentioned in this order will move under orders to be issued by the A.A. & Q.M.G.

4. Divisional Headquarters will remain at CANAPLES to-morrow 15th instant.

5. ACKNOWLEDGE.

J.D. Coleridge
Lieut Colonel,
Gen. Staff, 11th Division.

Issued at 5/pm

Copy No. 1. A.D.C. for G.O.C.
2. C.R.A.
3. C.R.E.
4. 32nd Inf. Bde.
5. 33rd Inf. Bde.
6. 34th Inf. Bde.
7. 6th E. Yorks Regt.
8. Signal Coy.
9. A.A. & Q.M.G.
10. A.D.M.S.
11. A.P.M.
12. 11th Divl. Train.
13. D.A.D.O.S.
14. Camp Comdt.
15. 4th Corps.
16. 2nd Corps.
17 & 18. War Diary.
19 & 20. File.

MARCH TABLE to accompany 11th Division Order No. 40.

Date.	Formation.	From.	To.	Route.	Remarks.
15th 33rd	(1) 33rd Inf. Bde. Group as shown in 11thDivl. Order No.39.	BONNEVILLE MONTRELET PIERFFES.	CONTAY VADENCOURT HARPONVILLE.	roads VALHEUREUX-Cross/200 yards South of the second X of ANGⁿ Mⁿ DE VALHEUREUX -LR VAL DE MAISON-HERISSART.	Head not to reach CONTAY before 12 noon. To be clear of HERISSART by 2-30 p.m.
	(2) 32nd Inf.Bde. Group as shown in 11th Div Order No.39.	BERTEAUCOURT PERNOIS HALLOY.	RUBEMPRE HERISSART.	HAVERNAS-WARGNIES-NAOURS-TALMAS-RUBEMPRE.	Not to enter HERISSART before 2-30 p.m.
	(3) 34th Inf.Bde. Group as shown in 11th Div Order No.39.	ST OUEN ST LEGER FRANSU FRANQUEVILLE SUROAMPS LA HAIE FARM HOUDENCOURT	BERTEAUCOURT PERNOIS HALLOY.	Any route.	Not to enter BERTEAUCOURT before 10-30 a.m.
16th Nov.	(4) 33rd Bde. Group.	CONTAY- VADENCOURT HARPONVILLE	THIEPVAL AREA.	SENLIS - BOEZINCOURT.	To be clear of WARLUY by 10-30 a.m.
"	(5) 32nd Bde. Group.	RUBEMPRE HERISSART.	AVELUY W.12.d.	CONTAY-WARLOY-SENLIS-BOUZINCOURT.	Head not to reach CONTAY before 1 p.m.
"	(6) 34th Bde. Group.	BERTEAUCOURT PERNOIS HALLOY	CONTAY VADENCOURT HARPONVILLE	HAVERNAS-WARGNIES-NAOURS-TALMAS-HERISSART.	Not to reach CONTAY before 2-30 p.m.
19th Nov	(7) 32nd Bde. Group.	AVELUY W.12.d.	N. BLUFFS Area.		
"	(8) 34th Bde. Group.	CONTAY VADENCOURT HARPONVILLE	AVELUY W.12.d.	SENLIS-BOUZINCOURT	

Note. Distance of 200 yards between Companies, and 400 yards between Battalions to be maintained on the march.

APPENDIX "F".

SECRET.

LOCATION TABLE showing probable disposition
of units of 11th. Division at 5 p.m. 14/11/16.

11th. Division.	H.Q.	CANAPLES.	
32nd. Infantry Brigade.	H.Q.	BERTEAUCOURT.	
8th. W. Yorks Regt.	H.Q.	HALLOY.	Bn. HALLOY.
6th. Yorks Regt.	H.Q.	PERNOIS.	Bn. PERNOIS.
8th. W. Ridings Regt.	H.Q.	BERTEAUCOURT.	Bn. BERTEAUCOURT.
6th. York & Lancs. Regt.	H.Q.	do	Bn. do
32nd. Machine Gun Company.		attached 18th. Division.	
32nd. L.T.M. Battery.		BERTEAUCOURT.	
33rd. Infantry Brigade.	H.Q.	BONNEVILLE.	
6th. Lincoln Regt.	H.Q.	FIEFFES.	Bn. FIEFFES.
6th. Border Regt.	H.Q.	BONNEVILLE.	Bn. BONNEVILLE.
7th. S. Stafford Regt.	H.Q.	do	Bn. do
9th. S. Foresters.	H.Q.	MONTRELET.	Bn. MONTRELET.
33rd. Machine Gun Company.		attached 19th. Division.	
33rd. L.T.M. Battery.		FIEFFES.	
34th. Infantry Brigade	H.Q.	ST. OUEN.	
8th. Northd. Fusiliers.		ST. OUEN.	Bn. ST. OUEN.
9th. Lancs. Fusiliers.		FRANQUEVILLE.	Bn. FRANQUEVILL.E.
5th. Dorset Regt.	H.Q.	ST. LEGER.	Bn. ST. LEGER.
11th. Manchester Regt.	H.Q.	FRANSU.	Bn. FRANSU.
34th. Machine Gun Company.		attached 39th. Division.	
34th. L.T.M. Battery.		MESNIL DOMQUEUR.	

Pioneer Battalion.

   6th. E. Yorks Regt.   H.Q. W.9.d.5.4. Sheet 57D.S.E.

C.R.E. 11th. Division.   H.Q. CANAPLES.

   67th. Field Co. R.E.)
   68th. " " ") detached from Division.
   86th. " " ")

Divisional R.A.   Detached from Division.

A.D.M.S., 11th. Division. H.Q. CANAPLES.

   33rd. Field Ambulance.   MONTRELET.
   34th. " "   LA HAIE FARM.
   35th. " "   BERTEAUCOURT.
   21st. Sanitary Section.   CANAPLES.

11th. Divisional Train.   H.Q. SURCAMPS.

   No. 1 Company.   attached R.A.
   No. 2 "   BERTEAUCOURT.
   No. 3 "   BONNEVILLE.
   No. 4 "   SURCAMPS.

11th. Divisional Supply Column. ST. LEGER.

   S.A.A. Sub-section.   ST. OUEN.

A.D.V.S., 11th. Division.   REDERIE FARM.

NOTE :- The section D.A.C. consists of about 21 G.S. Wagons and 12 Limbered G.S. Wagons.

APPENDIX "G"   SECRET.

LOCATION TABLE showing disposition of troops
of 11th.Division at 6 a.m. day after date
return is rendered.   15-11-16.

11th.Division.	H.Q.	CANAPLES.	
32nd.Infantry Brigade.	H.Q.	RUBEMPRE.	
9th.W.Yorks Regt.	H.Q.	HERISSART.	Bn. HERISSART.
6th.Yorks Regt.	H.Q.	do	Bn. do
8th.W.Ridings Regt.	H.Q.	RUBEMPRE.	Bn. RUBEMPRE.
6th.York & Lancs.Regt.	H.Q.	do	Bn. do
32nd.Machine Gun Company.		attached 18th.Division.	
32nd.L.T.M.Battery.		RUBEMPRE.	
33rd.Infantry Brigade.	H.Q.	CONTAY.	
6th.Lincoln Regt.	H.Q.	VADENCOURT.	Bn. VADENCOURT.
6th.Border Regt.	H.Q.	CONTAY.	Bn. CONTAY.
7th.S.Stafford Regt.	H.Q.	HARPONVILLE.	Bn. HARPONVILLE.
9th.S.Foresters.	H.Q.	VADENCOURT.	Bn. VADENCOURT.
33rd.Machine Gun Company.		attached 19th.Division.	
33rd.L.T.M.Battery.		VADENCOURT.	
34th.Infantry Brigade.	H.Q.	BERTEAUCOURT.	
8th.Northd.Fusiliers.	H.Q.	HALLOY.	Bn HALLOY.
9th.Lancs.Fusiliers.	H.Q.	PERNOIS.	Bn.PERNOIS.
5th.Dorset Regt.	H.Q.	PERNOIS.	Bn.PERNOIS.
11th.Manchester Regt.	H.Q.	BERTEAUCOURT.	Bn. BERTAUCOURT.
34th.Machine Gun Company.		attached 39th.Division.	
34th.L.T.M.Battery.		BERTEAUCOURT.	

Pioneer Battalion.

    6th.E.Yorks Regt.   H.Q. & Battn. W.8.d.5.4. (DOG'S LEG).

C.R.E., 11th.Division.   H.Q.   CANAPLES.

67th.Field Company. R.E.)
68th.   "   "   "   )   attached 18th.Division.
86th.   "   "   "   attached 19th.Division.

Divisional R.A.   H.Q.   TARA HILL. W.30.a.

A.D.M.S., 11th.Division. H.Q.   CANAPLES.

33rd.Field Ambulance.   HAPRONVILLE.
34th.   "   "   BERTEAUCOURT.
35th.   "   "   RUBEMPRE.
21st.Sanitary Section.   CANAPLES.

11th.Divisional Train. H.Q.

No. 1 Company.   attached R.A.
No. 2   "   HALLOY.
No. 3.   "   CONTAY.
No. 4   "   BERTEAUCOURT.

11th.Divisional Supply Column. ST. LEGER.

A.D.V.S. 11th.Division.   CANAPLES.

APPENDIX "H".   S E C R E T.

17th.Novr.1916

LOCATION TABLE showing position of units of 11th.Divn. at 6 a.m. day after date return is rendered.

11th.Division.	H.Q.	HEDAUVILLE.
32nd.Infantry Brigade.	H.Q.	LEALVILLERS.
9th.W.Yorks Regt.	H.Q. LEALVILLERS.	Bn. LEALVILLERS.
6th.Yorks Regt.	H.Q. do	Bn. do
8th.W.Ridings Regt.	H.Q. ACHEUX.	Bn. ACHEUX.
6th.York & Lancs. Regt.	H.Q. do	Bn. do
32nd. Machine Gun Company.	FORCEVILLE.	
32nd. L.T.M.Battery.		
33rd. Infantry Brigade.	H.Q.	HEDAUVILLE.
6th.Lincoln Regt.	H.Q. HEDAUVILLE.	Bn. HEDAUVILLE.
6th.Border Regt.	H.Q. VARENNES.	Bn. VARENNES.
7th.S.Stafford Regt.	H.Q. do	Bn. do
9th.Sherwood Foresters.	H.Q. HEDAUVILLE.	Bn. HEDAUVILLE.
33rd. Machine Gun Company.	FORCEVILLE.	
33rd. L.T.M.Battery.		
34th.Infantry Brigade.	H.Q.	PUCHEVILLERS.
8th.Northd. Fusiliers.	H.Q. do	Bn. PUCHEVILLERS.
9th.Lancashire Fusiliers.	H.Q. do	Bn. do
5th.Dorset Regt.	H.Q. RAINCHEVAL.	Bn. RAINCHEVAL.
11th. Manchester Regt.	H.Q. PUCHEVILLERS.	Bn. PUCHEVILLERS.
34th.Machine Gun Company.	FORCEVILLE.	
34th.L.T.M.Battery.	PUCHEVILLERS.	
Pioneer Battalion.		
6th.E.Yorks Regt.	H.Q. & Battn.	FORCEVILLE.
C.R.E., H.Q. 11th.Division.		HEDAUVILLE.
67th. Field Company. R.E.		
68th. " " "	FORCEVILLE.	
86th. " " "		
Divisional R.A.		
A.D.M.S., 11th. Division.	H.Q.	HEDAUVILLE.
33rd. Field Ambulance.	HEDAUVILLE	
34th. " "	PUCHEVILLERS.	
35th. " "	LEALVILLERS	
21st. Sanitary Section.	HEDAUVILLE.	
11th.Divisional Train.	H.Q.	RAINCHEVAL.
No. 1 Company.	attached R.A.	
No. 2 "		
No. 3 "	HEDAUVILLE.	
No. 4 "	RAINCHEVAL.	
11th. Divisional Supply Column.	H.Q.	
S.A.A. Sub-section.	PUCHEVILLERS.	
A.D.V.S., 11th. Division.	H.Q.	CONTAY.
22nd. Mobile Vet Section.	PUCHEVILLERS.	

APPENDIX "I".

SECRET.
18th. Novr. 1916.

LOCATION TABLE showing position of units of 11th.Division at 6 a.m. day after date return is rendered.

11th. Division.	H.Q.	HEDAUVILLE.
32nd. Infantry Brigade.	H.Q.	LEALVILLERS.
9th. W. Yorkshire Regt.	H.Q.	LEALVILLERS.
6th. Yorkshire Regt.	H.Q.	LEALVILLERS.
8th. W. Ridings Regt.	H.Q.	ACHEUX.
6th. York & Lancs. R.	H.Q.	ACHEUX.
32nd. Machine Gun Company.		FORCEVILLE. Q.31.b
33rd. Infantry Brigade.	H.Q.	HEDAUVILLE.
6th. Lincoln Regt.	H.Q.	Q.31.b.
6th. Border Regt.	H.Q.	VARENNES.
7th. S. Stafford Regt.	H.Q.	VARENNES.
9th. S. Foresters.	H.Q. c	Q.31.b.
33rd. Machine Gun Company.		FORCEVILLE.
34th. Infantry Brigade.	H.Q.	PUCHEVILLERS.
8th. Northd. Fusiliers.	H.Q.	PUCHEVILLERS.
9th. Lancs. Fusiliers.	H.Q.	do
5th. Dorset Regt.	H.Q.	do
11th. Manchester Regt.	H.Q.	do
34th. Machine Gun Company.		FORCEVILLE.

Pioneer Battalion.

6th. E. Yorks Regt.	H.Q.	FORCEVILLE.
C.R.E. 11th. Division.	H.Q.	HEDAUVILLE.
60th. Field Company.	R.E.)	
68th. " "	")	FORCEVILLE.
86th. " "	")	
Divisional R.A.;	H.Q.	TARA HILL.
A.D.M.S., 11th. Division.	H.Q.	HEDAUVILLE.
33rd. Field Ambulance.		HEDAUVILLE.
34th. " "		PUCHEVILLERS.
35th. " "		LEALVILLERS.
21st. Sanitary Section.		HEDAUVILLE.
11th. Divisional Train.	H.Q.	HEDAUVILLE.
No. 1 Company.		attached R.A.
No. 2 "		ACHEUX WOOD.
No. 3 "		HEDAUVILLE.
No. 4 "		RAINCHEVAL.
11th. Divisional Supply Col.	H.Q.	LEALVILLERS.
S.A.A., Sub-section.		PUCHEVILLERS.
A.D.V.S., 11th. Division.	H.Q.	HEDAUVILLE.
22nd. Mobile Vet. Section.		PUCHEVILLERS.

APPENDIX "J".   S E C R E T
                                 ==========   Copy No. 16

                                 19th Novr. 1916.

11th Division Order No. 4)
===========================

1. The moves shown in the attached March Table will be carried
   out tomorrow 20th November by the 32nd and 34th Brigades
   respectively.

2. In addition two battalions of the 32nd Inf. Bde. and 67th
   Field Coy. R.E. will be ready to move to DOG'S LEG W.9.d.
   tomorrow for work on roads under the orders of the C.R.E.
   11th Division.   Further details with regard to this move
   will follow.

3. Fifth Army orders with regard to intervals to be kept
   between formations on the march will be strictly complied
   with.

4. Completion of all moves to be reported by wire to this
   office.

5. ACKNOWLEDGE.

      Issued at 2.45 p.m.   [signature]
                                          for Lieut-Colonel.
                                          Gen. Staff. 11th Division.

Copy No.1. A.D.C. for G.O.C.
       2. C.R.A.
       3. C.R.E.
       4. 32nd Inf. Bde.
       5. 33rd Inf. Bde.
       6. 34th Inf. Bde.
       7. 8th E. Yorks Regt.
       8. Signal Coy.
       9. A.A. & Q.M.G.
      10. A.D.M.S.
      11. A.P.M.
      12. 11th Div. Train.
      13. D.A.D.O.S.
      14. 2nd Corps.
      15. 5th Corps.
   16 & 17. War Diary.
   18 & 19. File.

MARCH TABLE to accompany 11th Division Order No. 4/

Date.	Unit.	From.	To.	Route.	Remarks.
Novr.20th.	32nd Inf. Bde.(less here M.G. Coy) Battalions and 35th Field Ambulance (under orders of G.O.C. 32nd Inf. Bde.).	LEALVILLERS. ACHEUX	PUCHVILLERS.	ARQUEVES. RAINCHEVAL.	To clear LEALVILLERS by 11-30 a.m.
-do-	34th Inf. Bde.(less M.G. Coy.) and 34th Field Ambulance (under orders of G.O.C. 34th Inf. Bde.)	PUCHEVILLERS	LEALVILLERS ACHEUX.	TOUTENCOURT LEALVILLERS.	Not to enter LEALVILLERS before 1130 a.m.

APPENDIX "K".

SECRET.
Copy No. 19

11th Division Order No. 42.

20th. Novr. 1916.

Ref: Map 1/40,000 Sheet 57.D.
1/10,000 BEAUMONT.

1. The 11th Division (less Artillery) will (a) take over the front held by the 37th Division from the River ANCRE as far North as a line drawn from R.1.6.7.0 to Q.22.Central, relief to be completed by 6-0 a.m. on 21st instant. (b) place one battalion at disposal of G.O.C. 19th Division, South of the R. ANCRE in relief of a battalion of 61st Division.

2. Both reliefs will be carried out by the 33rd Inf. Bde. in accordance with attached Table "A", details to be arranged between Brigadiers and Commanding Officers concerned.

3. All Artillery arrangements for covering the front will remain unchanged.

4. The 37th Division have received orders to leave a proportion of Officers and N.C.O's per battalion and M.G. Company in the line until the night 21st/22nd.

5. Command of the line taken over from the 37th Division will pass to G.O.C. 11th Division on completion of relief.

6. Divisional Headquarters will remain at HEDAUVILLE for the present.

7. Completion of reliefs to be reported to Divl. Hd. Qrs.

8. ACKNOWLEDGE.

Issued at 12.30 a.m.

J.S. Coleridge
Lieut-Colonel.
Gen. Staff. 11th Div.

Copy No. 1. G.O.C.
2. C.R.A.
3. C.R.E.
4. 32nd Inf. Bde.
5. 33rd Inf. Bde.
6. 34th Inf. Bde.
7. 6th E. Yorks Regt.
8. Signals.
9. A.A. & Q.M.G.
10. A.D.M.S.
11. A.P.M.
12. 11th Div. Train.
13. D.A.D.O.S.
14. 2nd Corps.
15. 5th Corps.
16. 37th Divn.
17. 19th Divn.
18. 61st Divn.
19 & 20. War Diary.
21 & 22. File.

TABLE "A" referred to in 11th Division Order No. 42.

Date.	Unit.	From.	To.	ROUTE.	REMARKS.
20th Novr.	33rd Inf. Bde. H.Q. and 2 Battalions.	HEDAUVILLE and VARENNES.	Front Line Trenches.	HEDAUVILLE-ENGLEBELMER-MESNIL-HAMEL.	To relieve the 63rd Infantry Brigade.
do	One Battalion 33rd Inf. Bde.	HEDAUVILLE.	ST PIERRE DIVION.	Route as above.	To relieve one Battalion 61st Division and to be attached to 19th Division until 11th Division takes over line from 19th Division. Head of Column to reach Road junction Q.23.d.5.0. at 12 noon.
do	One Battalion 33rd Bde. 33rd M.G. Coy. 33rd L.T.M. Btty. 68th Field Coy.				Will remain in present billets until further orders, ready to move at short notice.

APPENDIX "L".   SECRET

                                                         Copy No. 24

        11th Division Order No. 46.   20/11/16.

Ref- Maps 1/40,000 Sheet 57.D.
         1/10,000 BEAUMONT.

1. The 11th Division (less Artillery) will on the nights of the
    21st/22nd Novr. and 22nd/23rd Novr. relieve the 19th Division
    on the front between Point R.21.a.6.8 approximately (STUMP ROAD
    exclusive) and the River ANCRE at the railway bridge at
    R.8.c.45.60.
        The relief will be completed by 6-0 a.m. on the 23rd Novr.

2. (a) On the night of the 21st/22nd Novr. the 34th Inf. Bde. will
    relieve the 56th Inf. Bde. from about R.14.Central to R.8.c.45.60.
    Relief to be completed by 6-0 a.m. 22nd Novr.

        The portion of the line North of the point R.14.a.5.5 being
    taken over by the 9th Sherwood Foresters (33rd Inf. Bde) who
    will be placed under the orders of the G.O.C. 34th Inf. Bde. for
    this purpose.
                    latter
        This portion of the line will pass under the command of G.O.C.
    33rd Inf. Bde. at 6-0 a.m. 23rd Novr. when G.O.C. 11th Division
    will assume command of the line.

    (b) On the night of the 22nd/23rd the 34th Inf. Bde. will
    relieve the 58th Inf. Bde. from about Point R.21.a.6.8 to
    R.14. Central. Relief to be completed by 6-0 a.m. 23rd.

3. Two Field Coys. R.E. and the Pioneer Battalion of 19th Division
    will remain in 2nd Corps Area and will be attached to 11th
    Division.

4. Movements and reliefs as shown in the attached March Table will
    take place on the dates therein specified.

5. All details regarding reliefs will be arranged direct between
    Brigades and Units concerned. G.O.C. 34th Inf. Bde. will
    report to this office the exact points of junction with
    Brigades on either flank, with sketch showing the dispositions
    of his Brigade.

6. The Field Ambulances of the Division will move under the orders
    of the A.D.M.S. Other units not mentioned will move under the
    orders of the A.A. & Q.M.G.

7. Divisional Headquarters will remain at HEDAUVILLE.

8. Completion of all reliefs to be reported to Divl. Hd. Qrs.

9. ACKNOWLEDGE.

                                        T. D. Colender
        Issued at 6/30 p.m.   Lieut-Colonel,
                                            Gen.Staff.11th Division.

        Copy No. 1. G.O.C.
               2. C.R.A.
               3. C.R.E.
               4. 32nd Inf.Bde.   Copy. No. 14. 2nd Corps.
               5. 33rd Inf.Bde.   15. 5th Corps.
               6. 34th Inf.Bde.   16. 37th Divn.
               7. 6th E. Yorks Regt.   17. 19th Divn. ×
               8. Signals.   18. 61st Divn.
               9. A.A. & Q.M.G.   19. 18th Divl. Arty. ×
              10. A.D.M.S.   20. 19th Divl. Arty.
              11. A.P.M.   21. 2nd Corps Arty. ×
              12. 11th Divl. Train.   22. 5th Corps Arty. ×
              13. D.A.D.O.S.   23 & 24. War Diary.
                                           25 & 26   File.

MARCH TABLE referred to in 11th Divl. Order No. 43.

Date.	Formation.	From.	To.	Route.	Remarks.
(1) 21st Nov.	1 Battn.33rd Inf. Bde.	N. BLUFFS AREA.	ST PIERRE DIVION.		To relieve one Battalion of 61st Div. and then proceed to line vide Order 43 Para 2.a.
(2) do	1 Battn. 33rd Inf. Bde. 33rd L.T.M. Btty. 33rd M.G. Coy. 68th Field Co.R.E.	HEDAUVILLE - VARENNES - FORCEVILLE.	33rd Inf. Bde. Area.	ENGLEBELMER - MESNIL.	To march under orders of G.O.C. 33rd Bde. but to clear HEDAUVILLE by 10-0 a.m.
(3) do	34th Inf. Bde. 85th Field Coy.R.E.	LEALVILLERS - ACHEUX - FORCEVILLE.	H.Q. St.PIERRE DIVION. 1 Bn. THIEPVAL. 2 Bns. SENLIS. 34th L.T.M.Btty. 1 Bn. BOUZINCOURT direct. 34th M.G.Co. 86th Fd. Co.R.E. do	ENGLEBELMER MESNIL.	Not to enter BOUZINCOURT before 12 noon. To move to THIEPVAL Area on 22nd Nov.
(4) do	32nd Inf.Bde. (less one Bttn)	PUCHEVILLERS	HEDAUVILLE and VARENNES.	TOUTENCOURT - HARPONVILLE.	Not to enter HEDAUVILLE before 12-30 p.m.
(5) 22nd Nov.	32nd Inf. Bde. (less one Battn).	HEDAUVILLE & VARENNES.	MARTINSART WOOD and huts at W.10.c. & W.9.d.	SENLIS - BOUZINCOURT.	Head not to leave HEDAUVILLE before 11-0 a.m.

APPENDIX "M".

SECRET. Copy No. 20

25th Novr. 1916.

11th Division Order No. 44.

Ref: Map. 1/40,000 Sheet 57.D.

1. The 2nd Corps and Divisional Areas have now been fixed. The area allotted to the 11th Division is shown on the attached Map.

2. The moves necessary to locate units within their own Divisional Areas will commence on Novr. 26th. The main moves to be carried out by units of this Division on the 26th. and 27th inst. are shown on the attached MARCH TABLE.

3. The A.A. & Q.M.G. will arrange for the moves and accommodation to-morrow of the detachments of 6th E. Yorks Regt. and 68th Field Coy. R.E. now in MARTINSART.

4. Advanced Divisional Hd. Qrs. will open at Q.26.c.0.4. at 12 noon on 26th instant.

5. ACKNOWLEDGE.

Ed Wright Capt
for Lieut-Colonel,
Gen. Staff. 11th Division.

Issued at 12 noon.

Copy No. 1. G.O.C.
2. C.R.A.
3. C.R.E.
4. 32nd Inf. Bde.
5. 33rd Inf. Bde.
6. 34th Inf. Bde.
7. 6th E. Yorks Regt.
8. Signals.
9. A.A. & Q.M.G.
10. A.D.M.S.
11. A.P.M.
12. 11th Divl. Train.
13. D.A.D.O.S.
14. 2nd Corps.
15. 5th Corps.
16. 37th Divn.
17. 19th Divn.

Copy No. 18. 61st Divn.
19. 19th Divl. Arty.
20 & 21. War Diary.
22 & 23. File.

MARCH TABLE to accompany 11th Division Order No. 44.

Date.	Formation.	From.	To.	Route.	Remarks.
Nov. 26th.	32nd Inf. Bde.	MARTINSART and vicinity.	ENGLEBELMER.		To clear MARTINSART by 8 a.m.
" "	67th Field Coy. R.E.	W.9.b.9.8.	MESNIL.		67th Field Coy. R.E. to march under orders of G.O.C. 32nd Bde.
Nov. 27th.	2 Battns 32nd Inf. Bde.	ENGLEBELMER.	FORCEVILLE.	via HEDAUVILLE.	Not to enter HEDAUVILLE before 5 p.m.

APPENDIX "H".   S E C R E T.

Copy No. 18

11th Division Order No. 45.

27th November 1916.

1. The 32nd Infantry Brigade will relieve the 33rd Infantry Brigade in the line during the nights of 28th/29th and 29th/30th November. Relief to be completed before 6 a.m. 30th November.

2. All arrangements for relief will be made between the Brigades concerned, moves taking place according to attached table. A sketch showing the line and dispositions handed over, will be forwarded by the 33rd Brigade to Divisional Head-Quarters.

3. The 33rd Brigade will arrange to leave a proportion of Coy. Officers, N.C.O's, and Machine Gunners in the line for 24 hours after the relief.

4. All schemes for defence, special maps or sketches, aeroplane photographs and all trench stores will be carefully handed over on relief.

5. The C.R.E. will arrange for the relief of the 68th Field Coy. R.E. by the 67th Field Coy. R.E. and will inform Brigadiers concerned and this office of the arrangements made.

6. The command will pass on completion of relief.

7. ACKNOWLEDGE.

Issued at 6/h

E.H.Wright Capt.
for
Lieut-Colonel,
Gen. Staff. 11th Division.

Copy No. 1. A.D.C. for G.O.C.
        2. 32nd Inf. Bde.
        3. 33rd Inf. Bde.
        4. 34th Inf. Bde.
        5. C.R.A.
        6. C.R.E.
        7. "Q".
        8. 6th ...
        9. Signals.
      10. A.D.M.S.
      11. A.P.M.
      12. Train.

Copy No. 14. C.R.A. 19th Div.
          15. 61st Divn.
          16. 7th Divn.
          17. 2nd Corps.
     18 & 19. War Diary.
     20 & 21. File.

Table referred to in 11th Divisional Order No. 45.

	Date.	Formation.	From.	To.	Route.	Remarks.
(1)	28th Nvr.	A Battn. 32nd Inf. Bde.	ENGLEBELMER.	Front line trenches.		
(2)	do	B Battn. 32nd Inf. Bde.	do	Support or Reserve Trenches.		NOTE.
(3)	do	A Battn. 33rd Inf. Bde.	Support or Reserve Trenches	ENGLEBELMER.		The relief of Machine Gun Coys.
(4)	do	B Battn. 33rd Inf. Bde.	Front Line.	Support or Reserve Trenches.		& Light Trench Mortar Batteries
(5)	29th Nvr.	C & D Battns 33rd Inf. Bde.	ENGLEBELMER.	Support or Reserve Trenches.		will be arranged by Brigade Commanders, those of the 33rd Brigade being billetted in ENGLEBELMER on relief.
(6)	do	B. Battn. 32nd Inf. Bde.	Support or Reserve Trenches.	Front line Trenches.		
(7)	do	Hd. Qrs. 33rd Inf. Bde.	ENGLEBELMER.	R.18.s.8.?.		
(8)	do	A. Battn. 33rd Inf. Bde.	ENGLEBELMER.	FORCEVILLE.	HEDAUVILLE.	
(9)	do	B. Bttn. 33rd Inf. Bde.	Support or Reserve Trenches.	FORCEVILLE.	AVELUY BOUZINCOURT HEDAUVILLE.	
(10)	do	H.Qrs. C & D Bttns. 33rd Inf. Bde.	Front Line & Support Trenches.	ENGLEBELMER.		

APPENDIX "O".

SECRET.

11 Corps.

The following scheme is submitted for the proposed attack on trench R.1.d.5.8 - R.1.c.7.9 and neighbouring defences.

1. OBJECTIVE
   (a) Front of attack 400 yards.
   (b) Distance of objective from assembly trench 500 yards.
   (c) Depth of objective (i) Single trench R.1.d.5.8 - R.1.c.7.8.
       (ii) Old gun-pits and occupied dug-outs from R.1.d.00.15 - R.1.c.95.45.
       (iii) Line of dug-outs in bank from R.1.d.5.8 - R.1.b.4.1.

2. POSITIONS OF ASSEMBLY.
   (a) New trench from R.7.b.3.8 to R.7.a.7.9, length about 300 yds.
   (b) New support trench R.7.b.3.5 - R.7.b.0.5, average distance between front and support trenches 250 yards.
   (c) Communication trenches
       (i) R.7.b.4.5 to R.7.b.4.7.
       (ii) ARTILLERY LANE.
   (d) Dug-outs and shell slits - - NIL.

3. METHOD OF ATTACK.
   (a) The advance will be made in 3 waves.

   Duty of each wave :-

   1st.Wave.   To take the objective viz., Trench R.1.d.5.8 - R.1.c.7.9, and clear same of all enemy and form out-post line for consolidating party.
               To leave a "Mopping up" party to deal with old gun pits, R.1.d.0.15 - c.95.45.

   2nd.Wave.   To advance 25 yards behind 1st.Wave to take objective. As soon as the objective is gained, they will drop back and consolidate a line 50 yds. S. of the objective, forming a strong point on the top of the bank at about R.1.d.3.6.

   3rd.Wave.   The garrisons of the present advanced posts consisting of 21 men per post (including the Lewis Gun detachment of each post) will follow the 2nd.wave at 25 yards distance, and assist in the consolidation of the position.
               The Lewis Guns will be pushed forward to cover the consolidation.

   (b) Positions of assembly for the above.:-

               1st. and 2nd.Waves in trench R.7.b.3.8 to R.7.a.7.9.
               3rd.Wave in present advance posts.

   (c) Special parties are required:
       (i) The battalion bombers will accompany the 1st.Wave moving up the PUISIEUX ROAD to :
           (1) Establish a block in ARTILLERY ALLEY at about R.1.d.70.95.
           (2) Destroy line of dug-outs in bank from R.1.d.5.8 to R.1.b.4.1 with "P" bombs.
       (ii) One platoon to follow above party and establish a strong point on bank about R.1.d.8.6 and to join up to outpost line at R.2.c.0.4.

4. ARTILLERY ARRANGEMENTS.

   (a) Preparation :
      (i) Destroy trench R.1.d.5.8 - 0.8 - 0.9-c.7.9.
     (ii)   do   line of dug-outs R.1.d.5.8 - b.4.1.
    (iii)   do   gun pits R.1.a.95.10 - 95.40.
     (iv)   do   ARTILLERY ALLEY.
      (v)   do   as much of PUISIEUX and River trenches on the SPUR in R.2.central as possible.
     (vi) Destroy all known M.G.emplacements, especially at R.1.c.5.9 and R.1.a.5.5.

   (b) Barrage:

      Length of advance 500 yards.
      Rate of advance 60 yards per minute.
      Time of barrage : ZERO to ZERO + 8
      Barrage is required on PUISIEUX and River trenches in R.2.central.
      At ZERO + 8 barrage to lift from objective on to GLORY LANE and on to PUISIEUX ROAD in northern half of R.1.a.
      A steady barrage to be maintained on R.2.central till dark.

   (c) Counter-Battery Work - as much as possible.

5. ZERO HOUR.

6. COVERING AEROPLANE.

   Aeroplane required to cover assembly 4 hours before ZERO.

7. WORK IN PREPARATION.
   (a) Completion and improvement of front assembly trench.
   (b) Digging new communication trenches:
      (i) R.7.b.4.4 - R.7.b.4.8.
     (ii) R.7.b.3.4 - R.7.b.3.8.(PUISIEUX ROAD).
    (iii) R.7.a.9.4 - R.7.a.7.9.(ARTILLERY LANE.).
   (c) Opening up and improvement of REDOUBT ALLEY.

   (d) Every endeavour will be made to dig outpost lines of right Battn. sector and to push out the advanced posts of the left Battn as far as possible.

8. ASSAULTING TROOPS.

   The attack will be carried out by the

   The 1st. and 2nd.Waves will consist of two coys in depth.
   The 3rd.Wave will consist of 3 platoons (garrisons of advanced posts) and 5 Lewis Guns.
   4th.Wave will consist of 1 Company to carry and assist in consolidation.
   Special parties: 1 platoon and battalion bombers.
   One company of the   to occupy the departure trench and advanced posts as soon as they are vacated by the attacking troops.

GLOSSARY.

Abbaye, Abb^e	Abbey.
Abreuvoir, Ab^r	Watering-place.
Abri de douaniers	Customs-shelter.
Aciérie	Steel works.
Aiguilles	Points (Ry.)
Allée	Alley, Narrow road.
Ancien - ne, Ancⁿ	Old.
Aqueduc	Aqueduct.
Arbre	Tree.
,, éventail	,, fan-shaped.
,, décharné	,, bare.
,, fourchu	,, forked.
,, isolé	,, isolated.
,, penché	,, leaning.
Arbrisseau	Small tree.
Arc	Arch.
Ardoisière, Ard^{re}	Slate quarry.
Arrêt	Halt.
Asile	Asylum.
,, des aliénés	Lunatic asylum.
,, d' ,,	
,, de charité	Asylum.
,, des pauvres	
,, de refuge	
Auberge, Aub^{ge}	Inn.
Aune	Alder-tree.
Bac	Ferry.
,, à traille	Ferry.
Bains	Baths.
Place aux bains	Bathing place.
Balise	Buoy, Beacon.
Banc de sable	Sand-bank.
,, vaseux	Mud-bank.
Baraque	Hut.
Barrage	Dam.
Barrière	Gate, Stile.
(Machine à) Bascule	Weigh-bridge.
Bassin	Dock, Pond.
,, d'échouage	Tidal dock.
Bassin de radoub	Dry dock.
Bateau-phare	Light-ship.
Blanchisserie	Laundry.
B.M. (borne milliaire)	Mile stone.
B^k (borne kilométrique)	
Boulonnerie	
Fab^e de boulons	Bolt Factory.
Bouée	Buoy.
Brasserie, Brass^{ie}	Brewery.
Briqueterie, Briq^{ie}	Brickfield.
Brise-lames	Breakwater.
Bureau de poste	Post office.
,, de douane	Custom house.
Butte	Butt, Mound.
Cabane	Hut.
Cabaret, Cab^t	Inn.
Câble sous-marin	Submarine cable.
Calvaire, Calv^{re}	Calvary.
Canal de dessèchement	Drainage canal.
Canal d'irrigation	Irrigation canal.
Fab^e de caoutchouc	Rubber factory.
Carrière, Carr^{re}	Quarry.
,, de gravier	Gravel-pit.
Caserne	Barracks.
Champ de courses	Race-course.
,, de manœuvres	Drill-ground.
,, de tir	Rifle range.
Chantier	Building yard.
,,	Ship yard.
,,	Dock yard.
Chantier de construction	Slip-way.
Chapelle, Ch^{lle}	Chapel.
Charbonnage	Colliery.
Château d'eau	Water tower.
Chaussée	Causeway, Highway.
Chemin de fer	Railway.
Cheminée, Ch^{ée}	Chimney.
Chêne	Oak tree.
Cimetière, Cim^{re}	Cemetery.
Clocher	Belfry.
Clouterie	Nail factory.
Colombier	Dove-cot.
Coron	Workman's dwellings.
Cour des marchandises	Goods yard.
,, aux ,,	
Couvent	Convent.
Crassier	Slag heap.
Croix	Cross.
Darse	Inner dock.
Démoli - e	Destroyed.
Détruit - e, Dét^t	
Déversoir	Weir.
Digue	Dyke, causeway.
Distillerie, Dist^{ie}	Distillery.
Douane	Custom-house.
Bureau de douane	
Entrepôt de douane	Custom warehouse.
Dynamitière, Dynam^{re}	Dynamite magazine.
Dynamiterie	Dynamite factory.
Écluse	Sluice, Lock.
Écrasette, Écl^{se}	Sluice.
École	School.
Écurie	Stable.
Église	Church.
Émaillerie	Enamel works.
Embarcadère, Emb^{re}	Landing-place.
Estaminet, Estam^t	Inn.
Étang	Pond.
Fabrique, Fab^e	Factory.
Fab^e de produits chimiques	Chemical works.
Fab^e de faïence	Pottery.
Faïencerie	
Ferme, F^{me}	Farm.
Filature, Fil^{re}	Spinning mill.
Fonderie, Fond^{ie}	Foundry.
Fontaine, Font^{ne}	Spring, fountain.
Forêt	Forest.
Forme de radoub	Dry dock.
Forge	Smithy.
Fosse	Mine, Pit.
Fossé	Moat, Ditch.
Four	Kiln.
,, à chaux	Lime-kiln.
Four à coke	Coke oven.
Ganterie	Glove Factory.
Gare	Station.
Garenne	Warren.
Garnison	Garrison.
Gazomètre	Gasometer.
Glacerie	
Fab^e de glaces	Mirror Factory.
Glacière	Ice factory.
Grue	Crane.
Gué	Ford.
Guérite	Sentry-box, Turret.
,, à signaux	Signal-box (Ry.)
Halte	Halt.
Hangar	Shed, Hangar.
Hôpital	Hospital.
Hôtel-de-Ville	Town hall.
Houillère	Colliery.
Huilerie	Oil factory.
Imprimerie, Imp^{ie}	Printing works.
Jetée	Pier.
Laminerie	Rolling mills.
Ligne de haute marée	High water mark.
,, de basse marée	Low ,, ,,
Maison Forestière, M^{on} F^{re}	Forester's house.
Malterie	Malt-house.
Marbrerie	Marble works.
Marais	Marsh.
Marais salant	Saltern, Salt marsh.
Marché	Market.
Mare	Pool.
Meule	Rick.
Minière	Mine.
Monastère	Monastery.
Moulin, Mⁱⁿ	Mill.
,, à vapeur	Steam mill.
Mur	Wall.
,, crénelé	Loop-holed wall.
Nacelle	
Orme	
Orphelinat	
Ossuaire	
Ouvrage	
Ouvrages	
Papeterie	
Parc	
,, à c^{...}	
,, à charb^{...}	
,, à pétrol^{...}	
Passage à p^{...}	
Passerelle, P^{...}	
Pépinière	
Peuplier	
Phare	
Pilier, Pil^r	
Plaine d'eau	
Pompe	
Ponceau	
Pont	
,, levis	
Poste	
Station P^{...}	
Poteau P^{...}	
Poterie	
Poudrière	
Magasin à p^{...}	
Prise d'eau	
Puits	
,, artésien	
,, d'aéra^{...}	
,, ventila^{...}	
,, de mi^{...}	
Quai	
,, aux bes^{...}	
,, aux p^{...}	
,, des	
Raccordement	
Raffinerie	
,, de	
Râperie	

[WAR DIARY]

General Staff.
11th Division

December 1916.

WAR DIARY

General Staff. 11th Div.

December 1916

Army Form C. 2118.

WAR DIARY
or
INTELLIGENCE SUMMARY
(Erase heading not required.)

11th. Division "G".

December.

Instructions regarding War Diaries and Intelligence Summaries are contained in F.S. Regs., Part II. and the Staff Manual respectively. Title Pages will be prepared in manuscript.

Place	Date	Hour	Summary of Events and Information	Remarks and references to Appendices
Q.26.c.0.4	1st.		Lt.Gen.WOOLLCOMBE left the Division to take over the command of IV Corps. Brig-Genl.ERSKINE temporarily assumed command of the Division. Pioneer Battalion and 2 Field Companies of the 19th. Division marched to rejoin their Division. From 11.30 a.m. to 12 noon bombardment of enemy's trenches carried out by the IV Corps Arty. in conjunction with the 18th. and 19th. Divnl.Artys. At 12 noon the Division passed under the orders of the IV Corps. Hostile artillery normal. Weather fine but cold. Poor visibility.	
do	2nd.		Hostile artillery slightly below normal. On the night 1st/2nd. the 18th. Divnl.Artillery were withdrawn. Divnl.front covered by 19th. Divnl.Arty. Weather cold and fine. Visibility poor.	
do	3rd.		Part of 11th.Divnl.Arty. took over the defence of part of the Divnl.front. 19th.Divnl.Arty. withdrawn. 10th.D.C.L.I.(Pioneers) and 5th. and 228th. Field Companies arrived from 2nd. Division to be attached to the Division for work in Divnl.Area. Hostile artillery normal. Weather fine. Visibility still very bad. A man belonging to 251st.Inf.Regt. surrendered to 34th.Bde. (normal).	
do	4th.		At 12 noon, 11th. Divn. took over the defence of the whole Divnl.front. Orders received from IV Corps for Divnl.Schools to assemble at ST. RIQUIER on 6th. inst. Reorganisation of Divnl.Arty. completed into 3 Bdes. Two of 3 - 6 gun 18 pdr. batteries and 1 - 4 gun How. Batty. One of 2 - 6 gun 18 pdr. battys and 2 - 4 gun How Battys. Enemy's shelling rather above normal with 77 mm. and 4.2", but very few heavy shells used. Visibility poor, weather cold but fine. Daily reports show that the enemy is doing a good deal of work in his trenches.	
do	5th.		Major General A.B.RITCHIE arrived to take over the command of the Division. Divisional School staff assembled at ST. RIQUIER. At 4 a.m. a patrol of the enemy's was captured, 2 wounded and one unwounded prisoners being taken. Prisoners belonged to 230 R.I.R. Visibility poor, cold and fine.	

Army Form C. 2118.

WAR DIARY
or
INTELLIGENCE SUMMARY

11th. Division "G".   December.

(Erase heading not required.)

Instructions regarding War Diaries and Intelligence Summaries are contained in F. S. Regs., Part II. and the Staff Manual respectively. Title Pages will be prepared in manuscript.

Place	Date	Hour	Summary of Events and Information	Remarks and references to Appendices
Q.W.26.c.0.4.	6th.		Divisional School opened at ST. RIQUIER. Hostile artillery slightly below normal. Fine weather but poor visibility. A man belonging to the 65th.K.I.R. was taken prisoner at about 7 a.m. by the 32nd.Inf.Bde.	
do	7th.		Hostile artillery normal. Operation order No. 46 issued with reference to portion of 11th. Divn. being line to be taken over by 61st.Divn. on night 8th/9th. Decr. 11th.Division No. G.S. 75 issued with reference to 33rd.Inf.Bde. taking over command of the Right Sector from 54th.Bde. and the method of holding the line until the relief of the Divn. Visibility poor. Weather fine.	App. "A". App. "B".
do	8th.		Situation unchanged. Hostile artillery less active than usual. Orders received that to co-operate with operations to be undertaken by the French, there would be an artillery bombardment on 5th.Army front on 11th. and 12th. December. At night the 183rd.Inf.Bde. (61st.Divn) took over from the 34th. Bde. the front line up to LUCKY WAY at R.14.d.9.3 exclusive. On completion of this relief, the command of this portion of the line passed to G.O.C. 61st.Division.	
do	9th.		Situation unchanged. ENGLEBELMER was shelled in the evening by a 5.9" H.V.Gun. At night the 33rd.Brigade relieved the 54th. Bde. in the Right Sector south of the ANCRE. Headquarters 33rd.Brigade at PAISLEY DUMP Q.50.c.7.2. 34th. Bde. moving to FORCEVILLE. LEALVILLERS - ARQUEVES Area with Headquarters at FORCEVILLE. Weather wet.	
do	10th.		Situation unchanged. Hostile artillery more active North of the River ANCRE. Proposed two days bombardment on 5th.Army front was postponed indefinitely. Two parties (each 100 strong) moved to THIEPVAL for work on Intermediate line under the Corps a third party of same strength being ordered to move there for same purpose on 12th. inst.	
do	11th.		Situation unchanged.	
do	12th.		do do Hostile Artillery fired intermittently throughout the day.	
do	13th.		do do Artillery active on both sides. Provisional Defence Scheme issued.	App "C".

Army Form C. 2118.

WAR DIARY
or
INTELLIGENCE SUMMARY

11th. Division "G".

December.

(Erase heading not required.)

Instructions regarding War Diaries and Intelligence Summaries are contained in F. S. Regs., Part II. and the Staff Manual respectively. Title Pages will be prepared in manuscript.

Place	Date	Hour	Summary of Events and Information	Remarks and references to Appendices
U.26.c.0.4	14th.		Situation unchanged. The enemy's front line north of the river was heavily bombarded by the Heavy and Divisional Artillery. Enemy's artillery was active throughout the day.	App. "D". Weekly operation report.
do	15th.		Situation unchanged. Intermittent artillery activity on both sides throughout the 24 hours. Divisional Order No.47 was issued of 32nd. by 34th. Bde. on Left Sector.	App "E". D.O. 47. d/15/12/16.
do	16th.		Situation unchanged. At night relief of 32nd. by 34th. Brigade commenced.	
do	17th.		Situation unchanged. Relief of 32nd. Brigade completed at night. The battalions of 33rd. Brigade also relieved at night in the Right Sector by two battalions of the same Brigade from ENGLEBELMER.	
do	18th.		Situation unchanged.	
do	19th.		Situation unchanged. Hostile artillery was active at intervals. At night for a short time BEAUCOURT was heavily bombarded. Weather cold and frosty, but dull.	
do	20th.		Situation unchanged. During night 19th/20th. one man out of a hostile patrol was killed in R.2.c. belonged to 135th. Regt (33rd.Divn) During the day the Heavy Artillery bombarded the enemy's trenches in R.14. and 15 for 3 hours with apparently good effect. Enemy's retaliation slight. Weather bright and frosty.	
do	21st.		Situation unchanged. During the night 20th/21st. a prisoner was taken in R.2.c. belonging to 230th. R.I.R. (50th. Res.Divn).	
do	22nd.		Situation unchanged. Artillery active on both sides.	
do	23rd.		Situation unchanged. Usual artillery activity.	
do	24th.		Situation unchanged. Artillery more active on both sides. Prisoner belonging to 85th. R.I.R. (18th.Divn) gave himself up in R.20.b. 54th.Res.Divn. have been relieved astride the ANCRE by 18th.Divnz Relief of 34th. by 32nd. Brigade in Left Sector commenced. South Westerly gale.	App "F". Letter No. G.S.377 d/22/12/16. App "G". letter GS. 594 d/23/12/16.

Army Form C. 2118.

WAR DIARY
or
INTELLIGENCE SUMMARY

11th. Division "G".

December.

(Erase heading not required.)

Instructions regarding War Diaries and Intelligence Summaries are contained in F. S. Regs., Part II. and the Staff Manual respectively. Title Pages will be prepared in manuscript.

Place	Date	Hour	Summary of Events and Information	Remarks and references to Appendices
W.26.c.0.4.	25th.		Situation unchanged. Bursts of fire from our artillery at stated hours were answered by the enemy but otherwise a quiet day. Relief of 34th. by 32nd.Bde. was completed at night. Two battalions of 33rd. Bde. were also relieved at night in the Right Sector by two battalions of the same Bde. from ENGLEBELMER. Weather dull, rain at intervals.	
do	26th.		Situation unchanged.	App "G". Monthly progress report with Map dated 26/12/16.
do	27th.		Situation unchanged. Enemy artillery activity was slightly above normal. Our artillery was also active. Our patrols were active at night but returned with only negative information. Aeroplane activity was greater on both sides but the enemy machines flew very high.	
do	28th.		Situation unchanged. Visibility poor owing to heavy mists but our artillery fired intermittently on enemy defences by day and night. Enemy artillery activity normal. Enemy M.Gs inactive. A man of the 2nd. Bav. R.I.R. gave himself up to the Left Battalion of the Left Brigade at 6 p.m.	
do	29th.		Situation unchanged. Visibility was poor owing to ground mists but our artillery kept up an intermittent fire by day and night. Enemy artillery activity normal. Enemy patrols were inactive.	
do	30th.		Situation unchanged. Visibility variable. Our Heavy Artillery and Divisional Artillery bombarded GRANDCOURT TRENCH for 3 hours. Enemy reply was feeble and consisted mostly of a shrapnel bombardment of our front line trenches. Enemy working parties were busy but were interrupted by our artillery fire.	
do	31st.		Situation unchanged. Our artillery fired on the enemy lines, communications, and working parties with effect throughout the day. Enemy artillery was rather more active, principally on our support lines and back areas. Wet day with fair intervals.	

J. D. Crosbie for
Brigadier General,
Commanding 11th. Division.

Army Form C. 2118.

WAR DIARY
or
INTELLIGENCE SUMMARY

(Erase heading not required.)

11th. Division "G".

DECEMBER 1916.

Summary of Events and Information

S U M M A R Y.

C A S U A L T I E S.

Killed.		Wounded.		Missing.	
O.	O.R.	O.	O.R.	O.	O.R.
6	106	18	403	–	12

J. D. Crichton Lt. Colonel
for Brigadier General,
Commanding 11th. Division.

APPENDIX "A"

SECRET   Copy No. 16

11th Division Order No. 46.   7th December 1916.

1. (a) On the night 8th/9th December the 61st Division will take over from the 11th Division the front line up to the LUCKY WAY exclusive. The 34th Inf. Bde. will be relieved on this portion of the front by the 183rd Inf. Bde. Relief to be completed by 6 a.m. 9th December.
   All details to be arranged direct between Brigades concerned.

   (b) The boundary between Divisions will then be the Post at R.14.d.9.3 and LUCKY WAY to Point R.20.b.2.7 (all to 11th Division) thence due south to the present boundary.

   (c) The portion of the front handed over will pass under the command of G.O.C. 61st Division on completion of relief which will be reported at once to D.H.Q.

2. (a) On night 9th/10th December the 34th Inf. Bde. will be relieved in the Right Sector by the 33rd Inf. Bde. Relief to be completed by 6 a.m. 10th December.
   All details to be arranged direct between Brigades concerned.

   (b) All schemes for defence, special maps or sketches, aeroplane photographs and all trench stores will be carefully handed over on relief.

   (c) Completion of relief and change of command will be reported to D.H.Q.

3. On relief the 34th Inf. Bde. will be accommodated as follows:-
   Headquarters and 2 Battalions FORCEVILLE, 1 Battalion LEALVILLERS, 1 Battalion ARQUEVES.

4. Moves in connection with the above reliefs will take place according to the attached March Table.

5. ACKNOWLEDGE.

                                            E.Wright Capt
                                            for
                                            Lieut-Colonel,
                                            Gen.Staff.11th Division.

Issued at 12-15 p.m.

        Copy No. 1. G.O.C.
              2. 32nd Inf. Bde.
              3. 33rd Inf. Bde.
              4. 34th Inf. Bde.
              5. C.R.A.
              6. C.R.E.
              7. Q.
              8. 6th E. Yorks Regt.
              9. Signals.
             10. A.D.M.S.
             11. A.P.M.
             12. D.A.D.O.S.
             13. Train.
             14. 61st Divn.
             15. IV Corps.
       16 & 17. War Diary.
       18 & 19. File.

MARCH TABLE referred to in 11th Division Order No. 46.

Date.	Unit.	From.	To.	Route.	
Dec. 8th.	1 Battalion 34th Bde.	THIEPVAL.	ARQUEVES	BOUZINCOURT-HEDAUVILLE-VARENNES-LEALVILLERS.	
Night Dec. 8th/9th.	1 Battalion 34th Bde.	LINE.	THIEPVAL.		On relief by 183rd Bde.
Dec. 9th.	1 Battalion 34th Bde.	THIEPVAL.	LEALVILLERS.	BOUZINCOURT-HEDAUVILLE-VARENNES.	By bus under arrangements to be made by A.A.Q.M.G
do	1 Battalion 61st Divn.	LEALVILLERS.	VARENNES.		Details to be arranged by G.O.C. 33rd Bde.
do	2 Battalions 33rd Bde.	FORCEVILLE.	ENGLEBELMER	via HEDAUVILLE.	
do	33rd Bde.(less 2 Bttns)	ENGLEBELMER.	Right Sector.		
do	34th Bde.(less 2 Bttns)	Right Sector.	FORCEVILLE.	BOUZINCOURT-HEDAUVILLE.	

The standing orders with regard to distances to be maintained between Companies and Battalions on the March will be observed.

11th Div.No.G.S.73.

APPENDIX B

TO: _____

1. With effect from the 10th instant, the G.O.C. 33rd Infantry Brigade will take over the Command of the Right Sector.

2. The Brigade will be disposed as under :-

   33rd Brigade less 2 Battalions.   In the Line
                                      ST PIERRE DIVION
                                      Old German Line.

   2 Battalions   ENGLEBELMER
                                      as Right Sector
                                      Reserve.

3. The Brigade will remain in the Right Sector until the Division is finally relieved; but the G.O.C. may relieve the 2 Battalions in the Line by the 2 Battalions from ENGLEBELMER whenever he considers it desirable.

4. As regards the Left Sector. This will be held alternately by the 32nd and 34th Brigades for short periods. The Brigade holding the line being disposed as the 32nd Brigade is at present, while the Brigade resting will be located at FORCEVILLE and LEALVILLERS or ARQUEVES.

5. All available accommodation in THIEPVAL will be allotted as under in order of precedence :-

   (a) 2 Field Oc's 2nd Division.
   (b) 300 Infantry 11th Division attached to the above.
   (c) Personnel 58th F.A.B.
   (d) 10th. D.C.L.I. (Pioneers) or R.A. Personnel as allotted by 4th Corps.

6. The C.R.E. will allot R.E. and Pioneers (6th E. Yorks R.) to Sectors as required and will arrange for their periodical reliefs.

7. ACKNOWLEDGE.

J. D. Coleridge
Lieut-Colonel,
Gen.Staff.11th Division.

H.Q. 11th Division.
7th Decr. 1916.

Copies to :   C.R.A.   A.P.M.
              C.R.E.   D.A.D.O.S.
              32nd Inf. Bde.   1V Corps.
              33rd Inf. Bde.
              34th Inf. Bde.
              6th E. Yorks Regt.
              Signals.
              "Q"
              A.D.M.S.

```
32nd.Inf.Bde.        4th.Corps.
33rd.  "    "        61st.Divn.
34th.  "    "        7th.Divn.
C.R.A.               4th.Corps R.A.    SECRET
C.R.E.
"Q"
6th.E.Yorks.                                           11th Div. No. G.S.197.
A.D.M.S.                    11th Division
Train.
A.P.M.                PROVISIONAL DEFENCE SCHEME.
```

                                                                APPENDIX C

1. **GENERAL.** In event of a general hostile attack the front line will be resolutely held, and the enemy, should he gain a footing, vigorously counter attacked, at first locally under Sector arrangements and later, if necessary, by the Divisional Reserve. Corps H.A., 11th Divl. Artillery, and Artilleries of ajacent Divl. Artilleries (if available) will act on "Defend 11th Division" and "Defend IV Corps" lines.

2. **ATTACK ON RIGHT SECTOR.** In event of an attack on the Right Sector only :

   (a) The Divl. Artillery will open as prearranged on the S.O.S. lines, and the Corps H.A., and the 61st Divl. R.A. (if available) will co-operate on the "Defend 11th Division" lines.

   (b) The G.O.C. Right Sector will organize local counter attacks, utilizing the Reserve Companies now located at THIEPVAL and ST PIERRE DIVION. This includes Infantry working parties quartered in THIEPVAL.

   (c) The G.O.C. Left Sector will co-operate by opening fire with all Machine Guns capable of covering the Right Sector.

   (d) The 2 Battalions now at ENGLEBELMER will march via MESNIL - Q.35.d.2.8 - PASSERELLE DE MAJENTA and will assemble at PAISLEY DUMP under orders of G.O.C. Right Sector.

   (e) The Reserve Brigade located at FORCEVILLE, ARQUEVES and LEALVILLERS will stand to arms ready to move at 2 hours notice.

3. **ATTACK ON LEFT SECTOR.** In event of an attack on the Left Sector only :

   (a) The Divl. Artillery will open as prearranged on S.O.S. lines. When the situation clears and it is evident that the attack is confined to the Left Sector front then the whole of the Divl Artillery will concentrate on that front under a prearranged scheme, and the Corps H.A., 37th and 61st.Divnl.Artilleries (if available) will co-operate on "Defend 11th.Division and Defend IV Corps Lines".

   (b) The G.O.C. Left Sector will organize local counter attacks utilizing his Reserve Battalions now located about STATION ROAD and in the old German lines.

   (c) The G.O.C. Right Sector will co-operate by opening fire with all Machine Guns capable of covering the Left Sector.

   (d) The 2 Battalions of the 33rd Brigade located at ENGLEBELMER will march via MESNIL and thence along the Railway line to Q.22. Central; from there they will proceed in artillery formation to STATION ROAD where they will assemble under orders of the G.O.C. Left Sector. HAMEL and the HAMEL - BEAUCOURT ROAD are to be avoided on account of the hostile barrage which is certain to be brought down on those localities.

(e) The Reserve Brigade will act as detailed in para 2 (e).

4. ATTACK ON DIVISION ON OUR RIGHT. In event of an hostile attack on the Division on our Right :

(a) The Divl. Artillery will act on "Defend 61st Division lines".

(b) The G.O.C. Right Sector will :

1. Co-operate by opening fire with all Machine Guns capable of covering the left of the Division on our right.

ii. Get his Reserve Companies under arms ready to move as required at ½ an hours notice.

(c) The G.O.C. Left Sector will get his Reserve Battalions under arms ready to move at ½ an hours notice.

(d) The 2 Battalions of the 33rd Brigade located at ENGLEBELMER will get under arms ready to move off at ½ an hours notice.

(e) The Reserve Brigade will get under arms ready to move off at 2 hours notice.

5. ATTACK ON DIVISION ON OUR LEFT. In event of an hostile attack on the Division of the 13th Corps on our left :

(a) The Divl. Artillery will act on "Defend 13th Corps lines".

(b) The G.O.C. Left Sector will :

1. Co-operate by opening fire with all Machine Guns capable of covering the right of the Division on our left.

ii. Get his Reserve Battalions under arms ready to move Northwards or North Eastwards as required at ½ an hours notice.

(c) The G.O.C. Right Sector will get his Reserve Companies under arms ready to move off at ½ an hours notice.

(d) The 2 Battalions 33rd Brigade located at ENGLEBELMER will get under arms ready to move off at ½ an hours notice.

(e) The Reserve Brigade will get under arms ready to move off at 2 hours notice.

6. DIVISIONAL HEAD QUARTERS.

In event of an attack the Divl. Head Quarters will remain At ENGLESART.

13th December 1916.

J.D. Coleridge
Lieut-Colonel,
Gen. Staff. 11th Division.

APPENDIX "D".

OPERATION REPORT.
For Week Ending 15th Decr. 1916.

No special operations have been carried out on this front during the past week.

Again, on the whole the enemy's artillery fire has been more active on the North than on the South of the River, though during the latter part of the week, more hostile shells than usual have fallen in the vicinity of SCHWABEN REDOUBT.

The outskirts of ENGLEBELMER were shelled by a 5.9" High Velocity gun on the evening of the 9th., MESNIL has also been frequently shelled.

Our own artillery have kept the enemy's defences and communications under almost continuous fire. One prearranged bombardment was carried out on the morning of the 13th inst., when RIVER and PUISIEUX trenches were heavily bombarded by our Heavy Artillery during the morning, while at 2-30 p.m. they were subjected to a two minutes intense bombardment by our Divisional Artillery.

Our snipers claim a few hits during the week, and our machine guns have fired on the enemy's communications with indirect fire.

Our patrols have been out each night and have gained useful information with regard to the enemy's defences, but have not met any hostile patrols.

The weather has been bad during the week, consequently all efforts have been concentrated on endeavouring to consolidate the line and dig communication trenches.

APPENDIX E

SECRET   Copy No. 17.

11th Division Order No. 47.   15th Decr. 1916.

1. The 34th Infantry Brigade will relieve the 32nd Infantry Brigade in the Left Sector in the Line during the nights of 16th/17th and 17th/18th December. Relief to be completed before 6 a.m. 18th December.

2. All arrangements for relief will be made between the Brigades concerned.

3. The 32nd Infantry Brigade will arrange to leave a proportion of Company officers, N.C.O's., and Machine gunners in the line for 24 hours after the relief.

4. All schemes for defence, special maps or sketches, aeroplane photographs and all trench stores will be carefully handed over on relief.

5. The command will pass on completion of relief.

6. On relief the 32nd Infantry Brigade will occupy the billets vacated by the 34th Infantry Brigade.

7. ACKNOWLEDGE.

Issued at 10.15 a.m.

Ed Wright Capt
for Lieut-Colonel,
Gen. Staff. 11th Division.

Copy No. 1. A.D.C. for G.O.C.
       2. 32nd Inf. Bde.
       3. 33rd Inf. Bde.
       4. 34th Inf. Bde.
       5. C.R.A.
       6. C.R.E.
       7. "Q"
       8. 6th E. Yorks Regt.
       9. Signals.
      10. A.D.M.S.
      11. A.P.M.
      12. 11th Div. Train.
      13. 61st Divn.
      14. 7th Divn.
      15. 1V Corps.
16 & 17. War Diary.
18 & 19. File.

APPENDIX F

COPY No. 15.

SECRET.   11th.Division No. G.S. 377.

1. The 34th.Bde. will be relieved by the 32nd. Bde. in the Left Sector on the nights 24th/25th. and 25th/26th. December.

2. All details will be arranged between Brigades concerned direct.

3. Detailed orders will be forwarded as soon as it it known what motor transport, if any, will be available.

4. ACKNOWLEDGE.

E.H.Wright Capt
for Lieut.Colonel,
Gen. Staff, 11th. Division.

```
Copy No.1 to    32nd.Inf.Bde.
        2       34th.  "   "
        3       C.R.A.
        4       C.R.E.
        5       33rd.Inf.Bde.
        6       "Q"
        7       6th.E.Yorks.
        8       Signals.
        9       A.D.M.S.
       10.      A.P.M.
       11.      D.A.D.O.S.
       12       11th.Div.Train.
    13 - 14     File.
    15 - 16     War Diary.
```

APPENDIX 'G'

11th.Division No. G.S. 394.

32nd.Inf.Bde.
34th. "   "
11th.Divn."Q".
IVth.Corps (for information).

Reference this office G.S. 377 of 22nd. and all subsequent correspondence, the relief of the 32nd. by 34th. Bde. must be carried out according to the attached programme.

ACKNOWLEDGE.

23rd.December 1916.

Lieut.Colonel,
Gen. Staff, 11th. Division.

S E C R E T.

Relief of 54th. Inf.Bde. by 52nd. Inf. Bde. nights 24th./25th. and 25th./26th. December.

Date.	Unit.	From.	To.	Remarks.
24th.Decr.	6th.Yorks Regt.(52nd.Bde).	FORCEVILLE.	Old German Fr nt Line.	By Route March.
-do-	9th.W.Yorks Regt.(52nd.Bde). and 52nd.M.G.Coy.	LEALVILLERS.	Front Line Right Sector.	By Bus to LANCASHIRE DUMP. Busses to be at LEALVILLERS at 10.30 a.m. and leave punctually at 11 a.m.
-do-	"A" Battn. (54th.Bde.) and 54th.M.G.Coy.	Old German Front Line.	LEALVILLERS.	By bus, leaving LANCASHIRE DUMP at 5 p.m. Busses will then return empty to LANCASHIRE DUMP.
-do-	"B" Battn.(54th.Bde).	Frontline. Right Sector	FORCEVILLE.	On relief by 9th.W.Yorks Regt. By bus, leaving BANCASHIRE DUMP about 11 p.m.

NOTE: Busses will remain for the night at FORCEVILLE, accommodation etc., being provided for drivers at Rest Camp.

P.T.O.

(contd).

Date.	Unit.	From.	To.	Remarks.
25th.Decr.	8th.York & Lancs.Regt. (32nd.Bde).	FORCEVILLE.	Support line.	By route march, to relieve "C" Battalion 34th.Bde. in support line.
-do-	8th.Duke of Wellington Regt.(32nd.Bde). and 32nd.T.M.Bty.(if required).	ARQUEVES.	Reserve Line.	By bus, to LANCASHIRE DUMP. Busses to be at ARQUEVES at 11 a.m. and leave at 11.30 a.m.
-do-	"C" Battalion (34th.Bde).	Support Line.	ARQUEVES.	By bus, on relief by 6th.York & Lancs.Regt. leaving LANCASHIRE DUMP about 8.30 p.m. Busses will then return empty to LANCASHIRE DUMP.
-do-	6th.Yorks Regt.(32nd.Bde).	Reserve Line.	Front line. Left Sector.	
-do-	"D" Battalion (34th.Bde).	Front Line. Left Sector.	FORCEVILLE.	By bus, on relief by 8th.Yorks Regt., leaving LANCASHIRE DUMP about 11 p.m.

NOTE: Busses will either remain at FORCEVILLE, as on night of 24th/25th December or return to their columns as required by IVth.Corps.

APPENDIX H

11th DIVISION.

	"C"	"D"
General Conditions. Front Line. (Brown).	Right consists of posts duck-boarded and being revetted. Centre & Left fairly good trench, though very wet - has an average depth of 6 feet.	Outposts are in fair condition - trench boarded and revetted. Posts 2,3 and 4 connected up with trench average depth 3 feet. SUVLA TRENCH is fairly good on right being in chalk and well traversed and trench-boarded. Centre and left very poor.
General Condition. Support Line. (Brown).	Right consists of posts duck-boarded and being revetted. Centre and left good trench fire - stepped and revetted. ~~posts.~~ Average depth 7 ft. ~~in front of trench.~~	Is very bad - practically uninhabitable, continually falling in.
General Condition. Reserve Line.	Right consist of posts duck-boarded and being revetted Centre and Left fairly good trench with posts in it, which are revetted, fire stepped and duck-boarded.	Is fairly good trench, not traversed, trench boards wholelength but very wet.
Entanglements. Front Line.	From the right to R.14.b.2.0 wire in front of all posts. From R.14.b.2.0 to Bridge Pt. 56 good belt of wire.	Posts have trip wire round them. SUVLA TRENCH has odd patches of wire at intervals along its front.
Entanglements. Support Line.	Short stretch of wire crossing COCKSHY AVENUE from R.14.a.7.3 to R.14.a.8.0. and on centre and left wire in front of posts.	Odd patches at intervals
Entanglements. Reserve Line.	NIL.	NIL.
Accomodation in Deep Dugouts completed. Front, Support and Reserve Lines.	Front Line. Two dugouts to hold 15 each, one dugout for 40 men. Support line. NIL. Reserve Line 13 dugouts to hold total of 140 men. Dugouts round R.20.c.9.2. hold one company.	Front Line NIL. Support Line. One dugout for 50 men. Reserve Line 14 dugouts and cave. Total accomodation 600.
Accomodation in Deep Dugouts under construction. Front, Support and Reserve Lines.	Front Line. NIL. Support Line. Two dugouts intended to hold 30 each. Reserve Line. One at R.20.c.7.5 to hold about 40. One at R.13.c.6.9 to hold 120.	~~Dugouts in Q.12.d.~~ ~~Brigade Headquarters.~~ Reserve Line. Dug-outs to accommodate 150 men in RAVINE. Q.12.d.

	"C"	"D"
M.G. Emplacements with deep dug-outs. Front, Support and Reserve Line.	Front Line. NIL. Support Line. 2 emplacements at R.14.c.90.05 with dug-out close by. Reserve Line. 4 emplacements as follows :- R.19.b.7.6. R.19.a.8.2. R.20.c.8.0. R.20.c.6.4.	Front Line. Two M.G. Emp: at QUARRY R.8.a.2.0. with dug-out for 10 men. Support Line. NIL. Reserve Line. M.G. Emp: at R.7.a.5.0. with dug-out at R.7.b.1.2.
M.G. Emplacements with deep dug-outs under construction. Front, Support and Reserve Line.	Front Line. NIL. Support Line. NIL. Reserve Line. One at each of : R.13.b.4.3. R.13.d.9.4. R.19.b.7.6.	

FRANCE.

$\frac{1}{20,000}$

1° 44′ W. of Brussels.

Places visible on map: Beaussart, Mailly-Maillet, Auchonvillers, Acheux, Vitermont, Forceville, Englebelmer, Mesnil, Varennes, Hedauville, Martinsart, Bouzincourt, Henencourt, Millencourt

G.S.G.S. 3742

1° 44′ W. of Brussels.

INSTRUCTIONS AS TO THE USE OF THE SQUS.

1. The large rectangles on the map, lettered P,Q,R, etc., are divided into squares of 1,000 yards side, which are numbered 1, 2, 3, etc. Each of these squares is sub-divided into four minor squares of 500 yards side. These minor squares are considered as lettered a, b, c, d. (See Square No. 5 in each rectangle). A point may thus be described as lying within Square B 6, M.6.b, etc.

2. To locate a point within a small square, consider the sides divided into tenths, and define the point by taking so many tenths from W. to E along Southern side, and so many from S. to N. along Western side: the S.W. corner always being taken as origin, and the distance along the Southern side being always given by the first figure. Thus the point Z would be 88 ; i.e. 8 divisions East and 8 divisions North from origin.

3. When more exact definition is wanted (on the 1: 20,000 or 1: 10,000 scales) use exactly the same method, divide sides into 100 parts and use four figures instead of two. Thus 0847 denotes 8s East and 47 parts North of origin from point X. Point Y is 5620.

4. Use 0 but not 10 either two or four figures; do not use fractions (8½, 4), etc.

REFER.

Any trench apparently organised for fire.
Enemy Other trenches. Important ones are shown by thick line. Old or disused by dotted line.
British front line trench
Entanglement or other obstacle
Ground cut up by Artillery fire
Mine craters   b. Mine craters fortified
Hedge, fence or ditch. (Unknown which)
Ditch with permanent water

NOTE.— ...

Scale 1:20,000

Yards 1000 500 0 1000 2000 3000 4000 5000 6000 7000

Metres 1000 500 0 1000 2000 3000 4000 5000 6000 7000

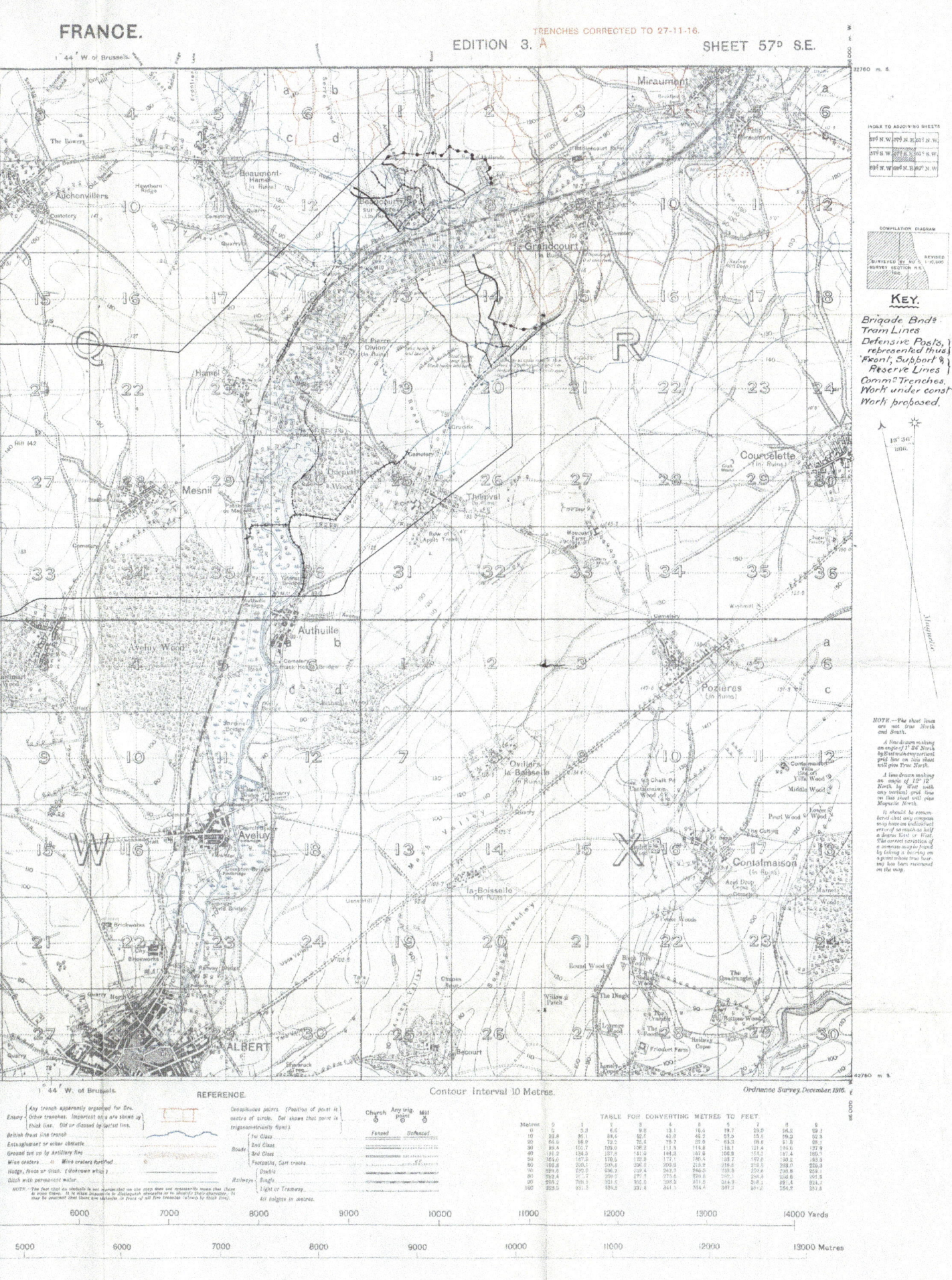

GLOSSARY.

Abbaye, Abb⁶	Abbey.
Abreuvoir, Ab'	Watering-place.
Abri de douaniers	Customs-shelter.
Aciérie	Steel works.
Aiguilles	Points (Ry.)
Allée	Alley, Narrow road
Ancien -ne, Anc⁶⁶ⁿ⁶	Old.
Aqueduc	Aqueduct.
Arbre	Tree.
,, éventail	,, fan-shaped.
,, déchárné	,, bare.
,, fourchu	,, forked.
,, isolé	,, isolated.
,, penché	,, leaning.
Arbrisseau	Small tree.
Arc	Arch.
Ardoisière, Ard⁶	Slate quarry.
Arrêt	Halt.
Asile	Asylum.
,, des aliénés	Lunatic asylum.
,, d'	
,, de charité	
,, des pauvres	Asylum.
,, de refuge	
Auberge, Aub⁶	Inn.
Aune	Alder-tree.
Bac	Ferry.
,, à traille	,,
Bains	Baths.
Place aux bains	Bathing place.
Balise	Boom, Beacon.
Banc de sable	Sand-bank.
,, vase	Mud-bank.
Baraque	Hut.
Barrage	Dam.
Barrière	Gate, Stile.
(Machine à) Bascule	Weigh-bridge
Bassin	Dock, Pond.
,, d'échouage	Tidal dock.
Bassin de radoub	Dry dock.
Bateau phare	Light-ship.
Blanchisserie	Laundry.
B.M. (borne milliaire)	Mile stone.
B⁶ (borne kilométrique)	
Boulonnerie Fabr⁶ de boulons	Bolt Factory.
Bouée	Buoy.
Brasserie, Brass⁶ⁿ⁶	Brewery.
Briqueterie, Briq⁶ⁿ⁶	Brickfield.
Brise-lames	Breakwater.
Bureau de poste	Post office.
,, de douane	Custom house.
Butte	Butt, Mound.
Cabane	Hut.
Cabaret, Cab⁶	Inn.
Câble sous-marin	Submarine cable.
Calvaire, Calv⁶	Calvary.
Canal de démolissement	Drainage canal.
Canal d'irrigation	Irrigation canal.
Fabr⁶ de caoutchouc	Rubber factory.
Carrière, Carr⁶	Quarry.
,, de gravier	Gravel-pit.
Caserne	Barracks.
Champ de course	Race-course.
,, manœuvres	Drill-ground.
,, tir	Rifle range.
Chantier	Building yard. Dock yard.
Chantier de construction	Slip-way.
Chapelle, Ch⁶⁶	Chapel.
Charbonnage	Colliery.
Château d'eau	Water tower.
Chaussée	Causeway. Highway.
Chemin de fer	Railway.
Cheminée, Ch⁶⁶	Chimney.
Chêne	Oak-tree.
Cimetière, Cim⁶⁶	Cemetery.
Clocher	Belfry.
Clouterie	Nail factory.
Colombier	Dove-cot.

Coron	Workmen's dwellings
Cour des marchandises	Goods yard.
Couvent	Convent.
Crassier	Slag heap.
Croix	Cross.
Darse	Inner dock.
Démoli -e	Destroyed.
Détruit -e, Détr	
Déversoir	Weir.
Digue	Dyke, causeway.
Distillerie, Dist⁶⁶	Distillery.
Douane	Custom-house
Bureau de douane	
Entrepôt de douane	Custom warehouse.
Dynamitière, Dynam⁶⁶	Dynamite magazine.
Dynamiterie	Dynamite factory.
Écluse	Sluice, Lock.
Éclusette, Écl⁶⁶	Sluice.
École	School.
Écurie	Stable.
Église	Church.
Émaillerie	Enamel works.
Embarcadère, Emb⁶⁶	Landing-place.
Estaminet, Estam'	Inn.
Étang	Pond.
Fabrique, Fabr	Factory.
Fabr⁶ de produits chimiques	Chemical works
Fabr⁶ de faïence	Pottery.
Ferme, F⁶⁶	Farm.
Filature, Fil⁶⁶	Spinning mill.
Fonderie, Fond⁶⁶	Foundry.
Fontaine, Font⁶⁶	Spring, fountain.
Forêt	Forest
Forme de radoub	Dry dock.
Forge	Smithy.
Fosse	Mine, Pit.
Fossé	Moat, Ditch.
Four	Kiln.
,, à chaux	Lime-kiln.

Four à coke	Coke oven.
Ganterie	Glove Factory.
Gare	Station.
Garenne	Warren.
Garnison	Garrison.
Gazomètre	Gasometer.
Glacerie Fabr⁶ de glaces	Mirror Factory.
Glacière	Ice factory.
Grue	Crane.
Gaz	Ford.
Guérite	Sentry-box, Turret.
,, à signaux	Signal-box (Ry.)
Halte	Halt.
Hangar	Shed, Haugar.
Hôpital	Hospital.
Hôtel-de-Ville	Town hall.
Houillière	Colliery.
Huilerie	Oil factory.
Imprimerie, Impr⁶⁶	Printing works.
Jetée	Pier.
Laminerie	Rolling mills.
Ligne de haute Laisse marée	High water mark.
,, de basse marée	Low
Maison Forestière Mⁿ For⁶⁶	Forester's house.
Malterie	Malt-house.
Marbrerie	Marble works.
Marais	Marsh.
Marais salant	Saltern. Salt marsh.
Marché	Market.
Mare	Pool.
Meule	Rick.
Minière	Mine.
Monastère	Monastery.
Moulin, M⁶⁶	Mill.
,, à vapeur	Steam mill.
Mur	Wall.
,, crénelé	Loop-holed wall.

Nacelle	
Orme	
Orphelinat	
Ossuaire	
Ouvrage	
Papeterie	
Parc	
,, à charb⁶⁶	
,, à pétrole	
Passage à niv⁶⁶	
Passerelle, P	
Pépinière	
Peuplier	
Phare	
Pilier, Pil⁶⁶	
Plaine d'ass⁶⁶	
Pompe	
Ponceau	
Pont	
,, levis	
Poste	
Station	
Poteau	
Poterie	
Poudrière, P	
Magasin à p	
Prise d'eau	
Puits	
,, artésien	
,, d'extr⁶⁶	
,, ventilat⁶⁶	
,, de sond⁶⁶	
Quai	
,, aux bes⁶⁶	
,, aux pass⁶⁶	
,, des f⁶⁶	
Raccordement	
Raffinerie	
Réparis	

APPENDIX H

TRENCH MAP.

FRANCE

SHEET 57D S.E.

EDITION 3. A

INDEX TO ADJOINING SHEETS

SCALE 20,000

Coke oven.	
Glass Factory.	
Station.	
Warren.	
Garrison.	
Gasometer.	
Mirror Factory.	
Ice factory.	
Crane.	
Ford.	
Sentry-box, Turret.	
Signal-box (Ry.)	
Halt.	
Shed, Hangar.	
Hospital.	
Town hall.	
Colliery.	
Oil factory.	
Printing works.	
Pier.	
Rolling mills.	
High water mark.	
Lock.	
Forester's house.	
Malt-house.	
Marble works.	
Marsh.	
Saltern.	
Salt marsh.	
Market.	
Post.	
Rick.	
Mine.	
Monastery.	
Mill.	
Steam mill.	
Wall.	
Loop-holed wall.	
Nacelle.	Ferry.
Orme.	Elm.
Orphelinat.	Orphanage.
Oseraie.	Osier-beds.
Ouvrage.	Fort.
Ouvrages hydrauliques.	Water works.
Papeterie.	Paper-mill.
Parc.	Park, yard.
,, aérostatique.	Aviation ground.
,, à charbon.	Coal yard.
,, à pétrole.	Petrol store.
Passage à niveau P.N.	Level-crossing.
Passerelle, Pass⁰⁰.	Foot-bridge.
Pépinière.	Nursery-garden.
Peuplier.	Poplar tree.
Phare.	Light-house.
Pilier, Pil⁰.	Post.
Plaine d'exercice.	Drill ground.
Pompe.	Pump.
Ponceau.	Culvert.
Pont.	Bridge.
,, levis.	Drawbridge.
Poste de garde-côte.	Coast-guard station.
Station.	
Poteau I⁰⁰.	Post.
Poterie.	Pottery.
Poudrière, Poud⁰⁰.	Powder magazine.
Magasin à poudre.	
Prise d'eau.	Water supply.
Puits.	Pit-head, Shaft, Well.
,, artésien.	Artesian well.
,, d'aérage.	
,, ventilateur.	Ventilating shaft.
,, de sondage.	Boring.
Quai.	Quay, Platform.
,, aux bestiaux.	Cattle platform.
,, aux marchandises.	Goods platform.
Raccordement.	Junction.
Raffinerie.	Refinery.
,, de sucre.	Sugar refinery.
Râperie.	Beet-root factory.
Remblai.	Embankment.
Remise des Machines.	Engine shed.
Réservoir, Rés⁰⁰.	Reservoir.
Route cavalière.	Bridle road.
Rubanerie.	Ribbon Factory.
Ruine.	
Ruines.	Ruin.
En ruine.	
Ruine - e.	
Sablière.	Sand-pit.
Sablonnière, Sablon⁰⁰.	
Sapin.	Fir tree.
Saule.	Willow tree.
Saunerie.	Salt-works.
Scierie, Sc⁰⁰.	Saw-mill.
Sondage.	Boring.
Source.	Spring.
Sucrerie, Suc⁰⁰.	Sugar factory.
Tannerie.	Tannery.
Tir à la cible.	Rifle range.
Tissage.	Weaving mill.
Tôlerie.	Rolling mill.
Tombeau.	Tomb.
Tour.	Tower.
Tourbière.	Peat-bog, Peat-bed.
Tourelle.	Small tower.
Tuilerie.	Tile works.
Usine à gaz.	Gas works.
,, électrique d'électricité.	Electricity works.
,, métallurgique.	Metal works.
,, à agglomérée.	Briquette factory.
Verrerie, Verr⁰⁰.	Glass works.
Viaduc.	Viaduct.
Vivier.	Fish Pond.
Voie de chargement - déchargement.	
,, d'évitement.	Siding.
,, formation.	
,, manœuvre.	
Zinguerie.	Zinc works.

Army Form C. 2118

WAR DIARY
or
INTELLIGENCE SUMMARY

(Erase heading not required.)

11th. DIVISION "G".

January 1917.

Instructions regarding War Diaries and Intelligence Summaries are contained in F. S. Regs., Part II. and the Staff Manual respectively. Title Pages will be prepared in manuscript.

Place	Date	Hour	Summary of Events and Information	Remarks and references to Appendices
Q.28.c.04.	1st.		Our artillery kept up an intermittent fire on the enemy lines and back areas by day and by night. Enemy artillery's activity was below normal throughout the day. Enemy working parties were in several places dispersed by our artillery fire. Visibility good.	
-do-	2nd.		Our artillery displayed their usual activity. Enemy artillery were more active than usual during the morning. FERDAN & COCKSHY trenches receiving most attention while the wiring parties in YELLOW LINE were also shelled. Our patrols were active during the night but gained no information. Fine day. Relief of 32nd. Bde. by 34th. Bde. in Left Sector completed.	
-do-	3rd.		Visibility bad. Our artillery was active and the enemy artillery fire was normal. Six prisoners were captured during the night by a patrol of the 6th. Lincolns. Prisoners belonged to 85th. F. Regt.	
-do-	4th.		Our artillery was active both by day and night. Enemy artillery was active during the morning but below normal after noon. Visibility fair.	
-do-	5th.		Usual activity by aour artillery. Enemy artillery fire normal. Our patrols had nothing to report. The 61st. Division is on our right and the 7th. Division of the XIII Corps on our left. Same aerial activity on both sides during the morning.	
-do-	6th.		From 12 noon to 12.14 p.m. a H.E. barrage was carried out on O.d.1. and O.d.2 with success. Enemy artillery fire normal. Our patrols had nothing to report. Our aeroplanes were active during the morning.	
-do-	7th.		Visibility bad all day. Normal fire by the artillery of both sides. A prisoner of the German Red Cross was taken during the night by the 33rd. Inf. Bde. Aeroplanes of both sides were up between 10 a.m. and 11 a.m.	
-do-	8th.		Our artillery was active all day particularly the Heavies. Enemy artillery was more active than usual. Considerable aerial activity but the enemy planes kept well behind their own lines. Our patrols had nothing to report.	
-do-	9th.	8 am.	A 48 hours bombardment of the enemy lines and back areas opposite the right of the XIII Corps and the left of IVth. Corps fronts commenced. Heavy and Divisional Artilleries all took part. The bombardment was intended to prepare the way for minor operations by the 7th. Division on our left.	

1875 Wt. W593/826 1,000,000 4/15 J.B.C.&A. A.D.S.S./Forms/C. 2118.

Army Form C. 2118

WAR DIARY
or
INTELLIGENCE SUMMARY

(Erase heading not required.)

11th. DIVISION "G".

JANUARY 1917.

Instructions regarding War Diaries and Intelligence Summaries are contained in F.S. Regs., Part II. and the Staff Manual respectively. Title Pages will be prepared in manuscript.

Place	Date	Hour	Summary of Events and Information	Remarks and references to Appendices
Q.26.c.0.4.	9th.		11th. Division., and 61st. Division on our right. Visibility was good. Enemy artillery fire normal.	APP. 1.
—do—	10th.		Bombardment continued by day and night. Enemy artillery fire was above normal and our front and support trenches were heavily shelled during the afternoon. Some aerial activity on the front part of our aeroplanes. Visibility was good.	
—do—	11th.	6.40 a.m.	In conjunction with an attack by the 7th. Division (on our left) on MUNICH TRENCH the 34th. Inf. Bde. attacked the spur in R.1.c. and d. (Sheet 57D. S.E.) at 6.40 a.m. under adequate Artillery barrage. The attack was carried out by the 5th. Dorsets and the objectives were captured with very few casualties. 14 Prisoners of the 135th. I. Regt. were captured in the "NEST" R.1.d.1.4.	APP. 2 O.O. No 52 d/8/1/17.
			A very heavy fog prevailed and it was impossible to see more than 50 yards until after 10 a.m. The work of consolidating the captured objectives was in progress when about 8.30 a.m. it was discovered that the platoon in the CHALK PIT had been attacked and driven out of it by a German bombing party who came out of an undetected dug-out on N. side of the PIT about R.1.d.1.1½. About the same time more Germans lined the bank about R.1.d.2.4 and began firing into our men from behind. Other parties of Germans estimated to be 200 strong attacked from about R.1.0.3.6. Fired into from front, flanks and rear the two Companies of the Dorsets withdrew to SUVLA TRENCH and original line of posts about 9.30 a.m.	

Our casualties were :—

	Killed.		Wounded.		Missing.	
	O.	O.R.	O.	O.R.	O.	O.R.
	1	19	3	44	?	90

| | | | Our artillery continued to be active during the rest of the day and night. Enemy's reply was heavy except between 10 p.m. and 4 a.m. SUVLA, CANAL and FERDAN TRENCHES receiving most attention. Our aeroplanes were active during the afternoon. | |
| —do— | 12th | | Visibility was poor during the day. The artillery of both sides was active during the day. SUVLA TRENCH being heavily shelled about 4 p.m. During the night one officer and 5 O.R. of the 1st. Bav. R.I.R. were captured by the 32nd. Inf. Bde. about R.2.c.0.3. | |

Army Form C. 2118

WAR DIARY
or
INTELLIGENCE SUMMARY

(Erase heading not required.)

11th. DIVISION "G".

JANUARY 1917.

Instructions regarding War Diaries and Intelligence Summaries are contained in F. S. Regs., Part II. and the Staff Manual respectively. Title Pages will be prepared in manuscript.

Place	Date	Hour	Summary of Events and Information	Remarks and references to Appendices
Q.26.c. 0.4.	13th.		The artillery of both sides was normal. Our patrols were active, and one sent out in R.14.d. encountered a hostile patrol. We fired on the enemy and claimed two hits. Another patrol reconnoitred in R.l.d. but encountered no enemy. Visibility was good and considerable movement was seen in L.31. and L.32 (Sheet 57D. S.E.).	
--do--	14th.		Our artillery was active during the day, and most of the fire was directed on the enemy's front line. Salvoes were also fired during the night. A big explosion was heard near BAILLESCOURT FARM about 2 a.m. Visibility was xxxx bad, and no movement could be observed.	
--do--	15th.		Visibility was poor throughout the day and little movement was seen. Divisional salvoes were fired by our artillery on enemy front and support lines during the afternoon. Patrols reconnoitred the area in R.l.d. (Sheet 57D. S.E.) between PUISIEUX ROAD and CHALK PIT, but no enemy movement was seen.	
--do--	16th.		At stated hours during the night and day our artillery fired Divisional salvoes. The enemy fired a few shells into ENGLEBELMER between 9.30 - 10.30 p.m. Visibility was bad and little movement seen. A patrol went along the whole front of the Right Brigade in front of the wire, but no enemy was seen.	
--do--	17th.	6.35 a.m.	In the early hours of the morning snow fell to the depth of several inches. At 6.35 a.m. the 32nd. Inf. Bde. under cover of our artillery barrage, attacked the German "NEST" and advanced works in R.l.c. and d. (Sheet 57 D. S.E.) with the intention of establishing a line of posts in R.l.d.8.5 - d.6.3 - d.45.40 - d.3.5 - d.2.4 - d.0.4 - c.6.3, in order to gain the crest of the spur and observation Northwards up the valley of the PUISIEUX ROAD. The attack, which was carried out by the 6th. Yorkshires on the left and the 6th. York and Lancasters on the right was xxxxxxxxxxxxxxxxxxxxxx successful, and the objective gained and consolidated. A counter-attack was reported at 10.5 a.m, but our artillery opened a barrage and the attack did not develop. The snow made all movement very visible. It would seem that the enemy evacuated the position and damaged some of his dug-outs prior to the attack. NOTE: The supposition was strengthened by the statement of a prisoner captured some days later.	

Army Form C. 2118.

WAR DIARY
or
INTELLIGENCE SUMMARY

(Erase heading not required.)

11th. Division "G"

JANUARY 1917.

Instructions regarding War Diaries and Intelligence Summaries are contained in F.S. Regs., Part II. and the Staff Manual respectively. Title Pages will be prepared in manuscript.

Place	Date	Hour	Summary of Events and Information	Remarks and references to Appendices

Q.26.c.0.4.	18th.		During the night posts were pushed forward to R.1.d.6.9 (Sheet 57D. S.E.), d.4.8 and d.6.9. The enemy were located in the gun-pit at R.1.b.0.1, from where Very Lights were being sent up. Patrols failed to get touch with the 7th. Division on our left flank. Our casualties during these operations were :-
			
			      Killed. Wounded. Missing.
			    O. O.R. O. O.R. O. O.R.
			    1 37 11 227 1 15
			
			 To safe-guard our position and to prevent the enemy counter-attacking from PUISIEUX ROAD or ARTILLERY ALLEY, at 4 p.m. a party of 50 men formed a strong point at the junction of these ways about R.1.d.6.9 and consolidated it. The relief of the Division by 63rd. Div.(R.N.) Divn. was begun. Two Battalions of 189th.Bde. relieved three Battalion of 32nd. Bde. in the line, while 2 Battalions each of 33rd. and 34th. Bdes. were relieved by 2 Battalions each of 188th. and 190th. Bdes.	

-do-	19th.		Artillery fire on both sides was normal. About 6.30 a.m. a platoon of the enemy was seen moving up PUISIEUX TRENCH. Further touch with the enemy North of R.1.d.(Sheet 57D.S.E.) was not obtained. It would appear he had withdrawn to a line of defence further back. The relief of 32nd. Bde. by 189th. Bde. of 33rd. Bde. by 188th. Bde., and of 34th. Bde. by 190th.Bde. was completed.	
-do-	20th.	12 noon.	The Command of the Divisional Area was assumed by G.O.C. 63rd. (R.N.)Div. at 12 noon. At that hour 11th. Div.H.Q. closed at Q.26.c.0.4 and opened at MARIEUX.	
MARIEUX. BERNAVILLE.	21st.		Div. H.Q. moved to BERNAVILLE, closing at MARIEUX and opening at BERNAVILLE at 11 a.m.	
BERNA- VILLE. YVRENCH.	22nd.		Div. H.Q. moved to YVRENCH, closing at BERNAVILLE and opening at YVRENCH at 11 a.m. The Division is concentrated in YVRENCH Area for training purposes.	
YVRENCH.	23rd.		Training. Hard frost and ground still covered with snow.	
-do-	24th.		Training continued. Weather fine and continued frost.	

Army Form C. 2118

WAR DIARY
or
INTELLIGENCE SUMMARY

11th. DIVISION "G".

January 1917.

(Erase heading not required.)

Instructions regarding War Diaries and Intelligence Summaries are contained in F. S. Regs., Part II. and the Staff Manual respectively. Title Pages will be prepared in manuscript.

Place	Date	Hour	Summary of Events and Information	Remarks and references to Appendices
YVRENCH.	25th.		Training continued. Weather fine and cold.	
-do-	26th.		Training continued. No change in weather.	
-do-	27th.		Training continued. No change in weather.	
-do-	28th.		Church parades. No change in weather.	
-do-	29th.		Training continued. No change in weather.	
-do-	30th.		Training continued. IV Corps order that the Division will be transferred to V Corps on or about March 1st. Another slight fall of snow.	
-do-	31st.		Training continued. Weather still fine and continued frost.	
	1st. February. 1917.			

Rodney Major
for Major General,
Commanding 11th. Division.

Army Form C. 2118

WAR DIARY
or
INTELLIGENCE SUMMARY

(Erase heading not required.)

Instructions regarding War Diaries and Intelligence Summaries are contained in F.S. Regs., Part II. and the Staff Manual respectively. Title Pages will be prepared in manuscript.

11th. DIVISION "G".

January 1917.

Place	Date	Hour	Summary of Events and Information	Remarks and references to Appendices
			S U M M A R Y.	

From 1st. to 20th. the Division was holding the trenches astride the ANCRE. Owing to continuous wet weather till 18th. inst. much work had to be done on all the trenches. The line North of the River was weakly held by a line of posts. Artillery on both sides was normal. The enemy's attitude was one of inactivity.

On 11th. inst. 34th. Bde. made an attack with 2 Coys. of 5th. Dorset Regt. in R.l.d. The objectives were gained, but a counter-attack by the enemy drove us back to our original line. On 17th. inst. the operation was repeated on a larger scale by 32nd. Bde. with 6th. York & Lancs. and 6th. Yorkshire Regts. and this time was successful.

On 20th. the Division was relieved in the line by 63rd.(R.N.) Division and moved to MARIEUX. On 21st. the move was continued to BERNAVILLE and on 23rd. the move was completed and the Division concentrated in YVRENCH Area. From 16th. to the end of the month there was a hard frost and the ground was covered with snow.

Total Prisoners captured during the month by the Division were :-
1 Officer.   26 Other Ranks.

Total casualties of the Division during the month were :-

Killed.		Wounded.		Missing.	
O.	O.R.	O.	O.R.	O.	O.R.
4	107	23	478	3	113

1st. February 1917.

(signed)

for Major General,

Commanding 11th. Division.

SECRET.   22nd. Jany. 1917.   11th. Division No. G.S. 50.

11th. Division Daily Location Return showing
position of units at 6 a.m. day after date return is rendered.

11th. Division   H.Q. YVRENCH.

32nd. Infantry Brigade. H.Q. PROUVILLE.
  9th. W. Yorks Regt. H.Q. DOMLEGER.
  6th. Yorkshire Regt. H.Q. AGENVILLE.
  8th. W. Ridings Regt. H.Q. BEAUMETZ.
  6th. York & Lancs. R. H.Q. PROUVILLE.
  32nd. M.G. Company.   do
  32nd. T.M. Battery.   do

33rd. Infantry Brigade. H.Q. CRAMONT.
  6th. Lincoln Regt.   H.Q. LE FESTEL & HANCHY.
  6th. Border Regt.   H.Q. CRAMONT.
  7th. S. Staffs. Regt. H.Q. CRAMONT.
  9th. S. Foresters.   H.Q. COULONVILLERS.
  33rd. M.G. Company.   MAISON ROLLAND.
  33rd. T.M. Battery.   -do-

34th. Infantry Brigade. H.Q. FRANSU.
  8th. Northd. Fusiliers. H.Q. DOMQUEUR.
  9th. Lancs. Fusiliers. H.Q. RIBEAUCOURT.
  5th. Dorset Regt.   H.Q. LE PLOUY.
  11th. Manchester Regt. H.Q. FRANSU.
  34th. M.G. Company.   MESNIL DOMQUEUR.
  34th. T.M. Battery.   -do-

6th. E. Yorks Regt. Pioneers. W.24.b.2.7.

11th. Divisional R.E.   H.Q. YVRENCH.
  67th. Field Company.)   W.11.d 9.4.
  68th.   "   "   )   and
  86th.   "   "   )   W.18.a 8.8.

11th. Divisional R.A.   H.Q. MAIZICOURT.   58th. F.A.B. MONTIGNY-LES-JONGLEURS.

D.A.C. & S.A.A. Sub-sect.   BEAUVOIR RIVIERE. 59th. F.A.B. BEALCOURT.

A.D.M.S. 11th. Division. H.Q. YVRENCH.   60th. F.A.B. MAIZICOURT.
  33rd Field Ambulance.   MAISON ROLLAND.
  34th. Field Ambulance.   BERNATRE.
  35th. Field Ambulance.   LONGVILLERS.

A.P.M., 11th. Division.   H.Q. YVRENCH.

D.A.D.O.S., 11th. Division. CONTEVILLE.

A.D.V.S., 11th. Division.   H.Q. YVRENCH.

11th. Divisional Train.   H.Q. YVRENCH.
  No. 2 Company.   PROUVILLE.
  No. 3   "   COULONVILLERS.
  No. 4   "   LE PLOUY.

11th. Divisional Supply Col. LE PLOUY, DOMQUEUR.

11th. Divisional Laundry.   DOMQUEUR. Billet No. A.3.

======================
S E C R E T
======================

Copy No. 22

11th Division Order No. 56.

18th January 1917.

1. The 11th Division (less Artillery) will march on the 19th and 20th January from the MARIEUX Area to the BERNAVILLE Area and on the 20th and 21st January to the YVRENCH Area.

   The Division will be clear of the MARIEUX Area by 12 noon on the 20th January.

   Moves to be carried out in accordance with attached March Tables.

   All columns will march closed up but an interval of 100 yards will be maintained between Battalions, Field Companies, Ambulances etc.,

2. Railheads will be on 20th January at BELLE EGLISE.

   21st " " CANAPLES.

   22nd. " " CONTEVILLE.

3. Units not mentioned in this order will move under the orders of the A.A. & Q.M.G.

4. D.H.Q. will close at MARIEUX at 11 a.m. on the 21st instant and will reopen at YVRENCH at 2 p.m. same day.

5. A list showing billeting accommodation in YVRENCH Area is issued with this order.

6. ACKNOWLEDGE.

Issued.

Copy No. 1. G.O.C.
       2. C.R.A.
       3. C.R.E.
       4. 32nd Inf. Bde.
       5. 33rd Inf. Bde.
       6. 34th Inf. Bde.
       7. 6th E. Yorks Regt.
       8. A.A. & Q.M.G.
       9. Signals.
       10. A.D.M.S.
       11. A.P.M.
       12. 11th Div. Train.
       13. Camp Comdt.
14 & 15. 63rd (R.N.) Divn.
       16. IV Corps.
       17. 7th Divn.
       18. 61st Divn.
       20. V Corps.
21 & 22. War Diary.
23 & 24. File.
       25. "Q" Rear.

Major,
for Lieut-Colonel,
Gen. Staff. 11th Division.

MOVE TABLE "A" ISSUED WITH 11th DIVISION ORDER No.56.

Date.	Unit.	From.	To.	Route.	Remarks.
(1) 20th Jany.	2 Battns.32nd Inf.Bde.	CANDAS.	32nd Bde. Area.	FIENVILLERS. BERNAVILLE.	To be clear of CANDAS BY 10 a.m.
(2) -do-	32nd.Inf.Bde.less 2 Ens.	RUBEMPRE. VAL DE MAISON. LA VICOGNE.	FIENVILLERS. BEUVILLE. DOMESMONT.	VAL DE MAISON.	Not to reach CANDAS before 10 a.m. To be clear by 12 noon. Bde. H.Q. FIENVILLERS.
(3) -do-	1 Battn.34th. Inf.Bde.	RAINCHEVAL. BEAUQUESNE. TERRA MESNIL.	CANDAS.	BEAUQUESNE. BEAUVAL.	Not to enter CANDAS before 12 noon. To be clear of RAINCHEVAL by 10 a.m.
(4) -do-	34th. Field Ambulance.	E.CLAIRFAYE.	PUCHEVILLERS.	RAINCHEVAL.	Not to reach RAINCHEVAL before 10 a.m.
(5) -do-	35th.Field Ambulance.	BEAUQUESNE.	VACQUERIE.	CANDAS. FIENVILLERS.	Under orders of 32nd. Inf.Bde.

NOTE: One Field Company is to be accommodated in each Brigade Area.

MOVE TABLE "B" ISSUED WITH 11th.DIVISION ORDER No.56.

Date.	Unit.	From.	To.	Route.	Remarks.
(A) 21st.Jany.	32nd.Inf.Bde. less 2 Battns.	FIENVILLERS. BEUBEUIL. DOMESCOURT.	32nd.Bde. Area.	Any route.	To be clear of FIENVILLERS by 9.30 a.m. Bde. H.Q. PROUVILLE.
(B) -do-	33rd.Inf.Bde.	PUCHEVILLERS.	GEZAINCOURT. LONGUEVILLETTE.	BEAUQUESNE. TERRA MESNIL.	Not to enter BEAUQUESNE before 9.30 a.m.
(C) -do-	2 Battns. 34th. Inf.Bde.	CANDAS.	34th.Bde. Area.	FIENVILLERS.	Not to enter FIENVILLERS before 9.30 a.m. To be clear of CANDAS by 10.30 a.m.
(D) -do-	34th.Inf.Bde. less 2 Battns.	RAINCHEVAL. BEAUQUESNE. TERR. MESNIL.	FIENVILLERS. BEUBEUIL.	BEAUVAL. CANDAS.	To be clear of BEAUQUESNE by 9.30 a.m.
(E) -do-	34th.Field Amb.	PUCHEVILLERS.	VACQUERIE.		Under orders of 34th. Inf.Bde.
(F) -do-	33rd. Field Amb.	VAL DE MAISON.	GEZAINCOURT.		Under orders of 33rd. Inf.Bde.
(G) -do-	35th.Field Amb.	V.CQUERIE.	LONGVILLERS.		Under orders of 32nd. Inf.Bde.
(H) -do-	Divnl.Sig.Coy (less Bde.Section.)	MARIEUX.	BERNAVILLE.	Any.	

MOVE TABLE "C" ISSUED WITH 11th.DIVISION ORDER No.56.

Date.	Unit.	From.	To.	Route.	Remarks.
(1) 22nd Jany.	33rd.Inf.Bde.	GEZAINCOURT. LONGUEVILLETTE.	33rd.Bde. Area.	FIENVILLERS.	Not to enter FIENVILLERS before 9.30 a.m. Bde. H.Q. CRAMONT.
(2) -do-	34th.Inf.Bde. less 2 Battns.	FIENVILLERS. BRUNEUIL.	34th.Bde. Area.	BERNEVILLE.	To be clear of FIENVILLERS by 9.30 a.m. Bde. H.Q. at LA PLOUY.
(3) -do-	33rd.Field Amb.	LE MEILLARD.	MAISON ROLLAND.		Under orders of 33rd.Inf.Bde.
(4) -do-	34th. Field Amb.	VACQUERIE.	BERNATRE.		Under orders of 34th. Inf.Bde.
(5) -do-	Divnl.Sig.Co. (less two sectors)	BERNAVILLE.	YVRENCH.	any.	

BILLETTING ACCOMMODATION. YVRENCH AREA.

No.	Place.	TOTAL ACCOMMDN.			WATER.			Remarks.	Allotted to
		Off.	O.Rs.	Horses.	Men.	Horses.			
1.	YVRENCH.	37	1,060	182	Pumps & wells.	Troughs reqd.			11th Divn. Hdqrs.
2.	CONTEVILLE.	14	550						11th Divn. Train.
3.	BERNATRE.	8	380						Fd. Amb. ?
4.	PROUVILLE.	36	1,527	21	4 wells.	5 ponds.			32nd Bde. Hdqrs, & 32nd Bde.
5.	LONGVILLERS.	27	865	110	7 "	Pond.			32nd Bde. and 1 Fd. Amb.
6.	DOMLEGER.	25	745	44	6 "	2 Ponds.			32nd Bde.
7.	AGENVILLE.	12	600		Wells.	Pond			32nd Bde.
8.	MAIZICOURT.	40	1,000		Wells.	Pond.		Pump and troughs reqd.	11th D.A., temp. to 32 Bde.
9.	ORAMONT.	52	1,175		10 wells.	Pond.			33rd Bde. H.Q. and 33rd Bde.
10.	HANCHY.	8	305	80	Wells.				33rd Bde.
11.	FESTEL.	5	100		Wells.				33rd Bde.
12.	MAISON ROLLAND.	30	1,000	50	Wells.	Pond.			33rd Bde. 1 Fd. Amb.
13.	COULONVILLERS.	23	1,014	70	5 wells.	3 ponds.			33rd Bde.
14.	YVRENCHEUX.	27	1,132	87	Wells.	Pond.			6th E.York. R. (P) temp. to 33rd Brigade.
15.	LE PLOUY.	30	600	65	Wells.	Pond.			34th Bde. H.Q. and 34th Bde.
16.	DOMQUEUR.	45	1,400	65	Wells.	Pond.			34th Bde.
17.	MESNIL DOMQUEUR.	23	800		Wells & Pumps.	Pond.			34th Bde.
18.	FRANSU.	25	700		Wells.	Pond.			34th Bde.
19.	BEAUMETZ.	29	949	105	Wells.	Wells only.			32nd Bde. temporarily to 34th Bde.
20.	MONT LOUIS FARM.	4	250	6	1 well.	Pond.		Well very poor.	11th D.A.C.
21.	BEALCOURT.	25	800		Wells.	River.		R. AUTHIE.	11th D.A.
22.	BEAUVOIR.	10	500		Wells.	River.		R. AUTHIE.	11th D.A.
23.	ST. ACHEUL.	10	265	105	7 wells.	Pond.		Troughs required.	11th D.A.
24.	MONTIGNY.	25	600	10	4 pumps. Wells & pumps.	Pond.		Troughs required.	11th D.A.

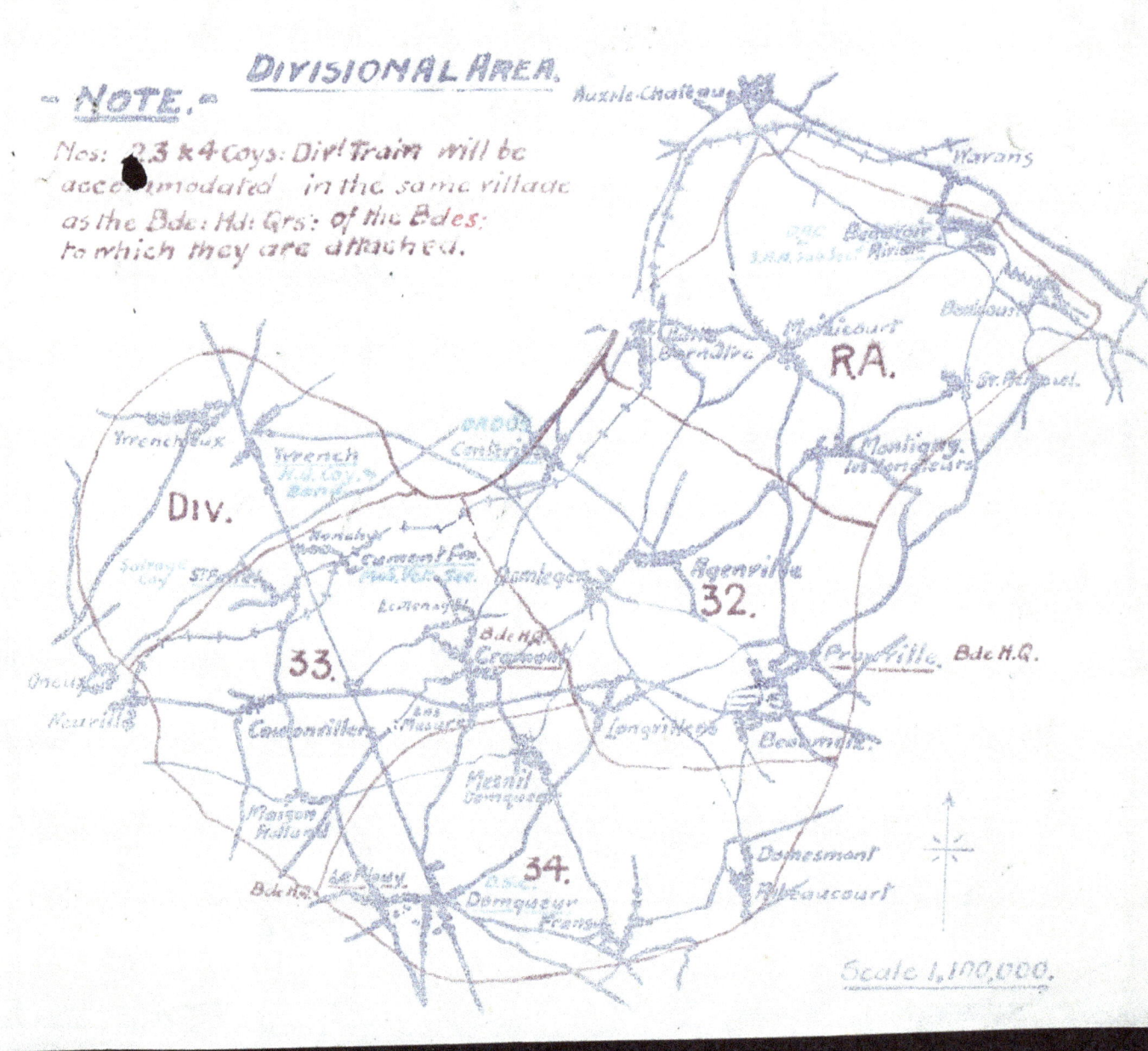

Artillery Orders follow later.

```
==========
S E C R E T
==========      11th Division Order No. 55.        Copy No. _____
```

Reference Maps   15th Jany. 1917.
1/5,000 BOIS D'HOLLANDE
        PENDANT COPSE
        BEAUMONT HAMEL
        REDAN. and
1/1,250 Special Map.

1. On a date to be communicated later the 11th Division will advance the line of forward posts in R.1.d. and c. to the West of a small ridge running East and West on the line

   (1) R.1.d.8.3.- (2) R.1.d.64.40.- (3) R.1.d.4.5.- (4) R.1.d.25.50

   (5) R.1.d.0.4.- (6) R.1.c.8.5. - (7) R.1.c.6.2. (on ARTILLERY

   LANE) (Marked green on special map):

   Posts 1 and 2 to guard the right flank and keep banks North of line R.1.d.7.5 to R.1.d.9.5 under fire.

   Posts 6 and 7 to guard the left flank.

   This will necessitate the capture of all German works between the above mentioned line and the existing forward posts (marked Blue on special map). These works are believed to be :-

   1. Dug-out and Machine Gun in Right Ridge R.1.d.4.3.

   2. Large dug-out in HOOK RIDGE R.1.d.3.3.

   3. CHALK PIT between HOOK RIDGE and LEFT RIDGE R.1.d.20.25.

   4. Strong points in LEFT RIDGE R.1.d.15.40 and R.1.d.17.45 with Machine Guns at latter place.

   5. Dug-out in LEFT RIDGE R.1.d.30.45.

   6. Dug-out at R.1.d.10.35 (COCKED HAT).

   7. Dug-out in ruined battery R.1.d.0.4 to R.1.d.0.3.

2. The 32nd Brigade is detailed for this task.

3. Simultaneously with this advance the 3 banks East of the PUISIEUX ROAD North of the line R.1.d.7.5 to R.1.d.9.5 will beraided by the 32nd Brigade; with the object of protecting the right flank of the main attack West of the Road and of destroying Machine Guns believed to be located about R.1.d.85.65 and R.1.d.7.7 and all dug-outs. The PUISIEUX ROAD about R.1.d.65.85 will also be searched.
   Raiding troops East of the Road will be back behind Green Line by ZERO + 80 minutes.

4. (a) The area to be captured contains a number of dug-outs which will be dealt with systematically, by especially equipped parties detailed for this duty. It is particularly important that the large dug-out in the HOOK RIDGE be blocked or blown in about R.1.d.4.5 and further North about R.1.d.4.6.

   (b) The objective once gained will be held by posts constructed so as to command the ground to the North. These posts will be consolidated as rapidly as possible. as well as a Support line R.1.d.35.20 - CHALK PIT - R.1.d.10.35 - R.1.d.0.4.
                       Material to assist in consolidation

-2-

consolidation will be dumped as far forward as possible prior to the attack.

(c) Every effort will be made to maintain touch with the new advanced line when gained, and no means of communication will be neglected.

(d) Careful arrangements will be made to ensure an adequate supply of S.A.A., grenades, rations and water for the attacking troops.

5. 1 Battalion 34th Brigade will march from FORCEVILLE to-morrow and will be located as under :-

H.Q. and 2 Companies, MESNIL ready to move forward into the old German front line near 32nd Bde. H.Q.

2 Companies ENGLEBELMER ready to move to MESNIL.

Moves to be completed by 4-30 p.m. 16th.

This battalion will be placed at the disposal of the O.C. 32nd Brigade up to mid-night 18th/19th instant.
Battalion H.Q. and 32nd Brigade H.Q. will be connected by a direct telephone wire.

6. Artillery arrangements for covering the attacks will be as shown on the Table attached.
In addition to the 11th Division Artillery the following artillery will be supporting the attack :-
63rd Division Artillery.
2 Brigades 61st Division Artillery.
Portion of 7th Division Artillery.
1 6" Howitzer Battery.
The 3rd., 4th., and 5th Corps Heavy Artillery will also support the attack by engaging various targets and in counter battery work.

7. The C.R.E. will place 2 Sections R.E., and 1 Company 6th East Yorks (Pioneers) at the disposal of the O.C. 32nd Brigade to :-

(a) Provide parties to assist in the blocking of the dug-out in the HOOK RIDGE.

(b) To consolidate on the night after the attack a line of posts R.1.d.35.20 - CHALK PIT - R.1.d.10.35 to R.1.d.0.4 to form a support line to the now forward posts.

8. The 32nd: and 33rd: Machine Gun Companies will carry out the tasks detailed in 11th Division Order No. 52 paras 6 and 7., and in addition a Vickers Gun will be pushed up near post 9 to keep HOOK RIDGE N. of R.1.d.4.5 under fire. Certain 5th Corps Machine Guns will also keep road junction R.1.d.6.9 and ARTILLERY ALLEY under continuous long range fire from ZERO hour onwards.

9. A contact aeroplane of the 4th Squadron R.F.C. marked with a black panel on each lower plane fixed in the centre of trailing edge will act with the attacking troops as soon as it is light enough to see.

Troops will light red flares in the bottom of shell holes at ZERO + 60 minutes and at intervals after that hour.

-3-

10. To supplement existing S.O.S. arrangements, each Company Commander will be provided with Very Light pistols, and in case of necessity the following subsidiary S.O.S. signals will be made use of :-

    3 Very Lights fired in quick succession

        1 to Right
        1 Vertically
        1 to Left.

Observers in rear seeing this signal will immediately send up the usual S.O.S. Rocket Signal.

11. To simulate an/attack, the Artillery of the 2nd., 18th., and 61st Divisions will bombard at ZERO

    COULEE and GRANDCOURT Trenches from M.8.a.11 to R.11.c.00

    and later

    BOOM RAVINE and SOUTH MIRAUMONT Trench from R.6.c.5.4 to R.10.b.2.8.

12. Brigade H.Q. will be at Q.18.a.8.2.

13. Orders regarding synchronising of watches will be issued later.

14. ZERO hour will be notified later.

15. ACKNOWLEDGE.

Issued at 6-30 p.m.

                      J. D. Coleridge.
                                Lieut-Colonel,
                        Gen.Staff.11th Division.

Copy No.1. A.D.C. for G.O.C.
     2. G.S.O.1.
     3. A.A. & Q.M.G.
     4. C.R.A.
     5. C.R.E.
     6. 32nd Inf.Bde.
     7. 33rd Inf. Bde.
     8. 34th Inf. Bde.
     9. 6th E. Yorks R. (P).
    10. Signals.
    11. A.D.M.S.
    12. IV Corps.
    13. 7th Division.
    14. 61st Division.
15 & 16. War Diary.
17 & 18. File.
    19. Gas Officer.
    20. 4th Squad. R.F.C.

To:- ....   11th. Division No. G.S. 869.

    ....
                                          S E C R E T.

           Reference 11th. Division Order No.55.

           The following will be inserted :-

Para 5.   The two battalions 33rd. Inf. Bde. at ENGLEBELMER
           will be held in readiness to move forward from ZERO
           hour onwards as follows :-

               6th. Borders.   Two companies will stand to
                                arms from ZERO hour in instant
                                readiness to move.
                                Two companies will remain in
                                billets ready to move from ZERO
                                hour.

               7th. S. Staffords. Will remain in billets ready
                                to move from ZERO hour.

           All roads and approaches to front line from
ENGLEBELMER will be at once reconnoitred by the officers of
these battalions.

Para 13.   Watches will be synchronised as laid down in
           IV Corps H.R.S. 609/14 dated 15/1/17 forwarded under
           11th. Division No. G.S. 861.

Para 14.   ZERO hour will be at 6.35 a.m. on 17th. January.

Para 9.   Erase last para and insert -

           " Troops will light red flares in the bottom
of shell holes at ZERO + 60 minutes and on signals
from contact aeroplane. The signals will be :-

(a)   The firing of a single white Very Light.

(b)   Blasts on a Klaxon horn.

           ACKNOWLEDGE.

                                                Major,
16th. January 1917.   Gen. Staff, 11th. Division.

To _____

Following amendments and additions in March Tables issued with 11th Division Order No. 54 of 14th January are published :-

	Date.	Unit.	From.	To.	Route.	Remarks.
1.	Jan.18th.	(a) 3 Battns 32nd. Inf. Bde.	Line.	RUBEMPRE.	By bus.	3 Battns. will occupy billets vacated by 2 Bns. 186th.Inf.Bde.
		(d) 34th.Inf.Bde. less 3 Battns.	FORCEVILLE.	RAINCHEVAL.		Bde.Hd.Qrs. to BEAUQUESNE.
2.	Jan.19th.	(b) 32nd.Inf.Bde. less 3 Battns.	Reserve Trenches Left Sector.	RAINCHEVAL.	By bus.	
	add (c)	1 Battn.34th. Inf.Bde.	Q.2c.c.O.4.	MARIEUX TAILLY.	By bus.	
3.	Jan.20th. add	11th.Div.Sig.Coy. (less Bde.sections)				

18th.January 1917.

R.[illegible] Major,
General Staff,11th.Division.

TO:- File   11th.Division No. G.S. 873.

PROVISIONAL.

AMENDMENTS TO 11th.DIVISION ORDER No.54.
==

The following amendments and additions are published with reference to Tables issued with 11th.Division Order No. 54 of 14th. January 1917. :-

1. <u>Jan.18th.</u> (a)   The 2 Battns. of 32nd.Inf.Bde. will be 6th. Yorkshire Regt. and 6th.York & Lancs.Regt. leaving 9th.W.Yorks Regt., 8th.W.Ridings Regt. and 11th. Manchester Regt. (34th.Inf.Bde) in reserve.

2. <u>Jan.18th.</u> (d)   Delete 34th.Inf.Bde. less 2 Battns. and substitute -

    1 Battn.   )
    M.G.Company.   )   34th.Inf.Bde.
    L.T.M.Battery.   )

3. <u>Jan.19th.</u> add -

    (e)   34th.Inf.Bde. H.Q. to BEAUQUESNE.

    (f)   1 Battn. 34th.Inf.Bde. from line to -

          Batt. FORCEVILLE.   Not to move before 4 p.m.

    this bn. will be joined by 1 Cd. from the Yellow Line en route.

4. <u>Jan.20th.</u>   Delete (c)

    substitute -

    (c)   1 Battn. 34th.Inf.Bde. from ARQUEVES to

          RAINCHEVAL.   )   To clear ARQUEVES
          BEAUQUESNE.   )
          TERRA MESNIL)   by 12 noon.

    (d)   1 Battn. 34th.Inf.Bde. from LEALVILLERS to
                                                    CANDAS.

          To be clear of LEALVILLERS by 12 noon.

add (e)   1 Battn. 34th.Inf.Bde. from FORCEVILLE to

          RAINCHEVAL.   )   Rpute - ACHEUX,
          BEAUQUESNE.   )   LEALVILLERS, and
          TERRA MESNIL)   ARQUEVES.

    not to reach ARQUEVES before 12 noon.

                                J. D. Coleridge Lieut.Colonel,
16th.January 1917.   General Staff, 11th. Division.

=============
S E C R E T.
=============

Copy No. 1....
18th. Jan. 1917.

11th. Division Order No. 54.

1. The 11th. Division (less Artillery) will be relieved in the line by the 63rd.(R.N.) Division (less Artillery) on 18th., 19th. and 20th. January, and will move to the MARIEUX Area in accordance with the attached Move Table.

2. All details of the relief of Infantry Brigades will be made direct between Brigadiers concerned.
Command of Brigade Sectors will pass to incoming Brigadiers at times to be fixed by Brigadiers concerned on the completion of the relief of the Sector.
Completion of reliefs will be reported to D.H.Q. by wiring the code word "IMBROS".

3. The 11th. Divnl. Artillery will remain in the line temporarily and will be attached to the 63rd.(R.N.) Division.

4.(a) The 3 Field Companies and 6th. E. Yorks Regt.(Pioneers) will pass under the orders of the C.E. IVth. Corps on 18th. January and from that date will be ready to move to new huts etc., Vide move Table "A".

(b) Permanent working parties attached to the 3 Field Companies, Divnl. R.E. will rejoin their units on the 17th. inst. under arrangements to be made direct between C.R.E. and Infantry Brigade Commanders.

(c) Permanent working parties on the YELLOW LINE will be relieved by parties from the 189th. Infantry Brigade on 19th. Jany. One officer per Company from 11th. Division will remain with companies of 189th. Infantry Brigade until 20th. inst. to hand over work.

(d) The R.E. Officer, superintending permanent R.A. and Infantry Artillery O.P. construction party will remain behind for a few days to explain the work to incoming Division.

5. The A.D.M.S. will arrange for the Medical reliefs vide attached programme, in consultation with A.D.M.S. 63rd.(R.N.) Divn.

6. The following troops attached or belonging to this Division will be attached to 63rd. (R.N.) Division from 12 noon on 20th. inst.

        11th. Divisional Artillery.
        175th. Tunnelling Company.

7. Separate instructions have been issued regarding the handing over of huts and billets, R.E. and Ordnance Stores, and Supplies.

8. Separate instructions have been issued regarding the handing over of maps, codes, trench stores etc.

9. Distances of 200 yards between companies and of 500 yards between larger units will be maintained during the march into the MARIEUX Area.

10/.

- 2 -

10. 11th Division Headquarters will close at Q.26.c.0.4. at 12 noon on 20th January and will reopen at HARIEUX at the same hour.

   G.O.C. 63rd (R.N.) Division will assume command of Divisional Area at 12 noon on 20th January.

11. All units not mentioned in this order will move under the orders of A.A. & Q.M.G.

12. ACKNOWLEDGE.

Issued at *12 noon*
J. D. Coleridge
Lieut-Colonel,
Gen. Staff. 11th Division.

```
Copy No. 1.   A.D.C. for G.O.C.
         2.   C.R.A.
         3.   C.R.E.
         4.   32nd Inf. Bde.
         5.   33rd Inf. Bde.
         6.   34th Inf. Bde.
         7.   6th E. Yorks Regt.
         8.   A.A. & Q.M.G.
         9.   Signals.
        10.   A.D.M.S.
        11.   A.P.M.
        12.   11th Div. Train.
        13.   Camp. Commdt.
    14 & 15   63rd.(R.N.) Divn.
        16    IV Corps.
        17    7th. Divn.
        18    C.R.E. YELLOW LINE.
        19    61st.Divn.
        20    V Corps.
    21 & 22   War Diary.
    23 & 24   File.
```

Move Table "A" issued with 11th D.O. No. 54.

Date.	Unit.	From.	To.	Route.	Remarks.
18th Jan.	(a) 2 Battns. 32nd Inf. Bde.	Line Left Sector.	RUBEMPRE-VAL DE MAISON - LA VIGOIGNE Area.	Move by bus.	On relief by 2 Battns. 189th Inf. Bde.
-do-	(b) 2 Battns. 33rd Inf. Bde.	ENGLEBELMER.	FORCEVILLE.		On relief by 2 Battns. 188th Inf. Bde.
-do-	(c) 35th Fd. Amb.	LANCASHIRE DUMP.	BEAUQUESNE.	RAINCHEVAL-LEALVILLERS.	Will be relieved by 1st Field Ambulance on night 18th/19th.
-do-	(d) 34th Inf. Bde.) less 2 Battns.)	FORCEVILLE.	RAINCHEVAL BEAUQUESNE TERRA MESNIL Area	ACHEUX LEALVILLERS ARQUEVES.	Not to pass LEALVILLERS before 12-30 p.m. Bde. Hd. Qrs. at BEAUQUESNE.
-do-	(e) 67th Fd. Coy. R.E. 68th Fd. Coy. R.E. 86th Fd. Coy. R.E. 6th E. Yorks Regt. (Pioneers).	Q.28.d.2.7. Q.30.d.2.2. N.3.d.3.7. {Q.26.b.1.1 { MESNIL. {Q.36.c.7.7.	To billets in W.11.d.9.4. & billets in W.18.a.2.@. USNA HILL. N.24.b.2.7.	Under orders to be given by IV Corps	Accommodation is equal to 3 Field Companies.

Move Table "B" issued with 11th D.O. No.54.

Date.		Unit.	From.	To.	Route.	Remarks.
19th Jan.	(a)	93rd Inf. Bde. less 2 Battns.	Trenches Right Sector.	ENGLEBELMER.	—	On relief by 188th Inf. Bde. Bde. Hd. Qrs. at FORCEVILLE.
—do—	(b)	72nd Inf. Bde. less 2 Battns.	Reserve Trenches & Left Sector.	RUDEMPRE—VAL DE MAISON— LA VICOIGNE Area.	By bus. Dismounted personnel by bus. Transport as for 33rd Field Ambulance.	Bde. Hd. Qrs. at RUDEMPRE.
—do—	(c)	33rd Field Amb.	Q.31.b.9.7. ENGLESART.	VAL DE MAISON.	RAINCHEVAL – LEALVILLERS – VAREINES – HEDAUVILLE.	On relief by No. 2 Field Ambulance night of 19th/20th.
—do—	(d)	2 Battns 32nd Inf. Bde.	RUBEMPRE VAL DE MAISON LA VICOIGNE.	CANDAS.	VAL DE MAISON.	

Move Table "C" issued with 11th D.O. No.54.

Date.	Unit.	From.	To.	Route.	Remarks.
20th Jan.	(a) 2 Battns 33rd Inf. Bde.	ENGLEBELMER.	PUCHEVILLERS.	By bus.	On relief by 2 Battns 188th Inf. Bde.
—do—	(b) 33rd Inf. Bde.) FORCEVILLE. loss 2 Battns.)		PUCHEVILLERS.	VARENNES HARPONVILLE TOUTENCOURT.	Not to pass TOUTENCOURT before 12 noon.
—do—	(c) 2 Battns 34th Inf. Bde.	ARQUEVES LEALVILLERS.	RAINCHEVAL BEAUQUESNE TERRA MESNIL.	ARQUEVES RAINCHEVAL.	To clear ARQUEVES by 12 noon.

To:-................... 11th.Division No. G.S. 714.

.... S E C R E T.

The following addition is to be made to 11th. Division Order No. 58.

" Para 2 (d), The 61st. Division will carry out a raid on "Z" day at the same time as the minor operations by 13th. Corps and 11th. Division".

9th.January 1917.
J. E. Coleridge Lieut.Colonel,
Gen. Staff, 11th.Division.

11th. DIVISION ORDER No.52.

SECRET.

Copy No. 17.

9th. Jan. 1917.

1. The XIIIth. Corps will be carrying out certain operations on X. Y. Z days. (dates will be notified later).

2. The IVth. Corps will render the following assistance:-

    (a) Bombardments in the proximity of the hostile line about to be attacked.

    (b) Deliberate bombardment and wire cutting on X. and Y. days and a simulation of an attack on Z day on

        i.   GRANDCOURT TRENCH from R.12.c.9.9 to R.16.c.9.8.

        ii. South MIRAUMONT Trench from R.6.c.5.5 to R.10.b.5.9.

        iii. New Trench from R.10.b.2.5 to R.10.c.2.8.

    (c) A minor operation by 11th.Division to destroy certain hostile M.G. Emplacements and push forward their own advanced posts in R.1.c. and d. to gain the ridge which runs East and West in that area.

3. As regards para 2 (c) above :-

    (a) The operation will be carried out on Z day by the Brigade occupying the line on that date, as the date is still somewhat uncertain both the 32nd. and 34th. Brigades will draw up plans for the attack.

    (b) The line to be occupied by posts will be R.1.d.8.4 - R.1.d.6.4 - R.1.d.4.5 - R.1.d.0.4½ - R.1.c.7.2 and will necessitate the capture of any German works South of that line including the works about R.1.d.0.4.

    (c) The posts when occupied will be immediately consolidated. Material for consolidation will be dumped as far forward as possible prior to the attack and parties for carrying material will be detailed to follow the assaulting troops.

    (d) The area to be captured is believed to contain a number of dug-outs, special arrangements will, therefore, be made to deal with any enemy who may be taking cover in them.

4. Prior to Z day, the Heavy Artillery will carry out the tasks detailed in attached Appendix "A".

5. Artillery barrage arrangements for covering the/attacks are as per Appendix "B" attached.

6. Arrangements will be made by the Brigades in the line to barrage with Machine Gun fire immediately previous to and during the assault the ground N. of the line mentioned in para 3 (b) and the approaches to this line. 33rd. M.G. Company will give especial attention to PUISIEUX TRENCH.

- 2 -

7. The 33rd.Inf.Bde. will not make any active demonstration, but O.G. 1 and 2 and GRANDCOURT will be kept under careful observation and machine gun and rifle fire will be brought to bear on any hostile troops seen to be moving in that neighbourhood.

8. The C.R.E. will place 2 sections R.E. and 1 Company 6th.E.Yorks Pioneers at the disposal of the Brigadier making the attack to:

    (a) Assist in consolidation.

    (b) Join up the existing adv nced posts to form a continuous line.

9. Brigade Headquarters will be at Q.18.a.8.2.

10. ZERO hour will be notified later.

11. ACKNOWLEDGE.

T. S. Coleridge Lieut.Colonel,
General Staff, 11th.Division

Issued at 1-0 pm

Copy No. 1 to A.D.C. for G.O.C.
        2   G.S.O. I.
        3   A.A. / Q.M.G.
        4   C.R.A.
        5   C.R.E
        6   32nd.Inf.Bde.
        7   33rd. "   "
        8   34th. "   "
        9   6th.E.Yorks.
       10   Signal Coy.
       11   A.D.M.S.
       12   IVth Corps
       13
       14   7th Division.
       15   61st. Division.
   16 & 17   War Diary.
   18 & 19   File.

APPENDIX "A".

HEAVY ARTILLERY TASKS.

        R.1.d.0.3.   Old gun pit.
        R.1.d.1.5.   Old gun pit.
        R.1.d.1½.2½   Rubble heap.
        R.1.d.3.5.   Chalk pit.
        R.1.d.5.8.to)
        R.1.b.3.1.)   Dug-outs.

About L.32.c.3.2. - 2.3. Consolidated shell-holes.

Trench system L.32. central :- L.32.b.0.2 - L.32.d.1.6 -
                             L.32.c.9.4 - L.32.d.0.0 -
                             R.2.b.0.9 - 0.6 - 3.7.

        R.2.b.9.2.   O.P.

=*=*=*=*=

APPENDIX "B" will be forwarded later.

SECRET.

Copy No..........

11th. DIVISION ORDER No. 51.   8th. Jan. 1917.

1. The 32nd. Inf. Bde. will relieve the 34th. Inf. Bde. in the Left Sector on the nights of the 10th/11th. and 11th/12th. January 1917.

2. Details to be arranged by Brigadiers concerned.

3. O.C. 32nd. Inf. Bde. will take steps to ensure that the work now in hand by the 34th. Inf. Bde. will be continued. Reconnaissances to begin without delay.

4. The same number of busses as were provided for the last relief will be available.

5. This order is liable to modification.

6. ACKNOWLEDGE.

J. D. Coleridge

Lieut. Colonel,
Gen. Staff, 11th. Division.

8th. January 1917.

```
Copy No. 1 to 32nd. Inf. Bde.
         2    34th.  "    "
         3    C.R.A.
         4    C.R.E.
         5    "Q".
       6 & 7  War Diary.
       8 & 9  File.
```

SECRET.

Copy No. 1st

11th Division Order No. 50.

5-1-17.

1. The 63rd Divl. Artillery will move tomorrow, 6th January into 11th Divl. Area, where it will come under orders of C.R.A. 11th Division.
    All arrangements have been made between C.R.A's concerned.

2. The Artillery covering the 11th Divisional Front will be grouped as follows from midnight 7th/8th inst.

    (a) 59th Group. (59th F.A.B.) under command of Lieut. Colonel A.F. THOMSON, R.F.A. H.Q. as at present.
    (b) 58th Group. (58th and 223rd F.A.Bs) under command of Lieut. Colonel W.H.HORTON. R.F.A. H.Q. as at present.
    (c) 60th Group. (60th & 317th F.A.Bs) under command of Lieut. Colonel L.H.D.BROUGHTON R.F.A. H.Q. as at present.
    (d) 315th Group. (315th F.A.B.) under command of Lieut.Colonel H.HIGGINBOTTOM R.F.A. H.Q. Q.34.a.4.0.

3. Positions of 63rd D.A. batteries as follows :-

    315th F.A.B.   A Bty.   Q.22.a.55.90.
                    B Bty.   Q.22.a.9.9.
                    C Bty.   Q.22.c.9.1.
                    D Bty.   Q.22.c.8.6.

    317th F.A.B.   A Bty.   Q.23.d.0.6.
                    B Bty.   Q.23.b.9.4.
                    C Bty.   R.25.a.5.7.
                    D Bty.   Q.24.c.7.5.

    223rd F.A.B.   A Bty.   R.26.d.0.4.
                    B Bty.   R.25.c.6.5.
                    C Bty.   R.25.c.4.6.
                    D Bty.   R.25.c.4.3.

4. 63rd D.A. Batteries will be in action ready to open fire by 6-0 a.m. 8th January.

5. 63rd D.A.C. will march to FORCEVILLE on afternoon of 6th January.

6. Distances to be observed on the march, at least 200 yards between batteries and similar units, and 500 yards between Brigades.

7. ACKNOWLEDGE.

Issued at 6 p.m.

for Lieut-Colonel,
Gen.Staff. 11th Division.

Copy No. 1. C.R.A.
        2. 32nd Inf. Bde.
        3. 33rd Inf. Bde.
        4. 34th Inf. Bde.
        5. A.A.& Q.M.G.
        6. Signals.
        7. A.D.M.S.
        8. A.P.M.
        9. 11th Div. Train.
        10. 63rd Div.
        11. 7th Div.
        12. 61st Div.
    13 & 14. War Diary.
    15 & 16. File.

Secret   Copy No

DEFENCE SCHEME

S E C R E T.

11th. DIVISION DEFENCE SCHEME.

INDEX.

Chapter 1. Description of the 11th. Division Area and Defensive System

1. Description of the Country.
2. Chief Tactical Features.
3. The Defensive System.
4. Projected Works.
5. Distribution of Troops.
6. Places of Assembly.
7. Lines of Approach.
8. Dug-out accomodation.

Chapter 2. Instructions as to the Action of the Troops.

1. Chief Objects to be kept in view.
2. General Principles.
3. Forms of Attack to be anticipated.
4. Action to be taken against various forms of attack.
5. Considerations affecting the Artillery Defence.
6. Artillery arrangements.

Chapter 3. Action of the Corps Reserve.

1. Corps Reserve.
2. Moves of Reserve Infantry Brigades.
3. Action of a fourth Division if allotted to support Division.

Chapter 4. Administrative Arrangements.

1. Supply of R.E. Materials.
2. Supply of Ammunition and Supplies.
3. Medical arrangements.
4. Stations of Traffic Control Posts and Battle Police.

APPENDICES.

Appendix 1.   Boundaries of Areas and Distribution of Troops.

Appendix 2. (a) Mutual Artillery Support between adjacent Divisions of 4th. and 13th. Corps.

(b) Mutual Artillery Support between Divisions of 4th. Corps.

(c) Action of 4th. Corps Heavy Artillery in case of hostile attack. "Defend 11th. Division".

(d) Position for reinforcing batteries and for defence of Rear Lines.

(e) S.O.S.

Appendix 3.   Supply of R.E. Stores and Materials.

Appendix 4.   Gas Alarms.

Appendix 5.   List of Dug-outs in 11th. Divisional Area.

Appendix 6.   Liaison between Infantry and Artillery.

Maps.

Map "A".   Boundaries of the Area generally and Tram Lines.

Map "B".   Trench Map showing rear lines and Machine gun positions.

Map "C".   Map showing 11th. Divisional Artillery Defensive barrages.

Map "D".   Bridges over the ANCRE.

Map "E".   Water Map.

Map "F".   Road Control Posts and Straggler's Posts Map.

Map "G".   Dug-out Map.

Map "H".   Communications.

H E A D Q U A R T E R S.

Headquarters IVth. Corps.   SENLIS.

Headquarters Right Division.   USNA HILL.

Headquarters Centre Division.   BOUZINCOURT. W.7.b.2.7.

Headquarters 11th.Division.   Q.26.c.0.4.

Headquarters Brigade holding)
            "C" Section.   )   PAISLEY DUMP, Q.30.c.7.2.

Headquarters Brigade holding)
            "D" Section.   )   Q.18.a.8.2.

Headquarters Support Brigade.   FORCEVILLE.

SECRET.

11th Division DEFENCE SCHEME.

January 1917.

CHAPTER 1.

Description of the 11th Division Area and Defensive System.

MAPS "A", "B" and "C".

1. DESCRIPTION OF THE COUNTRY.
The position held by the 11th Division lies on both banks of the River ANCRE. On the Left bank it has a length of about 1,200 yards, on the Right bank 1,600 yards, exclusive of the marshy valley of the river which is 400 yards across.

On the left bank the front line position follows down the slope of the spur facing GRANDCOURT from SCHWABEN REDOUBT to the River. As far South as R.14.d.9.3. there is a swampy depression (BATTERY VALLEY) separating it from the enemy's lines. The post at R.14.d.9.3 however is only separated from a hostile post about R.15.c.1.5. by a hundred yards of open ground.

The Reserve Line follows the old German trench called the HANSA LINE.

The Intermediate and Rearward Reserve Lines are shown on Map "B".

On the right bank of the ANCRE the position forms a sharp salient, and follows the lower slopes of three spurs which run down from CULINCAMPS to the River.

The front system, Firing, Support, and Reserve Lines, lies on the two foremost of these, and the Intermediate and Rearward Reserve Line on the rear one.

5.

The whole area is pulverised with shell holes and movement even - on foot in Winter, except after frost is most difficult. Trenches must be revetted directly they are dug otherwise they fall in immediately, those in existence require constant attention cleaning and draining. Except in the river valley the country is open.

The valley of the ANCRE is flooded in the Winter, and cannot be crossed except at made crossing places.

2. CHIEF TACTICAL FEATURES.

(a) The high ground round about SCHWABEN REDOUBT which gives cover and command and hence a great advantage over the enemy.

(b) The marshy valley of the ANCRE which hampers intercommunication.

(c) The spur on which BEAUCOURT stands; which, if lost would give the enemy command of the ANCRE Valley and spoil it as an avenue of approach.

3. THE DEFENSIVE SYSTEM.

The Defensive System consists of :-

(i) The Front System - Front Line, Support Line, Reserve Line (under construction).
(ii) The Intermediate Line (under construction).
(iii) The Reserve Line (now being reconnoitred).
(iv) Various Switches (not yet surveyed).

5. PROJECTED WORKS.

(a) Front System.

The Front, Support and Reserve Lines will be made continuous, as soon as the portions of the trench held by bodies of Infantry are made habitable.

Each Line will be well wired, and will have ample dug-out accomodation for its garrison.

The provision of at least one communication path per Brigade Front, and a boarded communication trench between Support and Front Line at least every 200 yards will be undertaken.

The Support Line has been so sited as to develop to the utmost the employment of Machine Guns, dug-outs for the Machine Guns being the first item to be constructed.

6.

(b) <u>The Intermediate Line</u> (YELLOW LINE) is in process of being wired, and dug-outs are being constructed, each designed for the accomodation of the Detachments of 2 Machine Guns and a Section of Infantry, at intervals of about 200 yards.

(c) <u>The Reserve Line</u>.

Work on this Line will be undertaken when the more forward Lines are completed.

(d) <u>Various Switches</u>.

Divisions are responsible for the reconnaissance, construction and maintenance of Switches from the Front System to the Intermediate Line. PEEL TRENCH is of the nature of a Switch.

Switches from the Intermediate to the Reserve Line will be reconnoitred, constructed and maintained by the Corps.

5. DISTRIBUTION OF TROOPS.

The Division is distributed as per Appendix I.

The Brigade at FORCEVILLE, LEALVILLERS, and ARQUEVES is portion of the Corps Reserve.

6. PLACES OF ASSEMBLY.

Generally speaking, on the left bank of the ANCRE assembly places are good up to the crest of the high ground. In front of the crest, on the gentle slopes, troops could be kept a short time concealed in shell holes if they were got up by night. In winter, both the trenches and shell holes are full of mud and water, and troops could not be kept in them for long.

The following are specially good assembly places:-

THIEPVAL WOOD.

On the right bank of the ANCRE there is a great deal of cover in the old German and British Lines.

AVELUY WOOD, Valley behind the MESNIL Ridge, and the BEAUMONT HAMEL Valley, afford good assembly places.

7. LINES OF APPROACH.

On the left bank of the ANCRE up to the crest, and up to the old German Front Line near the river, the approaches are covered from view. The enemy are likely to put up barrages on all roads and tracks however. Troops must, therefore, be prepared to move across the open unless it is seen that there is little shelling along roads and tracks.

Beyond the crest there is no cover from view.

The roads along the Valley of the ANCRE are likely to be heavily barraged, at any rate in front of HAMEL Village. Troops, in advancing, should therefore keep a little distance up the hill, and move across country.

On the right bank, the best plan would probably be to keep up the MESNIL Valley and drop over the hill N. of HAMEL, avoiding that village, and then keep along the lower slopes of the hill into the BEAUMONT HAMEL Valley.

8. DUG-OUT ACCOMODATION.

For dug-out accomodation see Appendix 5 and Map "G".

8.

CHAPTER II.

Instructions as to the Action of the Troops.

1. Chief Objects to be kept in view.

The underlying idea of the Defence is that the area: STUFF REDOUBT - SCHWABEN REDOUBT - BEAUMONT HAMEL will form the centre of resistance of the Fifth Army.

Should a heavy attack be developed against us during the winter, and retirement become inevitable, the plan would be gradually to withdraw our right flank to the Reserve Line, while still maintaining a hold, by means of the Switch Lines, upon the central defensive area.

In addition, it is important to hold on to the two minor tactical features mentioned in Section I, viz, the spur between COURCELETTE and MIRAUMONT, and the spur on which BEAUCOURT stands.

2. General Principles.

The broad principles of Defence in the event of a hostile attack, and of the front being driven in, are as follows :-

(When the front system is finished, the front line trench will be the line of resistance).

(a) Without definite orders to the contrary from Corps Headquarters, troops will not fall back from one line to any other, but will defend all points in their possession even if their flanks are turned. If a part of a line is temporarily lost, steps will be taken to connect up the flanks of the gap with the next line in rear. To this end, detached keeps and Machine Gun Emplacements will be of great assistance, and should be provided for in the plans of construction.

(b) Should the enemy succeed in penetrating and driving us out of our front defences, keeps and supporting points previously garrisoned, together with communication trenches prepared for fire both ways, and other auxiliary defences, will hold him up in pockets in which his flanks will be exposed to fire. Here also he will be counter-attacked by our Infantry, assisted by the fire of well protected Machine Guns in forward or flank positions screened from hostile observation.

(c) All subordinate Commanders must realise that no ground which might be held should be given up. The objective of every leader should be to deliver a counter-stroke as rapidly as possible. With this object in view, directly an attack is threatened, subordinate Commanders should usually reinforce their supports and reserves within the means at their disposal, so as to have sufficient troops immediately at hand to make local counter attacks. Unless this is done, time will be lost, and the opportunity for delivering an immediate counter attack gone.

Care must, however be taken not to expose troops to needless losses by crowding trenches with men for whose action there is not sufficient room. The counter attack, to be successful must be made at once, i.e. within a few minutes of the enemy having entered our trenches. If this cannot be done, the reserves must not be frittered away in partial attacks but collected for a well-prepared, organised and powerful counter attack executed in accordance with a definite plan.

(d) Troops designed for counter attack should be fresh and located where they are protected as far as possible from artillery fire. Preparation of protection for this purpose will be included in the scheme of work required in the Sector.

Reserves should be moved out of villages. These come under heavy shell fire, and it is very difficult to collect the men out of cellars and dug-outs, in them. They should be assembled in some of the trenches of the rear positions.

(e) Machine Gun Emplacements and Keeps which are not kept garrisoned should be manned, when any serious attack threatens.

The Defence of the rear lines should as far as possible be left to Machine Guns, and the Infantry looked on as a mobile reserve for counter attack, even if they have been placed in the rear line defences for the sake of cover.

All officers must consider the action to be taken by the troops under their command in the event of any of the above situations arising. They will study the communications in their area, and will think out plans for reinforcing their line where required; for launching counter attacks; and, in cases where no immediate local counter attack is possible, of manning the auxiliary defences within the limits of the area allotted to them, so as to hold the enemy until the higher commands have made their dispositions for dealing with the situation.

3. Forms of Attack to be anticipated.

Experience shows that the forms of attack to be anticipated are :-

(a) Raid with a view to causing damage, but with no intention on the part of the enemy of staying in our trenches.

(b) Trench snatching - Sudden local attacks assisted by mines, gas, flammenwerfer, and probably a moderate bombardment, intended to seize and hold some salient or other point in our lines.

(c) Local attacks with a limited objective, such as that made by the Germans on the BOIS DE GIVENCHY on February 21st. 1916, or the VIMY RIDGE on May 21st. 1916.

A large force of Heavy Artillery is concentrated and the desired spot is subjected to a most intense bombardment.

(d) A great attack on a wide front.

(e) Gas attacks.

As regards (a)

The best safeguards are :-

1. Vigilance.
2. Good wire.
3. Flank Machine Gun fire.
4. Proper methods for getting men out of dug-outs.

As regards (b)

The best safeguards are :-

1. The promptness of our own barrage in opening.
2. Enterprise of local commanders, good use of bombers and Lewis guns.

As regards (c)

The best safeguards are :-

1. The Artillery, Divisional and Heavy will make every effort to cut the hostile attack down before it can materialize.
2. Counter battery work will be vigorous.
3. The trenches subjected to the hostile bombardment will be flattened, so the Infantry must be disposed in depth, the front line held lightly and the troops in rear in dug-outs.
4. These troops in rear must be protected by wire, the Support and Reserves lines must therefore be strongly wired.
5. S.O.S. signals must be plentiful.
6. Local counter attacks must be thought out.

As regards (d)

1. The principles detailed for (c) apply equally.
2. Opportunities for a general counter attack by the Corps Reserve will arise.

As regards (e)

Gas attacks may be of several kinds :-
They may be followed by a raid or a great attack, or gas may simply be omitted in the hope of inflicting loss and no Infantry attack may follow.

11.

As regards the actual discharge of gas, this may take many forms, and every endeavour will no doubt be made by the enemy to increase the element of surprise and novelty. Speaking generally, however, the discharge of gas has two objects :-

i. To catch the enemy by surprise before they can put on their helmets. An attack of this kind would probably last from five to twenty minutes.

ii. To wear out the enemy's gas masks and exhaust the men. An attack of this kind might possibly last two hours, with intervals of slight discharges of gas and smoke.

Any given gas attack may aim at a combination of both the above methods, and it is fairly certain to be accompanied by a severe bombardment.

The beating off of an Infantry attack or raid following a gas discharge is very much the same as in the case of an attack following a bombardment: the principles laid down with reference to paras (c) and (d) above therefore hold good.

All available artillery will therefore be concentrated on the enemy's trenches opposite where the gas is being discharged in the same way as is laid down in para (c). All neighbouring Artillery will assist, and the action in case of "GAS 11th.DIVISION" will be the same as in the case of "DEFEND 11th.DIVISION" (See Chapter II para 8 and APPS. IIB & C.), the code word "GAS" being used in lieu of the code word "DEFEND".

Every endeavour will be made to smash up the enemy's attack before it leaves his trenches. It should be remembered, however, that a discharge of gas or smoke at any place may simply be a feint. The action of the artillery laid down under the order "DEFEND ..11th.Division...." or "GAS" .11th.Division" is only the first step of several which may have to follow, for the C.R.A. of the Division attacked must be prepared to modify the roles allotted to the various Batteries if circumstances demand it.

As regards the Infantry, if the gas discharge is accompanied by a heavy bombardment, the garrisons of the trenches bombarded should take refuge in their deep dugouts and be prepared to come out instantly when the artillery fire lifts. If there is little bombardment they will man the trenches. In any case, the gas curtains of the dug-outs will be let down.

During a gas attack Machine and Lewis Guns and their ammunition will be wrapped in blankets or waterproof sheets to prevent their being damaged by the gas.

The Corps orders as regards Gas Alarms and practice for them will be found in APPENDIX IV.

12.

4. Action to be taken against various forms of attack.
----

1. GENERAL.   In event of a general hostile attack the front line will be resolutely held, and the enemy, should he gain a footing vigorously counter attacked, at first locally under Sector arrangements, and later, if necessary, by the Divisional Reserve. Corps H.A. 11th.Divisional Artillery, and Artilleries of adjacent Divisional Artilleries (if available) will act on "Defend 11th.Division " and "Defend IV Corps lines".

2. ATTACK ON RIGHT SECTOR.   In event of an attack on Right Sector only:

   (a)   The Divisional Artillery will open as prearranged on the S.O.S. lines, and the Corps H.A. and the 61st.Divnl. R.A. (if available) will co-operate on the "Defend 11th.Division lines".

   (b)   The G.O.C. Right Sector will organise local counter attacks, utilising the Reserve Companies now located at THIEPVAL and ST. PIERRE DIVION. This includes Infantry working parties quartered in THIEPVAL.

   (c)   The G.O.C. Left Sector will co-operate by opening fire with all machine guns capable of covering the Right Sector.

   (d)   The 2 Battalions now at ENGLEBELMER will march via MESNIL - Q.35.d.2.8 - PASSERELLE DE MAJENTA, and will assemble at PAISLEY DUMP under orders of G.O.C. Right Sector.

   (e)   The Reserve Brigade located at FORCEVILLE, ARQUEVES, and LEALVILLERS will stand to arms ready to move at 2 hours notice.

3. ATTACK ON LEFT SECTOR.   In event of an attack on the left Sector only:

   (a)   The Divnl.Artillery will open as prearranged on S.O.S. lines. When the situation clears and it is evident that the attack is confined to the Left Sector front then the whole of the Divnl.Artillery will concentrate on that front under a prearranged scheme, and the Corps H.A., 37th. and 61st. Divnl. Artilleries (if available) will co-operate on "Defend 11th.Division and Defend IV Corps Lines".

   (b)   The G.O.C. Left Sector will organise local counter attacks utilising his Reserve Battalions now located about STATION ROAD and in the old German lines.

   (c)   The G.O.C. Right Sector will co-operate by opening fire with all Machine Guns capable of covering Left Sector.

   (d)   The 2 Battalions of 33rd.Inf.Bde. located at ENGLEBELMER will march via MESNIL and thence along the Railway line to Q.22. central; from there they will proceed in Artillery formation to STATION ROAD where they will assemble under orders of the G.O.C. Left Sector. HAMEL and the HAMEL - BEAUCOURT ROAD are to be avoided on account of the hostile barrage which is certain to be brought down on these localities.

   (e)   The Reserve Brigades will act as detailed in para 2 (e)

13.

4. <u>ATTACK ON DIVISION ON OUR RIGHT</u>. In event of an hostile attack on the Division on our Right :

   (a) The Divnl.Artillery will act on "Defend 61st.Division lines".

   (b) The G.O.C. Right Sector will :-

      i. Co-operate by opening fire with all Machine Guns capable of covering the left of the Division on our right.

      ii. Get his Reserve Companies under arms ready to move as required at ½ an hours notice.

   (c) The G.O.C. Left Sector will get his Reserve Battalions under arms ready to move at ½ an hours notice.

   (d) The 2 Battalions of the 33rd. Brigade located at ENGLEBELMER will get under arms ready to move off at ½ an hours notice.

   (e) The Reserve Brigade will get under arms ready to move off at 2 hours notice.

5. <u>ATTACK ON DIVISION ON OUR LEFT</u>. In event of an hostile attack on the Division of the 13th. Corps on our Left. :

   (a) The Divisional Artillery will act on "Defend 13th. Corps lines".

   (b) The G.O.C. Left Sector will:

      i. Co-operate by opening fire with all Machine Guns capable of covering the right of the Division on our left.

      ii. Get his Reserve Battalions under arms ready to move Northwards or North Eastwards as required at ½ an hours notice.

   (c) The G.O.C. Right Sector will get his Reserve Companies under arms ready to move off at ½ an hours notice.

   (d) The 2 Battalions 33rd. Brigade located at ENGLEBELMER will get under arms ready to move off at ½ an hours notice.

   (e) The Reserve Brigade will get under arms ready to move off at 2 hours notice.

6. <u>ACTION BY R.E. & PIONEERS</u>. In case of an attack the Field Companies and the 6th.E.Yorks will assemble in their billets and await orders.

5. Considerations affecting the Artillery Defence.

1. The position held by the Corps astride of the ANCRE possesses great advantages for observation and artillery enfilade fire.

2. The facilities for mutual support by enfilade fire within the Sectors of the Corps front, especially as regards the Centre and Left, are admirable. On the right, enfilade fire can be brought to bear from the centre and at long range from the left.

3. The Valley of the ANCRE offers endless positions for Howitzers and the high ground between MESNIL and AUCHONVILLERS commands the Valley and approaches, and provides positions for 60-pdrs. and 6" (Mark VII) guns, to enfilade the Corps front.

4. West of the ANCRE good observation is easily obtained between BEAUCOURT and AUCHONVILLERS.
This offers great advantages for counter-battery work.

5. Although the balance of the advantage of observation is in our hands, the enemy is enabled to overlook us from the North from the direction of SERRE and the high ground about MUNICH TRENCH.
The capture of these places is therefore of great importance to us. It would enable us to advance guns to the line THIEPVAL - SCHWABEN REDOUBT.

LOUPART WOOD enables the enemy to overlook the Corps position N.E. of the line POZIERES WINDMILL - STUFF REDOUBT, and the Valley of the ANCRE.

6. Owing to the soft friable nature of the ground, its broken condition due to shell fire, and state of the roads, great difficulties are experienced in supplying artillery with ammunition and material for construction of positions and observation posts. A properly organised system of light railways, which is in course of construction, is therefore of vital importance for any Scheme of Defence or Offence.

6. Artillery arrangements.

1. The Artillery of the 11th. Division covers frontally the enemy trenches in R.2.b., R.2.a., R.1. and Q.6., and both frontally and in enfilade the trenches in R.15. opposite Centre Division, O.G. 1 and 2, in R.14., and PUISIEUX and RIVER TRENCHES, R.8. and R.2.d. (the latter being at long range for enfilade guns).

2. The Heavy Artillery are at present in nine Groups. The Batteries are sited so that enfilade fire can be brought to bear on trenches in M.1., G.31., R.14., R.8., R.2., and L.32. from the South, and on trenches in M.7., R.12. central, R.11., R.10., R.6 and R.5 and R.3. from the West.

3. The XIII Corps R.A. assist IV Corps by enfilading trenches in R.4. R.3 and R.2.b from the West.

4.   The Heavy Artillery are particularly well-placed for Counter-Battery work on enemy Batteries North of the ANCRE, especially on the Group West of MIRAUMONT. The Grouping of the Heavy Artillery is to be re-arranged so that the Counter-Battery Group Commanders can call on 4 Heavy Artillery Group Commanders.

5.   In case of an attack, a concentration of fire would be brought to bear on assembly places, trenches and approaches opposite to where our trenches were being bombarded, and neutralising Counter-Battery fire would be carried out.

6.   Arrangements have been made with neighbouring Corps to support, in case of hostile attack, and a scheme for mutual support between Divisions has also been drawn up.

   The code words "DEFEND IV CORPS", "DEFEND 11th. DIVISION", etc., will be used between Corps or Divisions where artillery fire is necessary to repulse a hostile attack. The detail of these concentrations will be found in APPENDICES IIA, IIB, & IIC.
   Instructions have been circulated.

   In case of a gas attack - The call "GAS" will be substituted for "DEFEND" but the fire action of the artillery will be the same.

7.   The above arrangements will result in a concentrated fire being brought to bear quickly on the threatened front. The C.R.A. of the Division concerned, or the B.G.,C.H.A. will then be in a position to move the fire of any of the Batteries to meet the further requirements of the situation.

   For S.O.S. arrangements see Appendix 2 (c) and Map "C".

CHAPTER III.

ACTION OF CORPS RESERVE.

1. Corps Reserve.

The three rearmost Infantry Brigades of the three Divisions will form the Corps Reserve. In the event of any attack on a large scale on the IV or either of the neighbouring Corps, they will receive orders to be ready to move in one hour.

If the attack is sufficiently serious, the Divisional Commanders will move their supporting Brigades (or Battalions in the case of the Left Division) up close behind the front line system.

On this, the Infantry Brigades of the Corps Reserve will be moved up to take their places.

These moves will be carried out according to the requirements of each case, but the foremost of the moves to be carried out in case of an attack on various parts of the front, is given below.

2. Moves of Reserve Infantry Brigades.

(a) Attack on the Right or Right and Centre Divisions.

Reserve Infantry Brigade Right Division to OVILLERS, AVELUY, and POZIERES.

    "   "   "   Centre   "   to MARTINSART.

    "   "   "   Left   "   to BOUZINCOURT and SENLIS.

(b) Attack on whole Corps front on left bank of the ANCRE.

Reserve Infantry Brigade Right Division to OVILLERS, AVELUY, and POZIERES.

    "   "   "   Centre   "   to MARTINSART.

    "   "   "   Left   "   to ENGLEBELMER and FORCEVILLE.

(c) Attack along both banks of the ANCRE or on Right bank.

Reserve Infantry Brigade Right Division to NAB VALLEY and AVELUY.

    "   "   "   Centre. "   to MARTINSART.

    "   "   "   Left.   "   to ENGLEBELMER and FORCEVILLE.

(d) Attack on the Corps on our Left.

Reserve Infantry Brigade, Left Division, to ENGLEBELMER and FORCEVILLE.

3. Action of a fourth Division, if allotted to the Corps.

In the event of a Division resting in the back area being allotted to the Corps, it would move up into the areas vacated by the Reserve Infantry Brigades - a Brigade Group moving into each. The Artillery would either move into HERISSART, HARPONVILLE and ARQUEVES, or into villages at the front of the MARIEUX Area, and from there move into the Reserve positions already prepared by the Divisional Artillery.

CHAPTER IV

Administrative Arrangements.

1. Supply of RE. Materials.

The following Parks and Dumps are in existence :-

Army Park.	VARENNES.
Corps Parks.)	LEALVILLERS.
	PIONEER ROAD STATION (PUP)
Dumps.)	LANCASHIRE.
)	ENGLEBELMER.
)	HAMEL.

Source of Supply:

The main source of supply to the dumps is from PUP. Owing to railway transport difficulties PUP are not always able to meet requirements, in this case stores are obtained direct from LEALVILLERS and VARENNES.

Means of Transport.

Stores from PUP are conveyed to the dump by lorries or trestle wagons working under the orders of the Field Co. in rest. In the case of LANCASHIRE DUMP stores are also carried direct by rail.

Stores from LEALVILLERS and VARENNES are carried to the dumps on lorries supplied on demand by the C.E. IV Corps.

Issue of Stores from Dumps.

Stores are issued from the dumps on the authority of the Field Co. or H.Q., R.E., units supplying their own transport. In case of there being any shortage of any material in the dumps, authority is given by H.Q., R.E. for the units to draw direct on PUP.

Issue of Brushwood.

Brushwood is cut in AVELUY WOOD by 3 platoons of Infantry under the supervision of the E.Yorks Pioneers.

Units draw brushwood direct from the dump using their own transport.

(SEE APPENDIX III.)

2. Supply of Ammunition and Supplies.
----

1. System of Supply of S.A.A., Grenades, Rockets etc.

   Railhead ACHEUX.

   Ammunition is drawn by M.T. and carried to a Divisional Dump at LESNIL, where there is an officer in charge.

   Brigades and units draw what they require from the Divisional Dump, sending their own transport for this purpose. No.5
   All grenades are detonated before being issued.
   The Divisional Dump is replenished by lorry sent direct from Sub-Park who issue on receipt of a request from the Division.
   Corps sanction is required for issue of special stores such as S.O.S. rockets.

2. System of Supply of Rations etc.

   Railhead ACHEUX.

   Supplies are drawn by M.T. and dumped at Refilling point at P.21.a.5.5 on FORCEVILLE - BERTRANCOURT road, for all troops quartered W. of line drawn N. and S. through P.29. central.
   Refilling point at Q.22.a.2.8 on ENGLEBELMER-AUCHONVILLERS road for all troops E. of line drawn through N. and S. through P.29. central.

   Supplies are drawn from these refilling points by units and taken to their own Q.M. stores etc. where they are further divided up and issued.

3. Ration Dumps.

   Reserve of iron rations have been dumped at -
   i.   Q.25.a.6.9 containing 19,000 Iron Rations.

   ii. Q.28.c.6.8   "   10,000   "   "

   Dumps containing 2 days rations (less bread and fresh meat portion) for a total of 20,000 men and 6000 animals for use in case of a thaw after a severe frost are situated at :-

   (a) P.21.a.2.4.
   (b) Q.19.b.7.7.

   All the above dumps are controlled by the S.S.O.

4. Ordnance Stores.

   Ordnance stores are deposited at FORCEVILLE whence units using their own transport for this purpose.

3. Medical Arrangements.
----

1.   The front area is divided into two sectors divided
by the River ANCRE.
(1) Right Sector.   South of ANCRE, cleared by 35th. Field
                                Ambulance.
   Main Dressing Station. - LANCASHIRE DUMP. Q.35.c.8.3.

   Advanced Dressing Station. -
   (a) ST. PIERRE DIVION.   Q.10.d.9.0.
   (b) THIEPVAL.   R.25.b.8.3.

   Motor Ambulance Car Stations.
   (a) Q.24.c.7.8.
   (b) R.31.a.7.9.

        Cases are brought by hand from Regimental Aid Posts
to Advanced Dressing Station, where they are dressed.
They are then conveyed by hand carriage to motor ambulance car
station, from which they are conveyed in motor ambulance wagons
to LANCASHIRE DUMP. From there, evacuation is carried out by
No. 20, Motor Ambulance Convoy.
        In addition, there is a collecting Station at PAISLEY
DUMP (Q.30.a.7.4). This is not used at present, and is handed
over to 33rd.Inf.Bde. for use as temporary Headquarters.

(2) Left Sector. North of ANCRE, cleared by 33rd. Field Ambulance.

            Main Dressing Station.   Q.31.b.9.7.

            Advd. Dressing Station. MESNIL. Q.28.c.6.6.

            Advd. Bearer Post.   Q.18.b.5.8.

            Motor Ambulance Car Station.   Q.18.c.4.5.

        Cases are brought by hand from Regimental Aid Posts
to Advanced Bearer Posts where they are dressed. They are then
conveyed by hand carriage to motor ambulance car station, from
which they are conveyed in motor ambulance wagons to Advanced
Dressing Station, MESNIL. From there evacuation is carried out
by No.20 Motor Ambulance Convoy.
        In addition, there are three huts at Q.29.b.4.9.
These have been temporarily evacuated.

(3)   All casualties are disposed of as in (1) and (2) except
gassed cases, which are all conveyed to Main Dressing Station, of
Left Sector at Q.31.b.9.7 for treatment.

(4) Rest Station.
        This is under IV Corps at CLAIRFAYE (0.30.a.1.9) and
is at present run by 34th. Field Ambulance.

----
4. Station of Traffic Control Posts and Battle Police.

See Map "F".

APPENDIX 1.

BOUNDARIES OF AREAS AND DISTRIBUTION OF TROOPS.

BOUNDARIES.

1. The front held by the IV Corps extends from M.15.a.6.3 to R.7.a.7.9.

    The Eastern Boundary - between the IV Corps and the III Corps runs from M.15.a.6.3 to ALBERT - BAPAUME Road at M.21.c.3.8 thence as on attached Map "A".

    The Northern boundary - between the IV Corps and the XIII Corps, runs from R.1.c.7.0 South-westwards to Q.17.c.0.0., thence as on attached Map "A".

DISTRIBUTION OF TROOPS.

2. The 11th Division has :-

    Two Brigades holding the front system with four Battalions in front, and four Battalions in support at Q.12.d. (1 Btn) Q.17.b. (1 Btn.) and ENGLEBELMER (2 Btns.).

    One Brigade in Corps reserve at ARQUEVES (1 Btn.), LEALVILLERS (1 Btn.) and FORCEVILLE (2 Btns.).

3. The IV Corps front is divided into four sections, A., B., C., and D.

Left Division. "C" Section.

    Eastern boundary - LUCKY WAY - thence as on attached map "A".

    Western boundary - R.8.c.5.6 - RIVER ANCRE. attached map "A".

    "D" Section.

    Eastern boundary - as for Western boundary of "C" Section.

    Northern boundary - Northern boundary of IV Corps.

The boundaries between A., B., and C Sections are the boundaries between the Right, Centre and Left Divisions.

APPENDIX 11 (A).

MUTUAL ARTILLERY SUPPORT BETWEEN ADJACENT DIVISIONS OF IV AND XIII CORPS.

(1) **Divisional support to be given by Left Division IV Corps to Right Division XIII Corps.**

WARNING :-

"DEFEND XIII CORPS".

Two 18-Pdr batteries 58th Brigade R.F.A. enfilade Trench R.1.c.4½.4 to 2½.9.

One 18-Pdr battery 58th Brigade R.F.A. enfilade Trench R.1.c.2½.5 to 2.8.

(2) **Divisional support to be given by Right Division XIII Corps to Left Division IV Corps.**

WARNING :-

"DEFEND IV CORPS".

Three 18-Pdr Batteries R.F.A.

   (1) Barrage a line from R.1.c.6.7 to R.1.d.5.9.
   (2) Enfilade ARTILLERY ALLEY and Track immediately to the SOUTH of it.

APPENDIX 11 (B).

MUTUAL ARTILLERY SUPPORT BETWEEN DIVISIONS OF IV CORPS.

(1). <u>Divisional support to be given by Right and Left Divisions to Centre Division, IV Corps.</u>

    WARNING :-   "DEFEND 61st DIVISION".

<u>By.</u>   <u>Target.</u>

Right Division
  8 18-pdrs
  4 4.5" Hows.
  10 18-pdrs

Barrage GRANDCOURT Trench from R.11.d.1.4 - R.16.b.0.8.
Barrage R.12.a.5.0 - R.11.d.1.4.

Left Division
  30-18-pdrs.

1 Battery enfilade GRANDCOURT Trench from R.15.a. to W. MIRAUMONT ROAD.
1 Battery enfilade road from GRANDCOURT (exclusive) to PETIT MIRAUMONT and S. MIRAUMONT TRENCH.
3 Batteries search and sweep area bounded by GRANDCOURT TRENCH, GRANDCOURT ROAD, W. MIRAUMONT ROAD, SOUTH MIRAUMONT TRENCH & GRANDCOURT - PETIT MIRAUMONT ROAD.

(2) <u>Divisional support to be given by Centre Division IV Corps to Left Division IV Corps.</u>

    WARNING :-   "DEFEND 11th DIVISION".

<u>By.</u>   <u>Target.</u>

308th Brigade
(12-18 pdrs)
(8-4.5" Hows.)

2-18 pdr. batteries enfilade RIVER TRENCH & PUSIEUX TRENCH from their junction at R.2.d.3.9 SOUTHWARDS & sweep area between them.
1 How. battery on GRANDCOURT MAIN STREET.
1 How. battery on BEAUCOURT-MIRAUMONT ROAD.

306th Brigade
(12-18 pdrs.)

1 battery enfilade O.G.2. from R.15.c.1.5 NORTHWARDS and sweep area to STUMP ROAD.
1 battery enfilade STUMP ROAD from R.15.c.6.4 NORTHWARDS and sweep area to O.G.2.

APPENDIX 11 (C).

ACTION OF IVth. CORPS HEAVY ARTILLERY IN CASE OF HOSTILE ATTACK.

On receipt of warning, "DEFEND 11th. DIVISION", Heavy Artillery Groups will engage targets as shown below :-

UNIT	Nature.	Attack on Left. Div.	Centre. Div.	Right. Div.	TARGETS.
59th. Group.					
55 S.B.	9.2" How.	*	*		R.4.b.2.2.
		*	*		R.4.b.1½.6.
219 S.B.	6" How.	*			R.1.d.6.8 – b.4.4.
		*	*		R.14.b.9.1.
45th. Group.					
36 S.B.	8" How.	*			Sunken Road in L.32.d.
36th. Group.					
129 S.B.	9.2" How.	*			PUISIEUX & RIVER Trenches in R.2.d.
25th. Group.					
76 S.B.	9.2" How.	*			PUISIEUX & RIVER Trenches in R.2.a.
20 S.B.	8" How.	*	*		R.15.a.9.1 – 7.7.
157 S.B.	6" How.	*	*		R.15.b.3.0 – 3½.5.
27 S.B.	6" How.	*	*		R.9.b.6.3 – R.10.b.2.7.
40th. Group.					
72 S.B.	6" How.	*			Sunken Road. L.31.d.
10th. Group.					
30th. S.B.	8" How.	*	*		R.2.d.6.4.
62 S.B.	9.2" do (RX)	*	*		GRANDCOURT in R.9.c. & d.
173 S.B.	6" How.	*			R.2.a.0.0 – 5.6.
		*			R.3.a.6½.0 – b.0.3.
2nd. Group.					
24 H.B.	60- Pdr.	*	*		R.14.b.9.2 – 6.9.
122 H.B.	60- Pdr.	*			PUISIEUX & RIVER Trench in R.2.a. & b.
14 H.B.	60- Pdr.	*			PUISIEUX & RIVER Trench in R.2.d.
114 H.B.	60- Pdr.	*	*		South edge of GRANDCOURT.

Rate of fire will be :-

    60-Pdrs. & 4.7"   –   1 round per gun per minute.
    6" Hows.   –   1 " " How. " two minutes.
    8" & 9.2" How.   –   1 " " " " four minutes.

This rate of fire will be maintained till the situation clears.

APPENDIX II (D).

Positions for Reinforcing Batteries and for Defence of Rear Lines.

1. Re-inforcing positions :-

    58th. Bde. R.F.A.
    "A" Battery   R.25.c.5.6.
    "B" Battery.   R.25.a.5.6.
    "C" Battery.   R.26.d.1.4
    "D" Battery.   R.25.a.3.1½

    59th. Bde. R.F.A.
    "A" Battery.   R.33.b.4.2½.
    "B" Battery.   R.33.b.7.4½
    "C" Battery.   R.33.a.1.7
    "D" Battery.   R.32.b.5.5½

    60th. Bde. R.F.A.
    "A" Battery.   Q.23.c.6.7.
    "B" Battery.   Q.24.c.6.6
    "C" Battery.   Q.18.c.1½.1½
    "D" Battery.   Q.23.d.0.8.

2. Wire cutting positions :-

    58th. Bde. R.F.A.
    1 Section.   R.19.d.4½.1½
    1 Battery.   R.26.b.5.9.
    1 Battery.   R.26.c.2.3.
    1 Battery.   R.25.b.0.3.

    59th. Bde. R.F.A.
    For three 6 gun batteries. R.27.a.½.4½ (left flank of left battery) to R.27.a.6½.4½ (right flank of right battery).

    60th. Bde.R.F.A.   R.13.c.6.0.
                                Q.12.c.8.6.

    As practically the whole of the 11th.Divisional Artillery are in the process of making new primary positions, it will be some time before work can be commenced either on re-inforcing or wire cutting positions.

    Some of above re-inforcing positions are at present occupied by batteries pending the completion of their primary positions.

APPENDIX II (E).

S.O.S.

Defensive barrages will be as follows :-

58th. Bde. R.F.A.
- (1) 1 18-Pdr. Bty.   R.2.d.0.4 - R.2.c.1.8½.
- (2) 1 18-Pdr. Bty.   R.2.c.1.8½ - R.1.d.5.7
- (3) 1 18-Pdr. Bty.   R.1.d.5.7 - R.1.d.6.7
- (4) Howitzers.   Points R.1.d.6½.8., 6.9., 5.8., 4.9½.

59th. Bde. R.F.A.
- (5) 1 18-Pdr. Bty.   R.14.d.9.7 - R.14.b.6.2 - 5.5.
- (6) 1 18-Pdr. Bty.   R.14.b.5.5 - R.6.d.2.0 - 3.3.
- (7) 1 18-Pdr. Bty.   R.8.b.5.6 - R.2.d.0.4.
- (8) Howitzers.   Points R.15.c.5.9., R.14.b.9.2., R.8.d.5.1. and 5.4.

80th. Bde. R.F.A.
- (9) 1 18-Pdr. Bty.(A/80) R.1.d.9.8 - 2.5½.
- (10) 1 18-Pdr. Bty.(B/80) (2 guns) R.8.b.5.6 - 9.9.
- (11)   (2 guns) R.8.b.5.2½ -.7.4 - 9.5.
- (12)   (2 guns) R.8.d.5.4 ; 8.5 - N.9.c.1.6
- (13) 1 How. Bty.   Points R.8.b.6.9.,R.2.d.9.1., 8.5.,4.5.
- (14) 1 How Bty.   Points R.8.b.5.2½., 7.4. R.1.b.7½.5½., R.1.b.7.0.

108 (H) Battery R.G.A.
- (15) (2 guns).   R.2.a.1.3. and R.1.b.7½.0 (ARTILLERY ALLEY).
- (16) (2 guns).   R.9.a.7.2½ and 3.1½ (RAILWAY).
- (17) (2 guns)   R.3.c.2.3 and 1.6   (GRANDCOURT)

140 (S) Battery R.G.A.
- (18) (2 Hows).   R.2.b.0.6 and 0.5 (PUISIEUX TRENCH).
- (19) (2 Hows).   R.15.a.8.6 and 7.8 (STUMP ROAD).

Rate of Fire on Receipt of S.O.S.

First 2 minutes.   4 rounds per gun per minute.
After 2 minutes.   2 rounds "   "   "   "
till situation clears.

" SPECIAL SCHNAPPS " BARRAGE.

In the event of a localised attack on the positions North of the River round BOIS D'HOLLANDE, the following modified barrage may be ordered. The guns firing to the South of the River being lifted as follows, those firing to the North of the River remaining as already detailed.

Code name for this barrage is "SPECIAL SCHNAPPS".

59th. Bde. R.F.A.

Item (5)   6 18-Pdrs on to R.8.b.5.6 - R.2.d.4.5.

Item (6)   6 18-Pdrs. on to R.2.d.4.5 - R.2.c.5.7.

Item (8)   4 4.5" Hows. will be superimposed on 58th. F.A.B. Howitzers - Item (4)

60th. Bde. R.F.A.

Item (12)   Will be superimposed on Item (10)

108 (H) Battery R.G.A.

Item (17) (Two guns) will fire at Points R.8.b.7.7 and R.9.a.0.9 (MIRAUMONT ROAD).

140 (S) Battery R.G.A.

Item (19) (Two Hows) will fire at Points R.2.b.1.3 and R.2.d.2.8

APPENDIX 111.

SUPPLY OF R.E. STORES AND MATERIALS.

RAILHEAD.

1. Stores are consigned to PIONEER ROAD STATION (PUP). Certain stores are unloaded at AVELUY Siding and distributed from there in order to facilitate transport.

2. The main Corps Expense Store and Workshop is established alongside PIONEER ROAD STATION.

3. Divisions make their own arrangements for drawing stores - the 60 c.m. Light Railway is used for this purpose, as far as possible A Corps officer ("The Yard Master, AVELUY") making the necessary arrangements for the Divisions.

4. Stores are issued in bulk to the Divisions and "YELLOW LINE" and in detail to other units.

5. C's R.E. Divisions are responsible for the allocation and distribution of stores from the Divisional Dumps.

RIGHT DIVISION.

1. The Right Division Workshop is at OVILLERS POST (X.13.a.2.1) and the Main Dump is at POZIERES Road, X.9.b.9.7. These are supplied by road.

2. From the latter point stores are carried up by the Light Tramway to EAST MIRAUMONT ROAD North of COURCELETTE.

CENTRE DIVISION.

1. The Main Divisional Dump is at AVELUY Siding, W.17.a.5.7. and is supplied direct from the broad gauge railway.

2. The Centre Division has also a subsidiary Dump on TULLOCHS CORNER, R.33.d.7.2. This is supplied from AVELUY Siding by 60 c.m. track.

LEFT DIVISION.

The Main Divisional Dumps are at ENGLEBELMER and LANCASHIRE Dump, Q.35.d.1.3.; these are supplied by lorries from PIONEER ROAD.

APPENDIX IV.

STANDING ORDERS ON ACTION TO BE TAKEN DURING "GAS ALERT" AND DURING HOSTILE GAS ATTACKS.

1. **GAS ALERT.**

    Gas Alert will be ordered when the wind is in the dangerous quarter, no matter what the strength of the wind.

    Gas Alert will usually be ordered by Divisional Commanders. They are responsible for warning all units which are attached to them for administration, whether quartered within or outside their areas, also the Headquarters of any Army or Corps Heavy Artillery or troops which may be quartered in their areas. Brigade Headquarters or Battalion Commanders, however, are empowered to order a Gas Alert as a result of wind observations made by Company Gas N.C.O's. forwarded by Company Commanders, but such action will be reported immediately to the next higher formation.

    In the case of other Corps Troops, the order will be communicated to the S.O.R.A., S.O.R.E., and Camp Commandant at Corps H.Q., who will be responsible for conveying it to all Units with which each is concerned, not quartered in Divisional Areas.

    When the warning is received by Signals, it will automatically be communicated to those concerned. The Gas Alert will not be taken off without the authority of Divisional Commanders and in the case of Corps Troops, Corps H.Q.

2. **BEHAVIOUR DURING GAS ALERT.**

    <u>Inspection of Helmets.</u>

    (i) All helmets and box respirators will be carefully inspected and helmet or respirator inspection will be carried out daily.

    <u>Alert position for helmets.</u>

    (ii) All ranks not issued with box respirators, within 1,500 yards of the front line, will carry the first helmet on the chest in the "Alert" position: i.e., pinned through the container on to the shirt and rolled in such a manner as to protect the valve and leave the helmet suspended ready to put on the moment the jacket is opened.

    <u>Nothing to interfere with rapid adjustment of helmets.</u>

    (iii) The two top buttons of both jacket and great coat will be left undone. Men are forbidden to wear mackintosh sheets round their shoulders, or mufflers round their necks.

    (iv) The reserve/

(iv) The reserve helmet will be carried in the satchel attached to the belt, or slung from the left shoulder PERPENDICULARLY DOWNWARDS under the belt.

(v) In no circumstances will anything (rifle, second helmet, field glasses etc.) be slung across the chest in such a manner as to inrefere with the natural fall of the helmet when the jacket is opened or impede the rapid adjustment of the helmet.

(vi) Jackets will not be taken off within 1,000 yards of the front line.

(vii) Where box respirators are used, these will be carried in the "Alert" position and so adjusted that nothing slung across the chest shall interfere with the immediate use of the apparatus.

(viii) Officers and N.C.O's in charge of any Unit or party must see that the orders (i) to (vii) are strictly carried out, both for troops in front line trenches and for detached bodies of troops (working and carrying parties, etc.).

(ix) A man must never be without his helmet and respirator, and he must know how to adjust it quickly and securely.

Sentries etc.

(x) All working parties will have a sentry posted to give instant warning of a gas attack.

(xi) A sentry will be posted at each Strombos Horn or similar alarm device and instructed in its use.

(xii) A sentry will be posted to every dug-out holding more than ten men.

(xiii) A sentry will be posted to each group of two or three small dug-outs.

(xiv) A sentry will be posted to each Headquarters, Signal Office and independant body of men.

(xv) Arrangements will be made by the Officer in charge of the trench for warning the artillery observation post if there is one in the trench.

(xvi) Commanders of Units in billets within 12,000 yards of the front line trenches to organise a system of giving the alarm and rousing all men in cellars or houses.

(xvii) At night, sentries must have at least two men within reach of them, so that the alarm can be spread rapidly.

Men asleep).

Men asleep.

(xviii)   When a gas attack is probable, men in front line trenches will not sleep in dug-outs which are unprotected by blankets.

(xix)   Men sleeping in rearward lines or in works where they are allowed to take off their equipment, will sleep with on gas helmet or box respirator suspended round their necks, and must know exactly where their reserve helmets are to be found.

Company Gas N.C.Os.

(xx)   Company Gas N.C.Os will report to Company H.Q. in readiness to assist the Company Commander should a gas attack occur.

Ammonia Capsules.

(xxi)   Medical officers must see that a proper proportion of the ammonia capsules, or other first aid supplies for gas cases which are issued to them, are with stretcher bearers in the front line, in readiness for their immediate use after a gas attack.

Gas Alarm.

(i)   In the event of an enemy gas attack, the alarm will at once be given by all means available: by telephone, Strombos Horns, gongs, and, if necessary, by orderly. Sentries will warn all ranks in trenches, dug-outs, observation posts or mine shafts. In every Unit, arrangements must be made for a special signal to be given by gongs or other means.

The sound signals should be arranged in depth, so that troops in the front line are warned and, at the same time, sound signals in rear take up the alarm and spread it among the artillery, Reserve Infantry Brigades etc.

(ii)   All ranks will at once put on their helmets or box respirators, and stand to arms.

(iii)   All ranks in the front line are forbidden to move to a flank or to the rear. There must be as little movement and talking as possible.

(iv)   If troops in support or reserve lines of trenches remain in, or go into, unprotected dug-outs, they must continue to wear their anti-gas appliances.

Unnecessary movement to cease.

(v)   On the alarm being given, all bodies of troops or transport on the move, will halt and all working parties cease work until the gas cloud has passed.

(vi) If a relief /

(vi) If a relief is going on, Units should stand steady as far as possible, until the gas cloud has passed.

(vii) Supports and parties bringing up ammunition and grenades will only be moved up if the tactical situation demands.

Protected Dug-outs.

(viii) The blanket-doorways of protected dug-outs and cellars will be let down and carefully fixed in position.

4. Action during an enemy gas attack.

(i) Should the gas cloud be unaccompanied by an Infantry attack, a S.O.S. Signal will not be sent, but the message "GAS ATTACK, TRENCH ....".

Tactical Measures.

(ii) Men in dug-outs will stand ready to rush out at once should an Infantry attack develop. The troops in the front trenches will open a slow rate of rifle fire at once against the enemy trenches: occasional short bursts should be fired from Machine Guns to ascertain that these are in working order. All howitzers should be turned on the enemy's trenches from which the gas is being emitted, or in which the enemy infantry may be concentrating for the assault. It is the practice of the enemy infantry to retire to the second and third lines of the front trenches whilst gas is being discharged.
A light barrage by field guns should be put up in front of the enemy line, to prevent hostile patrols from following up the gas. No intense S.O.S. barrage will be employed at this stage.

(iii) Should an Infantry attack develop, the normal procedure of S.O.S. will be carried out.

(iv) Troops in the front line not affected by gas must be prepared to bring cross fire to bear on the enemy attempting to advance against a gassed portion of the line.

Movement.

(v) All movement must be reduced to a minimum. There should be as little moving about and talking as possible in the trenches. Men must be made to realise that, with the gas now used by the enemy, the observance of this order is essential for their safety.

5. Action/.

5. **Action after an enemy gas attack.**

   Removal of helmets.

   (i) Helmets and box respirators will not be removed after a gas attack until permission has been given by the Company Commander, who will, when possible, ascertain from Officers and N.C.Os who have been trained at the Divisional Gas School that it is safe to do so.

   (ii) Men in charge of anti-gas fans will use them as soon as the gas cloud has passed, so as to admit of helmets being removed.

   Preparation for a subsequent attack.

   (iii) So as to be ready for a subsequent gas cloud, all ranks will, when permission has been given to take off helmets, at once adjust the reserve (unused) helmets in the "Alert" position, folding up the helmets that have just been worn in gas, and putting them in the satchels in which the reserve helmets had been carried.

   A sharp look-out must be maintained for a repitition of the gas attack as long as the wind continues in the dangerous quarter.

   Similar precautions will be taken by men equipped with box respirators which, however, need not be exchanged but merely put back in the "Alert" position so as to be ready for immediate use if necessary.

   Clearing of Dug-outs.

   (iv) Dug-outs and cellars not protected during a gas attack must not be entered for four hours after the cloud has passed and must be ventilated freely. Thorough ventilation (natural, or by means of fires or anti-gas fans) is the only sure way of clearing a dug-out.

   If, after a gas attack, unprotected dug-outs have to be entered owing to heavy shelling, helmets or box respirators must be worn.

   Movement.

   (v) No man suffering from the effects of gas is to be allowed to walk to the dressing station.

   (vi) The clearing of trenches and dug-outs must not be carried out by men who have been affected by the gas.

   (vii) After a gas attack, troops in the front trenches are to be relieved of all fatigue and carrying work for 24 hours, by sending up working parties from Companies in rear.

   (viii) Horses /.

(viii) Horses which have been exposed to gas should not be worked for 24 hours if it can be avoided.

Cleaning of Arms

(ix) Rifles and Machine Guns must be cleaned after a gas attack. Oil cleaning will prevent corrosion for 12 hours, but the first opportunity must be taken to clean all parts in boiling water containing a little soda.

6. Action during a gas shell bombardment.

(i) Helmets or box respirators will be worn in the area shelled.

(ii) Arrangements must be made for giving a local alarm in the event of a sudden and intense bombardment with gas shells.

(iii) All dug-outs and shelters in the vicinity will be visited and any sleeping men roused.

7. Practice Gas Alarms.

Divisions will, from time to time, practice the "Gas Alarm".

This will be used to test :-

(i) The efficacy of the sound signals, and the time it takes to send the warning to all troops in the Divisional Area by telephone.

(ii) That every officer and man has his has helmet or respirator, and puts it on sufficiently quickly.

(iii) That all gas sentries know their posts and duties.

(iv) That the system of rousing Officers and men in cellars and dug-outs, is satisfactory.

(v) That all gongs are hanging clear of the parapet and have their strikers beside them.

APPENDIX VI

LIAISON BETWEEN INFANTRY AND ARTILLERY.

1. Liaison will be as follows :-

Right Brigade.	Right Battalion.	59th. F.A.B.
	Left Battalion.	59th. F.A.B.
Left Brigade.	Right Battalion.	60th. F.A.B.
	Left Battalion.	58th. F.A.B.

2. 58th. F.A.B. at Left Battalion Headquarters of Left Brigade will establish a night look out Post whose duty it will be to at once notify the liaison officer in case of S.O.S. Signals.

3. 59th. F.A.B. will either maintain its present look out post at SCHWABEN REDOUBT or establish one with Right Battalion, Right Brigade.

4. Duration of tours of duty as liaison officer.
48 hours, Left Battalion, Left Brigade.
48 hours, Right Battalion, Right Brigade.

APPENDIX V

DUG - OUTS.

SOUTH OF RIVER ANCRE.

and

NORTH OF RIVER ANCRE.

APPENDIX 5.

NORTH OF RIVER.

Location.	No.	Map Reference.	Capacity.	If occupied.	Being opened up.	Under construction.	Remarks.
SUVLA TRENCH.	1	R.8.a.1.4.	30 men.	No.		Yes.	25% completed.
	2	R.7.b.9.5.	30 "	No.		Yes.	-do-
	3	R.7.a.10.9	30 "	No.		Yes.	-do-
	4	R.7.a.9.9.	30 "	No.		Yes.	-do-
BEAUCOURT.	51	R.8.a.2.0.	50 "	Yes.			
	52	R.7.d.4.8	8 men, 3 offrs.	Yes.			
	53	R.7.d.5.9.	50 men.	Yes.			
	54	R.7.d.2.8.	15 "	Yes.			
	55	R.7.d.1.7	15 "	Yes.			
	56	R.7.c.9.5.	25 men, 8 offrs.	Yes.			
BEAUCOURT TRENCH.	57	R.7.c.6.6.	16 men.	Yes.			
"	58	R.7.c.6.7.	10 "	Yes.			
THE CAVE.	59	R.7.c.7.9	150 men, 4 offrs.	Yes.			BEAUCOURT CAVE being improved. Should eventually hold 200.
BEAUCOURT TRENCH.	60	R.7.a.5.2	25 men, 2 offrs.	Yes.			
"	61	R.7.a.1.3	25 " 6 "	No.			
"	62	R.7.a.0.4	25 " 1 "	No.			

Location.	No.	Map Reference.	Capacity.	If occupied.	Being Opened up.	Under construction.	Remarks.
BEAUCOURT TRENCH.	63	Q.19.d.8.1.	150 men, Prob. capacity.	No.		Yes.	75% complete.
"	64	Q.18.b.3.8	50, Prob.Capacity.	No		Yes.	60% complete
Along RAVINE.	65	Q.18.a.10.4.	NIL.	No		No.	Blown in
"	66	Q.18.a.9½.4	NIL.	No.		No.	Blown in
"	67	Q.18.a.9.4	200 men.	Yes.			
"	68	Q.18.a.8½.4	6 men, 6 offrs.	Yes.			
"	69	Q.18.a.8.4	10 men.	Yes.			
"	70	Q.18.a.7½.4	12 "	No.			
"	71	Q.18.a.7.4½	NIL.	No.		No.	Officers dug-out, marked in German.
"	72	Q.18.a.6½.5	220 men.	Yes.			
"	73	Q.18.a.6.5.	NIL.	No.		No.	) German dug-outs,
"	74	Q.18.a.5½.5	NIL.	No.		No.	) just started.
"	75	Q.18.a.5.6	14 men, 2 offrs.	Yes.			
"	76	Q.18.a.3½.4	60 " 3 "	Yes.			
RAILWAY ROAD.	151	Q.18.b.2.2	20 men, 2 offrs.	Yes.			

Location.	No.	Map Reference.	Capacity.	If Occupied.	Being Opened up	Under construction.	Remarks.
OLD GERMAN 3rd.Line.	152	Q.18.a.10.2	15 men	Yes.			
"	153	Q.18.a.9.2	15 "	Yes.			
"	154	Q.18.a.8½.2	10 " 2 offrs.	Yes.			} B.H.Q.
"	155	Q.18.a.8.2	10 " 2 "	Yes.			
"	156	Q.18.a.7.2	20 men.	Yes.			
"	157	Q.18.a.6.2	12 "	Yes.			
"	158	Q.18.a.5.2	16 "	Yes.			
"	159	Q.18.a.4.2	16 "	Yes.			
"	160	Q.18.a.3.2	20 "	Yes.			
"	161	Q.18.a.2½.2½	12 "	Yes.			
"	162	Q.18.a.2.3	4 "	Yes.			
"	163	Q.18.a.1.3	12 "	Yes.			
"	164	Q.18.a.0.4	19 "	Yes.			
"	165	Q.17.b.9.4	6 "	Yes.			
"	166	Q.17.b.6.5	15 "	Yes.			
"	167	Q.18.c.8.9	15 "	Yes.			
German 2nd.Line.	168	Q.18.c.7.9	16 "	Yes.			
"	169	Q.18.c.6.9¾	NIL.	No.			} Blown in.
"	170	Q.18.c.5.9¾	NIL.	No.			

Location.	No.	Map Reference.	Capacity.	If Occupied.	Being Opened up	Under construction.	Remarks.
German 2nd.Line.	171	Q.18.c.4.10	20 men.	Yes.			
"	172	Q.18.a.3.0	4 "	Yes.			
"	173	Q.18.a.2½.0	25 "	Yes.			
"	174	Q.18.a.2½.1	25 "	Yes.			
"	175	Q.18.a.1½.1	18 "	Yes.			
"	176	Q.18.a.1-1½	20 "	No.			Blown in
"	177	Q.18.a.½.2	25 "	Yes.			
"	178	Q.18.a.0.2	NIL.	No.			
"	179	Q.17.b.9.2	8 men	Yes.			
"	180	Q.17.b.8½.2	15 "	Yes.			
"	181	Q.17.b.7.3.	35 "	Yes.			
"	182	Q.17.b.7.2½	12 "	Yes.			
"	183	Q.17.b.6.2.	40 "	Yes.			
Old German 1st. Line.	184	Q.18.c.6.5	25 "	No.			Filled up.
"	185	Q.18.c.5.5½	25 "	Yes.			
"	186	Q.18.c.4½.5½	35 "	Yes.			
"	187	Q.18.c.3.6	2 "	N.			

Location.	No.	Map Reference.	Capacity.	If Occupied.	Being Opened up	Under construction.	Remarks.
Old German 1st. Line.	188	Q.18.c.2½.6	30 men.	Yes.			
"	189	Q.18.c.2.7	30 "	Yes.			
"	190	Q.18.c.2.8	20 "	No.			
"	191	Q.18.c.2.8½	NIL.	No.			Blown in.
"	192	Q.18.c.2.9	100 men.	Yes.			
"	193	Q.18.c.1½.9½	12 "	Yes.			
"	194	Q.18.c.1.10	25 "	No			Blown in.
"	195	Q.17.b.10.0	NIL.	No.			" "
"	196	Q.17.b.9.0	22 men.	No			" "
"	197	Q.17.b.8.½	16 "	Yes			
"	198	Q.17.b.7.1	60 "	Yes.			
"	199	Q.17.b.6.1	30 "	Yes.			
"	200	Q.17.b.5.1	30 "	No			Blown in.
"	201	Q.17.b.4.1	20 "	No.			" "
"	202	Q.17.b.3.1	18 "	No.			" "

APPENDIX V

SOUTH OF RIVER.

Location.	No.	Map Reference.	Capacity	If occupied.	Being Opened up.	Under construction.	Remarks.
Front Line.	1	R.14.d.9.6	15	Yes.			
do	2	R.14.c.95.00	40	Yes.			
do	3	R.14.c.65.00	20	Yes.			
do	4	R.14.c.80.15	50	Yes.			
do	5	R.14.d.2.9.	15	Yes.			
Support Line.	51	R.14.a.5.0.	30	No.	Yes.		60% completed.
do	52	R.14.a.4.1	50	No.	Yes.		60% complete
HINSA LINE.	115	R.13.b.4.2	10	Yes.			
do	114	R.13.b.40.17	10	Yes.			
do	113	R.13.b.42.10	10	Yes.			
do	112	R.13.b.45.05	10	Yes.			
do	111	R.13.d.61.88	8	Yes.			These are shafts which are being joined up underneath now by R.E.
do	110	R.13.d.65.85	8	Yes.			
do	109	R.13.d.70.78	8	Yes.			
do	108	R.13.d.7.7.	4	Yes.			
do	107	R.23.d.72.60	8	Yes.			These are shafts only.
do	106	R.13.d.85.55	4	Yes.			
do	105	R.13.d.90.49	8	Yes.			

Location.	No.	Map Reference.	Capacity.	If Occupied.	Being Opened up	Under construction.	Remarks.
HANSA LINE.	104	R.13.d.95.40	4	Yes.			
do	103	R.14.c.02.28	8	Yes.			
do	102	R.14.c.15.16	6	Yes.			
do	101	R.14.c.20.05	6	Yes.			
IRWIN TRENCH.	273	R.19.b.75.50	25	No.	Yes.		
do	272	R.19.b.6.4	25	No.	Yes.		
SPLUTTER ROAD.	270	R.20.c.2.8	20	No.	Yes.		
LUCKY WAY.	269	R.20.c.2.7	50	Yes.			
do	268	R.20.c.19.6	20	Yes.			
do	267	R.20.c.10.55	30	No.	Yes.		
PEEL TRENCH.	271	R.20.c.6.7	50	No.		Yes.	40' completed.
HESSIAN TRENCH.	258	R.20.c.7.4	20	Yes.			
do	257	R.20.c.72.34	20	Yes.			
do	256	R.20.c.76.28	20	Yes.			
do	255	R.20.c.80.23	25	Yes.			
do	254	R.20.c.86.15	25	Yes.			
do	253	R.20.c.91.10	25	Yes.			
do	252	R.20.c.98.08	25	Yes.			
do	251	R.20.d.05.03	25	Yes.			

Location.	No.	Map Reference.	Capacity.	Is Occupied.	Being Opened Up.	Under construction.	Remarks.
BULGAR TRENCH.	259	R.20.c.76.13	10	Yes.			
do	260	R.20.c.73.10	10	Yes.			
do	261	R.20.c.70.07	17	Yes.			
do	262	R.26.a.60.94	10	Yes.			
do	263	R.26.a.52.90	10	Yes.			
RANSOME TRENCH.	266	R.19.d.7.6	20	Yes.			
do	265	R.19.d.63.50	20	Yes.			
do	264	R.29.d.60.38	20	Yes.			
ST. PIERRE DIVION,	276	Q.24.b.7.9	50	Yes.			
MILL, FRENCH.	274	R.13.b.05.30	10	Yes.			
do	275	R.13.c.65.85	120	No.		Yes.	80' completed
ST. PIERRE LIVION.	284	Q.24.b.6.5 to Q.24.b.30.0.	300	Yes.			With a good deal of work to stop leaking and dry dugout up, would accord to 1000
do	283	Q.24.d.35.90	15	Yes.			
do	282	Q.24.d.40.85	15	Yes.			
do	281	Q.24.d.45.80	15	Yes.			
do	280	Q.24.d.48.78	15	Yes.			
do	279	Q.24.d.62.70	15	No.		Yes.	

Location.	No.	Map Reference.	Capacity.	If Occupied.	Being opened up	Under construction.	Remarks.
ST. PIERRE DIVISION.	278	Q.24.d.8.7.	15	No.	Yes.		
do	277	Q.24.d.85.62	15	No.	Yes.		
CENTRAL AVENUE, THIEPVAL.	301 to 331	R.25.b.2.9 to R.25.c.7.1.	500				In CENTRAL AVENUE, THIEPVAL there are 32 dugouts at present accomodating 500 men. Dugouts number 301-331 inclusive.
THIEPVAL.	338	R.25.c.90.35	14	Yes.			
do	349	R.25.a.05.50	9	Yes.			
do	340	R.25.d.09.70	6	Yes.			
do	341	R.25.d.1.8	30	Yes.			
do	342	R.25.d.1.9	7	Yes.			
do	343	R.25.b.2.2	15	Yes.			
do	344	R.25.b.25.25	22	Yes.			
do	345	R.25.b.4.3.	20	Yes.			
do	337	R.25.d.60.96	20	Yes.			
do	336	R.25.d.57.85	20	Yes.			
do	335	R.25.d.5.5	15	Yes.			
do	334	R.25.d.52.46	10	Yes.			

Location.	No.	Map Reference.	Capacity.	If Occupied.	Being opened up.	Under construction.	Remarks.
THIEPVAL	333	R.25.d.5.4.	15	Yes.			
do	332	R.25.d.5.1	40	Yes.			
PAISLEY DUMP. Brigade H.Q.	346	R.30.c.8.3	70	Yes.			

G S

11th DIVN

January 1917

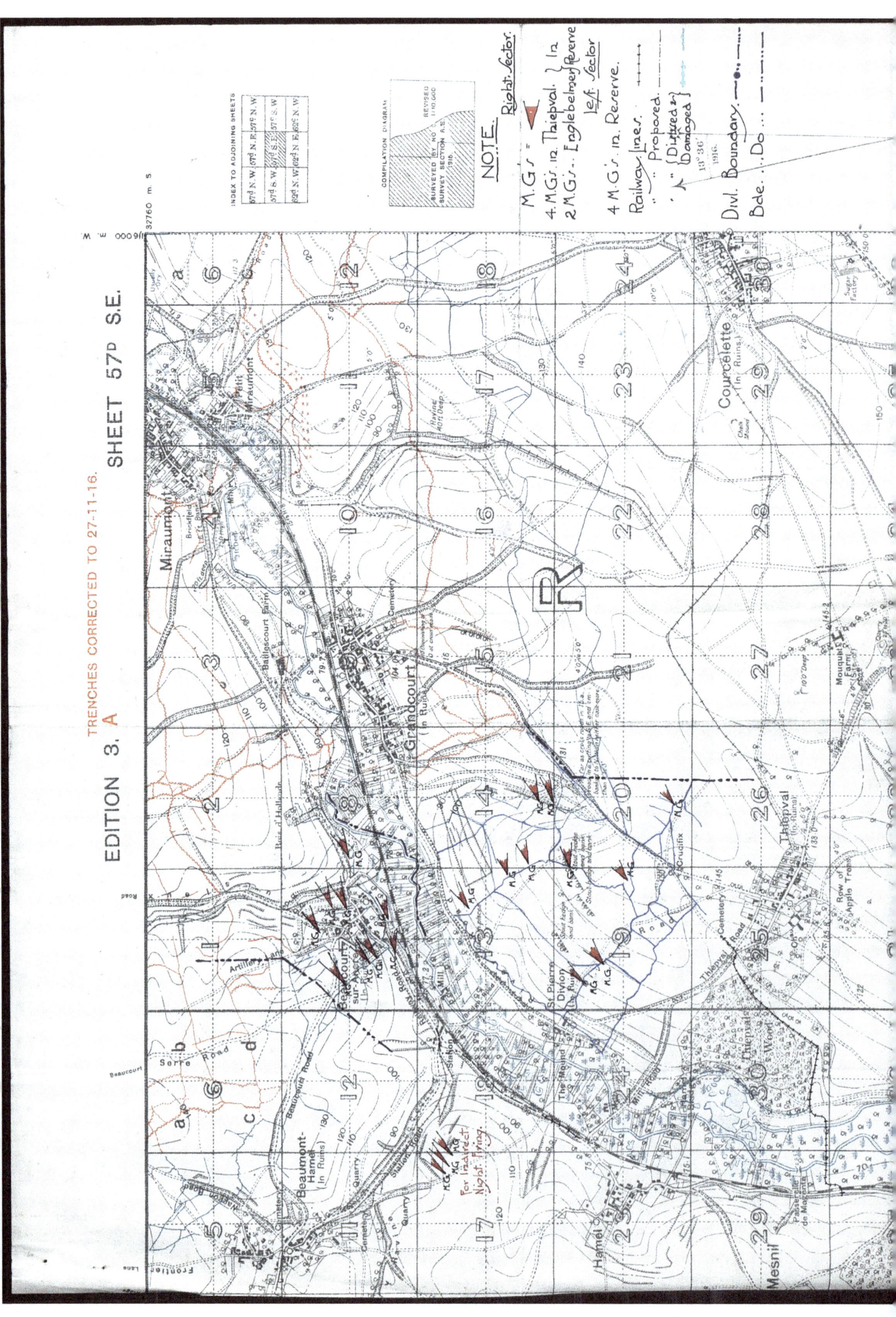

GLOSSARY.

Abbaye, Abbe	Abbey.
Abreuvoir, Abr	Watering-place.
Abri de douaniers	Customs-shelter.
Aciérie	Steel works.
Aiguilles	Points (Ry.)
Allée	Alley, Narrow road
Ancien -ne, Anc⁻ⁿᵉ	Old.
Aqueduc	Aqueduct.
Arbre	Tree.
,, éventail	,, fan-shaped.
,, débarmé	,, bare.
,, fourchu	,, forked.
,, isolé	,, isolated.
,, penché	,, leaning.
Arbrisseau	Small tree.
Arc	Arch.
Ardoisière, Ard⁻ⁿᵉ	Slate quarry.
Arrêt	Halt.
Asile	Asylum.
,, des } aliénés	Lunatic asylum.
,, d' }	
,, de charité	Asylum.
,, des pauvres	
,, de refuge	
Auberge, Aub⁻ᵍᵉ	Inn.
Aune	Alder-tree.
Bac	Ferry.
,, à traille	
Bains	Baths.
Place aux bains	Bathing place.
Balise	Boom, Beacon.
Banc de sable	Sand-bank.
,, vase	Mud-tank.
Baraque	Hut.
Barrage	Dam.
Barrière	Gate, Stile.
(Machine à) Bascule	Weigh-bridge.
Bassin	Dock, Pond.
,, d'échouage	Tidal dock.
,, de radoub	Dry dock.
Bateau phare	Light-ship.
Blanchisserie	Laundry.
B.M. (borne milliaire)	Mile stone.
B⁻ᵉ (borne kilométrique)	
Boulonnerie	Bolt Factory.
Fabᵉ de boulons	
Bouée	Buoy.
Brasserie, Brassⁱᵉ	Brewery.
Briqueterie, Briqᵗᵉ	Brickfield.
Brise-lames	Breakwater.
Bureau de poste	Post office.
,, de douane	Custom house.
Butte	Butt, Mound.
Cabane	Hut.
Cabaret, Cabᵗ	Inn.
Câble sous-marin	Submarine cable.
Calvaire, Calᵛᵉ	Calvary.
Canal de dessèchement	Drainage canal.
Canal d'irrigation	Irrigation canal.
Fabᵉ de caoutchouc	Rubber factory.
Carrière, Carʳᵉ	Quarry.
,, de gravier	Gravel-pit.
Caserne	Barracks.
Champ de courses	Race-course.
,, manœuvres	Drill-ground.
,, tir	Rifle range.
Chantier	Building yard.
,, construction	Ship yard.
	Dock yard.
Chapelle, Chˡˡᵉ	Chapel.
Charbonnage	Colliery.
Château d'eau	Water tower.
Chaussée	Causeway.
	Highway.
Chemin de fer	Railway.
Cheminée, Chⁿᵉᵉ	Chimney.
Chêne	Oak tree.
Cimetière, Cim⁻ʳᵉ	Cemetery.
Clocher	Belfry.
Clouterie	Nail factory.
Colombier	Dove-cot.
Corom	
Cour des } marchandises	Goods yard.
,, aux }	
Couvent	Convent.
Crassier	Slag heap.
Croix	Cross.
Darse	Inner dock.
Démoli -e, Dét⁻ᵉ	Destroyed.
Déversoir	Weir.
Digue	Dyke, causeway.
Distillerie, Disᵗⁱᵉ	Distillery.
Douane	Custom-house.
Entrepôt de douane	Custom warehouse.
Dynamiterie, Dynam⁻ᵐ	Dynamite magazine.
Dynamiterie	Dynamite factory.
Écluse	Sluice, Lock.
Échusette, Ecˡᵗᵉ	Sluice.
École	School.
Écurie	Stable.
Église	Church.
Émaillerie	Enamel works.
Embarcadère, Embᵉ	Landing-place.
Estaminet, Estamᵗ	Inn.
Étang	Pond.
Fabrique, Fabᵉ	Factory.
Fabᵉ de produits chimiques	Chemical works.
Fabᵉ de faïence	Pottery.
Faïencerie	
Ferme, Fᵐᵉ	Farm.
Filature, Fⁱˡᵉ	Spinning mill.
Fonderie, Fondⁱᵉ	Foundry.
Fontaine, Fontⁿᵉ	Spring, fountain.
Forêt	Forest.
Forme de radoub	Dry dock.
Forge	Smithy.
Fosse	Mine, Pit.
Fossé	Moat, Ditch.
Four	Kiln.
,, à chaux	Lime-kiln.
,, à coke	Coke oven.
Ganterie	Glove factory.
Gare	Station.
Garenne	Warren.
Garnison	Garrison.
Gazomètre	Gasometer.
Glacerie	Mirror works.
Fabᵉ de glaces	
Glacière	Ice house.
Grue	Crane.
Gué	Ford.
Guérite	Sentry-box.
,, à signaux	Signal box.
Halte	Halt.
Hangar	Shed.
Hôpital	Hospital.
Hôtel-de-Ville	Town-hall.
Houillère	Colliery.
Huilerie	Oil mill.
Imprimerie, Impʳᵉ	Printing works.
Jetée	Pier.
Laminerie	Rolling mill.
Ligne } de haute marée	High water line.
Laisse } de basse marée	Low water line.
Maison Forestière, Mⁿ Fᵉ	Forester's house.
Maîtrise	Master's house.
Marbrerie	Marble works.
Marais	Marsh.
Marais salant	Salt marsh.
Marché	Market.
Mare	Pool.
Meule	Rick.
Minière	Mine.
Monastère	Monastery.
Moulin, Mⁿ	Mill.
,, à vapeur	Steam Mill.
Mur	Wall.
,, crénelé	Loop-holed wall.

Workmen's dwellings

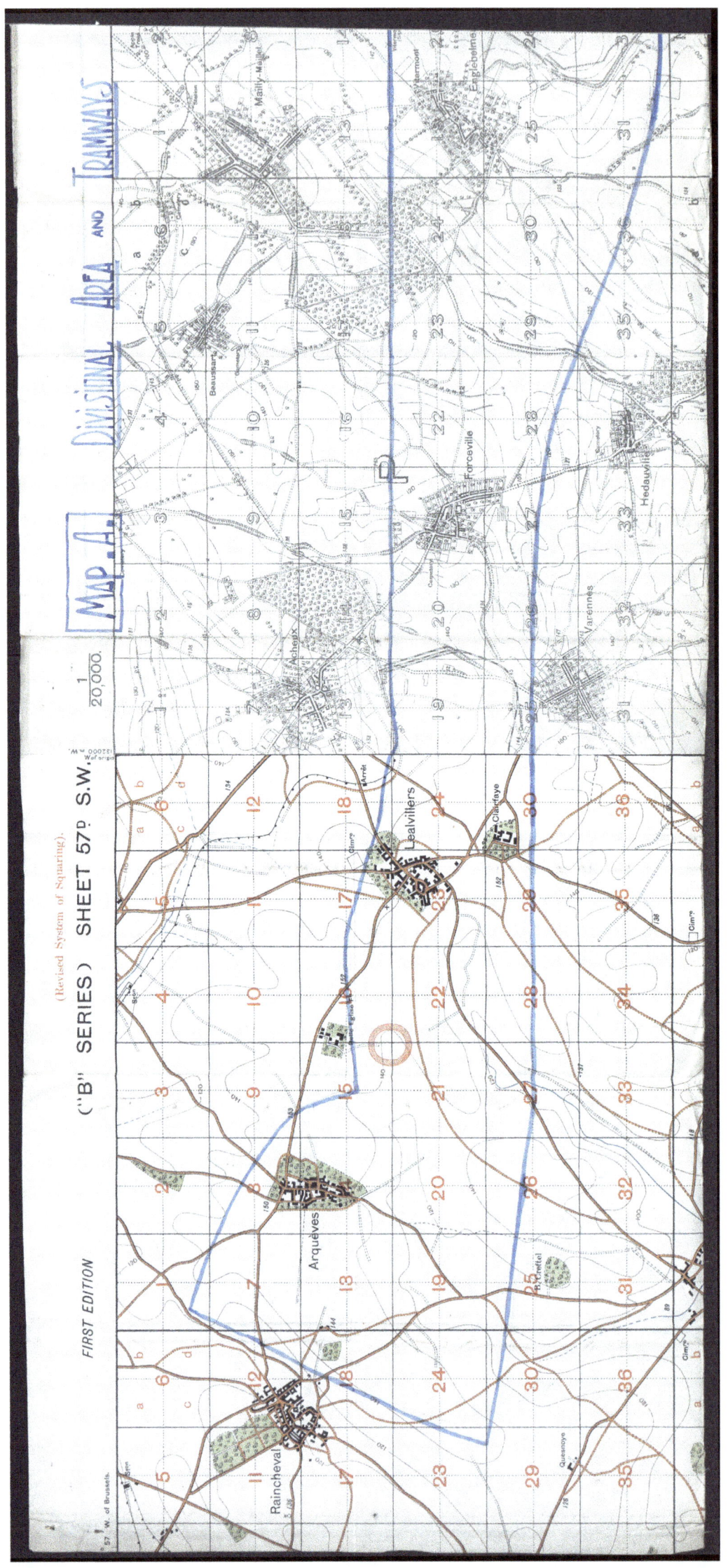

Map A. Divisional Area and Tramways

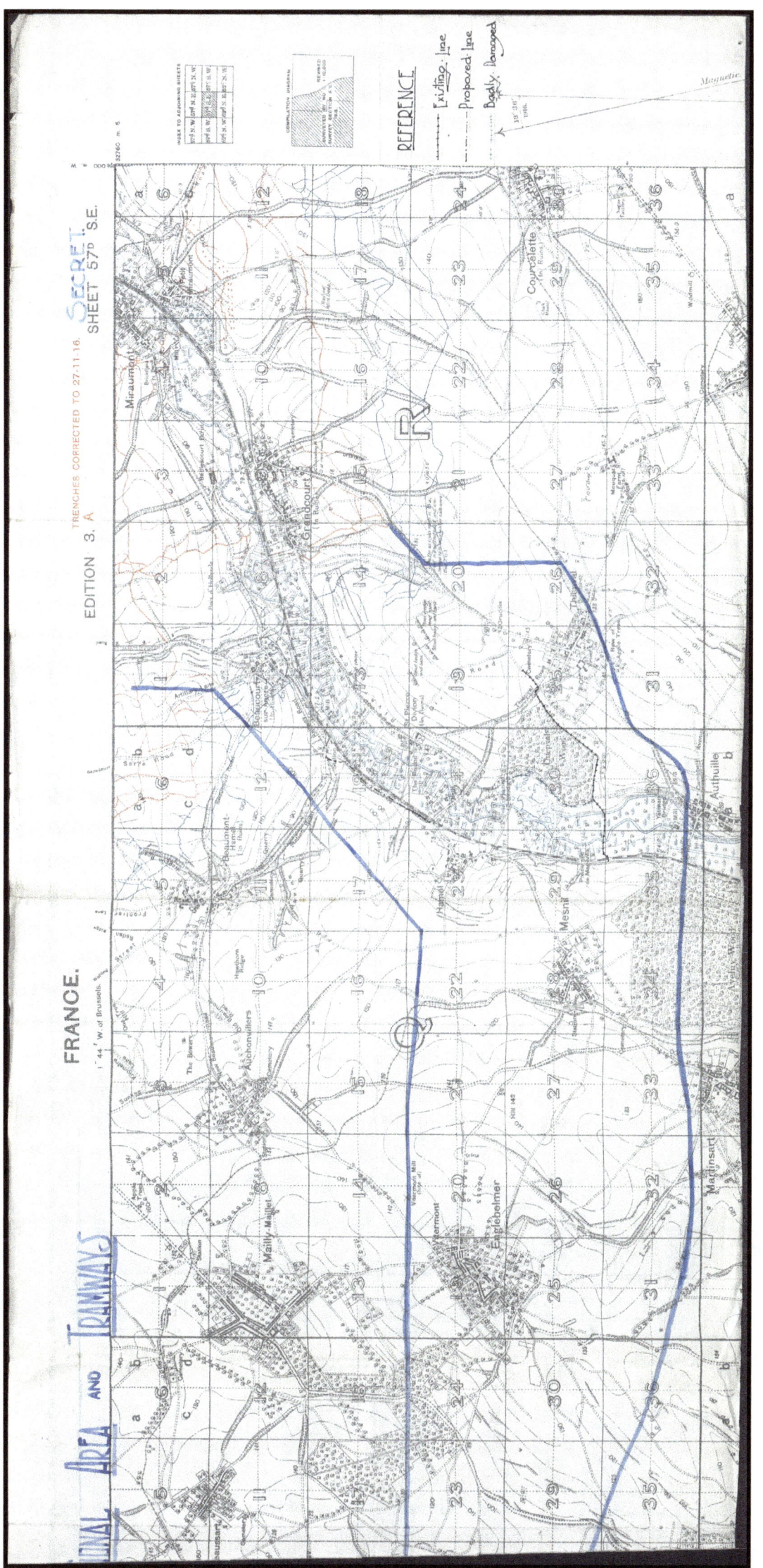

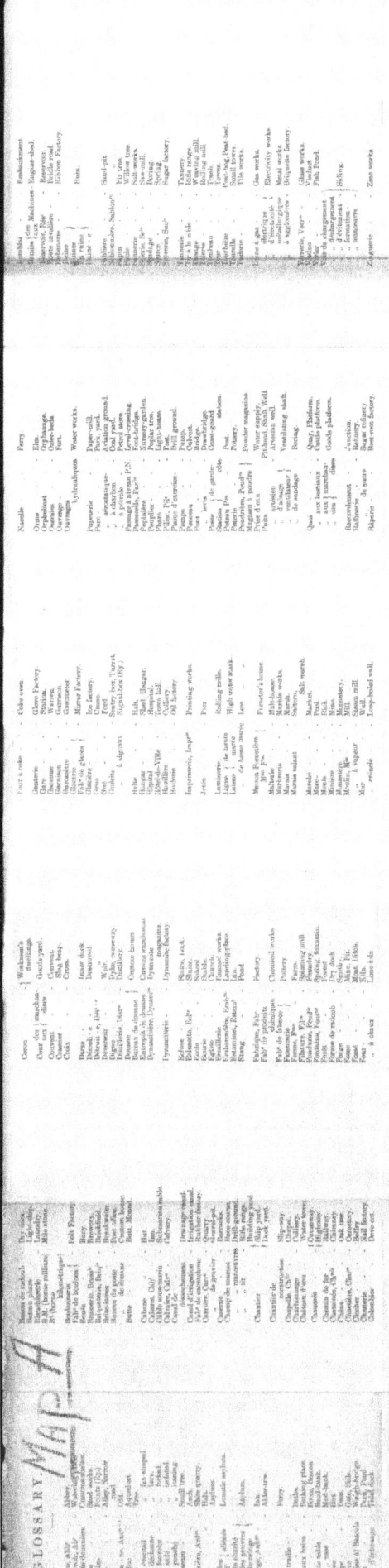

TRENCH MAP.
FRANCE.
SHEET 57D S.E.
EDITION 3. A

SCALE 1/20,000

INDEX TO ADJOINING SHEETS

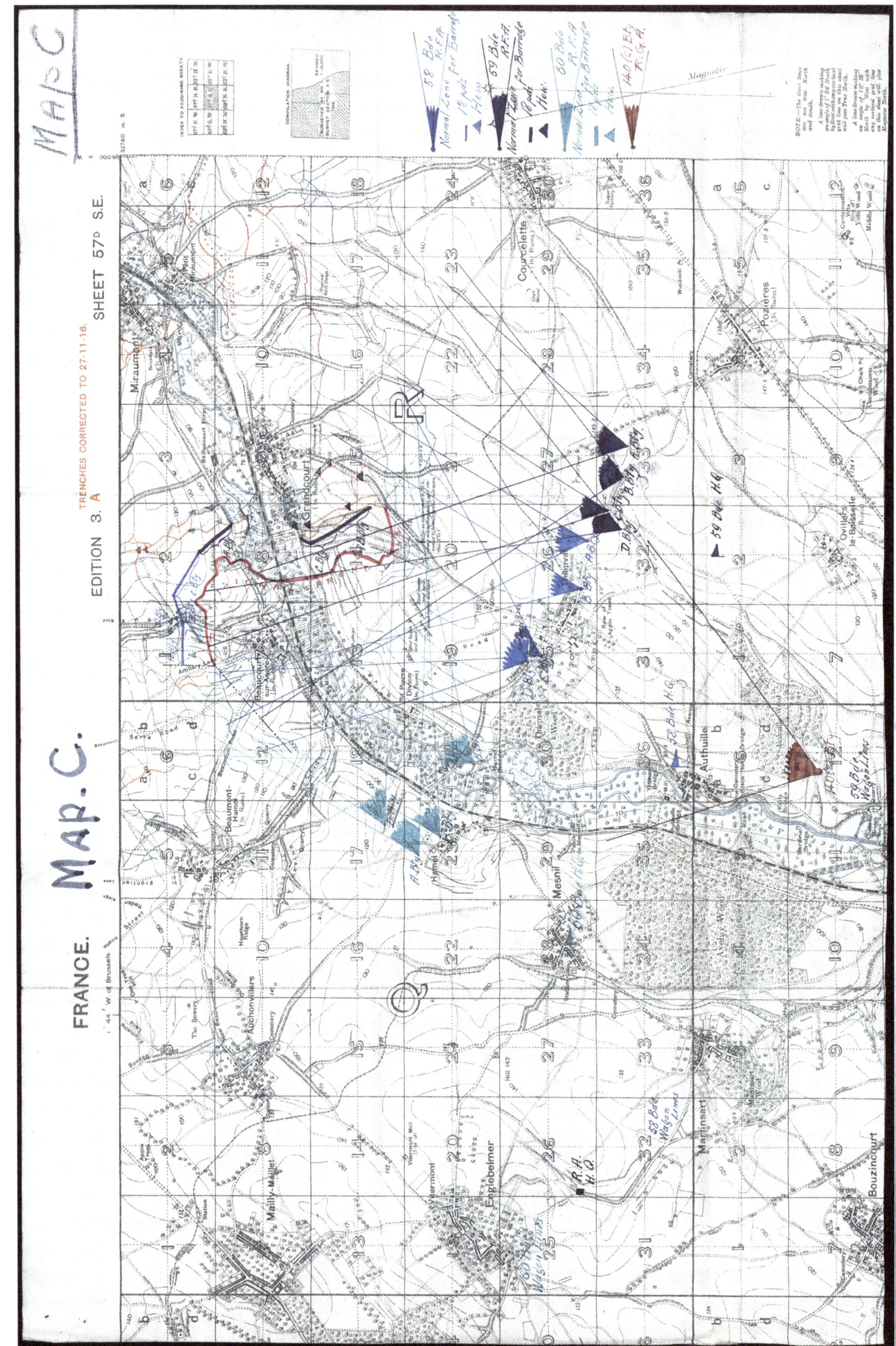

GLOSSARY.

Abbaye, Abʸᵉ	Abbey
Abreuvoir, Abʳ	Watering-place
Abri de douaniers	Customs shelter
Aciérie	Steel works
Aiguilles	Points (Ry)
Allée	Alley, Narrow road
Ancien — ne, Ancⁿ⁻ⁿᵉ	Old
Aqueduc	Aqueduct
Arbre	Tree
" oriental	" fan-shaped
" déchaussé	" bare
" fourché	" forked
" isolé	" isolated
" penché	" leaning
Arrimoirs	Small tree
Arc	Arch
Ardoisière, Ardʳᵉ	Slate quarry
Arrêt	Halt
Asile	Asylum
" d'aliénés	Lunatic asylum
" de charité	
" des pauvres	
" de refuge	
Auberge, Aubᵉ	Inn
Autel	Alder-tree
Bac	Ferry
Bains	Baths
Blanc aux bains	Bathing-place
Balise	Beacon
Banc de sable	Sand-bank
Banc de vase	Mud-bank
Barrage	Dam
Barrière	Gate, Stile
Bascule à Bascule	Weigh-bridge
Bassin	Dock, Pond
Bassin d'échouage	Tidal dock

Bassin de radoub	Dry dock
Bateau phare	Light-ship
Blanchisserie	Laundry
B. M. (borne milliaire)	Mile stone
Bⁿ (borne)	
Boulangerie	
Fabʳᵉ de boulons	Bolt Factory
Brasserie, Brassᵉ	Brewery
Briqueterie, Briqᵉ	Brickfield
Brise-lames	Breakwater
Bureau de poste	Post office
Butte	Custom house
	Butt, Mount
Cabane, Cabⁿᵉ	Hut
Cabaret, marin	Inn
Calvaire, Calⁿᵉ	Submarine cable
Casino de	Calvary
dessèchement	Drainage canal
Canal d'irrigation	Irrigation canal
Fabʳᵉ de caoutchouc	Rubber factory
Carrière, Carrᵉ	Quarry
Caserne	Barracks
Champ de courses	Race-course
" " manœuvres	Drill-ground
" " tir	Rifle range
Chantier	Building yard
" de construction	Ship yard
"	Dock yard
Chapelle, Chⁿᵉ	Chapel
Charbonnage	Colliery
Château d'eau	Water tower
Chaussée	Causeway
Chemin de fer	Railway
Cheminée, Chᵉᵉ	Chimney
Chêne	Oak tree
Cimetière, Cimᵉ	Cemetery
Cloche	Bell
Clocher	Steeple
Colombier	Dove-cot

Coron	Workmen's dwellings
Cour des marchandises	Goods yard
Ouvroir aux	
Ouvroir	Convent
Croix	Cross
Danse	Dance
Détroit — e, Détʳ	Strait
Déversoir	Weir
Digue	Dyke, Causeway
Distillerie, Distᵉ	Distillery
Douane	Custom house
Bureau de douane	
Entrepôt de douanes	Custom warehouse
Dynamiterie, Dynamᵉ	Dynamite magazine
	Dynamite factory
Écluse	Sluice, Lock
Échelette, Échʳᵉ	Sluice
École	School
Écurie	Stable
Église	Church
Émaillerie	Enamel works
Embarcadère, Embʳᵉ	Landing place
Établisemᵗ, Établmᵗ	
Étang	Pond
Fabrique, Fabʳᵉ	Factory
Fabᵉ de produits chimiques	Chemical works
Fabʳᵉ de faïence	Pottery
Faïencerie	
Ferme, Fᵉ	Farm
Filature, Filᵉ	Spinning mill
Fonderie, Fondᵉ	Foundry
Fontaine, Fonⁿᵉ	Spring, fountain
Forêt	Forest
Forme de radoub	Dry dock
Forge	Smithy
Fossé	Ditch, Pit
Four	Oven
" à chaux	Lime-kiln

Four à coke	Coke oven
Ganterie	Glove Factory
Gare	Station
Garenne	Warren
Garnison	Garrison
Gazomètre	Gas-meter
Glacerie	Mirror Factory
Glacière	Ice factory
Grue	Crane
Gué	Ford
Guérite	Sentry-box, Turret
" à signaux	Signal-box (Ry)
Halte	Halt
Hangar	Shed, Hangar
Hôpital	Hospital
Hôtel-de-Ville	Town hall
Houillère	Colliery
Huilerie	Oil factory
Imprimerie, Impʳᵉ	Printing works
Jetée	Pier
Lamaserie	
Ligne de haute	
Laisse de basse marée	High water mark
	Low
Maison Forestière, Mⁿ Forʳᵉ	Forester's house
Malterie	Malt-house
Marbrerie	Marble works
Marais salant	Salt marsh
Saltern	
Marché	Market
Mare	Pool
Moche	
Minière	Mine
Minoterie	Monastery
Moulin, Mⁿ	Mill
" à vapeur	Steam mill
Mur	Wall
Mur crénelé	Loop-holed wall

Nacelle	Ferry
Orme	Elm
Orphelinat	Orphanage
Ossuaire	Ossuary
Ouvrage	Fort
" hydrauliques	Water works
Papeterie	Paper-mill
Parc	Park, yard
" aérostatique	Aviation ground
" à charbon	Coal yard
Passage à niveau, P.N.	Level crossing
Passerelle, Passᵉ	Foot-bridge
Pépinière	Nursery-garden
Peuplier	Poplar tree
Phare	Light-house
Pilier, Pⁱ	Pier
Plaine d'exercice	Drill ground
Plateau	Pass, plateau
Pont	Bridge
Ponceau	Culvert
Poste de garde	Post
Station Pᵉ	Station
Poudrière, Poudʳ	Powder magazine
Magasin à poudre	
Prise d'eau	Water supply
Puits	Pit-head, Shaft, Well
" aréoien	Artesian well
" d'aérage	Ventilating shaft
Quai	Quay, Platform
" aux bestiaux	Cattle platform
" aux marchandises	Goods platform
Raccordement	Junction
Raffinerie	Refinery
" de sucre	Sugar refinery
Râperie	Beet-root factory

GLOSSARY.

Abbaye, Abb^e	Abbey.
Abreuvoir, Ab^r	Watering-place.
Abri de douaniers	Custom-shelter.
Aciérie	Steel works.
Aiguilles	Points (Ry.)
Allée	Alley, Narrow road.
Ancien -ne, Anc^{n -ne}	Old.
Aqueduc	Aqueduct.
Arbre	Tree.
" éventail	fan-shaped.
" décharné	bare.
" fourchu	forked.
" incliné	inclined.
" penché	leaning.
Arbrisseau	Small tree.
Arc	Arch.
Ardoisière, Ard^{re}	Slate quarry.
Arrêt	Halt.
Asile	Asylum.
" des aliénés	Lunatic asylum.
" d. de charité	
" des pauvres de refuge	Asylum.
Auberge, Aub^e	Inn.
Aune	Alder-tree.
Bac	Ferry.
" à traille	
Bains	Baths.
Place aux bains	Bathing place.
Balise	Boom, Beacon.
Banc de sable	Sand-bank.
" vase	Mud-bank.
Baraque	Hut.
Barrage	Dam.
Barrière	Gate, Stile.
(Machine à) Bascule	Weigh-bridge.
Bassin	Dock, Pond.
" d'échouage	Tidal dock.
Bassin de radoub	Dry dock.
Bateau phare	Light-ship.
Blanchisserie	Laundry.
B.M. (borne milliaire)	Mile stone.
B^k (borne kilométrique)	
Boulonnerie Fab^e de boulons	Bolt Factory.
Bouée	Buoy.
Brasserie, Bras^{ie}	Brewery.
Briqueterie, Briq^{ie}	Brickfield.
Brise-lames	Breakwater.
Bureau de poste	Post office.
" da douane	Custom house.
Butte	Butt, Mound.
Cabane	Hut.
Cabaret, Cab^t	Inn.
Câble sous-marin	Submarine cable.
Calvaire, Cal^{re}	Calvary.
Canal de desséchement	Drainage canal.
Canal d'irrigation	Irrigation canal.
Fab^e de caoutchouc	Rubber factory.
Carrière, Carr^{re}	Quarry.
" de gravier	Gravel-pit.
Caserne	Barracks.
Champ de courses	Race course.
" manœuvres	Drill-ground.
" tir	Rifle range.
Chantier	Building yard. Ship yard. Dock yard.
Chantier de construction	Slip-way.
Chapelle, Ch^{le}	Chapel.
Charbonnage	Colliery.
Château d'eau	Water tower.
Chaussée	Causeway.
Chemin de fer	Railway.
Cheminée, Ch^{ée}	Chimney.
Chêne	Oak-tree.
Cimetière, Cim^{re}	Cemetery.
Clocher	Belfry.
Clouterie	Nail factory.
Colombier	Dove-cot.
Coron	Workmen's dwellings.
Cour des marchandises	Goods yard.
Couvent	Convent.
Crassier	Slag heap.
Croix	Cross.
Darse	Inner dock.
Démoli -e	Destroyed.
Détruit -e, Dét^t	
Déversoir	Weir.
Digue	Dyke, causeway.
Distillerie, Dist^{ie}	Distillery.
Douane	Custom-house.
Bureau de douane	
Entrepôt de douane	Custom warehouse.
Dynamitière, Dynam^{re}	Dynamite magazine.
Dynamiterie, Dynam^{ie}	Dynamite factory.
Écluse	Sluice, Lock.
Écluette, Ecl^{te}	Sluice.
École	School.
Écurie	Stable.
Église	Church.
Émaillerie	Enamel works.
Embarcadère, Emb^{re}	Landing-place.
Établissement, Etab^{mt}	Inn.
Étang	Pond.
Fabrique, Fab^e	Factory.
Fab^e de produits chimiques	Chemical works.
Fab^e de faïence	Pottery.
Faïencerie	
Ferme, F^{me}	Farm.
Filature, Fil^{re}	Spinning mill.
Fonderie, Fond^{ie}	Foundry.
Fontaine, Font^{ne}	Spring, fountain.
Forêt	Forest.
Forme de radoub	Dry dock.
Forge	Smithy.
Fosse	Mine, Pit.
Fossé	Moat, Ditch.
Four	Kiln.
" à chaux	Lime-kiln.
Four à coke	Coke oven.
Ganterie	Glove Factory.
Gare	Station.
Garenne	Warren.
Garnison	Garrison.
Gazomètre	Gasometer.
Glacerie Fab^e de glaces	Mirror Factory.
Glacière	Ice factory.
Grue	Crane.
Gué	Ford.
Guérite	Sentry-box, Turret.
" à signaux	Signal-box (Ry.)
Halte	Halt.
Hangar	Shed, Hangar.
Hôpital	Hospital.
Hôtel-de-Ville	Town hall.
Houillère	Colliery.
Huilerie	Oil factory.
Imprimerie, Imp^{ie}	Printing works.
Jetée	Pier.
Laminerie	Rolling mills.
Ligne de haute laisse de marée	High water mark.
" de basse marée	Low
Maison Forestière M^{on} F^{re}	Forester's house.
Malterie	Malt-house.
Marbrerie	Marble works.
Marais	Marsh.
Marais salant	Salt marsh.
Marché	Market.
Mare	Pool.
Meule	Rick.
Minière	Mine.
Monastère	Monastery.
Moulin, Mⁱⁿ	Mill.
" à vapeur	Steam mill.
Mur	Wall.
" crénelé	Loop-holed wall.
Nacelle	
Orme	
Orphelinat	
Ossuaire	
Ouvrages	
Papeterie	
Parc	
" à charbon	
" à poudre	
Passage à niveau	
Passerelle, Pass^{le}	
Pépinière	
Peuplier	
Phare	
Pilier, Pil^r	
Plaine d'exercice	
Pompe	
Ponceau	
Pont	
" à lavis	
Pataire	
Poterie	
Poudrerie, Poud^{ie}	
Magasin à poudre	
Prise d'eau	
Puits	
" artésien	
" d'aérage	
" ventilateur	
" de sondage	
Quai	
" aux bateaux	
" aux marchandises	
Raccordement	
Raffinerie	
" de sucre	
Râperie	

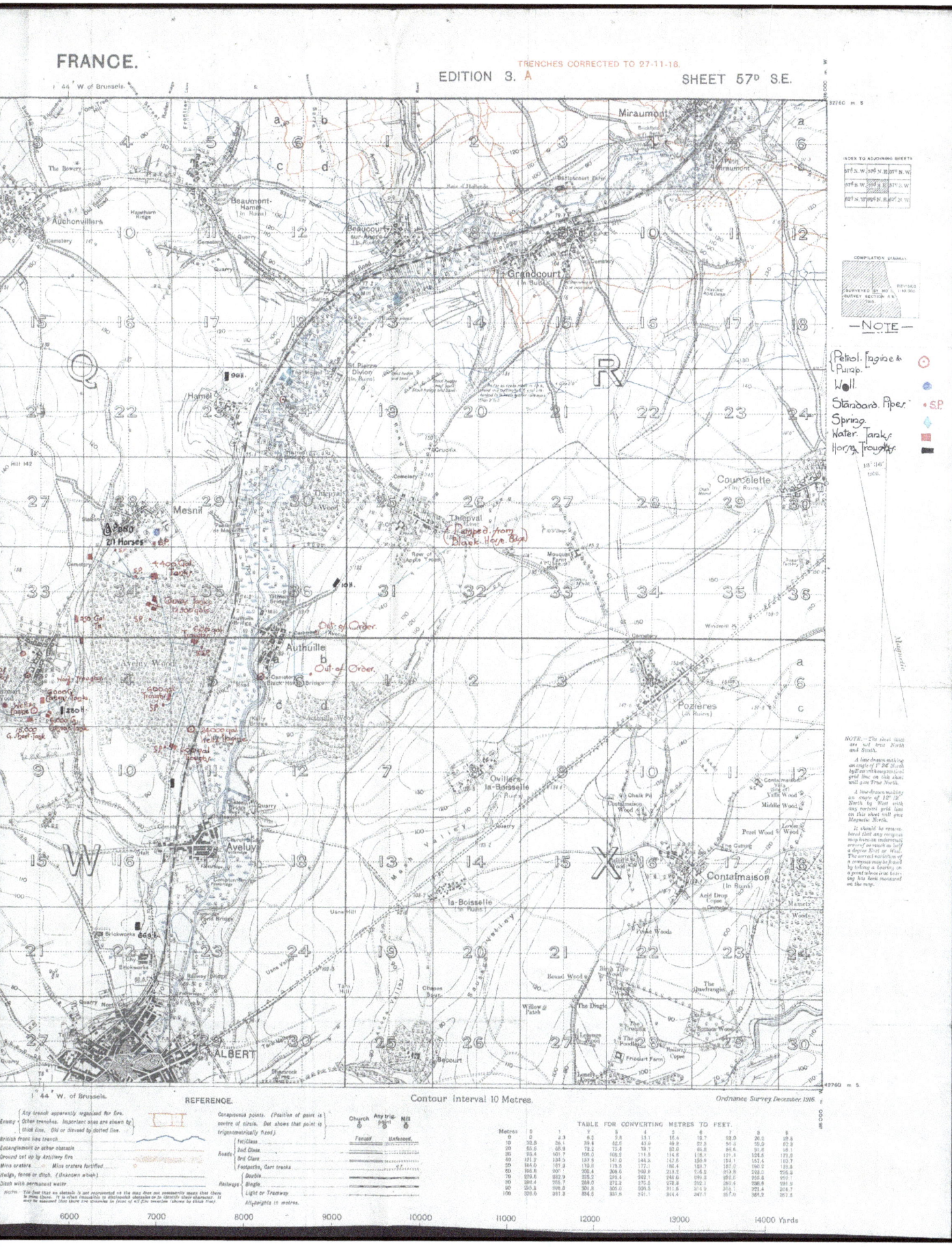

GLOSSARY.

Abbaye, Abb^e	Abbey
Abreuvoir, Ab^r	Watering-place
Abri de douaniers	Customs-shelter
Aciérie	Steel works
Aiguilles	Points (Ry.)
Allée	Alley, Narrow road
Ancien, -ne, Anc^{n,ne}	Old
Aqueduc	Aqueduct
Arbre	Tree
,, éventail	,, fan-shaped
,, ébranché	,, bare
,, fourchu	,, forked
,, isolé	,, isolated
,, penché	,, leaning
Arbrisseau	Small tree
Arc	Arch
Ardoisière, Ard^{re}	Slate quarry
Arrêt	Halt
Asile	Asylum
,, des aliénés	Lunatic asylum
,, d' ...	
,, de charité	
,, des pauvres, de refuge	Asylum
Auberge, Aub^{ge}	Inn
Aune	Alder-tree
Bac	Ferry
,, à traille	Ferry
Bains	Baths
Bains aux boues	Bathing place
Balise	Beacon
Banc de sable	Sand-bank
,, vase	Mud-bank
Baraque	Hut
Barrage	Dam
Barrière	Gate, Stile
(Machine à) Bascule	Weigh-bridge
Bassin	Dock, Pond
,, d'échouage	Tidal dock
Bassin de radoub	Dry dock
Bateau phare	Light-ship
Blanchisserie	Laundry
B.M. (borne milliaire)	Mile stone
B^e (borne kilométrique)	
Boulonnerie Fab^e de boulons	Bolt Factory
Bouée	Buoy
Brasserie, Brass^{ie}	Brewery
Briqueterie, Brig^{te}	Brickfield
Brise-lames	Breakwater
Bureau de poste	Post office
,, de douane	Custom house
Butte	Butt, Mound
Cabane	Hut
Cabaret, Cab^t	Inn
Câble sous-marin	Submarine cable
Calvaire, Calv^e	Calvary
Canal de dessèchement	Drainage canal
Canal d'irrigation	Irrigation canal
Fab^e de caoutchouc	Rubber factory
Carrière, Carr^e	Quarry
,, de gravier	Gravel-pit
Caserne	Barracks
Champ de courses	Race-course
,, manœuvres	Drill-ground
,, tir	Rifle range
Chantier	Building yard, Ship yard, Dock yard
Chantier de construction	Slip-way
Chapelle, Ch^{lle}	Chapel
Charbonnage	Colliery
Château d'eau	Water tower
Chaussée	Causeway, Highway
Chemin de fer	Railway
Cheminée, Ch^{ée}	Chimney
Chêne	Oak tree
Cimetière, Cim^{re}	Cemetery
Clocher	Belfry
Clouterie	Nail factory
Colombier	Dove-cot
Coron	Workmen's dwellings
Cour des marchandises, aux dises	Goods yard
Couvent	Convent
Cuvelier	Slag heap
Croix	Cross
Dame	Inner dock
Dépôt	
Détruit -e, Dét^{r,te}	Destroyed
Déversoir	Weir
Digue	Dyke, causeway
Distillerie, Dist^{ie}	Distillery
Douane	
Bureau de douane	Custom-house
Entrepôt de douane	Custom warehouse
Dynamitière, Dynam^{re}	Dynamite magazine
Dynamiterie	Dynamite Factory
Ecluse	Sluice, Lock
Eclusette, Ecl^{te}	Sluice
Ecole	School
Ecurie	Stable
Eglise	Church
Emaillerie	Enamel works
Embarcadère, Emb^{re}	Landing-place
Estaminet, Estam^t	Inn
Etang	Pond
Fabrique, Fab^e	Factory
Fab^e de produits chimiques	Chemical works
Faïencerie	Pottery
Ferme, F^{me}	Farm
Filature, Fil^{re}	Spinning mill
Fonderie, Fond^{ie}	Foundry
Fontaine, Font^{ne}	Spring, fountain
Forêt	Forest
Forme de radoub	Dry-dock
Forge	Smithy
Fosse	Mine, Pit
Fossé	Moat, Ditch
Four	Kiln
,, à chaux	Lime-kiln
Four à coke	Coke oven
Ganterie	Glove Factory
Gare	Station
Garenne	Warren
Garnison	Garrison
Gazomètre	Gasometer
Glacerie	
Fab^e de glaces	Mirror Factory
Glacière	Ice factory
Grue	Crane
Gué	Ford
Guérite	Sentry-box, Turret
,, à signaux	Signal-box (Ry.)
Halte	Halt
Hangar	Shed, Hangar
Hôpital	Hospital
Hôtel-de-Ville	Town hall
Houillère	Colliery
Huilerie	Oil factory
Imprimerie, Impr^{ie}	Printing works
Jetée	Pier
Laminerie	Rolling mills
Ligne de haute	High water mark
Laisse marée	
,, de basse marée	Low
Maison Forestière Mon. For^{re}	Forester's house
Malterie	Malt-house
Marbrerie	Marble works
Marais	Marsh
Marais salant	Saltern, Salt marsh
Marché	Market
Mare	Pool
Meule	Rick
Minière	Mine
Monnaierie	Monnaiery
Moulin, Mⁱⁿ	Mill
,, à vapeur	Steam mill
Mur	Wall
,, crénelé	Loop-holed wall
Nacelle	
Orme	
Orphelinat	
Ossemen	
Ouvrages	
Papeterie	
Parc	
,, à charbon	
,, à pétrole	
Passage à niveau	
Passerelle, Pas^{le}	
Peuplier	
Phare	
Pilier, Pil^r	
Plaine d'exercice	
Pompe	
Ponceau	
Pont	
,, levis	
Poste de garde	
Station	
Potasse	
Poterie	
Poudrière, Poud^{re}	
Magasin à poudre	
Prise d'eau	
Puits	
,, artésien	
,, d'aérage	
,, de ventilation	
,, de soude	
Quai	
,, aux bestiaux	
,, aux marchandises	
,, des voyageurs	
Raccordement	
Raffinerie	
Râperie	

TRENCH MAP.
FRANCE.
SHEET 57ᴅ S.E.
EDITION 3. A

INDEX TO ADJOINING SHEETS

SCALE 1/20,000

Four à coke	Coke oven.
Ganterie	Glove Factory.
Gare	Station.
Garenne	Warren.
Garnison	Garrison.
Gazomètre	Gasometer.
Glacerie	
Fab. de glaces	Mirror Factory.
Glacière	Ice factory.
Grue	Crane.
Gué	Ford.
Guérite à signaux	Sentry-box, Turret Signal-box (Ry.)
Halte	Halt.
Hangar	Shed, Hangar.
Hôpital	Hospital.
Hôtel de Ville	Town hall.
Houillère	Colliery.
Huilerie	Oil factory.
Imprimerie, Imp^rie	Printing works.
Jetée	Pier
Laminerie	Rolling mills.
Ligne de haute marée	High water mark.
Laisses de basse marée	Low " "
Maison Forestière, M^on F^re	Forester's house.
Malterie	Malt-house.
Marbrerie	Marble works.
Marais	Marsh.
Marais salant	Salt marsh.
Marché	Market.
Mare	Pool.
Meule	Rick.
Minière	Mine.
Monastère	Monastery.
Moulin, M^n	Mill.
" à vapeur	Steam mill
" cernelé	Loop-holed wall.

Nacelle	Ferry.
Orme	Elm.
Orphelinat	Orphanage.
Ossuaire	Osse-beds.
Ouvrage	Fort.
Ouvrages hydrauliques	Water works.
Papeterie	Paper-mill.
Parc	Park, paddock.
" aéronautique	Aviation ground.
" à charbon	Coal yard.
Passage à niveau P.N.	Level crossing.
Passerelle, à tab^le	Foot-bridge.
Pépinières	Nursery-garden.
Peuplier	Poplar tree.
Phare	Light-house.
Pilier, Pil^r	Post.
Plaine d'exercice	Drill ground.
Pompe	Pump.
Ponceau	Culvert.
Pont	Bridge.
" levis	Drawbridge.
Poste de garde côte	Coast-guard station.
Potelet P^ot	Post.
Poterie	Pottery.
Poudrière, Poud^re	Powder magazine
Magasin à poudre	
Prise d'eau	Water supply.
Puits	Pit-head, Shaft, Well.
" artésien	Artesian well.
" d'arage	Ventilating shaft.
" ventilateur	
" de sondage	Boring.
Quai	Quay, Platform.
" aux bestiaux	Cattle platform.
" des marchandises	Goods platform.
Raccordements	Junction.
Raffinerie	Refinery.
" de sucre	Sugar refinery
Bijoirie	Beet-root factory.

Remblai	Embankment.
Remise (des Machines)	Engine-shed.
Réservoir, Rés^r (eau)	Reservoir.
Route cochière	Bridle road.
Rubannerie	Ribbon Factory.
Ruine	} Ruin.
Ruines	
En ruine	
Ruiné - e	
Sablière	Sand-pit.
Sablonnière, Sablon^re	"
Sapin	Fir tree.
Saule	Willow tree.
Saunerie	Salt-works.
Scierie, Sc^ie	Saw-mill.
Sondage	Boring.
Source	Spring.
Sucrerie, Suc^re	Sugar factory.
Tannerie	Tannery.
Tir à la cible	Rifle range.
Tissage	Weaving mill
Tôlerie	Rolling mill
Tombeau	Tomb.
Tour	Tower.
Tourbière	Peat-bog, Peat-bed.
Tourelle	Small tower.
Tuilerie	Tile works.
Usine à gaz	Gas works.
" d'électricité	Electricity works.
" métallurgique	Metal works.
" à agglomérés	Briquette factory.
Verrerie, Verr^ie	Glass works.
Viaduc	Viaduct.
Vivier	Fish Pond.
Voie de chargement	} Siding.
" déchargement	
" d'évitement	
" formation	
" manœuvre	
Zinguerie	Zinc works.

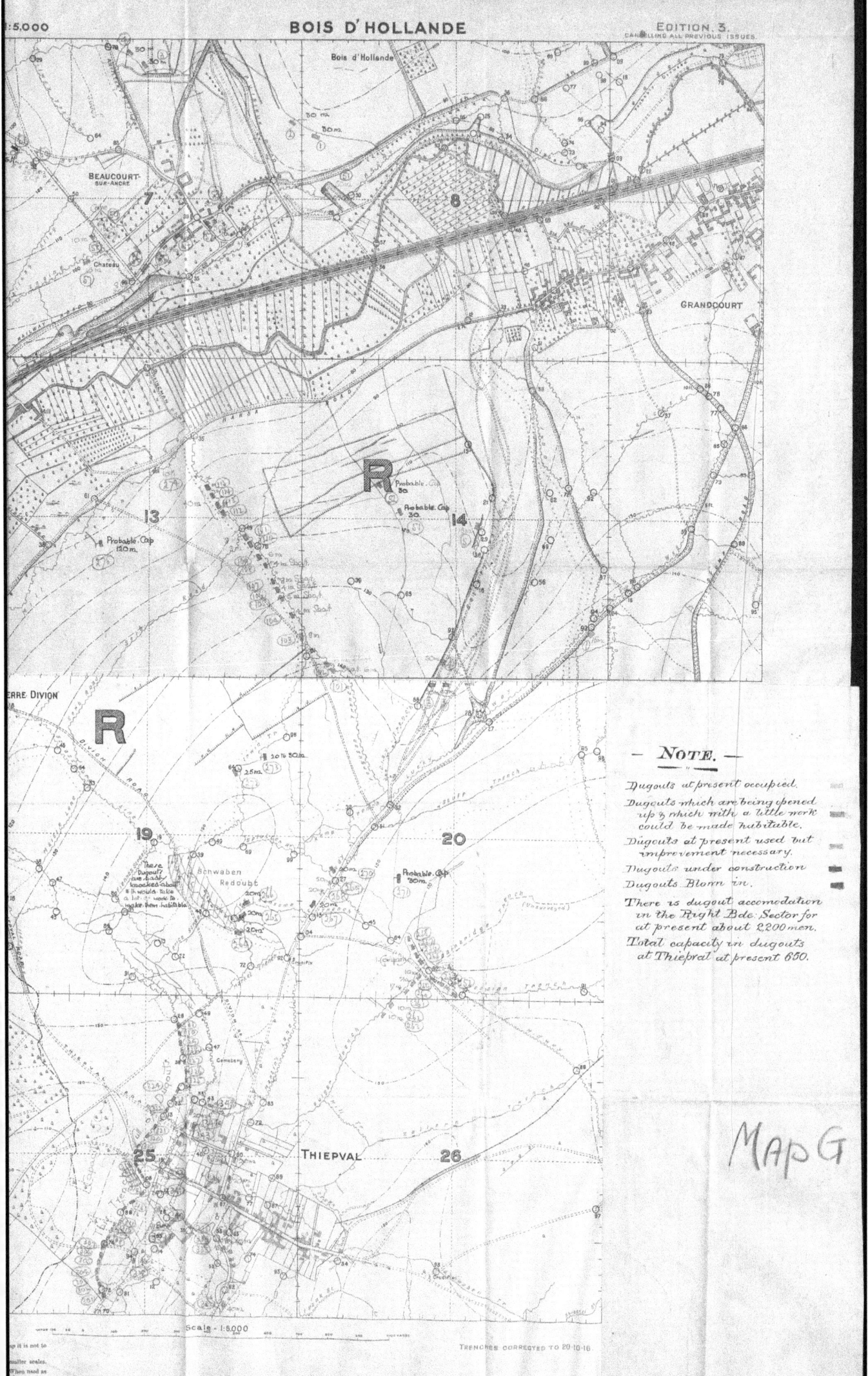

WAR DIARY.

11th. DIVISION "G".

FEBRUARY 1917.

Army Form C. 2118.

WAR DIARY
or
INTELLIGENCE SUMMARY.

11th. DIVISION. "G"   FEBRUARY 1917.

(Erase heading not required.)

Instructions regarding War Diaries and Intelligence Summaries are contained in F. S. Regs., Part II. and the Staff Manual respectively. Title pages will be prepared in manuscript.

Place	Date	Hour	Summary of Events and Information	Remarks and references to Appendices
YVRENCH	1st.		Training continued. Hard frost, and snow still on the ground.	
"	2nd.		Training continued. No change in weather.	
"	3rd.		Training continued. The Army Commander visits the Division and sees 2 Battalions in each Bde. at their training. No change in weather.	
"	4th.		Church parades. Weather unchanged.	
"	5th.		Training continued. Weather unchanged.	
"	6th.		Training continued. Weather unchanged.	
"	7th.		Training continued. Weather unchanged.	
"	8th.		Training continued. Weather unchanged.	
"	9th.		Training continued. Presentation of Medals by G.O.C. Weather unchanged.	
"	10th.		Training continued. Weather unchanged.	
"	11th.		Church parades. Weather unchanged.	
"	12th.		Training continued. Thaw sets in and weather mild.	
"	13th.		Training continued. Weather bright and mild.	
"	14th.		Training continued. Weather unchanged.	
"	15th.		Training continued. 33rd. Brigade leaves the YVRENCH Area and proceeds to AUTHIE to relieve 187th. Bde. of 62nd.Divn. on construction of railway in AUTHIE Valley. No change in weather.	
"	16th.		Training continued. Weather mild and some rain.	

Army Form C. 2118.

WAR DIARY
or
INTELLIGENCE SUMMARY.

11th. DIVISION "G"

FEBRUARY 1917.

(Erase heading not required.)

Instructions regarding War Diaries and Intelligence Summaries are contained in F.S. Regs., Part II. and the Staff Manual respectively. Title pages will be prepared in manuscript.

Place	Date	Hour	Summary of Events and Information	Remarks and references to Appendices
YVRENCH	17th.		Training continued. Weather dull and mild.	
"	18th.		Church parades. Order received from XIII Corps for Division (less Artillery) to move to CANAPLES Area on 20th. Feb. Order No.58. issued to this effect. Some rain.	APP.I. D.O. 58.
"	19th.		Training continued. Preliminary entraining order issued in view of Division becoming H.H.Q. reserve at noon on 20th. Feb. XIII Corps Order received for Artillery to join V Corps at ACHEUX on 22nd. February. Wet day.	APP.2 Entraining Order.
YVRENCH CANAPLES.	20th.		Division becomes G.H.Q. Reserve at 12 noon. Division (less Artillery and 33rd. Inf. Bde.) move to CANAPLES area. D.H.Q. close at YVRENCH and open at CANAPLES at 12 noon. 34th. Inf. Bde. continue training. Wet day.	APP.3 Location Table dated 20th.
CANAPLES	21st.		Training continued. Order received from V Corps for Division to move into MARIEUX Area on 23rd. and 24th. February and for M.G. Coys. to relieve M.G. Coys. of 7th. Division on 62nd. Division's front on 25th. Feb.	
"	22nd.		Training continued. Order No. 59 issued directing the move into V Corps area on 23rd. and 24th. Feb. and of M.G. Coys. to cond. Division's front by 25th. Feb. Weather dull and rainy.	APP.4. D.O. 59.
CANAPLES MARIEUX.	23rd.		Div. H.Q. and 32nd. Inf. Bde. move into V Corps area. Div. H.Q. close at CANAPLES at 12 noon and open at MARIEUX at the same hour. 34th. Inf. Bde. move to FIEFFES. Weather dull, and moving a matter of great difficulty owing to the bad state of the roads, which were in places almost impassable for transport. One Battalion of 32nd. Inf. Bde. detailed for working parties at BEAUVAL and its neighbourhood, and one battalion of 34th. Inf. Bde. for working parties at or near DOULLENS, in relief of parties from 7th. Division. Major R.F.GUY, D.S.O. leaves to take up appointment of G.S.O. 2 of 9th. Corps.	APP.5. Location Table dated 23rd.

WAR DIARY
or
INTELLIGENCE SUMMARY.

Army Form C. 2118.

11th. DIVISION "G"   FEBRUARY 1917.

(Erase heading not required.)

Instructions regarding War Diaries and Intelligence Summaries are contained in F.S. Regs., Part II. and the Staff Manual respectively. Title pages will be prepared in manuscript.

Place	Date	Hour	Summary of Events and Information	Remarks and references to Appendices
MARIEUX	24th.		34th. Inf. Bde. march to MARIEUX Area. 32nd. and 34th. M.G. Coys. march to 62nd. Division area. 33rd. M.G. Coy. not required. Order received from to cover their front. Order received that 33rd. M.G. Coy. not required. Order received from V Corps that 3 Battalions are required for work in II Corps area. Division Order No. 60 issued ordering 2 Battalions of 32nd. Inf. Bde. to march to II Corps area on 25th. and 1 Battalion of 34th. Inf. Bde. on 26th. Feb. Training continued by 32nd. Inf. Bde. Weather dull. News of enemy's retirement on V and II Corps front.	APP. 6. D.O.-60.A
"	25th.		2 Battalions of 32nd. Inf. Bde. march to II Corps area, but owing to enemy's retirement are no longer required for work there, and orders received that these battalions and the Battalion of 34th. Inf. Bde. are to be attached to 7th. Div., 19th.Div., 62nd. Div.; respectively for work in V Corps area. Training continued by 32nd. Inf. Bde. less 3 Battalions and by 34th. Inf. Bde. less 2 Battalions. Weather fine.	
"	26th.		Orders received that 33rd. M.G. Coy. go on 27th. Div. to help cover their front; also that 6th. EAST YORKS (Pioneers) and one Field Coy. R.E. be attached to 62nd. Division for work on BEAUCOURT Road under C.E., V Corps. Training continued by remaining 1½ Battalions of 32nd. Inf. Bde. and 2 Battalions of 34th. Inf. Bde. Weather fine, but the broken up state of the roads makes the question of transport and all movement a serious one.	
"	27th.		6th. E. Yorks (Pioneers) and 86th. Field Coy. R.E. march to the neighbourhood of BEAUMONT HAMEL and BEAUCOURT for work under C.E., V Corps. Weather fine, and training continued by remaining Battalions.	
"	28th.		Orders received for 2 Battalions to be sent to work on railway construction at ACHEUX, MAILLY MAILLET and COURCELLES. Weather fine and training continued by 1 Battalion of 32nd. Inf. Bde. and 2 Battalions of 34th. Inf. Bde. ESSEX Regt. takes up duties of G.S.O. 2 of the Division.	

2/3/17.

A.B. Ritchie
Major General,
Commanding 11th. Division.

Army Form C. 2118.

WAR DIARY
or
INTELLIGENCE SUMMARY.
(Erase heading not required.)

11th. DIVISION "G". FEBRUARY 1917.

Instructions regarding War Diaries and Intelligence Summaries are contained in F. S. Regs., Part II. and the Staff Manual respectively. Title pages will be prepared in manuscript.

Place	Date	Hour	Summary of Events and Information	Remarks and references to Appendices
			S U M M A R Y. ********************* Throughout the month the Division has been out of the line. From 1st. to 20th. training was carried out on in the YVRENCH Area. On 15th., 33rd. Inf. Bde. was sent to work on the AUTHIE VALLEY RAILWAY and remained detached for the rest of the month. On 20th. the Division moved to CANAPLES. Many working parties were called for and training onwards was more and more interfered with. On 23rd. the Division move to MARIEUX Area and came under V Corps. Each day more working parties were demanded, mostly for work on the railways, made urgently necessary by the retirement of the enemy, and by the end of the month there was only one Battalion left in the Division for training.	
	2/3/17.			

A.B. Ritchie
Major General,
Commanding 11th. Division.

SECRET   Copy No. 15

11th Division Order No. 57.   15th February 1917.

1. The 33rd Inf. Bde. and attached troops (less 33rd Field Ambulance) will march to the AUTHIE Area for certain work in relief of the 187th Infantry Brigade, as per Table attached.

   Work to commence on 17th instant.

2. The C.R.A. will detail as many wagons from the 11th D.A.C. as can be spared to accompany the 33rd Inf. Bde.

3. All details regarding taking over work, tools, and billets to be arranged between Infantry Brigades concerned.

4. ACKNOWLEDGE.

Issued at 3-30 p.m.

J. D. Coleridge, Lieut-Colonel,
Gen. Staff. 11th Division.

Copy No. 1. A.D.C. for G.O.C.
         2. G.S.O.1.
         3. A.A. & Q.M.G.
         4. C.R.A.
         5. C.R.E.
         6. 33rd Inf. Bde.
         7. Signals.
         8. A.D.M.S.
         9. A.P.M.
        10. 13th Corps.
        11. 5th Corps.
        12. 62nd Division.
        13. Officer i/c Rly. Construction, AUTHIE.
        14. Office.
    15 & 16. Diary.
        17. Spare.

MOVEMENT TABLE to accompany 11th Div. Order No. 57.

DATE.	UNIT.	FROM.	TO.	ROUTE	REMARKS.
15th.	33rd Inf. Bde. less 33rd Fd.Amb.	CRAMONT Area.	FIENVILLERS) CANDAS) MONTRELET) BONNEVILLE)	BERNAVILLE.	
do	No. 3 Coy. of the Train.	do	do		To march under the orders of A.A. & Q.M.G. Billets for night 15th/16th to be arranged by O.C. 33rd Inf. Bde.
16th.	33rd Inf.Bde. less 33rd Fd.Amb.	CANDAS Area.	AUTHIE- ST LEGER- BUS- THIEVRES- SARTON	Cross Roads N.of ROSEL FARM - BEAUQUESNE - MARIEUX.	Column to march under orders of O.C. 33rd Inf. Bde. Head of column to cross BEAUVAL - TALMAS Road at 10 a.m. Brigade Headquarters at AUTHIE.
do	No. 3 Coy. of the Train.				

11th. Division Order No. No. 58.   S E C R E T.

Ref. Map 1/100,000
LENS Sheet.   Copy No. 19

                                           18th. Feb. 1917.

1.   The 11th. Division (less Artillery and 33rd. Inf. Bde.) will move on 20th. Feb. to CANAPLES Area.

2.(a)   Moves will take place as ordered in attached March Table.

  (b)   The Artillery will move to 5th. Corps Area under orders to be issued seperately.

3.   No troops are to enter the new area before 12 noon.

4.   34th. Inf. Bde. will remain in the billets now occupied.

5.   33rd. Field Ambulance will move to BEAUVAL under orders to be issued by A.D.M.S.

        35th. Field Ambulance will remain at LONGVILLERS.

6.   Divisional Headquarters will close at YVRENCH at 12 noon and open at CANAPLES at the same hour.

7.   All units not mentioned will move under orders of A.A. & Q.M.G.

8.   ACKNOWLEDGE.

Issued at 6 p.m.

                                    F.G. Turner, Capt.
                                    for Lieut. Colonel,
                                    Gen. Staff, 11th. Division.

Copy No.1 to A.D.C. for G.O.C.   11. A.D.M.S.
        2.   G.S.O. I.   12. A.D.V.S.
        3.   O.R.A.   13. A.P.M.
        4.   O.R.E.   14. 11th. Div. Train.
        5.   32nd. Inf. Bde.   15. D.A.D.O.S.
        6.   33rd. "   "   16. Camp Commdt.
        7.   34th. "   "   17. 13th. Corps.
        8.   6th. E.Yorks.   18.) War Diary.
        9.   Signal Coy.   19.)
       10.   A.A. & Q.M.G.   20.) Office.
                                   21.)

MARCH TABLE TO ACCOMPANY 11th. DIVISION ORDER No. 58.

Unit.	From.	To.	Route.	Remarks.
Divnl.Hd.Qrs.	Present Billets.	CANAPLES.	DOMQUEUR - ST. OUEN - BERTEAUCOURT.	
Divnl.Sig.Coy.	-do-	-do-		
Field Coys. R.E.	-do-	PERNOIS.	DOMQUEUR - Cross Roads at E. in CHAUSSEE BRUNEHAUT-DOMART-ST.LEGER.	To move under order of C.R.E.
32nd.Inf.Bde.	-do-	FIEFFES (H.Q.) MONTRELET. BONNEVILLE.	BERNAVILLE-FIENVILLERS.	To move under orders of G.O.C. 32nd.Inf.Bde.
6th. E. Yorks.	-do-	PERNOIS.	DOMQUEUR- Cross Roads at B in CHAUSSEE BRUNEHAUT-DOMART-ST.LEGER.	To move under orders of O.C. Battalion.
H.Q. Divnl.Train.	-do-	CANAPLES.		To move under orders of A.A. & Q.M.G.
34th. Field Ambulance.	-do-	CANAPLES.	DOMLEGER--BEAUMETZ-BERNAVILLE.	To move under orders of A.D.M.S.

PROPOSED LOCATIONS IN CANAPLES Area.

UNIT.	LOCATION.
Divisional Headquarters.	CANAPLES.
Divisional Signal Company.	CANAPLES.
H.Q. Divisional Engineers.	CANAPLES.
3 Field Coys. R.E.	PERNOIS.
H.Q., 32nd. Inf. Bde.	FIEFFES.
1 Battalion.	FIEFFES.
1 Battalion.	MONTRELET.
2 Battalions.	BONNEVILLE.
M.G. Company.	MONTRELET.
T.M. Battery.	MONTRELET.
1 Company Train.	FIEFFES.
6th. E. Yorks Regt. (Pioneers).	PERNOIS.
H.Q., Divisional Train, A.S.C.	CANAPLES.
34th. Field Ambulance.	CANAPLES.
Supply Column.	ST. LEGER.
Mobile Veterinary Section.	ST OUEN.
Sanitary Section.	CANAPLES.

To:-..................   11th. Division No. GMS. 304.

    ....

    Attached is a provisional copy of orders for

the entraining of the Division.

    Entraining tables will follow.

                                 F.G. Turner, Capt.
                                    for Lieut. Colonel,

19th. February 1917.   General Staff, 11th. Division.

S E C R E T.

Copy No........

Feby. 1927.

11th. Division Preliminary Entraining Order.

1.   Begin The 11th. Division is in G.H.Q. Reserve, and is to be prepared to entrain at 24 hours notice. The entrainment will be from three stations - CANDAS, DOULLENS. N. and DOULLENS S.

2.   The entrainment will be undertaken in three Brigade Groups, in accordance with attached Table.

    32nd. Inf. Bde. from DOULLENS South.

    33rd. " " " " "

    34th. " " " CANDAS.

In the order for the entrainment, ZERO hour at which the first train leaves the first station will be named, and trains will leave each station at probably about 4 hour intervals.

The approximate length of journey will also be notified.

3.   The following details will be found by Brigades :-

(a)   1 Officer (Major or Captain) of the Bde. Staff, or of Infantry Company travelling in last train will receive all instructions at Brigade H.Q. and be sent to the entraining station at least 6 hours before ZERO to represent the Bde. Staff there, to organise entraining parties, to arrange their billets, to control traffic at entraining station, to find out watering arrangements etc.,. He will travel in last train from his station.

(b)   A party of approximately 2 officers and 200.R.R. for detraining duties will be detailed from first unit entraining at each station.

(c)   Another party of 3 officers, (or 4 officers) and 200 O.R. will be detailed for entraining duties, these will be found by units shown in tables.

4.   The A.P.M. will detail military police to control traffic on the approaches to the station. No troops or transport will be allowed in the station yard until the R.T.O. is ready.

5. (a)   All trains consist of 1 officers' carriage,; 17 flat trucks, 30 covered trucks.

 (b) (i) Each flat truck will take an average on four axles.

  (ii) Each covered truck will take 6 H.D. horses .
       or 8 L.D. horses or mules
       or 40 men.

 (c)   No personnel or stores will be allowed in the brake vans at each end of the train, or on the roofs of the trucks. No covered trucks should be used for baggage.

(2)

6. (a) <u>INFANTRY BATTALIONS</u>. The transport will arrive at the entraining station 3 hours before the departure of the train, and the personnel one and a half hours.

(b) <u>OTHER UNITS</u>. Will arrive complete 3 hours before the departure of the train.

7. Arrangements will be made for resting accomodation near entraining stations so that units can remain there in the event of the trains being late in starting.

8. A complete marching out state showing the numbers of men, horses, G.S. limbered, G.S. and two wheeled wagons and bicycles will be sent down with the transport of every unit, so that accomodation in the train can be checked by the R.T.O. at the beginning of the entrainment, limbered G.S. wagons being counted as 2 - 2 wheeled on the state.

9. Supply and baggage wagons will accompany <u>their own units in every case</u>.

10. The entrainment of all units must be completed half an hour before the time of departure of train, when it will be moved from the loading siding.

11. Breast ropes for horse trucks must be provided by the Units themselves; ropes for lashing vehicles on the flat trucks will be provided by the Railway. Units will take steps now to complete required number of breast ropes.

12. Piquets must be provided at all stops for each end of the train to prevent troops leaving.

13. Battery Commanders are responsible for assisting in the entrainment of the sub-section or other portion of the D.A.C. travelling with their Batteries.

14. ACKNOWLEDGE.

F.G. Turner, Capt
for Lieut. Colonel,
Gen. Staff, 11th. Division.

19th. Feby. 1917.

Copy No.		
1) 2)		C.R.A.
3.		C.R.E.
4) 5) 6) 7)		32nd. Inf. Bde.
		33rd. " "
8) 9)		34th. " "
10.		6th. E. Yorks.
11.		Signals.
12.		Divnl. Train.
13.		A.A. & Q.M.G.
14.		A.D.M.S.
15.		A.D.V.S.
16.		A.P.M.
17.		D.A.D.O.S.
18 - 19.		War Diary.
20 - 21.		File.

SECRET.

Copy No........
20th. Feb. 1917.

11th. Division Supplementary Entraining Order.

1. Reference para 2, of Preliminary Order,

   33rd. Inf. Bde. from DOULLENS South,

   should read   "   "   North.

2. If the entrainment takes place from two stations, 32nd. and 34th. Brigades will go from CANDAS.

   33rd. Brigade   "   "   " DOULLENS.

3. If three stations are used, loading parties will be provided as under. In each case there will be 2 officers and 200 O.R. in each party.

   CANDAS.
      8th. Northd. Fus. to provide for trains Nos. 1, & 4.
      9th. Lancs. Fus.   "   "   "   "   " 7 & 10.
      5th. Dorset Regt. "   "   "   "   " 13 & 16.
      11th. Manchesters "   "   " remainder.

   DOULLENS NORTH.
      6th. Lincoln Regt. to provide for trains Nos. 2, & 5.
      6th. Border Regt. "   "   "   "   " 8 & 11.
      7th. S. Staffs. Regt." "   "   "   " 14 & 17.
      9th. Notts & Derby. " "   "   "   " 20.
      6th. E. Yorks (Pnrs)" "   " remainder.

   DOULLENS SOUTH.
      9th. West Yorks   to provide for trains Nos. 3, & 6.
      6th. Yorkshires   "   "   "   "   " 9 & 12.
      8th. W. Ridings.   "   "   "   "   " 15 & 18.
      6th. York & Lancs."   "   " remainder.

4. If two stations are used, loading parties will be arranged as under.

   CANDAS.
      8th. Northd. Fus. to provide for trains Nos. 1, & 3.
      9th. Lancs. Fus.   "   "   "   "   " 5 & 7.
      5th. Dorset Regt. "   "   "   "   " 9 & 11.
      11th. Manchesters. "   "   "   "   " 13 & 15.
      9th. W. Yorks.   "   "   "   "   " 17 & 19.
      6th. Yorkshires   "   "   "   "   " 21 & 23.
      8th. W. Ridings.   "   "   "   "   " 25 & 27.
      6th. York & Lancs. "   "   " remainder.

   DOULLENS.
      6th. Lincolns. to provide for trains Nos. 2 & 4.
      6th. Borders.   "   "   "   "   " 6 & 8.
      7th. S. Staffs." "   "   "   "   " 10 & 12.
      9th. Notts & Derby. " "   "   " 14.
      6th. E. Yorks(Pnrs). " " remainder.

2.

5. Troops will entrain in full marching order, carrying on the man, the unconsumed portion of the days' rations.

6. Supplies for the day following the day of entrainment will be loaded on the train in the Supply wagons of the Divnl. Train.

7. Only authorised baggage and transport will be loaded on the train.

8. Blankets and all other surplus baggage and kit will be dumped at one spot in each village and a guard with 3 days' rations left in charge.

Sites for the dumps should be selected forthwith.

9. Entraining tables attached.

F.G. Turner, Capt.
for Lieut. Colonel,
Gen. Staff, 11th. Division.

20th. February 1917.

Copy No. 1)
2) C.R.A.
3   CRE
4)
5) 32nd Inf. Bde.
6)
7) 33rd Inf. Bde.
8)
9) 34th Inf. Bde.

Copy No. 10. 6th E. Yorks.
11. Signals.
12. Divnl. Train.
13. A.A. & Q.M.G.
14. A.D.M.S.
15. A.D.V.S.
16. A.P.M.
17. D.A.D.O.S.
18 & 19. War Diary.
20 & 21. File.
22. 13th Corps G.
23. 13th Corps Q.

PROGRAMME OF MOVE OF 11th DIVISION. No.1.

From Fifth Army.
  Entraining Stations
  A. CANDAS.
  B. DOULLENS NORTH.
  C. DOULLENS SOUTH.

To:-
  Detraining Stations.
  A.
  B.
  C.

Train No. From Stations			SERIAL NUMBERS	Date	Marche	Time due to leave	Time due to arrive	Remarks
A	B	C						
1	2	3	4	5	6	7	8	9
1	-	-	1131					
-	2	-	1121					
-	-	3	1111					
4	-	-	1130,31a,35,36,37.					
-	5	-	1120,21a,25,26,27.					
-	-	6	1110,11a,15,16,17.					
7	-	-	1132					
-	8	-	1122					
-	-	9	1112					
10	-	-	1132a,90,93.					
-	11	-	1122a,23a,85.					
-	-	12	1112a,88,92.					
13	-	-	1133					
-	14	-	1123					
-	-	15	1113					
16	-	-	1133a,34a,86.					
-	17	-	1123b,24a,89,91.					
-	-	18	1113a,14a,84.					
19	-	-	1134					
-	20	-	1124					
-	-	21	1114					
22	-	-	1151,81a.					
-	23	-	1179					
-	-	24	1142.81f.					
25	-	-	1152,81b.					
-	26	-	1180					
-	-	27	1102,40,78,80a,96,97, 98,99.					
28	-	-	1153,81c.					
-	29	-	1141,81e.					
-	-	30	1143,81g.					
31	-	-	1154,81d.					
-	32	-	1181,87a.					
-	-	33	1144,81h.					
34	-	-	1150,79a,95.					
-	35	-	1104a,05,24b.					
-	-	36	1104,14b.					
37	-	-	1101,08,34b,83,87.					

DOULLENS.
19-2-17

Lieut.
for D.A.D.R.T.(V)

The trains will leave at the rate of 6 marches per station per day.

PROGRAMME OF MOVE OF 11th DIVISION - No.2.

From Fifth Army.To.-
   Entraining Stations.   Detraining Stations.
   A. CANDAS   A.
   B. DOULLENS.   B.

Train No. From Stns		SERIAL NUMBERS	Date	Marchs	Time due to leave	Time due to arrive	Remarks.
A	B						
1	2	3	4	5	6	7	8
1	-	1131			0-00		
-	2	1121			2-00		
3	-	1130,31a,35,36,37.			4-00		
-	4	1120,21a,25,26,27.			6-00		
5	-	1132			8-00		
-	6	1122			10-00		
7	-	1132a,90,93.			12-00		
-	8	1122a,23a,85.			14-00		
9	-	1133			16-00		
-	10	1123			18-00		
11	-	1133a,34a,88.			20-00		
-	12	1123b,24a,89,91.			22-00		
13	-	1134			0-00		
-	14	1124			2-00		
15	-	1101,08,34b,83,87.			4-00		
-	16	1141,81e.			6-00		
17	-	1111			8-00		
-	18	1142,81f.			10-00		
19	-	1110,11a,15,16,17.			12-00		
-	20	1102,40,78,80a,96,97,98,99.			14-00		
21	-	1112			16-00		
-	22	1143,81g.			18-00		
23	-	1112a,88,92.			20-00		
-	24	1144,81h.			22-00		
25	-	1113			0-00		
-	26	1151,81a.			2-00		
27	-	1113a,14a,84.			4-00		
-	28	1152,81b.			6-00		
29	-	1114			8-00		
-	30	1153,81c.			10-00		
31	-	1179			12-00		
-	32	1154,81d.			14-00		
33	-	1180			16-00		
-	34	1150,79a,95.			18-00		
35	-	1181,87a.			20-00		
-	36	1104a,05,24b.			22-00		
37	-	1104,1114b.			0-00		

                                                                                               Lieut.
                                                                                       for D.A.D.R.T.(V)

DOULLENS.
   19-2-17.

TABLE "D" - 11th DIVISION.

UNIT	SERIAL NUMBER	DESCRIPTION
DIVISIONAL UNITS.	1101	Divisional H.Q.
	1102	H.Q. Divisional Artillery.
	1104	20 Off. 500 O.R. and transport less 4 G.S.& Teams of 6th E.York.Pioneers.
	1104 a	Remainder of 6th E.Yorks Pioneers.
	1105	H.Q.& No.1 Section Div.Signals.
	1108	Salvage Company.
32nd INFANTRY BRIGADE.	1110	Brigade H.Q.
	1111	33 Off. 700 O.R. and transport of 9th West Yorks.
	1111 a	Remainder of 9th West Yorks.
	1112	33 Off. 700 O.R. and transport of 6th Yorks.
	1112 a	Remainder of 6th Yorks.
	1113	33 Off. 700 O.R. and transport of 8th West Riding.
	1113 a	Remainder of 8th West Riding.
	1114	33 Off. 700 O.R. and transport of 6th York & Lancs.
	1114 a	5 Off. 200 O.R. of 6th York & Lancs.
	1114 b	Remainder of 6th York & Lancs.
	1115	Brigade Section Signals.
	1116	Machine Gun Company.
	1117	Brigade T.M.B.
33rd INFANTRY BRIGADE.	1120	Brigade H.Q.
	1121	33 Off. 700 O.R. and transport of 6th Lincolns.
	1121 a	Remainder of 6th Lincolns.
	1122	33 Off. 700 O.R. and transport of 6th Borders.
	1122 a	Remainder of 6th Borders.
	1123	33 Off. 700 O.R. and transport of 7th S.Staffs.
	1123 a	5 Off. 200 O.R. of 7th S.Staffs.
	1123 b	Remainder of 7th S.Staffs.
	1124	33 Off. 700 O.R. and transport of 9th Notts & Derby.
	1124 a	7 Off. 300 O.R. of 9th Notts & Derby.
	1124 b	Remainder of 9th Notts & Derby.
	1125	Brigade Section Signals.
	1126	Machine Gun Company.
	1127	Brigade T.M.B.
34th INFANTRY BRIGADE.	1130	Brigade H.Q.
	1131	33 Off. 700 O.R. and transport of 8th Northumberland Fusrs.
	1131 a	Remainder of 8th Northd.Fusrs.
	1132	33 Off. 700 O.R. and transport of 9th Lancs.Fusrs.
	1132 a	Remainder of 9th Lancs Fusrs.
	1133	33 Off. 700 O.R. and transport of 5th Dorsets.
	1133 a	Remainder of 5th Dorsets.
	1134	33 Off. 700 O.R. and transport of 11th Manchesters.
	1134 a	5 Off. 200 O.R. of 11th Manchesters
	1134 b	Remainder of 11th Manchesters.
	1135	Brigade Section Signals.
	1136	Machine Gun Company.
	1137	Brigade T.M.B.

Table "D" - 11th Division (continued)

UNIT	SERIAL NUMBER	DESCRIPTION
58th BRIGADE R.F.A.	1140	Brigade H.Q.
	1141	"A" Battery.
	1142	"B" Battery.
	1143	"C" Battery.
	1144	"D" Battery.
59th BRIGADE R.F.A.	1150	Brigade H.Q.
	1151	"A" Battery.
	1152	"B" Battery.
	1153	"C" Battery.
	1154	"D" Battery.
DIVISIONAL AMMUNITION COLUMN,	1178	H.Q., D.A.C.
	1179	No.1 Section D.A.C. less 1 Sub-section.
	1179 a	One Sub-section of No.1 Section D.A.C.
	1180	No.2 Section D.A.C. less 1 Sub-section.
	1180 a	One Sub-section of No.2 Section D.A.C.
	1181	No.4 Section D.A.C. less 32 G.S.& Teams.
	1181 a	4 G.S.& Teams of No.4 Section D.A.C.
	1181 b	4 " " "
	1181 c	4 " " "
	1181 d	4 " " "
	1181 e	4 " " "
	1181 f	4 " " "
	1181 g	4 " " "
	1181 h	4 " " "
DIVISIONAL ENGINEERS.	1183	H.Q. Divisional Engineers.
	1184	67th Field Company R.E.
	1185	68th " " "
	1186	86th " " "
DIVISIONAL TRAIN.	1187	H.Q. Divisional Train.
	1187 a	H.Q. Coy. " "
	1188	No.2 Coy. " "
	1189	No.3 Coy. " "
	1190	No.4 Coy. " "
MEDICAL UNITS	1191	33rd Field Ambulance.
	1192	34th " "
	1193	35th " "
VETERINARY UNIT	1195	22nd Mobile Veterinary Section.
TRENCH MORTAR BATTERIES.	1196	X.11 T.M.B.
	1197	Y.11 T.M.B.
	1198	Z.11 T.M.B.
	1199	V.11 T.M.B.

S E C R E T.   20th. Feby. 1917.   11th. Division No. G.S. 300.

11th. Division Location Table showing position
of units at 6 a.m. day after date return is rendered.

11th. Division   H.Q. CANAPLES.

32nd. Infantry Brigade. H.Q. FIEFFES.
  9th. W. Yorks Regt.   H.Q. and Bn.   )
  6th. Yorkshire Regt.   H.Q. and Bn   )   MONTRELET.
  8th. W. Riding Regt.   H.Q. and Bn.   )
  6th. York & Lancs. R. H.Q. and Bn.   )   BONNEVILLE.
  32nd. M.G. Company.   )
  32nd. T.M. Battery.   )

33rd. Infantry Brigade. H.Q. AUTHIE.
  6th. Lincoln Regt.   H.Q. and 3 Coys. ST. LEGER.
                                1 Coy.   AUTHIE.
  6th. Border Regt.   H.Q. and 3 Coys. COIGNEUX.
                                1 Coy.   BUS LES ARTOIS.
  7th. S. Staffs. Regt. H.Q. and Bn.   BUS LES ARTOIS.
b 9th. S. Foresters   H.Q. and 2 Coys. FAMECHON.
                                1 Coy.   SARTON.
                                1 Coy.   FRESCHVILLERS.
  33rd. M.G. Company.   AUTHIE.
  33rd. T.M. Battery.   AUTHIEULE.

34th. Infantry Brigade. H.Q. FRANSU.
  8th. Northd. Fusiliers H.Q. and Bn. DOMQUEUR.
  9th. Lancs. Fusiliers H.Q. and Bn. RUBEAUCOURT.
  5th. Dorset Regt.   H.Q. and Bn. LE PLOUY.
  11th. Manchester Regt. H.Q. and Bn. FRANSU.
  34th. M.G. Company.   MESNIL DOMQUEUR.
  34th. T.M. Battery.   -do-

6th. E. Yorks Regt. (Pioneers).   PERNOIS.

11th. Divisional R.E.   H.Q.   CANAPLES.

  3 Field Companies.   PERNOIS.

11th. Divisional R.A.   H.Q.) Moving on 21st.)
  58th. F.A.B.   ) HEM, HARDINVAL,) Moving on 22nd.
  59th. "   ) GEZAINCOURT,   )
  60th. "   ) OCCOCHES.   ) to ACHEUX.
                              OUTREBOIS.   )

A.D.M.S., 11th. Division.   CANAPLES.
  33rd. Field Ambulance.   BEAUVAL.
  34th.   "   "   CANAPLES.
  35th.   "   "   LONGVILLERS.

A.P.M., 11th. Division.   CANAPLES.

D.A.D.O.S., 11th. Division.   CANAPLES.

A.D.V.S., 11th. Division.   CANAPLES.
  22nd. Mobile Vet. Section.   BERNEUIL.

11th. Divisional Train. H.Q.   CANAPLES.
  Headquarter Company.   Attached 11th. D.A.
  No. 2 Company.   FIEFFES.
  No. 3   "   Attached 33rd. Brigade.
  No. 4   "   DOMESMONT.

11th. Divisional Supply Col.   LE PLOUY DOMQUEUR.

```
===========
S E C R E T                                           Copy No. 24
===========
```

11th Division Order No.59.

Ref. Map 1/100,000   22nd Feby. 1917.
   LENS Sheet.
----

1. The 11th Division (less Artillery and 33rd Inf. Bde.) will move from CANAPLES Area into Vth Corps Area on 23rd and 24th February.
   One Brigade group will arrive in Vth Corps Area on 23rd February, and the remainder of the Division on 24th February.

2. The Machine Gun Companies are placed at the disposal of G.O.C. 62nd Division from 10 a.m. 25th February for the purpose of relieving the Machine Gun Companies of 7th Division now covering the front of 62nd Division. They will join 62nd Division on 24th February.

3. Moves will take place as ordered in attached March Table.

4. Divl. Hd. Qrs. will close at CANAPLES at 12 noon 23rd February, and open at BARIEUX at the same hour.

5. All units not mentioned in the March Tables will move under orders of A.A. & Q.M.G.

6. Billets will be in accordance with attached list.

7. ACKNOWLEDGE.

Issued at *12 noon*   F.G. Turner, Capt.
                                                 for Lieut-Colonel,
                                                 Gen. Staff. 11th Division.

Copy No. 1. A.D.C. for G.O.C.
        2. G.S.O 1.
        3. C.R.A.   Copy No. 14. 11th Div. Train.
        4. C.R.E.   15. D.A.D.O.S.
        5. 32nd Inf. Bde.   16. Camp Comdt.
        6. 33rd Inf. Bde.   17. 13th Corps 'G'
        7. 34th Inf. Bde.   18. 13th Corps 'Q'
        8. 6th E. Yorks Regt.   19. 5th Corps 'G'
        9. Signal Coy.   20. 5th Corps 'Q'
       10. A.A. & Q.M.G.   21. 62nd Div.
       11. A.D.M.S.   22. 7th Div.
       12. A.D.V.S.   23 & 24. War Diary.
       13. A.P.M.   25 & 26. Office.

MARCH TABLE TO ACCOMPANY 11th DIVISION ORDER No.59.

Date.	Unit.	From.	To.	Route.	Remarks.
23rd.	Div. Hd. Qrs.	Present billets.	MAIZIEUX.		Under orders of G.P.T. to clear present billets by 9 a.m.
do.	Div. Signal Coy.	do	do		
do.	Field Coys. R.E.	do	HARLEUX TERRA-MESNIL RAINCHEVAL.	HAVERNAS - MAOURS - VAL-DE-MAISON.	
do.	32nd Inf. Bde.	do	BEAUQUESNE (H.Q.) TERRA-MESNIL.	VALHEUREUX - Cross roads N. of FERME DU-ROSEL.	To be clear of present billets by 9 a.m. Must be in new billets by 1.30 p.m.
do	34th Inf. Bde.	do	FIEFFES (H.Q.) MONTRELET BONNEVILLE.	FRANQUEVILLE - BERNEUIL.	Not to enter new billets before 10 a.m.
do.	34th M.G. Coy.	do	BEAUQUESNE.	BERNAVILLE-CANDAS-BEAUVAL.	Must not cross main TALMAS-DOULLENS road between 2.30 pm. and 3.30 p.m.
do.	34th Fd. Amb.	do	BEAUQUESNE.	VALHEUREUX-Cross roads N. of FERME DU-ROSEL.	Under orders of A.D.M.S. Must be in new billets by 1.50 p.m.
do.	35th Fd. Amb.	do	BERNEUIL.	BEAUMETZ-BERNAVILLE.	Under orders of A.D.M.S.

MARCH TABLE TO ACCOMPANY 11th. DIVISION ORDER No. 59. (contd)

Date.	Unit.	From.	To.	Route.	Remarks.
4th.	34th. Inf. Bde.	FIEFFES (H.Q.) MONTRELET. BONNEVILLE.	BEAUQUESNE. (H.Q.) RAINCHEVAL.	VALHEUREUX - Cross Roads N. of FERME - DU-ROSEL - BEAUQUESNE.	To clear billets by 10 a.m.
-do-	55th. Fd. Amb.	BERNEUIL	BEAUVAL.	BONNEVILLE - VALHEUREUX.	Under orders of A.D.M.S.
-do-	8th. E. Yorks.	PERNOIS.	BEAUQUESNE.	HAVERNAS - NAOURS- Cross Roads N. of FERME-DU-ROSEL.	Under orders of O.C. Battr. Not to clear billets before 10 a.m.
24th.	32nd. M.G. Coy. 33rd. " " 34th. " "	BEAUQUESNE. FIENVICH. BEAUQUESNE.	62nd. Division Area.		Details to follow.

PROPOSED DISTRIBUTION OF BILLETS IN NEW AREA.

D.H.Q.	MARIEUX.
32nd. Inf. Bde. H.Q.	BEAUQUESNE.
2 Battalions.	"
32nd. M.G. Company.	"
32nd. T.M. Battery.	"
Remainder of Brigade.	TERRA MESNIL.
34th. Inf. Bde. H.Q.	BEAUQUESNE.
1 Battalion.	"
Remainder of Brigade.	RAINCHEVAL.
Field Coys. R.E.	MARIEUX.
	TERRA MESNIL.
	RAINCHEVAL.
34th. Field Amb.	BEAUQUESNE.
35th. " "	BEAUVAL.
6th. E. Yorks (Pnrs).	BEAUQUESNE.

S E C R E T.　　　　　　Feb. 23rd. '17.　　　　11th. Division No. G.S. 340

11th. Division Location Table showing position
of units at 6 a.m. day after date return is rendered.

11th. Division.	H.Q. MARIEUX.
32nd. Infantry Brigade.	H.Q. BEAUQUESNE.
9th. W. Yorks Regt.	H.Q. and Bn. BEAUQUESNE.
6th. Yorkshire Regt.	H.Q. and Bn. TERRA MESNIL.
8th. W. Riding Regt.	H.Q. and Bn. BEAUQUESNE.
6th. York & Lancs. R	H.Q. and Bn. TERRA MESNIL.
32nd. M.G. Company.	BEAUQUESNE.
32nd. T.M. Battery.	-do-
33rd. Infantry Brigade.	H.Q. FAMECHON.
6th. Lincoln Regt.	H.Q. and 3 Coys. STLEGER.
	1 Coy. THIEVRES.
6th. Border Regt.	H.Q. and Bn. COIGNEUX.
7th. S. Staffs Regt.	H.Q. and Bn. BUS LES ARTOIS.
9th. S. Foresters	H.Q. and 2 Coys. FAMECHON.
	1 Coy. SARTON.
	1 Coy. FRESCHVILLERS.
33rd. M.G. Company.	THIEVRES. Moving to MAILLY WOOD.
33rd. T.M. Battery.	AUTHIEULE.
34th. Infantry Brigade.	H.Q. FIEFFES. Moving to BEAUQUESNE. on 24th.
8th. Northd. Fusiliers	H.Q. and Bn. MONTRELET. Moving to RAINCHEVAL.
9th. Lancs. Fusiliers	H.Q. and Bn. BONNEVILLE.　"　"　GEZAINCOURT.
5th. Dorset Regt.	H.Q. and Bn. FIEFFES.　"　"　RAINCHEVAL.
11th. Manchester Regt.	H.Q. and Bn. BONNEVILLE.
34th. M.G. Company.	BEAUQUESNE.　"　"　62nd. Div. Area.
34th. T.M. Battery.	MONTRELET.
6th. E. Yorks Regt. (Pioneers).	PERNOIS.
11th. Divisional R.E.	H.Q. MARIEUX.
67th. Field Company.	MARIEUX.
68th.　"　"	TERRA MESNIL.
96th.　"　"	RAINCHEVAL.
11th. Divisional R.A.	H.Q.)
58th. F.A.B.	) ACHEUX WOOD Go into action on night
59th.　"	)　　23rd.　　23rd./24th.
60th.　"	)
D.A.C.	FORCEVILLE.
A.D.M.S., 11th. Division.	MARIEUX.
33rd. Field Ambulance.	BEAUVAL.
34th.　"　"	BEAUQUESNE.
35th.　"　"	BERNEUIL.
A.P.M., 11th. Division.	MARIEUX.
D.A.D.O.S., 11th. Division.	CANAPLES.
A.D.V.S., 11th. Division.	MARIEUX.
22nd. Mobile Vet. Section.	MARIEUX.
11th. Divisional Train.	H.Q. MARIEUX.
Headquarters Company.	Attached 11th. D.A.
No. 3 Company.	Attached 33rd. Bde.
11th. Divisional Supply Col.	MARIEUX.

==========
S E C R E T.   Copy No.......
==========
                                24th. Feby. 1917.

11th. DIVISION ORDER No.60.

Ref. Map. 57D. 1/40,000
----

1. Two Battalion of 32nd. Inf. Bde. will march tomorrow 25th. Feb. to II Corps area to relieve 2 Battalions of 7th. Division in their present work.

   One battalion will be attached for work to 2nd. Division and will march to ALBERT tomorrow. Billets will be provifed by Town Major ALBERT.

   The second Battalion will be attached to 18th. Division This Battalion will be billeted tomorrow night as follows :-

   300 at AVELUY and the remainder in hutsand tents,

   at ENGLEBELMER.

   The work of the second battalion will be in Square W.6.

2. One battalion of 34th. Inf. Bde. will march to II Corps Area on 26th. Feby. Half the battalion will work with 2nd. Division and will be billeted in OVILLERS Huts at X.7.d.8.1., where billeting representative should report to Town Major. The other half battalion will work with 18th. Division and will be billeted at DONNETS POST, W.12.d.8 3.

3. These Battalions will rejoin their Brigades on March 3rd.

4. 11th. Manchester Regt. and 34th. L.T.M. Battery will march to 34th. Inf. Bde. area on 25th. Feby.

5. March Table attached.

6. ACKNOWLEDGE.

Issued at 5 p.m.   (Sd). F.G.TUNRER, Captain,

                                for Lieut. Colonel,

                        Gen. Staff, 11th. Division.

Copy No. 1 to Vth. Corps.
      2   32nd. Inf. Bde.
      3   34th. "   "
      4.   7th. Division.
      5   2nd. Division.
      6   18th. Division.
      7   "Q"
      8   II Corps.
      9   Office
   10 -11   Diary.

MARCH TABLE TO ACCOMPANY 11th.DIVISION ORDER No.60.

Date.	Unit.	From.	To.	Route.	Remarks.
25th.	11th. Manchester Regt.	BONNEVILLE.	TERRA MESNIL.	VALHEUREUX - Cross Roads North of FERME DU-ROSEL - BEAUQUESNE.	No restrictions to time.
"	34th. L.T.M. Battery.	MONTRELET.	TERRA MESNIL.	—do—	
"	1 Battn. 32nd. Inf.Bde.	TERRA MESNIL.	ALBERT.	RAINCHEVAL— ACHEUX.	To clear present billets by 9 a.m.
"	1 Battn. 32nd. Inf.Bde.	TERRA MESNIL.	300 AVELUY. remainder ENGLEBELMER.	—do—	
26th.	1 Battn. 34th. Inf.Bde.	RAINCHEVAL.	H.Q., and ½ Battn. to X.7.d. ½ Battn. to W.12.d.	ACHEUX - BOUZINCOURT— ABELUY.	

WAR DIARY.

General Staff.   11th Division.

March, 1917.

Army Form C. 2118.

WAR DIARY
or
INTELLIGENCE SUMMARY.

11th. DIVISION "G".

MARCH 1917.

(Erase heading not required.)

Instructions regarding War Diaries and Intelligence Summaries are contained in F. S. Regs., Part II and the Staff Manual respectively. Title pages will be prepared in manuscript.

Place	Date	Hour	Summary of Events and Information	Remarks and references to Appendices
MARIEUX.	1st.		Weather foggy. 9th. W. Yorks Regt. moved to COURCELLES for work, and 11th. Manchester Regt. moved to VARENNES, less 2 coys. to MAILLY MAILLET for work on light railway.	
"	2nd.		No change, except that 33rd. M.G. Coy. rejoined its Brigade.	
"	3rd.		No change. Frost at night.	
"	4th.		No change. Fine day. One battalion of 34th. Inf. Bde.(5th. Dorset Regt.) ordered to move to MAILLY MAILLET for work on SUCRERIE-SERRE Road. under 7th. Division.	
"	5th.		5th. Dorset Regt. moved to MAILLY MAILLET. Whole of 32nd. and 34th. Inf. Bdes. now employed on work on communications under V Corps. In future Daily Location reports of units will be found in Appendix 1. About 2" of snow fell during the night and, thawing before afternoon, made the roads worse than before.	
"	6th.		No change. Fine day.	
"	7th.		No change. Cold drying wind.	
"	8th.		Very cold wind with snow at intervals. 2 Medium T.M. Batteries ordered to be ready to move elsewhere by rail. G.O.C. attended conference at V Corps H.Q.	
"	9th.		Snow at intervals throughout day. Cold in morning. G.O.C. visited BEAUCOURT to reconnoitre means of communication to 62nd. Div's front. Brigadier General H.R.DAVIES assumed command of 33rd. Inf. Bde. A.A. & Q.M.G. proceeded to G.H.Q. French Army, CLAREMONT for 3 day's attachment. H.Q. and 1 Section of 68th. Field Coy. R.E. to BEAUSSART.	
"	10th.		Weather bad. No change.	
"	11th.		Fine day. G.O.C. visited PUISIEUX to reconnoitre means of communication.	
"	12th.		Fine morning. 8th. North'd. Fusiliers ordered up to front line to b.23.d. by 62nd. Division.	

Army Form C. 2118.

WAR DIARY
or
INTELLIGENCE SUMMARY.

11th. DIVISION "G". MARCH 1917.

(Erase heading not required.)

Instructions regarding War Diaries and Intelligence Summaries are contained in F.S. Regs., Part II. and the Staff Manual respectively. Title pages will be prepared in manuscript.

Place	Date	Hour	Summary of Events and Information	Remarks and references to Appendices
MARIEUX.	12th.		Fine morning. Heavy showers in the afternoon. No change.	
"	13th		Showery weather. 8th. Northd. Fusiliers ordered up to Front line in L.23.d. by 62nd. Division.	
"	14th.		Showery weather. One Coy. 8th. Northd. Fusiliers advanced round to EAST of ACHIET LE PETIT but when dawn broke found they were unsupported and had to withdraw. Order received from V Corps that 11th. Division will leave the 5th. Army on or about 21st. March and move to 1st. Army.	
"	15th.		Fine day. Order received from V Corps that Army Commander intends to operate in N.E. direction with a view to cutting off the enemy troops in front of 3rd. Army, South of ARRAS, and that move of 11th. Division may possibly be postponed.	
"	16th.		Fine day. 8th. Northd. Fusiliers were relieved from Front Line during the night, and went into billets at FORCEVILLE. Their casualties in action amounted to 1 Officer killed, 10 O.R. killed and 44 O.R. wounded. 32nd. M.G. Coy. rejoined their Brigade at BEAUQUESNE.	
"	17th.		Fine day. Letter of appreciation received from G.O.C. 62nd. Division for good work done by 8th. Northd. Fusiliers and 32nd. and 34th. M.G. Coys. during their attachment to 62nd. Division. (see Appendix).	APP. 2.
"	18th.		Fine day. G.O.C. reconnoitred ACHIET LE GRAND Area.	
"	19th.		Half of guns of Div. Arty. withdrawn from their positions in the line. Wet afternoon.	
"	20th.		Wet day. Remainder of Div. Arty. withdrawn from the line to BUS. 34th. M.G. Company rejoined their Brigade at BEAUQUESNE.	
"	21st.		Fine day. Order received from V Corps for 11th. Division to move to 5th. Army staging Area (BEAUVAL) on or about 31st. March., preparatory to transfer to 3rd. Army.	

Army Form C. 2118.

WAR DIARY
or
INTELLIGENCE SUMMARY.

11th. DIVISION "G".

MARCH 1917.

(Erase heading not required.)

Instructions regarding War Diaries and Intelligence Summaries are contained in F. S. Regs., Part II. and the Staff Manual respectively. Title pages will be prepared in manuscript.

Place	Date	Hour	Summary of Events and Information	Remarks and references to Appendices
MARIEUX	22nd.		Order received from V Corps for working parties to cease after 23rd. and for 11th. Division to concentrate in MARIEUX Area by evening of 24th. for a week's training prior to joining 3rd. Army. Div. Operation Order No. 61 consequently issued ordering concentration of Infantry, the Artillery remaining at BUS LEZ ARTOIS. See Appendix.	APP. III
"	23rd.		Fine day and drying wind. No change.	
"	24th.		Division concentrated in MARIEUX Area. G.O.C. and G.S.O. I attended conference at 18th. Corps H.Q. Army received transferring 11th. D.A. to 18th. Corps with temporary Order from 3rd. Div. Op. Order No. 62 issued. See Appendix detachment to 6th. Corps.	APP. IV
"	25th.		Church parades. Cleaning up. Letter of appreciation received from G.O.C. 62nd. Division for good work done by 6th. E. Yorks Regt. (Pioneers) during their attachment to 62nd. Division. (See Appendix).	APP. V
"	26th.		Dull rainy day. Training carried out. Lecture by 18th. Corps Commander at D.H.Q.	
"	27th.		Some snow. Training continued. G.O.C. inspected Div. Arty. on the march to 3rd. Army.	
"	28th.		Fine day. Training continued.	
"	29th.		Wet day. Training continued. Wire received from V Corps cancelling move of Div. (less Arty) on April 1st.	
"	30th.		Fine day. Training continued.	
"	31st.		Fine morning. Heavy rain in afternoon. Training continued.	

4/4/17.

W.B. Ritchie
Major General,
Commanding 11th. Division.

Army Form C. 2118.

WAR DIARY
or
INTELLIGENCE SUMMARY.

11th. DIVISION "G".   MARCH 1917.

(Erase heading not required.)

Place	Date	Hour	Summary of Events and Information	Remarks and references to Appendices
			S U M M A R Y.	
			The work on the communications to the Front Line made urgently necessary by the retreat of the Germans was carried on. The few remaining Battalions left for training were soon taken, and by 5th. the whole of the 32nd. and 34th. Inf. Bdes. were engaged on this work under V Corps. Meanwhile, the 33rd. Inf. Bde. were continuing their work on the AUTHIE VALLEY Railway begun in February. 32nd. and 34th. M.G. Coys. were attached to 62nd. Division to help cover their front, while 8th. Northd. Fusiliers (also attached to 62nd. Division) were suddenly ordered into the line on 14th., to help in the operations against ACHIET-LE-PETIT, and remained in the line for 3 days. Both these M.G. Coys. and 8th. Northd. Fusiliers did excellent work and a letter of thanks was received from G.O.C., 62nd. Division. On 14th. the transfer of Division to 1st. Army was ordered, but this was subsequently cancelled and a move to 3rd. Army ordered. All working parties ceased on 23rd. and the Division concentrated for a week's training before moving to 3rd. Army on April 1st., but this move was postponed. At the end of the month the Division was still under V Corps and training in MARIEUX Area.	
4/4/17.				

W.P. Pitchu   Major General,

Commanding 11th. Division.

WAR DIARY.

March, 1917.

APPENDIX I

LOCATION OF UNITS.

War Diary

SECRET.   5th/3/'17.   11th. Division No. G.S. 446

11th. Division Location Table shewing position
of units at 6 a.m. day after date return is rendered.

11th. Division.	H.Q. RARIEUX.
32nd. Infantry Brigade.	H.Q. BEAUQUESNE.
9th. W. Yorks Regt.	H.Q. and Bn. COURCELLES.
6th. Yorkshire Regt.	H.Q. and Bn. BERTRANCOURT.
8th. W. Riding Regt.	H.Q. and Bn. BEAUQUESNE.
6th. York & Lancs. Regt.	H.Q. and 2 Coys. BUS.
	2 Coys. BEAUSSART.
32nd. M.G. Company.	Attached 62nd. Division.
32nd. T.M. Battery.	BEAUQUESNE.
33rd. Infantry Brigade.	H.Q. FALFOMON.
6th. Lincoln Regt.	H.Q. and 3 Coys. GOUIN.
	1 Coy. THIEVRES.
6th. Border Regt.	H.Q. and Bn. COIGNEUX.
7th. S. Staffs Regt.	H.Q. and Bn. BUS LES ARTOIS.
9th. S. Foresters.	H.Q. and 2 Coys. FALFOMON.
	1 Coy. FRESCHVILLERS.
	1 Coy. SARTON.
33rd. M.G. Company.	SARTON.
33rd. T.M. Battery.	AUTHIEULE.
34th. Infantry Brigade.	H.Q. BEAUQUESNE.
8th. Northd. Fusiliers.	H.Q. and Bn. Attached 62nd. Divn. Q.11.c.
9th. L. Fusiliers.	H.Q. GEZAINCOURT.
	Bn. DOULLENS Area.
5th. Dorset Regt.	H.Q. and Bn. MAILLY MAILLET. P.6.d.
11th. Manchester Regt.	H.Q. and 2 Coys. VARENNES.
	2 Coys. MAILLY MAILLET.
34th. M.G. Company.	Attached 62nd. Division.
34th. T.M. Battery.	BEAUQUESNE.
6th. E. Yorks Regt. (Pioneers).	Q.17.A.8.8.
11th. Divisional R.E.	H.Q. RARIEUX.
67th. Field Company.	BEAUQUESNE.
68th. " "	RARIEUX.
86th. " "	Q.18.A.9.8.

11th. Divisional R.A.	H.Q. VAUCHELLES.	**11th. Divisional Train.**
58th F.A.B.	MAILLY MAILLET.	T. H.Q., RARIEUX.
59th. "	Q.8.c.5.8.	H.Q.,Coy. VAUCHELLES.
		No.2 Coy. BEAUQUESNE.
D.A.C.	FORCEVILLE.	No.3 Coy. RARIEUX.
S.A.A. Subsection.	BEAUQUESNE.	No.4 Coy. RAINCHEVAL.
A.D.M.S., 11th. Division.	RARIEUX.	**11th. Divisional Supply Col.**
33rd. Field Ambulance.	BEAUVAL.	
34th. " "	BEAUQUESNE.	BEAUQUESNE.
35th. " "	BEAUVAL.	
		11th. Divnl. School.
A.P.M. 11th. Division.	RARIEUX.	
		ST. RIQUIER.
D.A.D.O.S., 11th. Division.	RAINCHEVAL.	
		11th. Divnl. Laundry.
A.D.V.S., 11th. Division.	RARIEUX.	
22nd. Mobile Vet. Section.	RARIEUX.	Billet 44, RAINCHEVAL.

SECRET.   6th. March 1917.   11th. Division No. G.S. 452.

War Diary.

11th. Division Location Table showing position
of units at 6 a.m. day after date return is rendered.

11th. Division.   H.Q. MARIEUX.

32nd. Infantry Brigade. H.Q. BEAUQUESNE.
  9th. W. Yorkshire Regt. H.Q. and Bn. COURCELLES.
  6th. Yorkshire Regt.   H.Q. and Bn. BERTRANCOURT.
  8th. W. Riding Regt.   H.Q. and Bn. BEAUQUESNE.
  6th. York & Lancs. R.   H.Q. and 2 Coys. BUS.
                               2 Coys. BEAUSSART.
  32nd. M.G. Company.   Attached 62nd. Division.
  32nd. T.M. Battery.   BEAUQUESNE.

33rd. Infantry Brigade. H.Q. FAMECHON.
  6th. Lincoln Regt.   H.Q. and 3 Coys. COUIN.
                                1 Coy. THIEVRES.
  6th. Border Regt.   H.Q. and Bn.   COIGNEUX.
  7th. S. Staffs. Regt.   H.Q. and Bn.   BUS LES ARTOIS.
  9th. S. Foresters.   H.Q. and 2 Coys FAMECHON.
                                1 Coy.   FRESCHVILLERS.
                                1 Coy.   SARTON.
  33rd. M.G. Company.   SARTON.
  33rd. T.M. Battery.   AUTHIEULE.

34th. Infantry Brigade. H.Q. BEAUQUESNE.
  8th. Northd. Fusiliers. H.Q. and Bn. Q.11.c.
  9th. Lancs. Fusiliers. H.Q. GEZAINCOURT.
                          Bn. DOULLENS Area.
  5th. Dorset Regt.   H.Q. and Bn. MAILLY MAILLET. P.6.d.
  11th. Manchester Regt. H.Q. and 2 Coys. VARENNES.
                               2 Coy. MAILLY MAILLET.
  34th. M.G. Company.   Attached 62nd. Division.
  34th. T.M. Battery.   BEAUQUESNE.

6th. E. Yorks Regt. (Pioneers).
                          H.Q. and 1 Coy. Q.16.b.2.2.
                                1 Coy. MESNIL.
                                1 Coy. Q.18.a.d.
                                1 Coy. Q.18.a.5.2.

11th. Divisional R.E.
  67th. Field Company.   H.Q. MARIEUX.
  68th. Field Company.   BEAUQUESNE.
  86th. Field Company.   MARIEUX.
                               Q.18.a.9.8.

11th. Divisional R.A. H.Q. VAUCHELLES.
  58th. F.A.B.   MAILLY MAILLET.
  59th. "   Q.5.c.5.c.
  D.A.C.   FORCEVILLE.
  S.A.A. Subsection.   BEAUQUESNE.

A.D.M.S., 11th. Division.
  33rd. Field Ambulance. MARIEUX.
  34th.   "   "   BEAUVAL.
  35th.   "   "   BEAUQUESNE.
                          BEAUVAL.

A.P.M., 11th. Division. MARIEUX.

D.A.D.O.S., 11th. Division. RAINCHEVAL.

A.D.V.S., 11th. Division. MARIEUX.
  22nd. Mobile Vet. Section. MARIEUX.

11th. Divnl. Train.
  H.Q.,   MARIEUX.
  H.Q. Coy.   VAUCHELLES.
  No. 2 Coy.   BEAUQUESNE.
  No. 3 Coy.   MARIEUX.
  No. 4 Coy.   RAINCHEVAL.

11th. Divnl. Supply Col.
                  BEAUQUESNE.

11th. Divnl. School.
                  ST. RIQUIER.

11th. Divnl. Laundry.
  Billet 44. RAINCHEVAL.

S E C R E T.   8th. March 1917.   11th. Division No. G.S. 452.

11th. Division Location Table showing position of units at 6 a.m. day after date return is rendered.

11th. Division.   H.Q. MARIEUX.

32nd. Infantry Brigade.   H.Q. BEAUQUESNE.
- 9th. W. Yorkshire Regt.   H.Q. and Bn. COURCELLES.
- 6th. Yorkshire Regt.   H.Q. and Bn. BERTRANCOURT.
- 8th. W. Riding Regt.   H.Q. and Bn. BEAUQUESNE.
- 6th. York & Lancs. R.   H.Q. and 2 Coys. BUS.
        2 Coys. BEAUSSART.
- 32nd. M.G. Company.   Attached 62nd. Division.
- 32nd. T.M. Battery.   BEAUQUESNE.

33rd. Infantry Brigade.   H.Q. FAMECHON.
- 6th. Lincoln Regt.   H.Q. and 3 Coys. COUIN.
        1 Coy. THIEVRES.
- 6th. Border Regt.   H.Q. and Bn. COIGNEUX.
- 7th. S. Staffs. Regt.   H.Q. and Bn. BUS LES ARTOIS.
- 9th. S. Foresters.   H.Q. and 2 Coys FAMECHON.
        1 Coy. FRESCHVILLERS.
        1 Coy. SARTON.
- 33rd. M.G. Company.   SARTON.
- 33rd. T.M. Battery.   AUTHIEULE.

34th. Infantry Brigade.   H.Q. BEAUQUESNE.
- 8th. Northd. Fusiliers.   H.Q. and Bn. Q.11.c.
- 9th. Lancs. Fusiliers.   H.Q. GEZAINCOURT.
        Bn. DOULLENS Area.
- 5th. Dorset Regt.   H.Q. and Bn. MAILLY MAILLET. P.6.d.
- 11th. Manchester Regt.   H.Q. and 2 Coys. VARENNES.
        2 Coy. MAILLY MAILLET.
- 34th. M.G. Company.   Attached 62nd. Division.
- 34th. T.M. Battery.   BEAUQUESNE.

6th. E. Yorks Regt. (Pioneers).
    H.Q. and 1 Coy. Q.16.b.2.2.
    1 Coy. MESNIL.
    1 Coy. Q.18.a.d.
    1 Coy. Q.18.a.5.2.

11th. Divisional R.E.   H.Q. MARIEUX.
- 67th. Field Company.   BEAUQUESNE.
- 68th. Field Company.   MARIEUX.
- 86th. Field Company.   Q.18.a.9.8.

11th. Divisional R.A.   H.Q. VAUCHELLES.
- 58th. F.A.B.   MAILLY MAILLET.
- 59th. "   Q.5.c.5.c.
- D.A.C.   FORCEVILLE.
- S.A.A. Subsection.   BEAUQUESNE.

A.D.M.S., 11th. Division.
- 33rd. Field Ambulance.   MARIEUX.
- 34th. "   "   BEAUVAL.
- 35th. "   "   BEAUQUESNE.
        BEAUVAL.

A.P.M., 11th. Division.   MARIEUX.

D.A.D.O.S., 11th. Division.   RAINCHEVAL.

A.D.V.S., 11th. Division.   MARIEUX.
- 22nd. Mobile Vet. Section.   MARIEUX.

11th. Divnl. Train.
H.Q., MARIEUX.
H.Q. Coy. VAUCHELLES.
No.2 Coy. BEAUQUESNE.
No.3 Coy. MARIEUX.
No. 4 Coy. RAINCHEVAL.

11th. Divnl. Supply Col.
BEAUQUESNE.

11th. Divnl. School.
ST. RIQUIER.

11th. Divnl. Laundry.
Billet 44. RAINCHEVAL.

S E C R E T. 8th. March 1917. 11th. Division No. G.S. 470.

11th. Division Location Table showing position
of units at 6 a.m. day after date return is rendered.

11th. Division H.Q. MARIEUX.

32nd. Infantry Brigade. H.Q. BEAUQUESNE.
9th. W. Yorks Regt. H.Q. and Bn. COURCELLES.
6th. Yorkshire Regt. H.Q. and Bn. BERTRANCOURT.
8th. W. Riding Regt. H.Q. and Bn. BEAUQUESNE.
6th. York & Lancs R. H.Q. and 2 Coys. BUS.
                          2 Coys. BEAUSSART.
32nd. M.G. Company. Attached 62nd. Division.
32rd. T.M. Battery. BEAUQUESNE.

33rd. Infantry Brigade. H.Q. FARECHON.
6th. Lincoln Regt. H.Q. and 3 Coys. ST. LEGER.
                          1 Coy. THIEVRES.
6th. Border Regt. H.Q. and Bn. COIGNEUX.
7th. S. Staffs.Regt. H.Q. and Bn. BUS LES ARTOIS.
9th. S. Foresters. H.Q. and 2 Coys. FARECHON.
                        1 Coy. SARTON.
                        1 Coy. FRESCHVILLERS.
33rd. M.G. Company. SARTON.
33rd. T.M. Battery. AUTHIEULE.

34th. Infantry Brigade. H.Q. BEAUQUESNE.
8th. Northd. Fusiliers H.Q. and Bn. Q.11.c.
9th. Lancs. Fusiliers H.Q. GEZAINCOURT.
                      Bn. DOULLENS Area.
5th. Dorset Regt. H.Q. and Bn. MAILLY MAILLET. P.6.d.
11th. Manchester Regt. H.Q. and 2 Coys. VARENNES.
                      2 Coys. MAILLY MAILLET.
34th. M.G. Company. Attached 62nd. Division.
34th. T.M. Battery. BEAUQUESNE.

6th. E. Yorks Regt. (Pioneers).
             H.Q. and 1 Coy. Q.18.h.2.2.
             1 Coy. MESNIL.
             1 Coy. Q.18.a.
             1 Coy. Q.18.a.5.2.

11th. Divisional R.E. H.Q. MARIEUX.
67th. Field Company. BEAUQUESNE.
68th.   "   "   MARIEUX.
96th.   "   "   Q.18.a.9.9.

11th. Divisional R.A. H.Q. VAUCHELLES.
58th. F.A.B. MAILLY MAILLET.
59th.   Q.5.c.5.8.
D.A.C.   FORCEVILLE.
S.A.A. Subsection. BEAUQUESNE.

A.D.M.S., 11th. Division.
33rd. Field Ambulance. MARIEUX.
34th.   "   "   BEAUVAL.
35th.   "   "   BEAUQUESNE.
                       BEAUVAL.

P.M., 11th. Division. MARIEUX.

A.D.O.S., 11th. Division. RAINCHEVAL.

D.V.S., 11th. Division. MARIEUX.
22nd. Mobile Vet. Section. MARIEUX.

11th. Divnl. Train.
H.Q., MARIEUX.
H.Q., Coy. VAUCHELLES.
No. 2 Coy. BEAUQUESNE.
No. 3 Coy. MARIEUX.
No. 4 Coy. RAINCHEVAL.

11th. Divnl. Supply Column.
         BEAUQUESNE.

11th. Divnl. School.
         ST. RIQUIER.

11th. Divnl. Laundry.
Billet 44. RAINCHEVAL.

S E C R E T.　　　　9th. March '17.　　11th. Division No. G.S. 481.

11th. Division Location Table showing position
of units at 6 a.m. day after date return is rendered.

11th. Division.　　　　　H.Q. MARIEUX.

32nd. Infantry Brigade. H.Q. BEAUQUESNE.
 9th. W. Yorks Regt.　H.Q. and Bn. COURCELLES.
 6th. Yorks Regt.　　　H.Q. and Bn. BERTRANCOURT.
 8th. W. Riding Regt. H.Q. and Bn. BEAUQUESNE.
 6th. York & Lancs. R H.Q. and 2 Coys. BUS.
         2 Coys. BEAUSSART
 32nd. M.G. Company.　　Attached 62nd. Division.
 32nd. T.M. Battery.　　　BEAUQUESNE.

33rd. Infantry Brigade. H.Q. FALECHON.
 6th. Lincoln Regt.　H.Q. and 3 Coys. ST. LEGER.
        1 Coy. THIEVRES.
 6th. Border Regt.　H.Q. and Bn.　COIGNEUX.
 7th. S. Staffs.Regt. H.Q. and Bn.　BUS LES ARTOIS.
 9th. S. Foresters　H.Q. and 2 Coys. FALECHON.
        1 Coy. FRESCHVILLERS.
        1 Coy. SARTON.
 33rd. M.G. Company.　　　SARTON.
 33rd. T.M. Battery.　　　AUTHIEULE.

34th. Infantry Brigade. H.Q. BEAUQUESNE.
 8th. Northd. Fusiliers H.Q. and Bn. Q.11.c.
 9th. Lancs. Fusiliers H.Q. GEZAINCOURT.
        Bn. DOULLENS Area.
 5th. Dorset Regt.　H.Q. and Bn. MAILLY MAILLET. P.6.d.
 11th. Manchester Regt. H.Q. and 2 Coys. VARENNES.
        2 Coys. MAILLY MAILLET.
 34th. M.G. Company.　Attached 62nd. Division.
 34th. T.M. Battery.　　　BEAUQUESNE.

6th. E. Yorks Regt. (Pioneers).
    H.Q. and 1 Coy. Q.16.b.2.2.
    1 Coy. MESNIL.
    1 Coy. Q.18.a.
    1 Coy. Q.18.a.5.2.

11th. Divisional R.E.　H.Q. MARIEUX.
 67th. Field Company.　BEAUQUESNE. - Moving to LOUVENCOURT.
 68th.　"　　"　　　　BEAUSSART.
 6th.　　"　　"　　　　Q.18.a.9.8.

11th. Divisional R.A.　H.Q. VAUCHELLES.
 58th. F.A.B.　　　MAILLY MAILLET.
 59th.　"　　　　Q.5.c.5.6　　　　　11th. Divnl. Train.
 D.A.C.　　　　　　FORCEVILLE.　　　　H.Q., MARIEUX.
 S.A.A. Subsection.　BEAUQUESNE.　　　H.Q. Coy. VAUCHELLES.
            No. 2　"　BEAUQUESNE.
A.D.M.S., 11th. Division.　MARIEUX.　　　No. 3　"　SARTON.
 33rd. Field Ambulance.　BEAUVAL.　　　No. 4　"　RAINCHEVAL.
 34th.　"　　　"　　　　BEAUQUESNE.
 35th.　"　　　"　　　　BEAUVAL.　　　　11th. Divnl. Supply Col.

A.P.M., 11th. Division.　MARIEUX.　　　　　　BEAUQUESNE.

D.A.D.OS., 11th. Division. RAINCHEVAL.　　11th. Divnl. School.

              ST. RIQUIER.

A.D.V.S., 11th. Division　MARIEUX.
 22nd. Mobile Vet. Section. MARIEUX.　　11th. Divnl. Laundry.

             Billet 44. RAINCHEVAL.

SECRET.   10th. March '17.   11th. Division No. G.S. 487.

11th. Division Weekly Location Table showing
position of units at 6 a.m. Sunday March 11th. 1917.

11th. Division.   H.Q. MARIEUX.

32nd. Infantry Brigade.   H.Q. BEAUQUESNE. Moving to P.20.b.5.5 on 11th.
  9th. W. Yorks Regt.   H.Q. and Bn. COURCELLES.
  6th. Yorkshire Regt.   H.Q. and Bn. BERTRANCOURT.
  8th. W. Riding Regt.   H.Q. and Bn. BEAUQUESNE.
  6th. York & Lancs. R.   H.Q. and 2 Coys. BUS.
                                2 Coys. LEAUSJART.
  32nd. M.G. Company.   Attached 62nd. Division.
  32nd. T.M. Battery.   BEAUQUESNE.

33rd. Infantry Brigade.   H.Q. FALECHON.
  6th. Lincoln Regt.   H.Q. and 3 Coys. COUIN.
                                1 Coy. THIEVRES.
  6th. Border Regt.   H.Q. and Bn. COIGNEUX.
  7th. S. Staffs. Regt.   H.Q. and Bn. BUS LES ARTOIS.
  9th. S. Foresters.   H.Q. and 2 Coys. FALECHON.
                                1 Coy. FRESCHVILLERS.
                                1 Coy. SARTON.
  33rd. M.G. Company.   SARTON.
  33rd. T.M. Battery.   AUTHIEULE.

34th. Infantry Brigade.   H.Q. BEAUQUESNE.
  8th. Northd. Fusiliers. H.Q. and Bn. G.11.c.
  9th. Lancs. Fusiliers.   H.Q. GEZAINCOURT.
                           Bn. DOULLENS Area.
  5th. Dorset Regt.   H.Q. and Bn. MAILLY MAILLET. P.6.d.
  11th. Manchester Regt.   H.Q. and 2 Coys. VARENNES.
                                2 Coys. MAILLY MAILLET.
  34th. M.G. Company.   Attached 62nd. Division.
  34th. T.M. Battery.   BEAUQUESNE.

6th. E. Yorks Regt. (Pioneers).
                           H.Q. and 1 Coys. Q.16.b.2.2.
                                1 Coy. Q.18.a.
                                1 Coy. MESNIL.
                                1 Coy. Q.18.a.5.2.

11th. Divisional R.E.   H.Q. MARIEUX.
  67th. Field Company.   LOUVENCOURT.
  68th.   "   "   BEAUSSART.
  86th.   "   "   Q.18.a.9.8.

11th. Divisional R.A.   H.Q. VAUCHELLES.
  58th. F.A.B.   MAILLY MAILLET
  59th. "   Q.5.c.5.6.   11th. Divisional Train.
  D.A.C.   FORCEVILLE.   H.Q., Rxx. MARIEUX.
  S.A.A. Subsection.   BEAUQUESNE.   H.Q., Coy. VAUCHELLES.
                                               No. 2 Coy. BEAUQUESNE.
A.D.M.S., 11th. Division. MARIEUX.   No. 3 Coy. SARTON.
  33r. Field Ambulance.   BEAUVAL.
  34th.   "   "   BEAUQUESNE.   11th. Divisional Supply Col.
  35th.   "   "   (BOIS LALEAU.   I.27.c.1.7.
                          (I.10.c.7.7

A.P.M., 11th. Division.   MARIEUX.   11th. Divisional School.

D.A.D.G.S., 11th. Division. RAINCHEVAL.   ST. RIQUIER.

A.D.V.S., 11th. Division. MARIEUX.   11th. Divisional Laundry.
  22nd. Mobile Vet. Section. MARIEUX.
                                               Billet 44. RAINCHEVAL.

S E C R E T.

War Diary

11th. March 1917.   11th. Division No. G.S. 591.

11th. Division Location Table showing position of units at 6 a.m. day after date return is rendered.

11th. Division.   H.Q. MARIEUX.

32nd. Infantry Brigade.   H.Q.   P.20.b.5.5. Moving to BEAUQUESNE.
  9th. W. Yorks Regt.   H.Q. and Bn. AUCHONVILLERS.
  6th. Yorkshire Regt.   H.Q. and Bn. BERTRANCOURT.
  8th. W. Riding Regt.   H.Q. and Bn. BEAUQUESNE.
  6th. York & Lancs. R.   H.Q. and 2 Coys. BUS.
                        2 Coy. BEAUSSART.

  32nd. M.G. Company.   Attached 62nd. Division.
  32nd. T.M. Battery.   BEAUQUESNE.

33rd. Infantry Brigade.   H.Q. FAMECHON.
  6th. Lincoln Regt.   H.Q. and 2 Coys. ST. LEGER.
                        2 Coys. THIEVRES.
  6th. Border Regt.   H.Q. and Bn. COIGNEUX.
  7th. S. Staffs. Regt.   H.Q. and Bn. BUS LES ARTOIS.
  9th. S. Foresters   H.Q. and 2 Coys. FAMECHON.
                        1 Coy. SARTON.
                        1 Coy. FRESCHVILLERS.
  33rd. M.G. Company.   SARTON.
  33rd. T.M. Battery.   AUTHIEULE.

34th. Infantry Brigade.   H.Q. BEAUQUESNE.
  5th. Northd. Fusiliers.   H.Q. and Bn. Q.11.c.
  9th. Lancs. Fusiliers.   H.Q. GEZAINCOURT.
                        Bn. DOULLENS Area.
  5th. Dorset Regt.   H.Q. and Bn. MAILLY MAILLET .P.6.d.
  11th. Manchester Regt.   H.Q. and 2 Coys. VARENNES.
                        2 Coys. MAILLY MAILLET.
  34th. M.G. Company.   Attached 62nd. Division.
  34th. T.M. Battery.   BEAUQUESNE.

6th. E. Yorks Regt. (Pioneers).
                    H.Q. and 1 Coy. Q.16.b.2.2.
                    1 Coy. Q.18.a.
                    1 Coy. MESNIL.
                    1 Coy. Q.18.a.5.2.
                    (Moving to

11th. Divisional R.E.   H.Q. MARIEUX.) COIGNEUX.   **Attached Troops.**
  67th. Field Company.   LOUVENCOURT.   50th. A.S.P., TERRA MESNIL.
  68th.   "   "   BEAUSSART.
  86th.   "   "   Q.18.a.9.8.   Town Major   BEAUQUESNE.

11th. Divisional R.A.   H.Q. BUS LES ARTOIS.
  58th. F.A.B.   STAR WOOD.   **11th. Divisional Train.**
  59th.   "   K.24.a.0.7.   H.Q.,   MARIEUX.
  D.A.C.   FORCEVILLE.   H.Q., Coy.   VAUCHELLES.
  S.A.A. Subsection.   BEAUQUESNE.   No. 2 Coy.   BEAUQUESNE.
                                    No. 3 Coy.   SARTON.

A.D.M.S., 11th. Division.   MARIEUX.   No. 4 Coy.   RAINCHEVAL.
  33rd. Field Ambulance.   BEAUVAL.
  34th.   "   "   BEAUQUESNE.   **11th. Divisional Supply Col.**
  35th.   "   "   { BOIS LALEAU.
                          I.10.c.7.7.   I.27.c.1.7.
A.P.M., 11th. Division.   MARIEUX.

                                    11th. Divisional School.

D.A.D.O.S., 11th. Division.   RAINCHEVAL.
                                    ST. RIQUIER.

A.D.V.S., 11th. Division.   MARIEUX.
  22nd. Mobile Vet. Section   MARIEUX.   **11th. Divisional Laundry.**

                                    Billet 44.   RAINCHEVAL.

War Diary

S E C R E T.   12th. March 1917.   11th. Division No. G.S. 510.

11th. Division Location showing position of units at 6 a.m. day after date return is rendered.

11th. Division	H.Q. MARIEUX.
32nd. Infantry Brigade.	H.Q. BEAUQUESNE.
9th. W. Yorkshire Regt.	H.Q. and Bn. AUCHONVILLERS.
6th. Yorkshire Regt.	H.Q. and Bn. BERTRANCOURT.
8th. W. Riding Regt.	H.Q. BEAUQUESNE.
	2 Coys. AUCHONVILLERS.
6th. York & Lancs. Regt.	H.Q. and 2 Coys. BUS.
	2 Coys. BEAUSSART.
32nd. M.G. Company.	Attached 62nd. Division. FORCEVILLE.
32nd. T.M. Battery.	BEAUQUESNE.
33rd. Infantry Brigade.	H.Q. FAMECHON.
6th. Lincoln Regt	H.Q. and 2 Coys. ST. LEGER.
	2 Coy. THIEVRES.
6th. Border Regt.	H.Q. and Bn. COIGNEUX
7th. S. Staffs Regt.	H.Q. and Bn. BUS LES ARTOIS.
9th. S. Foresters	H.Q. and 2 Coys. FAMECHON.
	1 Coy. FRESCHVILLERS.
	1 Coy. SARTON.
33rd. M.G. Company.	SARTON.
33rd. T.M. Battery.	AUTHIEULE.
34th. Infantry Brigade.	H.Q. BEAUQUESNE.
8th. Northd. Fusiliers.	H.Q. and Bn. Q.11.c.
9th. Lancs. Fusiliers.	H.Q. GEZAINCOURT.
	Bn. DOULLENS Area.
5th. Dorset Regt.	H.Q. and Bn. MAILLY MAILLET. P.6.d.
11th. Manchester Regt.	H.Q. and 2 Coys. VARENNES.
	2 Coys. MAILLY MAILLET.
34th. M.G. Company.	Attached 62nd. Division. ENGLEBELMER.
34th. T.M. Battery.	BEAUQUESNE.
6th. E. Yorks Regt. (Pioneers).	
	H.Q. and 1 Coy. Q.16.b.2.2.
	1 Coy. Q.18.a.
	1 Coy. MESNIL.
	1 Coy. Q.18.a.5.2.
11th. Divisional R.E.	H.Q. COIGNEUX.
67th. Field Company.	LOUVENCOURT.
68th. " "	BEAUSSART.
86th. " "	Q.18.a.9.8.
11th. Divisional R.A.	H.Q. BUS LES ARTOIS.
58th. F.A.B.	STAR WOOD.
59th. "	K.24.a.0.7.
D.A.C.	FORCEVILLE.
S.A.A. Subsection.	BEAUQUESNE.
A.D.M.S., 11th. Division.	MARIEUX.
33rd. Field Ambulance.	BEAUVAL.
34th. " "	BEAUQUESNE.
35th. " "	BOIS LALEAU I.10.c.7.7.
A.P.M. 11th. Division.	MARIEUX.
D.A.D.O.S., 11th. Division.	RAINCHEVAL.
A.D.V.S., 11th. Division.	MARIEUX.
22nd. Mobile Vet. Section.	MARIEUX.

Attached Troops.
50th. A.S.P., TERRA MESN

Town Major. BEAUQUESNE.

11th. Divisional Train.
H.Q., MARIEUX
H.Q., Coy. VAUCHELLES.
No.2 Coy. BEAUQUESNE.
No.3 Coy. SARTON.
No.4 Coy. RAINCHEVAL.

11th. Divisional Supply Co
I.27.c.1.7.

11th. Divisional School
ST. RIQUIER.

11th. Divisional Laundry.
Billet 44. RAINCHEVAL.

WAR DIARY

S E C R E T. 13th. March 1917. 11th. Division No. G.S. 524.

11th. Division Location Table showing position
of units at 6 a.m. day after date return is rendered.

11th. Division   H.Q. MARIEUX.

32nd. Infantry Brigade.   H.Q. FORCEVILLE. P.20.b.5.5.
  9th. W. Yorks Regt.   H.Q. and Bn. AUCHONVILLERS. (Q.9.c.5.8).
  6th. Yorkshire Regt.   H.Q. and Bn. BERTRANCOURT.
  8th. W. Riding Regt.   H.Q.   BEAUQUESNE.
                          2 Coys. AUCHONVILLERS.
  6th. York & Lancs. R.   H.Q. and 2 Coys. BUS.
                          2 Coys. BEAUSSART.
  32nd. M.G. Company.   Attached 62nd. Division. FORCEVILLE.
  32nd. T.M. Battery.   BEAUQUESNE.

33rd. Infantry Brigade.   H.Q. FAMECHON.
  6th. Lincoln Regt.   H.Q. and 2 Coys. ST. LEGER.
                          2 Coys. THIEVRES.
  6th. Border Regt.   H.Q. and Bn. COIGNEUX.
  7th. S. Staffs. Regt.   H.Q. and Bn. BUS LES ARTOIS.
  9th. S. Foresters.   H.Q. and 2 Coys. FAMECHON.
                          1 Coy. SARTON.
                          1 Coy. FRESCHVILLERS.
  33rd. M.G. Company.   SARTON.
  33rd. T.M. Battery.   AUTHIEULE.

34th. Infantry Brigade.   H.Q. BEAUQUESNE.
  8th. Northd. Fusiliers H.Q. and Bn. Q.11.c.
  9th. Lancs. Fusiliers   H.Q. GEZAINCOURT.
                          Bn. DOULLENS Area.
  5th. Dorset Regt.   H.Q. and Bn. MAILLY MAILLET. P.6.d.
  11th. Manchester Regt. H.Q. and 2 Coys. VARENNES.
                          2 Coys. MAILLY MAILLET.
  34th. M.G. Company.   Attached 62nd. Division. ENGLEBELMER.
  34th. T.M. Battery.   BEAUQUESNE.

6th. E. Yorks Regt. (Pioneers).
                          H.Q. and 1 Coy. Q.16.b.2.2
                          1 Coy. Q.18.a.
                          1 Coy. MESNIL.
                          1 Coy. Q.18.a.5.2.

11th. Divisional R.E.   H.Q. COIGNEUX.   Attached Troops.
  67th. Field Company.   LOUVENCOURT.   50th. A.S.P., TERRA MESNIL
  68th.   "   "   BEAUSSART.
  86th.   "   "   Q.16.a.9.8.   Town Major   BEAUQUESNE.

11th. Divisional R.A.   H.Q. BUS LES ARTOIS.
  58th. F.A.B.   STAR WOOD.
  59th.   "   K.24.a.0.7.
D.A.C.   FORCEVILLE.   11th. Divisional Train.
S.A.A. Subsection.   BEAUQUESNE.   H.Q.,   MARIEUX.
                                              H.Q., Coy. VAUCHELLES.
A.D.M.S., 11th. Division. MARIEUX.   No.2 Coy. BEAUQUESNE.
  33rd. Field Ambulance. BEAUVAL.   No. 3 Coy. SARTON.
  34th. Field Ambulance. BEAUQUESNE.   No.4 Coy. RAINCHEVAL.
  35th. Field Ambulance. { BOIS LALEAU.
                          { I.10.c.7.7.   11th. Divnl. Supply Col.

A.P.M., 11th. Division.   MARIEUX.   I.27.c.1.7.

D.A.D.O.S., 11th. Division. RAINCHEVAL.   11th. Divisional School.

A.D.V.S., 11th. Division. MARIEUX.   ST. RIQUIER.
  22nd. Mobile Vet. Section. MARIEUX.   11th. Divnl. Laundry.

                                              Billet 44. RAINCHEVAL.

WAR DIARY

S E C R E T. 14th. March 1917. 11th. Division No. G.S. 531.

11th. Division Location Table showing position
of units at 6 a.m. day after date return is rendered.

11th. Division. H.Q. MARIEUX.

32nd. Infantry Brigade. H.Q. BEAUQUESNE.
  9th. W. Yorks Regt. H.Q. and Bn. AUCHONVILLERS. Q.9.c.5.8.
  6th. Yorkshire Regt. H.Q. and Bn. BERTRANCOURT.
  8th. W. Riding Regt. H.Q. BEAUQUESNE.
      2 Coys. AUCHONVILLERS.
  6th. York & Lancs. Regt. H.Q. and 2 Coys. BUS.
      2 Coys. BEAUSSART.
  32nd. M.G. Company. Attached 62nd. Division. FORCEVILLE.
  32nd. T.M. Battery. BEAUQUESNE.

33rd. Infantry Brigade. H.Q. FAMECHON.
  6th. Lincoln Regt. H.Q. and 2 Coys. ST. LEGER.
      2 Coys. THIEVRES.
  6th. Border Regt. H.Q. and Bn. COIGNEUX.
  7th. S. Staffs. Regt. H.Q. and Bn. BUS LES ARTOIS.
  9th. S. Foresters. H.Q. and 2 Coys. FAMECHON.
      2 Coys. SARTON.
      1 Coy. FRESCHVILLERS.
  33rd. M.G. Company. SARTON.
  33rd. T.M. Battery. AUTHIEULE.

34th. Infantry Brigade. H.Q. BEAUQUESNE.
  8th. Northd. Fusiliers. H.Q. and Bn. Attached 62nd. Division. L.25.d.
  5th. Lancs. Fusiliers. H.Q. GEZAINCOURT.
      Bn. DOULLENS Area.
  5th. Dorset Regt. H.Q. and Bn. MAILLY MAILLET. P.6.d.
  11th. Manchester Regt. H.Q. and 2 Coys. VARENNES.
      2 Coys. MAILLY MAILLET.
  34th. M.G. Company. Attached 62nd. Division. ENGLEBELMER.
  34th. T.M. Battery. BEAUQUESNE.

6th. E. Yorks Regt. (Pioneers).
      H.Q. and 1 Coy. Q.16.b.2.2.
      1 Coy. MESNIL.
      1 Coy. Q.18.a.5.2.
      1 Coy. Q18.a.

11th. Divisional R.E. H.Q. COIGNEUX.
  67th. Field Company. LOUVENCOURT.
  68th. " " BEAUSSART.
  86th. " " Q.18.a.9.8.

11th. Divisional R.A. H.Q. BUS LES ARTOIS.
  58th. F.A.B. STAR WOOD.
  59th. " K.24.a.0.7.
  D.A.C. FORCEVILLE.
  S.A.A. Subsection. BEAUQUESNE.

A.D.M.S., 11th. Division. MARIEUX.
  33rd. Field Ambulance. BEAUVAL.
  34th. " " BEAUQUESNE.
  35th. " " (BOIS LALEAU.
      (I.10.c.7.7.

A.P.M., 11th. Division. MARIEUX.

D.A.D.O.S., 11th. Division. RAINCHEVAL.

A.D.V.S., 11th. Division. MARIEUX.
  22nd. Mobile Vet. Section. MARIEUX.

Attached Troops.
50th. A.S.P., TERRA MESNIL.
Town Major. BEAUQUESNE.

11th. Divisional Train.
H.Q., MARIEUX
H.Q., Coy. VAUCHELLES.
No.2 Coy. BEAUQUESNE.
No.3 " SARTON.
No.4 " RAINCHEVAL.

11th. Divisional Supply Col.
I.27.c.1.7.

11th. Divisional School.
ST. RIQUIER.

11th. Divisional Laundry.
Belfast 44. RAINCHEVAL.

WAR DIARY

SECRET.   15th./3/1917.   11th. Division No. G.S. 542.

11th. Division Location Table showing position
of units at 6 a.m. day after date return is rendered.

11th. Division.   H.Q. MARIEUX.

32nd. Infantry Brigade.   H.Q. BEAUQUESNE.
  9th. W. Yorks Regt.   H.Q. and Bn. AUCHONVILLERS.   Q.9.c.5.8.
  6th. Yorkshire Regt.   H.Q. and Bn. BERTRANCOURT.
  8th. W. Riding Regt.   H.Q.   BEAUQUESNE.
                                   2 Coys. AUCHONVILLERS.
  6th. York & Lancs. Regt.   H.Q. and 2 Coys. BUS.
                                   2 Coys. BEAUSSART.
  32nd. M.G. Company.   Attached 62nd. Division. FORCEVILLE.
  32nd. T.M. Battery.   BEAUQUESNE.

33rd. Infantry Brigade.   H.Q. FAMECHON.
  6th. Lincoln Regt.   H.Q. and 2 Coys. ST. LEGER.
                                   2 Coys THIEVRES.
  6th. Border Regt.   H.Q. and Bn. COIGNEUX.
  7th. S. Staffs. Regt.   H.Q. and Bn. BUS LES ARTOIS.
  9th. S. Foresters.   H.Q. and 2 Coys. FAMECHON.
                                   1 Coy. SARTON.
                                   1 Coy. FRESCHVILLERS.
  33rd. M.G. Company.   SARTON.
  33rd. T.M. Battery.   AUTHIEULE.

34th. Infantry Brigade.   H.Q. BEAUQUESNE.
  8th. Northd. Fusiliers.   H.Q. and Bn. Attached 62nd. Division. L.23.d.
  9th. Lancs. Fusiliers.   H.Q. GEZAINCOURT.
                                   Bn. DOULLENS Area.
  5th. Dorset Regt.   H.Q. and Bn. MAILLY MAILLET. P.6.d.
  11th. Manchester Regt.   H.Q. and 2 Coys. VARENNES.
                                   2 Coys. MAILLY MAILLET.
  34th. M.G. Company.   Attached 62nd. Division.
  34th. T.M. Battery.   BEAUQUESNE.

6th. E. Yorks Regt. (Pioneers).
                                 H.Q. and 1 Coy. Q.16.b.2.2.
                                   1 Coy. Q.18.a.
                                   1 Coy. LESNIL.
                                   1 Coy. Q.18.a.5.2.

11th. Divisional R.E.   H.Q. COIGNEUX.   Attached Troops.
  67th. Field Company.   LOUVENCOURT.
  68th.   "   "   BEAUSSART.   50th. A.S.P., TERRAMESNIL
  86th.   "   "   Q.18.a.9.8.
                                                             Town Major   BEAUQUESNE.
11th. Divisional R.A.   BUS LES ARTOIS.
  58th. F.A.B.   STAR WOOD.
  59th.   "   K.24.a.0.7.
  D.A.C. & S.A.A. Subsection.   FORCEVILLE.
                                                             11th. Divisional Train.
A.D.M.S., 11th. Division.   MARIEUX.   H.Q.,   MARIEUX.
  33rd. Field Ambulance.   BEAUVAL.   H.Q., Coy.   VAUCHELLES.
  34th.   "   "   BEAUQUESNE.   No. 2 Coy.   BEAUQUESNE.
  35th.   "   "   { BOIS LALEAU.   No. 3 Coy.   SARTON.
                              { I.10.c.7.7.   No. 4 Coy.   RAINCHEVAL.

A.P.M., 11th. Division.   MARIEUX.   11th. Divisional Supply Col.

D.A.D.O.S., 11th. Division.   RAINCHEVAL.   I.27.c.1.7.

A.D.V.S., 11th. Division.   MARIEUX.   11th. Divisional School.
  22nd. Mobile Vet. Section.   MARIEUX.
                                                             ST. RIQUIER.

                                                             11th. Divisional Laundry.

                                                             Billet 44. RAINCHEVAL.

S E C R E T.   16th. March '17.   11th. Divn. No. G.S. 538.

WAR Diary

11th. Division Location Table showing position of units at 6 a.m. day after date return is rendered.

11th. Division.   H.Q. MARIEUX.

32nd. Infantry Brigade. H.Q. BEAUQUESNE.
- 9th. W. Yorks Regt.   H.Q. and Bn. AUCHONVILLERS. Q.9.c.5.8.
- 6th. Yorkshire Regt. H.Q. and Bn. BERTRANCOURT.
- 8th. W. Riding Regt. H.Q. &C. BEAUQUESNE.
                        2 Coys. AUCHONVILLERS.
- 6th. York & Lancs. R. H.Q. and 2 Coys. PUS.
                        2 Coys. BEAUSSART.
- 32nd. M.G. Company.   BEAUQUESNE.
- 32nd. T.M. Battery.   BEAUQUESNE.

33rd. Infantry Brigade. H.Q. FAMECHON.
- 6th. Lincoln Regt.   H.Q. and 2 Coys. THIEVRES.
                        2 Coys. ST. LEGER.
- 6th. Border Regt.   H.Q. and Bn. COIGNEUX.
- 7th. S. Staffs. Regt. H.Q. and Bn. BUS LES ARTOIS.
- 9th. S. Foresters.   H.Q. and 2 Coys. FAMECHON.
                        1 Coy. SARTON.
                        1 Coy. FRESCHVILLERS.
- 33rd. M.G. Company.   SARTON.
- 33rd. T.M. Battery.   AUTHIEULE.

34th. Infantry Brigade. H.Q. BEAUQUESNE.
- 8th. Northd. Fusiliers H.Q. and Bn. FORCEVILLE.
- 9th. Lancs. Fusiliers. H.Q. GEZAINCOURT.
                         Bn. DOULLENS Area
- 5th. Dorset Regt.   H.Q. and Bn. MAILLY MAILLET. P.6.d.
- 11th. Manchester Regt. H.Q. and 2 Coys. VARENNES.
                         2 Coys. MAILLY MAILLET.
- 34th. M.G. Company.   Attached 62nd. Division.
- 34th. T.M. Battery.   BEAUQUESNE.

6th. E. Yorks Regt. (Pioneers).
- H.Q. and 1 Coy.   Q.16.b.2.2.
- 1 Coy.   Q.18.a.
- 1 Coy.   MESNIL.
- 1 Coy.   Q.18.a.5.2.

11th. Divisional R.E.   H.Q. COIGNEUX.
- 67th. Field Company. LOUVENCOURT.
- 68th.   "   "   BEAUSSART.
- 86th.   "   "   Q.18.a.9.8.

11th. Divisional R.A.   H.Q. BUS LES ARTOIS.
- 58th. F.A.B.   STAR WOOD.
- 59th.   "   K.24.a.0.7.
- D.A.C. & S.A.A. Subsection.   FORCEVILLE.

A.D.M.S., 11th. Division.   MARIEUX.
- 33rd. Field Ambulance.   BEAUVAL.
- 34th.   "   "   BEAUQUESNE.
- 35th.   "   "   { BOIS LALEAU.
                           { I.10.c.7.7.

A.P.M., 11th. Division.   MARIEUX.

R.A.D.O.S., 11th. Division.   RAINCHEVAL.

A.D.V.S., 11th. Division.   MARIEUX.
- 22nd. Mobile Vet. Section.   MARIEUX.

Attached Troops.

- 50th. A.S.P. TERRA MES.
- Town Major   BEAUQUESNE

11th. Divisional Train.
- H.Q.,   MARIEUX.
- H.Q., Coy.   VAUCHELLES.
- No.2 Coy.   BEAUQUESNE.
- No. 3 "   SARTON.
- No. 4 "   RAINCHEVAL.

11th. Divisional Supply C
- I.27.c.1.7.

11th. Divisional School.
- ST. RIQUIER.

11th. Divisional Laundry.
- Billet 14.   RAINCHEVAL.

WAR DIARY

S E C R E T   17th March, 1917.   11th Div.No.G.S.566.

11th Division Weekly Location Table showing position of units at 6 a.m. Sunday, 18th March, 1917.

11th Division.	H.Q. MARIEUX.
32nd Infantry Brigade.	H.Q. BEAUQUESNE.
9th W. Yorks Regt.	H.Q. & Bn. AUCHONVILLERS. Q.9.c.5.8.
6th Yorkshire Regt.	H.Q. & Bn. BERTRANCOURT.
8th W. Riding Regt.	H.Q. & Bn BEAUQUESNE.
	2 Coys. AUCHONVILLERS
6th York & Lanc. Regt.	H.Q. & 2 Coys. BUS
	2 Coys. BEAUQUESNE.
32nd M.G. Coy.	BEAUQUESNE.
32nd T.M. Battery.	BEAUQUESNE.
33rd Infantry Brigade.	H.Q. FAMECHON.
6th Lincoln Regt.	H.Q. & 2 Coys. THIEVRES.
	2 Coys. ST LEGER.
6th Border Regt.	H.Q. & Bn. COIGNEUX.
7th S. Staffs Regt.	H.Q. & Bn. BUS LE ARTOIS.
9th Sh. Foresters.	H.Q. & 2 Coys. FAMECHON.
	1 Coy. SARTON.
	1 Coy. FRESCHVILLERS.
33rd M.G. Coy.	SARTON.
33rd T.M. Battery.	AUTHIEULE.
34th Infantry Brigade.	H.Q. BEAUQUESNE.
8th North'd Fus.	H.Q. & Bn. FORCEVILLE. Moving to RAINCHEVAL on 18th.
9th Lancs. Fus.	H.Q. GEZAINCOURT. Bn. DOUELENS Area.
5th Dorset Regt.	H.Q. & Bn. MAILLY MAILLET. P.6.d.
11th Manchester Regt.	H.Q. & 2 Coys. VARENNES.
	2 Coys. MAILLY MAILLET.
34th M.G. Coy.	Attached 62nd Division.
34th T.M. Battery.	BEAUQUESNE.
6th E. Yorks Regt. (P).	H.Q. & 1 Coy. Q.16.b.2.2.
	1 Coy. Q.18.a.
	1 Coy. MESNIL.
	1 Coy. Q.18.a.5.2.
11th Divl. R.E.	H.Q. COIGNEUX.
67th Field Coy.	LOUVENCOURT.
68th Field Coy.	TEAUSSART.
86th Field Coy.	Q.18.a.9.8.
11th Divl. R.A.	H.Q. BUS LES ARTOIS.
58th F.A.B.	STAR WOOD.
59th F.A.B.	STAR WOOD.
D.A.C. & S.A.A. Sub-Section.	BUS LES ARTOIS.
A.D.M.S. 11th Div.	MARIEUX.
33rd Field Amb.	BEAUVAL.
34th " "	BEAUQUESNE.
35th " "	(BOIS LALEAU.
	(I.10.c.7.7.
A.P.M. 11th Div.	MARIEUX.
D.A.D.O.S. 11th Div.	RAINCHEVAL.
A.D.V.S. 11th Div.	MARIEUX.
22nd Mobile Vet. Section.	MARIEUX.

ATTACHED TROOPS.

50th A.S.P.	TERRA MESN
Town Major.	BEAUQUESNE
11th Divl. Train.	
H.Q.	MARIEUX.
H.Q. Coy.	VAUCHELLES.
No. 2 Coy.	BEAUQUESNE
No. 3 Coy.	SARTON.
No. 4 Coy.	RAINCHEVAL
11th Divl. Supply Col.	
	I.27.c.1.7.
11th Divl. School.	ST RIQUIER.
11th Divl. Laundry.	
Billet 44.	RAINCHEVAL.

S E C R E T.　　　　　　　　　18th March 1917.　　11th. Division No. G.S. 568.

11th. Division Location Table showing position
of units at 6 a.m. day after date return is rendered.

11th. Division.	H.Q. MARIEUX.

32nd. Infantry Brigade.　　H.Q. BEAUQUESNE.
- 9th. W. Yorks Regt.　　H.Q. and Bn. AUCHONVILLERS.
- 6th. Yorkshire Regt.　　H.Q. and Bn. BERTRANCOURT.
- 8th. W. Riding Regt.　　H.Q.　　BEAUQUESNE.
　　　　　　　　　　　　1½ Coys.　AUCHONVILLERS.
- 6th. York & Lancs. Regt. H.Q. and 2 Coys. BUS.
　　　　　　　　2 Coys. Attached 7th. Division.
- 32nd. M.G. Company.　　BEAUQUESNE.
- 32nd. T.M. Battery.　　　-do-

33rd. Infantry Brigade.　　H.Q. FAMECHON.
- 6th. Lincoln Regt.　　H.Q. and 2 Coys. THIEVRES.
　　　　　　　　　　　　2 Coys. ST. LEGER.
- 6th. Border Regt.　　H.Q. and Bn. COIGNEUX.
- 7th. S. Staffs. Regt.　H.Q. and Bn. BUS LES ARTOIS.
- 9th. S. Foresters.　　H.Q. and 2 Coys. FAMECHON.
　　　　　　　　　　1 Coy. SARTON.
　　　　　　　　　　1 Coy. FRESCHVILLERS.
- 33rd. M.G. Company.　　SARTON.
- 33rd. T.M. Battery.　　AUTHIEULE.

34th. Infantry Brigade.　　H.Q. BEAUQUESNE.
- 8th. Northd. Fusiliers. H.Q. and Bn. FORCEVILLE.
- 9th. Lancs. Fusiliers. H.Q. GEZAINCOURT.
　　　　　　　　　　Bn. DOULLENS Area.
- 5th. Dorset Regt.　　H.Q. and Bn. MAILLY MAILLET.
- 11th. Manchester Regt. H.Q. and 2 Coys. VARENNES
　　　　　　　　　　2 Coys. MAILLY MAILLET.
- 34th. M.G. Company.　　Attached 62nd. Division.
- 34th. T.M. Battery.　　BEAUQUESNE.

6th. E. Yorks Regt. (Pioneers).
　　H.Q. and 1 Coy. Q.16.b.2.2.
　　　　1 Coy. MESNIL.
　　　　1 Coy. Q.18.a.5.2.
　　　　1 Coy. Q.23.a.

11th. Divisional R.E.　　H.Q. MARIEUX.
- 67th. Field Company.　　LOUVENCOURT.
- 68th.　　"　　"　　BEAUSSART.
- 86th.　　"　　"　　Q.18.a.9.8.

11th. Divisional R.A.　　BUS LES ARTOIS.
- 58th. F.A.B.　　STAR WOOD.
- 59th.　　"　　STAR WOOD.
- D.A.C. & S.A.A. Subsection. BUS LES ARTOIS.

A.D.M.S., 11th. Division.　MARIEUX.
- 33rd. Field Ambulance.　　BEAUVAL.
- 34th.　　"　　"　　BEAUQUESNE.
- 35th.　　"　　"　　{ BOIS LALEAU.
　　　　　　　　　　　I.10.c.7.7.

A.P.M., 11th. Division.　　MARIEUX.

D.A.D.O.S., 11th. Division.　RAINCHEVAL.

A.D.V.S., 11th. Division.　MARIEUX.
- 22nd. Mobile Vet. Section. MARIEUX.

ATTACHED TROOPS.
50th. A.S.P.
　　TERRA MESNIL
Town Major, BEAUQUESNE

11th. Divisional Train.
- H.Q.,　　　MARIEUX.
- H.Q. Coy.　VAUCHELLES.
- No. 2 Coy.　BEAUQUESNE.
- No. 3 Coy.　SARTON.
- No. 4 Coy.　RAINCHEVAL.

11th. Divnl. Supply Col.
　　　　I.27.c.1.7.

11th. Divnl. School.
　　　　ST. RIQUIER.

11th. Divnl. Laundry.
　　Billet 44. RAINCHEVAL.

WAR DIARY

S E C R E T.   19th. March 1917.   11th. Division No. G.S. 580.

11th. Division Location Table showing Position
of units at 6 a.m. day after date return is rendered.

11th. Division.	H.Q. MARIEUX.
32nd. Infantry Brigade.	H.Q. BEAUQUESNE.
9th. W. Yorkshire Regt.	H.Q. and Bn. AUCHONVILLERS.
6th. Yorkshire Regt.	H.Q. and Bn. MAILLY WOOD.
8th. W. Riding Regt.	H.Q. BEAUQUESNE.
	1 Coys. AUCHONVILLERS.
6th. York & Lancs. Regt.	H.Q. and Bn. K.33.a.2.8.
32nd. M.G. Company.	BEAUQUESNE.
32nd. T.M. Battery.	-do-
33rd. Infantry Brigade.	H.Q. FALECHON.
6th. Lincoln Regt.	H.Q. and 2 Coys. THIEVRES.
	2 Coys. ST. LEGER.
6th. Border Regt.	H.Q. and Bn. COIGNEUX.
7th. S. Staffs Regt.	H.Q. and Bn. BUS LES ARTOIS.
9th. S. Foresters.	H.Q. and 2 Coys. FALECHON.
	1 Coy. FRESCHVILLERS.
	1 Coy. SARTON.
33rd. M.G. Company.	SARTON.
33rd. T.M. Battery.	AUTHIEULE.
34th. Infantry Brigade.	H.Q. BEAUQUESNE.
8th. Northd. Fusiliers.	H.Q. and Bn. FORCEVILLE.
9th. Lancs. Fusiliers.	H.Q. GEZAINCOURT.
	Bn. DOULLENS Area.
8th. Dorset Regt.	H.Q. and Bn. MAILLY MAILLET.
11th Manchester Regt.	H.Q. and 2 Coys. VARENNES.
	2 Coys. MAILLY MAILLET.
34th. M.G. Company.	FORCEVILLE. Moving to BEAUQUESNE 20th.
34th. T.M. Battery.	BEAUQUESNE.
6th. E. Yorks Regt. (Pioneers).	
	H.Q. and 1 Coy. Q.16.b.2.2.
	1 Coy. Q.18.a.
	1 Coy. MESNIL.
	1 Coy. Q.18.a.5.2.

Unit	Location	ATTACHED TROOPS.	
11th. Divisional R.E.	H.Q. MARIEUX.		
67th. Field Company.	LOUVENCOURT.	50th. A.S.P.,	TERRA MESNIL.
68th. " "	DEAUSSART.	Town Major,	BEAUQUESNE.
86th. " "	Q.18.a.9.8.		

Unit	Location	11th. Divisional Train.	
11th. Divisional R.A.	H.Q. BUS LES ARTOIS.		
58th. F.A.B.	STAR WOOD.	H.Q.	MARIEUX.
59th. "	STAR WOOD.	H.Q., Coy.	VAUCHELLES.
D.A.C. & S.A.A. Subsection.	BUS LES ARTOIS.	No.2 Coy.	BEAUQUESNE.
		No. 3 Coy.	SARTON.
A.D.M.S., 11th. Division.	H.Q. MARIEUX.	No. 4 Coy.	RAINCHEVAL.
33rd. Field Ambulance.	BEAUVAL.		
34th. " "	BEAUQUESNE.	**11th. Divnl. Supply Col.**	
35th. " "	(BOIS LALEAU.		
	(I.10.c.7.7.		I.27.c.1.7.
A.P.M., 11th. Division.	MARIEUX.		
		11th. Divnl. School.	
D.A.D.O.S., 11th. Division.	RAINCHEVAL.		
			ST. RIQUIER.
A.D.V.S., 11th. Division.	MARIEUX.		
22nd. Mobile Vet. Section.	MARIEUX.	**11th. Divnl. Laundry.**	
		Billet 44.	RAINCHEVAL.

WAR DIARY

S E C R E T.   20th. March 1917.   11th. Division No. G.S. 590.

11th. Division Location Table showing position
of units at 6 a.m. day after date return is rendered.

11th. Division.   H.Q. MARIEUX.

32nd. Infantry Brigade.   H.Q. BEAUQUESNE.
  9th. W. Yorkshire Regt.   H.Q. and Bn. AUCHONVILLERS.
  6th. Yorkshire Regt.   H.Q. and Bn. MAILLY WOOD.
  8th. W. Riding Regt.   H.Q.   BEAUQUESNE.
                            1¾ Coys. AUCHONVILLERS.
  6th. York & Lancs. R.   H.Q. and Bn. EUSTON CAMP. K.33.a.2.8.
  32nd. M.G. Company.   BEAUQUESNE.
  32nd. T.M. Battery.   -do-

33rd. Infantry Brigade.   H.Q. FALECHON.
  6th. Lincoln Regt.   H.Q. and 2 Coys. THIEVRES.
                                   2 Coys. ST. LEGER.
  6th. Border Regt.   H.Q. and Bn.   COIGNEUX.
  7th. S. Staffs. Regt.   H.Q. and Bn.   BUS LES ARTOIS.
  8th. S. Foresters.   H.Q. and 2 Coys. FALECHON.
                                   1 Coy. FRESCHVILLERS.
                                   1 Coy. SARTON.
  33rd. M.G. Company.   SARTON.
  33rd. T.M. Battery.   AUTHIEULE.

34th. Infantry Brigade.   H.Q. BEAUQUESNE.
  8th. Northd. Fusiliers.   H.Q. and Bn. FORCEVILLE.
  9th. Lancs. Fusiliers.   H.Q.   GEZAINCOURT.
                            Bn.   DOULLENS Area.
  5th. Dorset Regt.   H.Q. and Bn. MAILLY MAILLET.
  11th. Manchester Regt.   H.Q. and 2 Coys. VARENNES.
                                   2 Coys. MAILLY MAILLET.
  34th. M.G. Company.   BEAUQUESNE.
  34th. T.M. Battery   -do-

6th. E. Yorks Regt. (Pioneers).
                            H.Q. and 1 Coy. Q.16.b.2.2.
                                   1 Coy. Q.18.a
                                   1 Coy. MESNIL.
                                   1 Coy. Q.18.a.5.2.

11th. Divisional R.E.   H.Q. MARIEUX.   ATTACHED TROOPS.
  67th. Field Company.   LOUVENCOURT.
  68th.   "   "   BEAUSSART.   50th. A.S.P.,   TERRA MESNIL.
  85th.   "   "   Q.18.a.9.8.   Town Major.   BEAUQUESNE.

11th. Divisional R.A.   H.Q. BUS LES ARTOIS.
  58th. F.A.B.   STAR WOOD. Bus
  59th.   "   STAR WOOD. Bus   11th. Divisional Train.
  D.A.C. & S.A.A. Subsection. BUS LES ARTOIS.
                                               H.Q.,   MARIEUX.
                                               H.Q., Coy.   VAUCHELLES.
A.D.M.S., 11th. Division. MARIEUX.   No. 2 Coy.   BEAUQUESNE.
  33rd. Field Ambulance.   BEAUVAL.   No. 3 Coy.   SARTON.
  34th.   "   "   BEAUQUESNE.   No. 4 Coy.   RAINCHEVAL.
  35th.   "   "   (BOIS LALHAU
                            (I.10.c.7.7.   11th. Divisional Supply Col.

A.P.M., 11th. Division.   MARIEUX.   I.27.c.1.7.

D.A.D.O.S., 11th. Division. RAINCHEVAL.   11th. Divisional School.

A.D.V.S., 11th. Division. MARIEUX.   ST. RIQUIER.
  22nd. Mobile Vet. Section. MARIEUX.   11th. Divisional Laundry.

                                               Billet 44.   RAINCHEVAL.

WAR DIARY

S E C R E T.   21st March 1917.   11th. Division No. G.S. 590.

Location Table showing position of units at 6 a.m. day after date return is rendered.

11th. Division.   H.Q. MARIEUX.

32nd. Infantry Brigade. H.Q. BEAUQUESNE.
  9th. W. Yorkshire Regt. H.Q. and Bn. AUCHONVILLERS.
  6th. Yorkshire Regt.   H.Q. and Bn. MAILLY WOOD.
  8th. W. Riding Regt.   H.Q.   BEAUQUESNE.
                          1¾ Coys. AUCHONVILLERS.
  6th. York & Lancs. R. H.Q. and Bn. EUSTON CAMP. K.33.a.2.8.
  32nd. M.G. Company.   BEAUQUESNE.
  32nd. T.M. Battery.   -do-

33rd. Infantry Brigade. H.Q. FAMECHON.
  6th. Lincoln Regt.   H.Q. and 2 Coys. THIEVRES.
                         2 Coys. ST. LEGER.
  6th. Border Regt.   H.Q. and Bn.   COIGNEUX.
  7th. S. Staffs. Regt. H.Q. and Bn.   BUS LES ARTOIS.
  9th. S. Foresters.   H.Q. and 2 Coys. FAMECHON.
                         1 Coy. FRESCHVILLERS.
                         1 Coy. SARTON.
  33rd. M.G. Company.   SARTON.
  33rd. T.M. Battery.   AUTHIEULE.

34th. Infantry Brigade. H.Q. BEAUQUESNE.
  8th. Northd. Fusiliers. H.Q. and Bn. FORCEVILLE.
  9th. Lancs. Fusiliers. H.Q. GEZAINCOURT.
                          Bn. DOULLENS Area.
  5th. Dorset Regt.   H.Q. and Bn. MAILLY MAILLET.
  11th. Manchester Regt. H.Q. and 2 Coys. VARENNES.
                          2 Coys. MAILLY MAILLET.
  34th. M.G. Company.   BEAUQUESNE.
  34th. T.M. Battery   -do-

6th. E. Yorks Regt. (Pioneers).
                          H.Q. and 1 Coy. Q.16.b.2.2.
                          1 Coy. Q.18.a
                          1 Coy. MESNIL.
                          1 Coy. Q.18.a.5.2.

11th. Divisional R.E.   H.Q. MARIEUX.   ATTACHED TROOPS.
  67th. Field Company.   LOUVENCOURT.
  68th.   "   "   BEAUSSART.   50th. A.S.P., TERRA MESNIL.
  86th.   "   "   Q.18.a.9.8.   Town Major.   BEAUQUESNE.

11th. Divisional R.A.   H.Q. BUS LES ARTOIS.
  58th. F.A.B.   BUS.
  59th.   "   BUS.   11th. Divisional Train.
  D.A.C. & SI.A.A. Subsection. BUS LES ARTOIS.
                                           H.Q.,   MARIEUX.
                                           H.Q., Coy.   VAUCHELLES.
A.D.M.S., 11th. Division.   MARIEUX.   No. 2 Coy.   BEAUQUESNE.
  33rd. Field Ambulance. BEAUVAL.   No. 3 Coy.   SARTON.
  34th.   "   "   BEAUQUESNE.   No. 4 Coy.   RAINCHEVAL.
  35th.   "   "   (BOIS LALLIAU
                          (I.10.c.7.7.   11th. Divisional Supply Col.

A.P.M., 11th. Division.   MARIEUX.   I.27.c.1.7.

D.A.D.O.S., 11th. Division. RAINCHEVAL.   11th. Divisional School.

A.D.V.S., 11th. Division.   MARIEUX.   ST. RIQUIER.
  22nd. Mobile Vet. Section. MARIEUX.   11th. Divisional Laundry.

                                           Billet 44.   RAINCHEVAL.

S E C R E T.   22nd. March 1917.   11th. Divn. No. G.S. 610.

11th. Division Location Table showing position
of units at 6 a.m. day after date return is rendered.

11th. Division.   H.Q. MARIEUX.

32nd. Infantry Brigade   H.Q. BEAUQUESNE.
  9th. W. Yorkshire Regt.   H.Q. and Bn. AUCHONVILLERS.
  6th. Yorkshire Regt.   H.Q. and Bn. MAILLY WOOD.
  8th. W. Riding Regt.   H.Q.   BEAUQUESNE.
                              1½ Coys. AUCHONVILLERS.
  6th. York & Lancs. Re. H.Q. and Bn. EUSTON CAMP. K.33.a.2.8.
  32nd. M.G. Company.   BEAUQUESNE.
  32nd. T.M. Battery.   -do-

33rd. Infantry Brigade.   H.Q. FAMECHON.
  6th. Lincoln Regt.   H.Q. and 2 Coys. THIEVRES.
                             2 Coys. ENTHIE.
  6th. Border Regt.   H.Q. and Bn. COIGNEUX.
  7th. S. Staffs. Regt.   H.Q. and Bn. BUS LES ARTOIS.
  9th. S. Foresters.   H.Q. and 2 Coys. FAMECHON.
                         1 Coy. FRESCHVILLERS.
                         1 Coy. SARTON.
  33rd. M.G. Company.   SARTON.
  33rd. T.M. Battery.   AUTHIEULE.

34th. Infantry Brigade.   H.Q. BEAUQUESNE.
  8th. Northd. Fusiliers.   H.Q. and Bn. FORCEVILLE.
  9th. Lancs. Fusiliers.   H.Q. GEZAINCOURT.
                        Bn. DOULLENS Area.
  5th. Dorset Regt.   H.Q. and Bn. MAILLY MAILLET.
  11th. Manchester Regt.   H.Q. and 2 Coys VARENNES.
                        2 Coys. MAILLY MAILLET.
  34th. M.G. Company.   BEAUQUESNE.
  34th. T.M. Battery.   -do-

6th. E. Yorks Regt. (Pioneers).
                      H.Q. and 1 Coy. Q.16.b.2.2.
                         1 Coy. Q.18.a.
                         1 Coy. MESNIL.
                         1 Coy. Q.18.a.5.2.

11th. Divisional R.E.   H.Q.   MARIEUX.   ATTACHED TROOPS.
  67th. Field Company.   LOUVENCOURT.
  68th.   "   "   BEAUSSART.   50th. A.S.P.,
  86th.   "   "   Q.18.a.9.8.   TERRA MESNIL.
                                                       Town Major. BEAUQUESNE.
11th. Divisional R.A.   H.Q. BUS LES ARTOIS.
  58th. F.A.B.   BUS.
  59th. "   BUS.
  D.A.C. & S.A.A. Subsection.   BUS LES ARTOIS.   11th. Divisional Train.
                                                        H.Q.,   MARIEUX.
A.D.M.S., 11th. Division.   MARIEUX.   H.Q., Coy.   VAUCHELLES.
  33rd. Field Ambulance.   BEAUVAL.   No. 2 Coy.   BEAUQUESNE.
  34th.   "   "   BEAUQUESNE.   No. 3 Coy.   SARTON.
  35th.   "   "   (BOIS LaLEAU   No. 4 Coy.   RAINCHEVAL.
                                         (I.10.c.7.7.
                                                     11th. Divnl. Supply Col.
A.P.M., 11th. Division.   MARIEUX.
                                                                  I.27.c.1.7.
D.A.D.O.S., 11th. Division.   RAINCHEVAL.
                                                 11th. Divnl. School.

A.D.V.S., 11th. Division.   MARIEUX.   ST. RIQUIER.
  22nd. Mobile Vet. Section.   MARIEUX.
                                                 11th. Divnl. Laundry.

                                                 Billet 44. RAINCHEVAL.

WAR DIARY

HORNE. 22nd. March 1917.   11th. Division No. G.S. 618

11th. Division Location Table, showing position
of units at 6 a.m. day after date return is rendered.

11th Division.	H.Q. MARIEUX.	
32nd. Infantry Brigade.	H.Q. BEAUQUESNE.	
9th. W. Yorkshire Regt.	H.Q. and Bn. AUCHONVILLERS.	) Moving to
6th. Yorkshire Regt.	H.Q. and Bn. MAILLY WOOD.	) LOUVENCOURT
8th. W. Riding Regt.	H.Q. BEAUQUESNE.	) RAINCHEVAL.
	1½ Coys. AUCHONVILLERS.	) VAUCHELLES.
6th. York & Lancs. Regt.	H.Q. and Bn. EUSTON CAMP.K.33.a.2.8.	) on 24th.
32nd. M.G. Company.	BEAUQUESNE.	
32nd. T.M. Battery.	-do-	
33rd. Infantry Brigade.	H.Q. BEAUCHON. Moving to SARTON 24th.	
6th. Lincoln Regt.	H.Q. and 2 Coys. THIEVRES.	)
	2 Coys. AUTHIE.	) Moving to
6th. Border Regt.	H.Q. and Bn. COIGNEUX.	)
7th. S. Staffs. Regt.	H.Q. and Bn. BUS LES ARTOIS.	) SARTON and
9th. S. Foresters.	H.Q. and 2 Coys. BEAUCHON.	)
	1 Coy. FRESCHVILLERS.	) ORVILLE on
	1 Coy. SARTON.	)
33rd. M.G. Company.	SARTON.	) 24th.
33rd. T.M. Battery.	AUTHIEULE.	
34th. Infantry Brigade.	H.Q. BEAUQUESNE.	
8th. Northd. Fusiliers.	H.Q. and Bn. FORCEVILLE.	) Moving to
9th. Lancs. Fusiliers.	H.Q. GEZAINCOURT.	) TERRA MESNIL.
	Bn. DOULLENS Area.	) BEAUQUESNE.
5th. Dorset Regt.	H.Q. and Bn. MAILLY MAILLET.	) SARTON. on
11th. Manchester Regt.	H.Q. and 2 Coys. VARENNES.	) 24th.
	2 Coys. MAILLY MAILLET.	)
	BEAUQUESNE.	
34th. M.G. Company.		
34th. T.M. Battery.	-do-	
6th. E. Yorks Regt. (Pioneers).		
	H.Q. and 1 Coy. Q.16.b.2.2.	) Moving to
	1 Coy. Q.18.a.	)
	1 Coy. MESNIL.	) ARQUEVES. on
	1 Coy. Q.18.a.5.2.	) 24th.

ATTACHED TROOPS.

11th. Divisional R.E.	H.Q. MARIEUX.	
67th. Field Company.	LOUVENCOURT) Moving	50th. A.S.P.,
68th. " "	BEAUSSART.) to	TERRA MESNIL.
86th. " "	Q.18.a.9.8.) MARIEUX	Town Major, BEAUQUESNE.
	) on 24th.	

11th. Divisional R.A.	H.Q. BUS LES ARTOIS.	
58th. F.A.B.	-ditto-	
59th. "	-ditto-	11th. Divisional Train.
D.A.C. & S.A.A. Subsection.	-ditto-	H.Q., MARIEUX.
		H.Q., Coy. VAUCHELLES.
		No. 2 Coy. BEAUQUESNE.
R.A.M.S. 11th. Division.		No. 3 Coy. SARTON.
33rd. Field Ambulance.	MARIEUX.	No. 4 Coy. RAINCHEVAL.
34th. " "	BEAUVAL.	
35th. " "	BEAUQUESNE.	
	BOIS LALEAU.	11th. Divnl. Supply Col.
	I.10.c.7.7.	
		I.27.c.1.7.
A.P.M., 11th. Division.	MARIEUX.	
D.A.D.O.S., 11th. Division.	RAINCHEVAL.	11th. Divnl. School.
		ST. RIQUIER.
A.D.V.S., 11th. Division.	MARIEUX.	
22nd. Mobile Vet. Section.	MARIEUX	11th. Divnl. Laundry.
		Billet 44. RAINCHEVAL.

WAR Diary

SECRET.   24th March 1917.   11th. Division No.G.S. 626.

11th. Division Weekly Location Table showing position of Units at 6 a.m. Sunday, 25th. March 1917.

11th. Division.	H.Q.	MARIEUX.

32nd. Infantry Brigade.	H.Q.	BEAUQUESNE.
9th. Yorks Regt.	H.Q. and Bn.	LOUVENCOURT.
6th. Yorkshire Regt.	H.Q. and Bn.	VAUCHELLES.
8th. W. Riding Regt.	H.Q. and Bn.	RAINCHEVAL.
6th. York & Lancs. R.	H.Q. and Bn.	LOUVENCOURT.
32nd. M.G. Company.		BEAUQUESNE.
32nd. T.M. Battery.		-do-

33rd. Infantry Brigade.	H.Q.	SARTON.
6th. Lincoln Regt.	H.Q. and Bn.	ORVILLE.
6th. Border Regt.	H.Q. and Bn.	SARTON.
7th. S. Staffs Regt.	H.Q. and Bn.	SARTON.
9th. S. Foresters.	H.Q. and Bn.	ORVILLE.
33rd. M.G. Company.		SARTON.
33rd. T.M. Battery.		THIEULE.

34th. Infantry Brigade.	H.Q.	BEAUQUESNE.
8th. Northd. Fus.	H.Q. and Bn.	TERRA MESNIL.
9th. Lancs. Fus.	H.Q. and Bn.	TERRA MESNIL.
5th. Dorset Regt.	H.Q. and Bn.	BEAUQUESNE.
11th. Manchester Regt.	H.Q. and Bn.	BEAUQUESNE.
34th. M.G. Company.		BEAUQUESNE.
34th. T.M. Battery.		BEAUQUESNE.

6th. E. Yorks Regt. (Pioneers).		ARQUEVES.

11th. Divisional R.E.	H.Q.	MARIEUX.
67th. Field Company.		MARIEUX.
68th. Field Company.		MARIEUX.
86th. Field Company.		MARIEUX.

11th. Divisional R.A.	H.Q.	BUS LES ARTOIS.
58th. F.....		-do-
59th. "		-do-
D.A.C. & S..... Subsection.		-do-

A.D.M.S., 11th. Division.	MARIEUX.
33rd. Field Ambulance.	BEAUVAL.
34th. " "	BEAUQUESNE.
35th. " "	VAUCHELLES.

A.P.M., 11th. Division.	MARIEUX.
D.A.D.O.S., 11th. Division.	RAINCHEVAL.
A.D.V.S., 11th. Division.	MARIEUX.
22nd. Mobile Vet. Section.	MARIEUX.

ATTACHED TROOPS.

50th. A.S.P., TERRA MESNIL.

Town Major, BEAUQUESNE.

11th. Divisional Train.	
H.Q.,	MARIEUX.
H.Q. Coy.	VAUCHELLES.
No. 2 Coy.	BEAUQUESNE.
No. 3 Coy.	SARTON.
No. 4 Coy.	RAINCHEVAL.

11th. Divnl. Supply Col.

I.87.c.1.7.

11th. Divnl. School.

ST. RIQUIER.

11th. Divnl. Laundry.

Billet 44. RAINCHEVAL.

WAR DIARY

S E C R E T   25th March, 1917.   11th Div. No. G.S. 639.

11th Division Location Table showing position of units at 6 a.m. day after date return is rendered.

11th Division.   H.Q. MARIEUX.

32nd Infantry Brigade.   H.Q. BEAUQUESNE.
9th W. Yorkshire Regt.   H.Q. & Bn. LOUVENCOURT.
6th Yorkshire Regt.   H.Q. & Bn. VAUCHELLES.
8th W. Riding Regt.   H.Q. & Bn. RAINCHEVAL.
6th York & Lancs. Regt.   H.Q. & Bn. LOUVENCOURT.
32nd M.G. Coy.   BEAUQUESNE.
32nd T.M. Battery.   do

33rd Infantry Brigade.   H.Q. SARTON.
6th Lincoln Regt.   H.Q. & Bn. ORVILLE.
6th Border Regt.   H.Q. & Bn. SARTON.
7th S. Stafford Regt.   H.Q. & Bn. SARTON.
9th Sherwood Foresters.   H.Q. & Bn. ORVILLE.
33rd M.G. Coy.   SARTON.
33rd T.M. Battery.   do

34th Infantry Brigade.   H.Q. BEAUQUESNE.
8th North'd Fusiliers.   H.Q. & Bn. TERRA MESNIL.
9th Lancs. Fusiliers.   H.Q. & Bn. TERRA MESNIL.
5th Dorset Regt.   H.Q. & Bn. BEAUQUESNE.
11th Manchester Regt.   H.Q. & Bn. BEAUQUESNE.
34th M.G. Coy.   BEAUQESNE.
34th T.M. Battery.   BEAUQUESNE.

6th E. Yorks Regt. (Pioneers)   ARQUEVES.

11th Divisional R.E.   H.Q. MARIEUX.
67th Field Company. R.E.   do
68th " " "   do
86th " " "   do

11th Divisional R.A.   H.Q. BUS LES ARTOIS.
58th F.A.B.   do
59th F.A.B.   do
D.A.C. & S.A.A. Sub-Section.   do

A.D.M.S. 11th Division.
33rd Field Ambulance.   MARIEUX.
34th " "   BEAUVAL.
35th " "   BEAUQUESNE.
     VAUCHELLES.

A.P.M. 11th Division.   MARIEUX.

D.A.D.O.S. 11th Division.   RAINCHEVAL.

A.D.V.S. 11th Division.   MARIEUX.
22nd Mobile Vet. Section.   MARIEUX.

11th Divisional Train.   H.Q. MARIEUX.
No.1. Company.   VAUCHELLES.
No.2. "   BEAUQUESNE.
No.3. "   SARTON.
No.4. "   RAINCHEVAL.

11th Divisional Supply Column.   I.27.c.1.7.

11th Divisional School.   ST RIQUIER.

11th Divisional Laundry.   Billet 44. RAINCHEVAL.

ATTACHED TROOPS

50th A.S.P.
     TERRA MESNIL.

Town Major
     BEAUQUESNE.

SECRET   26th March, 1917.   11th Div. No. G.S. (4)

War Diary

11th Division Location Table shewing position of units at 6 a.m. day after date return is rendered.

<u>11th Division.</u>	H.Q.	MARIEUX.
<u>32nd Infantry Brigade.</u>	H.Q.	LOUVENCOURT.
9th W. Yorkshire Regt.	H.Q. & Bn.	LOUVENCOURT.
6th Yorkshire Regt.	H.Q. & Bn.	VAUCHELLES.
8th W. Riding Regt.	H.Q. & Bn.	RAINCHEVAL.
6th York & Lancs. Regt.	H.Q. & Bn.	LOUVENCOURT.
32nd M.G. Coy.		BEAUQUESNE.
32nd T.M. Battery.		do
<u>33rd Infantry Brigade.</u>	H.Q.	SARTON.
6th Lincoln Regt.	H.Q. & Bn.	ORVILLE.
6th Border Regt.	H.Q. & Bn.	SARTON.
7th S. Stafford Regt.	H.Q. & Bn.	SARTON.
9th Sherwood Foresters.	H.Q. & Bn.	ORVILLE.
33rd M.G. Coy.		SARTON.
33rd T.M. Battery.		do
<u>34th Infantry Brigade.</u>	H.Q.	BEAUQUESNE.
8th North'd Fusiliers.	H.Q. & Bn.	TERRA MESNIL.
9th Lancs. Fusiliers.	H.Q. & Bn.	TERRA MESNIL.
5th Dorset Regt.	H.Q. & Bn.	BEAUQUESNE.
11th Manchester Regt.	H.Q. & Bn.	BEAUQUESNE.
34th M.G. Coy.		BEAUQESNE.
34th T.M. Battery.		BEAUQUESNE.
<u>6th E. Yorks Regt. (Pioneers)</u>		ARQUEVES.
<u>11th Divisional R.E.</u>	H.Q.	MARIEUX.
67th Field Company. R.E.		do
68th " " "		do
86th " " "		do
<u>11th Divisional R.A.</u>	H.Q.	BUS LES ARTOIS.
58th F.A.B.		do
59th F.A.B.		do
D.A.C. & S.A.A. Sub-Section.		do
<u>A.D.M.S. 11th Division.</u>		MARIEUX.
33rd Field Ambulance.		BEAUVAL.
34th " "		BEAUQUESNE.
35th " "		VAUCHELLES.
<u>A.P.M. 11th Division.</u>		MARIEUX.
<u>D.A.D.O.S. 11th Division.</u>		RAINCHEVAL.
<u>A.D.V.S. 11th Division.</u>		MARIEUX.
2nd Mobile Vet. Section.		MARIEUX.
<u>11th Divisional Train.</u>	H.Q.	MARIEUX.
No.1. Company.		VAUCHELLES.
No.2. "		BEAUQUESNE.
No.3. "		SARTON.
No.4. "		RAINCHEVAL.
<u>11th Divisional Supply Column.</u>		I.27.c.1.7.
<u>11th Divisional School.</u>		ST RIQUIER.
<u>11th Divisional Laundry.</u>	Billet 44.	RAINCHEVAL.

```
ATTACHED TROOPS

50th A.S.P.
   TERRA MESNIL.

Town Major
   BEAUQUESNE.
```

War Diary

SECRET.   27th March 1917.   11th Division No. G. 658.

11th Division Location Table showing position
of units at 6 a.m. day after date return is rendered.

11th. Division.	H.Q. MARIEUX.
32nd. Infantry Brigade.	H.Q. LOUVENCOURT.
9th. W. Yorkshire Regt.	H.Q. and Bn. LOUVENCOURT.
6th. Yorkshire Regt.	H.Q. and Bn. VAUCHELLES.
8th. W. Riding Regt.	H.Q. and Bn. RAINCHEVAL.
6th. York & Lancs. R.	H.Q. and Bn. LOUVENCOURT.
32nd. M.G. Company.	BEAUQUESNE.
32nd. T.M. Battery.	-do-
33rd. Infantry Brigade.	H.Q. SARTON.
6th. Lincoln Regt.	H.Q. and Bn. ORVILLE.
6th. Border Regt.	H.Q. and Bn. SARTON.
7th. S. Stafford Regt.	H.Q. and Bn. SARTON.
9th. S. Foresters.	H.Q. and Bn. ORVILLE.
33rd. M.G. Company.	SARTON.
33rd. T.M. Battery.	SARTON.
34th. Infantry Brigade.	H.Q. BEAUQUESNE.
8th. Northd. Fusiliers.	H.Q. and Bn. TERRA MESNIL.
9th. Lancs. Fusiliers.	H.Q. and Bn. TERRA MESNIL.
5th. Dorset Regt.	H.Q. and Bn. BEAUQUESNE.
11th. Manchester Regt.	H.Q. and Bn. BEAUQUESNE.
34th. M.G. Company.	BEAUQUESNE.
34th. T.M. Battery.	BEAUQUESNE.
6th. E. Yorks Regt.	H.Q. and Bn. ARQUEVES.

ATTACHED TROOPS.
50th. A.S.P., TERRA MESNIL.
Town Major, BEAUQUESNE.

11th. Divisional R.E.	H.Q. MARIEUX.
67th. Field Company.	MARIEUX.
68th. " "	MARIEUX.
86th. " "	MARIEUX.
11th. Divisional R.A.	H.Q. HEM. Moving to BOUBERS on 28th.
58th. F.A.B.	HEM. Moving to BOUBERS on 28th.
59th. "	OCCOCHES. Moving to CONCHY sur CANCHE on 28th.
D.A.C. & S.A.A. Subsection.	OUTREBOIS. Moving to VACQUERIE le BOUCQ and FORTEL on 28th.
A.D.M.S., 11th. Division.	MARIEUX.
33rd. Field Ambulance.	BEAUVAL.
34th. " "	BEAUQUESNE.
35th. " "	VAUCHELLES.
A.P.M., 11th. Division.	MARIEUX.
A.D.V.S., 11th. Division.	MARIEUX.
22nd. Mobile Vet. Section.	MARIEUX.
D.A.D.O.S., 11th. Division.	RAINCHEVAL.
11th. Divisional Train.	H.Q. MARIEUX.
No. 1 Company.	LE QUESNEL FARM. Moving to BOUBERS on 28th.
No. 2 "	BEAUQUESNE.
No. 3 "	SARTON.
No. 4 "	RAINCHEVAL.
11th. Divisional Supply Column.	M.27.a.1.7.
11th. Divisional School.	ST. RIQUIER.
11th. Divisional Laundry.	Billet 44. RAINCHEVAL.

SECRET.   28th. March 1917.   11th. Division No. G. 678.

11th. Division Location Table showing position of units at 6 a.m. day after date return is rendered.

****

11th. Division.	H.Q. MARIEUX.
32nd. Infantry Brigade.	H.Q. LOUVENCOURT.
9th. W. Yorkshire Regt.	H.Q. and Bn. LOUVENCOURT.
6th. Yorkshire Regt.	H.Q. and Bn. VAUCHELLES.
8th. W. Riding Regt.	H.Q. and Bn. RAINCHEVAL.
6th. York & Lancs. Regt.	H.Q. and Bn. LOUVENCOURT.
32nd. M.G. Company.	BEAUQUESNE.
32nd. T.M. Battery.	-do-
33rd. Infantry Brigade.	H.Q. SARTON.
6th. Lincoln Regt.	H.Q. and Bn. ORVILLE.
6th. Border Regt.	H.Q. and Bn. SARTON.
7th. S. Staffs. Regt.	H.Q. and Bn. SARTON.
9th. S. Foresters.	H.Q. and Bn. ORVILLE.
33rd. M.G. Company.	SARTON.
33rd. T.M. Battery.	SARTON.
34th. Infantry Brigade.	H.Q. BEAUQUESNE.
8th. Northd. Fusiliers.	H.Q. and Bn. TERRA MESNIL.
9th. Lancs. Fusiliers.	H.Q. and Bn. TERRA MESNIL.
5th. Dorset Regt.	H.Q. and Bn. BEAUQUESNE.
11th. Manchester Regt.	H.Q. and Bn. BEAUQUESNE.
34th. M.G. Company.	BEAUQUESNE.
34th. T.M. Battery.	BEAUQUESNE.
6th. E. Yorks Regt. (Pioneers).	ARQUEVES.
11th. Divisional R.E.	H.Q. MARIEUX.
67th. Field Company.	MARIEUX.
68th. " "	MARIEUX.
86th. " "	MARIEUX.
11th. Divisional R.A.	H.Q. BOUBERS.
58th. F.A.B.	BOUBERS.
59th. "	CONCHY sur CANCHE.
D.A.C. & S.A.A. Subsection.	VACQUERIE le BOUCQ and FORTEL.
A.D.M.S., 11th. Division.	MARIEUX.
33rd. Field Ambulance.	BEAUVAL.
34th. " "	BEAUQUESNE.
35th. " "	VAUCHELLES.
A.P.M., 11th. Division.	MARIEUX.
A.D.V.S., 11th. Division.	MARIEUX.
22nd. Mobile Vet. Section.	MARIEUX.
D.A.D.O.S., 11th. Division.	RAINCHEVAL.
11th. Divisional Train.	H.Q. MARIEUX.
No. 1 Company.	OUTREBOIS. Moving to BOUBERS.
No. 2 "	BEAUQUESNE.
No. 3 "	SARTON.
No. 4 "	RAINCHEVAL.
11th. Divisional Supply Column.	I.27.c.1.7.
11th. Divisional School.	ST. RIQUIER.
11th. Divisional Laundry.	Billet 44. RAINCHEVAL.

ATTACHED TROOPS.
50th. A.S.P., TERRA MESNIL
Town Major, BEAUQUESNE.

WAR Diary

S E C R E T   29th March, 1917.   11th Div. No. G.S.683.

11th Division Location Table showing position
of units at 6 a.m. day after date return is rendered.

11th Division.	H.Q.	MARIEUX.
32nd Infantry Brigade.	H.Q.	LOUVENCOURT.
9th W. Yorkshire Regt.	H.Q. and Bn.	LOUVENCOURT.
6th Yorkshire Regt.	H.Q. and Bn.	VAUCHELLES.
8th W. Riding Regt.	H.Q. and Bn.	RAINCHEVAL.
6th York & Lancs Regt.	H.Q. and Bn.	LOUVENCOURT.
32nd M.G. Coy.		BEAUQUESNE.
32nd T.M. Btty.		BEAUQUESNE.
33rd Infantry Brigade	H.Q.	SARTON.
6th Lincoln Regt.	H.Q. and Bn.	ORVILLE.
6th Border Regt.	H.Q. and Bn.	SARTON.
7th S. Staffs Regt.	H.Q. and Bn.	SARTON.
9th Sherwood For.	H.Q. and Bn.	ORVILLE.
33rd M.G. Coy.		SARTON.
33rd T.M. Btty.		SARTON.
34th Infantry Brigade	H.Q.	BEAUQUESNE.
8th North'd Fusiliers.	H.Q. and Bn.	TERRA MESNIL.
9th Lancs. Fusiliers.	H.Q. and Bn.	TERRA MESNIL.
5th Dorset Regt.	H.Q. and Bn.	BEAUQUESNE.
11th Manchester Regt.	H.Q. and Bn.	BEAUQUESNE.
34th M.G. Coy.		BEAUQUESNE.
34th T.M. Btty.		BEAUQUESNE.
6th E. Yorks Regt. (Pioneers)		ARQUEVES.
11th Divisional R.E.	H.Q.	MARIEUX.
67th Field Coy. R.E.		MARIEUX.
68th " " "		MARIEUX.
86th " " "		MARIEUX.
11th Divisional R.A.	H.Q.	BOUBERS.
58th F.A.B.		BOUBERS.
59th "		CONCHY sur CANCHE.
D.A.C. & S.A.A. Sub-section.		VACQUERIE le BOUCQ and FORTEL.
A.D.M.S. 11th Division.		MARIEUX.
33rd Field Ambulance.		BEAUVAL.
34th " "		BEAUQUESNE.
35th " "		VAUCHELLES.
A.P.M. 11th Division.		MARIEUX.
A.D.V.S. 11th Division.		MARIEUX.
32nd Mobile Vet. Section.		MARIEUX.
D.A.D.O.S. 11th Division.		RAINCHEVAL.
11th Divisional Train.	H.Q.	MARIEUX.
No. 1 Company.		VAUCQUERIE LE BOUCQ.
No. 2 "		RAINCHEVAL.
No. 3 "		SARTON.
No. 4. "		BEAUQUESNE.
11th Divisional Supply Column.		I. 27. c. 1.7.
11th Divisional School.		ST RIQUIER.
11th Divisional Laundry.		RAINCHEVAL. (Billet 44).

ATTACHED TROOPS.

50th A.S.P.   TERRA MESNIL.

Town Major,   BEAUQUESNE.

War Diary

S E C R E T.   30th March 1917.   11th Division No. G.S. 694.

11th Division Location Table showing position of Units at 6 a.m. on March 31st. 1917.

<u>11th. Division.</u>	H.Q. MARIEUX.
<u>32nd. Infantry Brigade.</u>	H.Q. LOUVENCOURT.
9th. W. Yorkshire Regt.	H.Q. and Bn. LOUVENCOURT.
6th. Yorkshire Regt.	H.Q. and Bn. VAUCHELLES.
8th. W. Riding Regt.	H.Q. and Bn. RAINCHEVAL.
6th. York & Lancs. Regt.	H.Q. and Bn. LOUVENCOURT.
32nd. M.G. Company.	BEAUQUESNE.
32nd. T.M. Battery.	BEAUQUESNE.
<u>33rd. Infantry Brigade.</u>	H.Q. SARTON.
6th. Lincoln Regt.	H.Q. and Bn. ORVILLE.
6th. Border Regt.	H.Q. and Bn. SARTON.
7th. S. Staffs. Regt.	H.Q. and Bn. SARTON.
9th. S. Foresters	H.Q. and Bn. ORVILLE.
33rd. M.G. Company.	SARTON.
33rd. T.M. Battery.	SARTON.
<u>34th. Infantry Brigade.</u>	H.Q. BEAUQUESNE.
8th. Northd. Fusiliers.	H.Q. and Bn. TERRA MESNIL.
9th. Lancs. Fusiliers	H.Q. and Bn. TERRA MESNIL.
5th. Dorset Regt.	H.Q. and Bn. BEAUQUESNE.
11th. Manchester Regt.	H.Q. and Bn. BEAUQUESNE.
34th. M.G. Company.	BEAUQUESNE.
34th. T.M. Battery.	BEAUQUESNE.
6th. E. Yorks Regt. (Pioneers).	ARQUEVES.
<u>11th. Divisional R.E.</u>	H.Q. MARIEUX.
67th. Field Company.	MARIEUX.
68th. " "	MARIEUX.
86th. " "	MARIEUX.

ATTACHED TROOPS.
50th. A.S.P., TERRA MESNIL.
Town Major, BEAUQUESNE.

<u>11th. Divisional R.A.</u>	H.Q.)
58th. F.A.B.	) MONTENESCOURT.
59th. "	)
D.A.C.	)
S.A.A. Subsection.	LOUVENCOURT.
<u>A.D.M.S., 11th. Division.</u>	MARIEUX.
33rd. Field Ambulance.	BEAUVAL.
34th. " "	BEAUQUESNE.
35th. " "	VAUCHELLES.
<u>A.P.M., 11th. Division.</u>	MARIEUX.
<u>A.D.V.S., 11th. Division.</u>	MARIEUX.
22nd. Mobile Vet. Section.	MARIEUX.
<u>D.A.D.C.S., 11th. Division.</u>	RAINCHEVAL.
<u>11th. Divisional Train.</u>	MARIEUX.
No. 1 Company.	VACQUERIE le BOUCQ.
No. 2 "	RAINCHEVAL.
No. 3 "	SARTON.
No. 4 "	BEAUQUESNE.
<u>11th. Divisional Supply Column.</u>	I.27.c.1.7.
<u>11th. Divisional School.</u>	ST. RIQUIER.
<u>11th. Divisional Laundry.</u>	RAINCHEVAL. Billet 44.

War Diary

S E C R E T.   31st. March 1917.   11th. Division No. G.S. 708.

11th. Division Weekly Location Table showing position of Units at 6 a.m. Sunday April 1st. 1917.

11th. Division.	H.Q. MARIEUX.
32nd. Infantry Brigade.	H.Q. LOUVENCOURT.
9th. W. Yorkshire Regt.	H.Q. and Bn. LOUVENCOURT.
6th. Yorkshire Regt.	H.Q. and Bn. VAUCHELLES.
8th. W. Riding Regt.	H.Q. and Bn. RAINCHEVAL.
6th. York & Lancs. R.	H.Q. and Bn. LOUVENCOURT.
32nd. M.G. Company.	BEAUQUESNE.
32nd. T.M. Battery.	BEAUQUESNE.
33rd. Infantry Brigade.	H.Q. SARTON.
6th. Lincoln Regt.	H.Q. and Bn. ORVILLE.
6th. Border Regt.	H.Q. and Bn. SARTON.
7th. S. Staffs. Regt.	H.Q. and Bn. SARTON.
9th. S. Foresters.	H.Q. and Bn. ORVILLE.
33rd. M.G. Company.	SARTON.
33rd. T.M. Battery.	SARTON.
34th. Infantry Brigade.	H.Q. BEAUQUESNE.
8th. Northd. Fusiliers	H.Q. and Bn. TERRA MESNIL.
9th. Lancs. Fusiliers.	H.Q. and Bn. TERRA MESNIL.
5th. Dorset Regt.	H.Q. and Bn. BEAUQUESNE.
11th. Manchester Regt.	H.Q. and Bn. BEAUQUESNE.
34th. M.G. Company.	BEAUQUESNE.
34th. T.M. Battery.	BEAUQUESNE.
6th. E. Yorks Regt. (Pioneers).	ARQUEVES.
11th. Divisional R.E.	H.Q. MARIEUX.
67th. Field Company.	MARIEUX.
68th. " "	MARIEUX.
86th. " "	MARIEUX.

ATTACHED TROOPS.

50th. A.S.P.,	TERRA MESNIL.
Town Major,	BEAUQUESNE.

11th. Divisional R.A. H.Q.)	
58th. F.A.B.)	
59th. ")	MONTENESCOURT.
60th. ")	
D.A.C.)	
S.A.A. Subsection.	LOUVENCOURT.
A.D.M.S., 11th. Division.	MARIEUX.
33rd. Field Ambulance.	BEAUVAL.
34th. " "	BEAUQUESNE.
35th. " "	VAUCHELLES.
A.P.M., 11th. Division.	MARIEUX.
A.D.V.S., 11th. Division.	MARIEUX.
22nd. Mobile Vet. Section.	MARIEUX.
D.A.D.O.S., 11th. Division.	RAINCHEVAL.
11th. Divisional TRAIN. H.Q.	MARIEUX.
No. 1 Company.	LATTRE ST. QUENTIN.
No. 2 "	RAINCHEVAL.
No. 3 "	SARTON.
No. 4 "	BEAUQUESNE.
11th. Divisional Supply Col.	I.27.c.1.7.
11th. Divisional School.	ST. RIQUIER.
11th. Divisional Laundry.	RAINCHEVAL., Billet 44.

Appendix 2

Headquarters,
11th. Division.

Please accept our grateful thanks for the loan of the 32nd. and 34th. Machine Gun Companies. Needless to say, these Companies have been of the greatest assistance to the Division during the time they have been attached to it. They have performed very good work and I would be much obliged if you would convey my grateful thanks to the Officers Commanding these two Companies for all the good work they did while attached to the 62nd. Division.

I have also to thank you for the use of the 8th. Northumberland Fusiliers, which were used in the line in the following circumstances. A few days ago it became necessary to reinforce the 187th. Brigade, which was in the line. I applied to the Corps for leave to move up one of my Battalions, which was at work on the Railway near BEAUCOURT. I was informed, however, that the work was so important that it would be better to take any other Battalion, that was close by, rather than disturb the railway construction work. The Battalion that was nearest happened to be the 8th. Northumberland Fusiliers and, as there was little time to lose, I ordered them up. The Battalion did very well indeed and I am proud to have had it under my Command even for so short a time.

I hope the Officer Commanding this Battalion may be informed how much I appreciate the good work he did while attached to the 187th. Brigade.

(Sd). W.P.BRAITHWAITE.,
Major General,
Commanding 62nd. Division.

16th. March. 1917.

Appx III

===========
S E C R E T.
===========

Copy No. 14

22nd. March 1917.

11th. Division Operation Order No.61.

1. The Division will cease to find working parties after March 23rd. and will be concentrated for training by the evening of March 24th. as shown on the attached Table.

The R.A., Field Ambulances, and Train Coys. A.S.C. will not move.

2. No restrictions as to roads, except for lorries, routes for which will be issued by "Q", 11th. Division.

3. The usual March intervals will be maintained.

4. ACKNOWLEDGE.

W.B. Charles Major

Issued at...7.p.m.

for Lieut. Colonel,
General Staff, 11th. Division.

Copy No. 1 to A.D.C. for G.O.C.
  2. C.R.A.
  3. C.R.E.
  4. 32nd. Inf. Bde.
  5. 33rd.   "   "
  6. 34th.   "   "
  7. 6th. E. Yorks Regt.
  8. A.D.M.S.
  9. A.D.V.S.
  10. A.P.M.
  11. Signals.
  12. "Q"
  13. 11th. Div. Train.
14 - 15. War Diary.
  16. File.

17 - 18. V Corps "G".
  19. V Corps "Q".
  20. 7th. Division.
  21. 62nd. Division.

March Table showing Moves 24th. March, issued with 11th. Div. Operation Order. No.61.

No.	Formation or Unit.	Area of Concentration.	Available Capacity.	Remarks.
1.	1.E.	MARIEUX (3 Field Coys).	21 Offrs. 840 O.R.	The detachment 67th. Field Coy. will clear VARENNES by 8 a.m. 24th. The 86th. Field Coy. is not to enter AUCHONVILLERS before 11.15 a.m.
2.	32nd. Inf. Bde.	LOUVENCOURT. RAINCHEVAL. VAUCHELLES.	107 Offrs. 2291 O.R. 30 " 1610 O.R. 54 " 1525 O.R.	Brigade H.Q., 32nd. E.G. Coys., 32nd. T.M.B. remain at BEAUQUESNE. No troops 32nd. Inf. Bde. to move West of FORCEVILLE before 10 a.m.
3.	33rd. Inf. Bde.	SARTON. ORVILLE. *	75 Offrs. 2000 O.R. 2 Battalions.	Brigade H.Q., SARTON. The L.T.M.Bty. to stay at AUTHIEULE. * Town Major's Office is at AMPLIER.
4.	34th. Inf. Bde.	TERRA MESNIL. BEAUQUESNE. SARTON.	46 Offrs. 1245 O.R. 65 " 2000 O.R. 20 " 500 O.R.	Bde. H.Q., 34th. M.G. Coy., 34th.L.T.M.B. remain BEAUQUESNE. All troops 34th. Brigade to be West of FORCEVILLE by 10 a.m.
5.	6th. Yorks Regt.	ARQUEVES.	32 Offrs. 940 O.R.	Not to enter FORCEVILLE before 12 noon.

NOTE:- Billetting parties under an Officer per Unit will report to Town Major s concerned as early as possible on 24th. March.

War Diary   *Appendix IV*

SECRET   Copy No. 16

11th Division Operation Order No. 62.

24/3/17.

1. The 11th Divisional Artillery (less the S.A.A. Sections and Grenade wagons) will be transferred to the XVIII Corps and attached temporarily to the VI Corps, and will move as detailed in para 3.

2. The 59th Brigade R.F.A. will remain at BUS if any further cases of STOMATITIS occur.

3. MOVES.

   (a) 27th March from BUS to OUTREBOIS Artillery Area. Orders as to routes and times will be issued later.

   (b) 28th and 29th March as detailed in Third Army Order No. 156 of the 23rd March, 1917.

4. The usual march intervals will be maintained.

5. ACKNOWLEDGE.

Issued at 8 pm

Charles Major
Lieut-Colonel,
Gen. Staff. 11th Division.

Copy No. 1. C.R.A.
2. Q.
3. Train.
4. A.D.M.S.
5. A.D.V.S.
6. Signals.
7. A.P.M.
8. V Corps G.
9. V Corps Q.
10. XVIII Corps G.
11. XVIII Corps Q.
12. VI Corps G.
13. VI Corps Q.
14. Third Army.
15. 2nd Division.
16 & 17. War Diary.
18. File.

Appendix V

62nd. Division.   "G".

I would like to express my appreciation of the very excellent work carried out by the 6th.(Pioneer) Battn. E. Yorks Regt. whilst working with men on forward roads during the past 3 weeks.

I shall be glad if you will kindly convey to Colonel Cowper and his officers my thanks for the energetic and efficient manner in which they assisted me in the supervision of this urgent work, and to all ranks of the Battalion my gratitude and admiration for the goodspirit in which they have so strenuously applied them-selves to getting it pushed forward.

(Sd). R.F.GILLAM, Lt.Col., R.E.
C.R.E., 62nd. Division.

24-3-17.

==

11th. Division.

Forwarded.

I would like to add my appreciation of the excellent work carried out by the 6th. E. Yorks Battn. (Pioneers).

(Sd). W.P.BRAITHWAITE.,
Major General,
Commanding 62nd. Division.

25-3-17.

11th. DIVISION "G".

WAR DIARY.

April 1917.

Army Form C. 2118.

WAR DIARY
or
INTELLIGENCE SUMMARY.

(Erase heading not required.)

11th. DIVISION "G".

April., 1917.

Instructions regarding War Diaries and Intelligence Summaries are contained in F. S. Regs., Part II. and the Staff Manual respectively. Title pages will be prepared in manuscript.

Place	Date	Hour	Summary of Events and Information	Remarks and references to Appendices
MARIEUX.	1st.		Fine morning with heavy showers in the afternoon. Church Parades and cleaning up. No Change.	For location of units see App.1.
"	2nd.		Wet day. Order received from 18th. Corps for the Division to move and be concentrated in "D" area (see Appendix) Third Army by 7th. Training continued.	
"	3rd.		Sharp frost at night. Fine day. Training continued.	
"	4th.		Rain at first, cleared up later. Training continued.	
"	5th.		Fine day. Training continued. Brigadier and one Staff Officer per Brigade went to reconnoitre 21st. Divn. area about BOYELLES.	
		7.15 pm.	The Division *, is placed in G.H.Q. Reserve, ready to move at 24 hours notice. Administrative arrangments as before. * (less Artillery) vide Fifth Army wire G.986 dated 5th. inst.	
	6th.		A very fine morning. Rain later. Training continued.	
	7th.		Training.	
	8th.		Sunday. Fine day.	
	9th.		Rained hard in the early morning. Training continued.	
		2.45 pm.	The Division ordered to be ready to move at six hours notice to SOUASTRE area, if ordered to join the 18th. Corps. Summary~of~Information~regarding~operations~~etc~to~be~found~in~App.~II.	App.II.
	10th.		Snow and squalls from S.W. Training continued.	
	11th.		Showers.	
		12.36 pm.	Fifth Army wire G.124 received 12.36 p.m. saying that the 11th. Division is placed under Fifth Army and allotted to Vth. Corps.	
		2.32 pm.	Fifth Corps wire B.312 received. moving Division forthwith to MAILLY - LOUVENCOURT - ACHEUX	
		3.30 pm	11th. Division O.O. 63 accordingly issued under G.856 ordering Brigade Groups to move.	App III.(1)
		10 p.m.	Move completed by 9.30 p.m.	

Army Form C. 2118.

WAR DIARY
or
INTELLIGENCE SUMMARY.
(Erase heading not required.)

11th. DIVISION "G".   April., 1917.

Instructions regarding War Diaries and Intelligence Summaries are contained in F.S. Regs., Part II. and the Staff Manual respectively. Title pages will be prepared in manuscript.

Place	Date	Hour	Summary of Events and Information	Remarks and references to Appendices
ACHEUX.	12th.		Vth. Corps ordered Div. H.Q. to ACHEUX instead of ENGLEBELMER. D.H.Q. accordingly opened at noon at ACHEUX.	
"	13th.		Training continued. Fine day.	
"	14th.		Training continued. Dry and fine.	
"	15th.		Sunday. G.S.O. 2, Major Charles (Essex Regt.) left on appointment as G.S.O. 1 40th. Divn. and was relieved by Major J.M.R. HARRISON (R.A.).	
"	16th.		Training continued. Weather squally. 32nd. Bde. employed on Salvage.	
"	17th.		Training continued. (less 32nd. Bde.) Sleet and snow with bright intervals.	
"	18th.		Training continued. Orders received from Vth. Corps, Divn. (less Artillery) move on 19th., take over from 5th. Aust. Divn. by noon 21st. and come under orders of 1 Anzac Corps. Brigades etc. warned. Order No.64 issued for the march on 19th. inst.	App.III (2)
"	19th.		Divn.(less Artillery) completed 1st. March to 1 Anzac Corps Area, 32nd. Bde. group to OVILLERS and AVELUY, 33rd. Bde. Group to BOUZINCOURT and SENLIS., 34th. Bde. Group to Huts in W.10. Pioneers to SENLIS. Order No. 65 issued for further moves on 20th., and 21st. and details of taking over. Divn. H.Q. remain at ACHEUX till 21st. Short course assembles at Divnl. School now located at VAUCHELLES.	App.III (3)
"	20th.		G.O.C., with G.S.O. I, visited 5th. Australian Division H.Q. and 1 Anzac Corps H.Q. Division (less Artillery) completed 2nd. day's march. 32nd. Bde. group to BEAULENCOURT. RIENCOURT and camps in N.11., relieving 15th. Australian Inf. Bde. Bde. H.Q. SUCRERIE in N.24. central. 33rd. Bde. Group to THILLOY and GREVILLERS (H.Q., THILLOY) relieving 14th. Australian Inf. Bde. 6th. E. Yorks (Pioneers) to camp at SPRING GARDENS in X.9. central. G.S.O. 2 proceeded to 5th. Australian Div. H.Q. in N.11. central as Liaison Officer.	
"	21st.			

Army Form C. 2118.

WAR DIARY
or
INTELLIGENCE SUMMARY.
(Erase heading not required.)

11th. DIVISION "G".

April., 1917.

Instructions regarding War Diaries and Intelligence Summaries are contained in F. S. Regs., Part II. and the Staff Manual respectively. Title pages will be prepared in manuscript.

Place	Date	Hour	Summary of Events and Information	Remarks and references to Appendices
N.11 central. near BAPAUME.	21st.		33rd. Inf. Bde. Group completed march to FREMICOURT, BANCOURT, HAPLINCOURT and BAPAUME (H.Q., FREMICOURT) and relieved 8th. Australian Inf. Bde. The Army Commander saw the South Staffords, Sherwood Foresters and 6th. E. Yorks Regt. on the march and personally complimented their respective C.O's on their march discipline. Pioneers marched to I.26 central and relieved 5th. Australian Pioneer Bn. G.O.C., 11th. Division took over Command from G.O.C., 5th. Australian at 12 noon. Orders received for 11th. Division to take over front from 1st. Aust. Divn. by 9 a.m. 25th. B.G.,G.S., 1st. Anzac Corps visited D.H.Q. and explained various details of policy. G.S.O. I visited 1st. Aust. Divn. to arrange details of relief. Warning order sent to all concerned.	App.III(4)
"	22nd.		Bright fine day. Good visibility. Wind E. of N. Order No. 66 for relief of 1st. Aust. Divn. issued to all concerned. C.R.E. and G.S.O.II reconnoitred position in J.32.a. for Adv. Divnl. Hd.Qrs. G.O.C.,1st. Aust.Divn. visited D.H.Q. in the evening. Much hostile aeroplane activity, one of our balloons brought down and 3 of our aeroplanes forced to land, hostile machines well over the line and as far West as BAPAUME and THILLOY. C.R.A.	
"	23rd.		At 9.30 a.m./5th. Australian Div. Artillery visited D.H.Q. and explained his dispositions to G.O.C. At 10 a.m. the G.O.C. held a Conference of Brigadiers and Bde. and Divnl. Staff Officers at which were discussed Questions of Relief, Defensive Policy, Anti-Gas Arrangments. The Army Commander visited D.H.Q. in the afternoon, he suggested the advisability of advancing the posts in K.26.c.	App.II(1)
"	24th.		First half of relief of 1st. Aust. Divn. completed. Corps Commander visited D.H.Q. G.O.C. inspected progress of work on BEAUMETZ-MORCHIES line. Reconnaissance made of ground in K.26.c. with a view to advancement of posts.	

Army Form C. 2118.

WAR DIARY
or
INTELLIGENCE SUMMARY.

11th. DIVISION "G".   April, 1917.

(Erase heading not required.)

Instructions regarding War Diaries and Intelligence Summaries are contained in F. S. Regs., Part II. and the Staff Manual respectively. Title pages will be prepared in manuscript.

Place	Date	Hour	Summary of Events and Information	Remarks and references to Appendices
N.11 central.	25th.		Relief of 1st. Aust. Divn. completed. G.O.C.,11th.Division assumed command at 9 a.m. During the night 24/25th. the 8th. West Riding Regt. advanced their posts slightly on the Right of the Divisional Sector. BEAUMETZ was shelled during the night and DEMICOURT and DOIGNIES during the day. Large party of the enemy seen in PRONVILLE at 2.30 p.m. and dispersed by our 18-pdrs.	
"	26th.		During the night LOUVERAL was heavily shelled. Posts of the right Bn. were pushed forward on the extreme Right. During the day hostile artillery caused us some casualties in K.19.c. and shelled our Support Line at intervals. Much hostile aeroplane activity, machines flying low, a bomb was dropped in I.29.c.	
"	27th.		Our posts on the Right were advanced along the line of the CANAL DU NORD from HAVRINCOURT WOOD, north to the Railway. Hostile artillery less active, visibility poor. Wind at last changed from E. of N. to almost due West.	
"	28th.		At 2.30 a.m. Gas was discharged by projectors from the neighbourhood of DEMICOURT against hostile trenches about Lock 6. Discharge was successful and a good cloud formed. Very little hostile artillery retaliation. During the night an Officers' Patrol reconnoitred the SLAG HEAP about K.20.central. During the day hostile shelling was intermittent but light. Left Brigade Headquarters were shelled by 10.5 cm. Hows. Much aerial activity. Wind W. by N.	App.III($). Appendices II(2) & II(3).
"	29th.		During the night SLAG HEAP in K.20.central was again reconnoitred, patrol was heavily fired on by M.Gs. and had to withdraw. LOUVERVAL was heavily shelled by 15 cm. hows. during the morning, some 300 rounds falling in the village in an hour. Poor visibility, but much aerial activity, in which two of our machines were driven down. Orders issued for another Gas Discharge on the morning of the 30th.	App.III(7)
"	30th.		Wind being variable between N.E. and N.W. at 2 a.m. Gas discharge did not take place. During the night the enemy advancing under cover of the Canal Cutting rushed a small advanced post about K.26.central, and 5 men of the 8th. West Riding Regt. are missing, the enemy barraged the supporting post heavily with T.M's and Rifle grenades fire. The post was re-established almost immediately. LOUVERVAL shelled during the day. Much aerial activity. Provisional Defence Scheme of the Division forwarded to all concerned.	App.II(4)

Army Form C. 2118.

WAR DIARY
or
INTELLIGENCE SUMMARY.

11th. DIVISION "G".

April 1917.

(Erase heading not required.)

Instructions regarding War Diaries and Intelligence Summaries are contained in F. S. Regs., Part II. and the Staff Manual respectively. Title pages will be prepared in manuscript.

Place	Date	Hour	Summary of Events and Information	Remarks and references to Appendices
			NOTE: Map References from April 25th. - 30th. refer to Map 1/40,000, Sheet 57C.	
	3/5/17.		[signature] A.B. Ritchie Major General, Commanding 11th. Division.	

Army Form C. 2118.

WAR DIARY
or
INTELLIGENCE SUMMARY.
(Erase heading not required.)

11th. DIVISION. "G". April 1917.

S U M M A R Y.

At the beginning of the month the Division was still training in the MARIEUX area under Vth. Corps, but expecting to move at short notice to the 3rd. Army.

On 2nd. April an order was received from 18th. Corps for the Division to be concentrated in "D" Area, Third Army by 7th.

On 5th. April the Division was placed in G.H.Q. Reserve ready to move at 24 hour's notice. Administration meanwhile still to be by Vth. Corps.

On 9th. April the Division was ordered to be ready to move at 6 hours notice to SOUASTRE area if ordered to join XVIII Corps.

Meanwhile training was being carried on, but on 11th. April a wire from V Corps was received stating the Division was placed under Fifth Army and allotting it to V Corps. V Corps then wired an order to move further forward. This move was carried out before night and Div. H.Q. moved the following day to ACHEUX.

Training was again carried on, and on 18th. April an order was received for the Division to take over from 5th. Aust. Divn. (in Reserve to I Anzac Corps) by 21st.April. This was done and on 22nd. April an order was received for the Division to relieve 1st. Aust. Divn. holding the Right Sector of the Corps Front, by 25th. The relief was staisfactorily carried out.

From 25th. onwards the Division was in the line, but no important operations were carried out.

Casualties.

Killed.		Wounded.		Missing.	
O.	O.R.	O.	O.R.	O.	O.R.
2	37	15	158	-	7

3/5/17.

AS Ritchie Major General,
Commanding 11th. Division.

DIVISIONAL INSTRUCTIONS & MISCEALANEOUS.

APPENDIX 11

APPENDIX II (2)

S E C R E T.

11th. Division No. G.S. 999.

32nd. Inf. Bde.
33rd. " "
34th. " "
C.R.E.
C.R.A., 5th.Aust.D.A.
C.R.A., 11th. D.A.(for information).

11th. DIVISION INSTRUCTIONS No.1.

1. Although the rôle of the Division is at present defensive, every effort must be made to advance our lines sufficiently near to the HINDENBURG LINE to enable us to carry out an attack upon it, whenever required to do so.

2. With this end in view plans must be drawn up for the following enterprises and submitted to D.H.Q. as soon as possible.

   (i) Assault and capture of the SLAG HEAP in K.20.central (by 32nd. Inf. Bde.).

   (ii) Capture of hostile trench running from K.26.central to K.20.b.3.2 (by 33rd. Inf. Bde.).

   (iii) Establishment of a Bridgehead about K.26.b.3.0 (by 33rd. Inf. Bde.).

3. Every effort must be made to keep up the men's "offensive spirit", patrolling will be vigorous and small raids carried out.

4. Men must be encouraged to use their rifles whenever possible and especial attention will be given to sniping.

5. The enemy must be annoyed by long-range machine gun fire at night.   (K.3.a.)
   HAVRINCOURT, THE SLAG HEAP, LOCK No.6, /and any other localities where the enemy are known to congregate should receive especial attention.
   Guns employed on this work should not fire from their permanent emplacements but from other positions especially selected for the purpose, guns on completion of their task to be removed at once.

6. The Division on our left has had great success lately in cutting German wire entanglements with Bangalore torpedoes. The employment of these weapons is to be considered and your affiliated Field Companies instructed to prepare a number of these torpedoes without delay.

7. The C.R.E. must give attention to possible crossing of the Canal, and the construction of bridges about K.32.a.7.9, K.26.central, K.20.d.2.6. Material, therefore, should be collected at convenient sites.

28th. April., 1917.

J. D. Coleridge Lieut. Colonel,
General Staff, 11th. Division.

APPENDIX II (1)

S E C R E T.

11th. Division No. G.S. 946.

32nd. Inf. Bde.
33rd. "   "
34th. "   "
C.R.A.   Signals.
C.R.E.   D.G.O.
A.D.M.S.
"Q".

The following are notes at a Conference held at D.H.Q. this morning :-

1. <u>Description of Divisional Front.</u>

The G.O.C. described the front about to be taken over by the Division, and made suggestions as to the Locations of Units.

2. <u>Method of Defence.</u>

The G.O.C. read :-

(a) Some Notes forwarded by 1st. Anzac Corps on the subject.
(b) 1st. Anzac S.2124 which gave nomenclature of all various lines.

The G.O.C. drew attention to the importance of constructing posts consisting of firing and support trenches connected by defensible communication trenches. (vide sketch).

[sketch: Fire trench / Support trench in road]

It was also pointed out that numerous sunken roads in the neighbourhood greatly facilitated the construction of defences on these lines.

3. <u>Relief's.</u>

It was decided to maintain 2 Brigades in the front line and the 3rd. Brigade in the Reserve.
Brigades will, therefore, remain for 12 days in the front line and 6 days in the reserve.
For the first period the 32nd. and 33rd. Brigades will be in the line and the 34th. Brigade in Reserve.

4. <u>Sanitation.</u>

The G.O.C. drew especial attention to the importance of Sanitation.
Every Unit is to construct proper latrines, urinals and refuse pits, and troops are to be warned that nothing reflects so descreditably on Units as a dirty camp.

/5. O.P's.

5. **O.P's.**

(a) There are good O.P's in C.28.b. whence the left sector can be viewed.

(b) S.E. of HERMIES, whence the right sector can be viewed. Approach can be made south of ridge - D.25 - 26 - 27 - 28 - 29 along South of village and across railway to about D.25.a.2.8.

(c) J.20.d. where it isproposed to establish a Div. O.P.

As British positions overldok the enemy's lines to a great extent, observation should be easy.

6. **Dumps.**
Every effort will be made to establish dumps containing R.E. and other stores as far forward as possibloo.

7. **Gas Alarms.**

The Divisional Gas Officer was instructed to establish a system of Gas Alarm Signals from forward areas to Divisional Headquarters.
He was directed to get in touch with sector and Reserve Brigade Commanders.

8. **Medical Arrangments.**

The .A.D.M.S. described medical arrangments he proposed to make.
Forward Dressing Stations will be established at :-

```
J.28.b.8.2.
J.16.c.6.8.
J.7.d.7.0.
```

9. **R.E. and Pioneers.**

(a) The C.R.E. will plan and construct village defences and those in the BEAUMETZ - MORCHIES line, in conjunction with Brigadiers concerned.

(b) Field Companies, and Pioneer Battalion will be employed as under :-

67th. Field Company.		Right Subsector.
68th. " "		Left Subsector.
86th. " "		BEAUMETZ - MORCHIES Line and Back Area.

Pioneer Battalion at work on roads.

10. **Miscellaneous.**

The G.O.C. drew attention to the following points :-

(a) The importance of HAVRINCOURT and BOURSIES.
(b) The importance of arranging posts in a systematic manner, firing line, supports, and reserves.
(c) The distances between posts will vary according to ground.
(d) The 32nd. and 33rd. Brigades will have their M.G. Coys. and L.T.M.B's completely at their disposal.
1st. Anzac Corps will be asked to supplement 34th. M.G. Company in BEAUMETZ-MORCHIES line with 2 sections Corps M.G's.

3.

(e) Continuity of work will be strictly adhered to. Companies as far as possible to work on same area.

(f) Company, platoon and section organisation will be strictly adhered to.

(g) Every man to be impressed with the fact that he is is the first place a rifleman, bomber and Lewis Gunner etc., afterwards.

(h) All subordinate Commanders to be impressed with the fact that the counter attack is the "soul of the defence".

Local counter-attacks must be launched within 10 minutes of the enemy attack, and every Commander keep a Reserve for this purpose.

(i) The importance of reconnaissance and patrolling, and the mastery of "No Man's Land".

(j) Subordinate Commanders must be taught to study the ground and to get practice in map reading.

(k) Attention is drawn to the fact that the enemy usually approaches by means of roads and depressions.

These are to be kept under cross Lewis and Machine Gun fire.

(l) All tents, huts and shelters to be camouflaged without delay.

Green and brown daubs are sufficient. It is unnecessary to cover the whole tent, shelter or hut.

(m) When sentries or look-out men detect hostile aircraft they must make use of a pre-arranged signal, such as a whistle.

Men should not gaze upwards at aeroplanes as this merely draws attention, they should lie down and remain motionless till the plane has passed over.

(n) Artillery arrangments for covering the front were explained and the methods of Liaison in use.
S.O.S. Signal (Very Pistols and Rockets,
Green, Red, Green).

(o) Present communications from front to rear are simple and good.

Lateral communications are indifferent. These will be improved and a Visual system brought into use.

(p) All ranks to be warned against entering standing houses and dug-outs which are still no doubt mined.

(q) No water to be drunk unless passed by Medical authority. The C.R.E. togive especial attention to water supply.

(r) Posts to be systematically numbered from right to left. Those in Right Sector, prefix letter "R".
Left Sub-sector "L".
BEAUMETZ-MORCHIES Line, "D".

/(s)

(s)   All posts in front line to be provided where possible with Artillery boards.

(t)   To assist movement across country, by day and night, a system of direction posts to be established. These posts will be provided by the R.E.

(u)   The front system must invariably be carefully approached. Positions are not to be given away by undue movement.

J. D. Coleridge
Lieut. Colonel,

23rd. April., 1917.   General Staff, 11th. Division.

```
=========
S E C R E T                                  11th Div. No. G.S. 3.A.
=========
```

32nd Inf. Bde.

C.R.A. 5th Aus. D.A.)
33rd Inf. Bde.   ) (for information).
34th Inf. Bde.   )
C.R.E.   )

11th Division Instructions No. 2.

1.   It would appear from 32nd Inf. Bde. Intelligence Summary, from 6 a.m. on 27/4/17 to 6 a.m. on 28/4/17, that the "SLAG HEAP" in K.20. Central is either abandoned by the enemy, or lightly held by him.

2.   The following action will be carried out to-night.

   (1) The SLAG HEAP will be reconnoitred by the same Officers patrols which visited it last night.

   (2) In event of these patrols reporting, either that the position has been vacated by the enemy or is merely lightly held by him, the SLAG HEAP will be occupied by our troops, and consolidated before morning. (As surprise is aimed at it is suggested that no "barrage" be employed).

3.   The advance will be systematically carried out, and the advancing lines supported by sufficient troops. The 5th Aust. D.A. will be in observation and prepared to open fire should occasion arise.

4.   The SLAG HEAP will, when occupied, be held as inconspicuously as possible, Lewis guns will be brought into position and will occupy positions likely to sweep the enemy's lines of approach for a counter attack.
        All men not on look out or with the Lewis guns will shelter in the ditches believed to exist South and West of the SLAG HEAP.

5.   In event of the SLAG HEAP being found to be occupied in force, a coup-de-main will be impossible and the position will have to be taken after artillery preparation and under a barrage.

6.   ACKNOWLEDGE.

                            (Signed)   J. D. COLERIDGE, Lt-Col.
H.Q. 11th Division.
                                       General Staff. 11th Division
28th April, 1917.

Secret. APPENDIX II (4)

Copy no 17

DEFENCE SCHEME
(Provisional)

HEADQUARTERS.

Headquarters 1st ANZAC Corps........   Advanced G.29.b.8.6.
     "   "   "   "   ....   Rear   X.14.a.7.3.
Headquarters 20th Division..........   LITTLE WOOD. P.26.b.5.0.
Headquarters 2nd Australian Division...............   H.15.c.4.3.
Headquarters 11th Division.........................   N.11, Central
Headquarters Right Brigade.........................   J.20.c.6.7.
Headquarters Left Brigade..........................   I.11.c.5.6.
Headquarters Reserve Brigade.......................   FREMICOURT)
                                                       I.25.b.4.6)

SECRET   Copy. No. 17

Reference 1/40,000 Map.   11th DIVISION.
        Sheet.57.C.
                              DEFENCE SCHEME. (Provisional)

                                        (vide Map)

DESCRIPTION   (1) The Division occupies the Main HERMIES RIDGE and a
OF THE   series of low, undulating spurs which run out from it
COUNTRY.   in a North Easterly direction.

                    There is practically no woodland East of the VELU
                    WOOD. In dry weather all arms can move across country
                    except in the villages and where Sunken Roads occur.
                    The ground is quite open, and the field of view is
                    remarkable.

                    There are a number of villages in the area which
                    materially affect the system of defence, and placed in
                    a proper state of defence they form invaluable support-
                    ing points and pivots of manoeuvre.

                    The area contains a number of Sunken roads, which are
                    invaluable for concealing reserves and machine gun
                    emplacements, and hence greatly assist in the defensive.

                    The whole area looks down on the German HINDENBURG
                    Line (except just West of HAVRINCOURT) which is in
                    consequence under direct observation.

BOUNDARIES.   (2) The front occupied by the Division is 12,000 yards
                    in length.

                    Boundaries : Southern Boundary.O.15.d.4.2 - O.9.c.8.1.-
                                    O.12.a.3.7. - J.34.c.8.4.- K.28.c.6.3.

                                 Boundary between   H.23.d.5.0 - I.14.Central
                                 Divisional Sub-   I.9.d.0.0 - I.10.Central
                                 sectors.   I.5.d.2.3 - O.30.Central
                                    D.19.b.5.0 - D.14.d.5.0 - D.15.b.1.9.

                                 Northern Boundary.I.31.Central - J.13.Central
                                    J.6.d.2.0.

DIVISIONAL   (3) The Divisional Policy, while defensive for the present
POLICY.   owing to the great extent of front held, is to system-
                    atically advance our lines sufficiently close to the
                    HINDENBURG Line to enable us to launch an attack against
                    it when occasion arises. Every opportunity will be
                    taken to harass and demoralize the enemy. Patrolling
                    and sniping will be active.

DEFENSIVE   (4) The Defensive System consists of :-
SYSTEM.
                            (i)   The Front System.
                            (ii) The BEAUMETZ - MORCHIES Line.
                            (iii) The YTRES - BEUGNY Line.

                    (i) The Front System. Will consist of a series of
                    posts containing garrisons varying from 2 to 4 sections
                    disposed so as to form Firing Line, Supports and
                    Reserves. These posts will be so sited as to mutually
                    support one another. Machine and Lewis Guns will be
                    employed in combination so as to develop a maximum of
                    fire power and to sweep all approaches.

                                                            /The Front

- 2 -

The Front System also includes the following villages :-

> HERMIES
> DEMICOURT
> BOURSIES
> DOIGNIES
> LOUVERVAL

these will be placed in a state of defence as supporting points.

The Front System is the Line of Resistance.

(ii) The BEAUMETZ - MORCHIES Line consists of a series of Infantry and Machine Gun posts (for details see Appendix 1.) This line also includes the villages of BEAUMETZ, MORCHIES, VELU, LEBUCQUIERE and BEUGNY, these will be placed in a state of defence as Supporting Points.

(iii) The YTRES - BEUGNY Line is still further in rear and is at present garrisoned by the 11th: and 12th: Australian Battalions, and the 3rd Australian Machine Gun Coy. This line also includes the villages of HAPLINCOURT and FREMICOURT, these will be placed in a state of defence as Supporting Points.

DISTRIBUTION. (5) (a) The Front System will be held by 2 Brigades, the line of demarcation between them being as detailed in para. 2.

(b) The BEAUMETZ - MORCHIES Line will be held by 2 Battalions and 2 Sections Machine Gun Company from the Divisional Reserve.

(c) The Divisional Reserve. The Reserve Brigade less 2 Battalions and 2 Sections Machine Gun Company will be located West of the BEAUMETZ - MORCHIES Line ready to move as required.

(d) The 6th E. Yorks (Pioneers) and 3 Field Coys. will stand to near their bivouacs ready to move in case of emergency.

(For detailed dispositions of the Division see Appendix 2.)

ACTION IN CASE OF ATTACK. (6) Every commander must realise, that "the counter attack" is the soul of the defence; and should the enemy happen to enter our lines he will be vigorously counter attacked at once. With this purpose in view every commander will keep in hand a reserve ready to counter attack at the shortest notice.

NUCLEUS GARRISONS. (7) In event of Reserves being called forward, as indicated above, nucleus garrisons will be told off to hold each locality vacated, until the situation is cleared up. This system will ensure that strong tactical points are not abandoned, and are held should it be necessary for the advanced troops to fall back.

/ARTILLERY (8).

- 3 -

ARTILLERY. (8) (a) For the present the 5th. Australian D.A. and attached Army F.A. Brigades will cover the Divisional Front as under :-

    3rd.(Army) Brigade A.F.A.   Covering from K.31.a.8.8
    ("A" Group).   to J.6.d.7.0.

    6th.(Army) Brigade A.F.A.   Covering from J.6.d.7.0
    ("D" Group).   to D.16.c.7.9.

    13th. Brigade A.F.A.   Covering from D.16.c.7.9
    ("B" Group).   to D.20.a.2.5.

    (b) Artillery Liaison Officers will live with the H.Q's of Battalions and Brigades in the Front System

    (c) The Artillery S.O.S. lines will be arranged to deal with possible direction of attacks instead of a complete barrage line.

    (d) Infantry Brigadiers will detail Artillery escorts in addition to those already found on application being made by O.R.A. 5th.Aust. D.A.

ENGINEERS & PIONEERS. (9) (a) One Field Company will work in each Sub-sector of the Front System.

    (b) One Field Company will work West of the BEAUMETZ-MORCHIES Line under orders of the C.R.E.

    (c) The 6th. E. Yorks (Pioneers) will work on roads West of the BEAUMETZ-MORCHIES Line under Corps arrangments issued through the C.R.E.

MISCELLANEOUS. (10)(a) Supply of R.E. Material. Instructions are issued herewith under Appendix III.

    (b) Supply of Ammunition and Supplies. Instructions will be issued later in Appendix IV.

    (c) Medical Arrangments. Instructions are issued herewith under Appendix V.

    (d) Situation of Traffic Control and Battle Posts, will be issued in Map form later. Appendix VI.

J. D. Coleridge
Lieut-Colonel,
General Staff. 11th Division.

28th April, 1917.

Copy No. 1 A.D.C. for G.O.C.   6. 34th.Inf.Bde.   11. Train.
         2 C.R.A.,11th.Divn.   7. 6th.E.Yorks.   12. 1st.Anzac Corps.
         3. E.R.E.   8. Signal Coy.   13. 2nd. Aust. Divn.
         4 32nd. Inf. Bde.   9. "Q"   14. 1st.   "   "
         5. 33rd. "   "   10 A.D.M.S.   15 C.R.A.5th.Aust.Div
                                                                      16. 20th.Divn.
                                                      17 - 18 War Diary.
                                                      19 - 20 File.

APPENDIX I.

HOECHIES - BEAUMETZ Line.

Machine Gun Emplacements.

No. of Post.	Location.	Description of Post.	M.G. Emplacements.
No.33.	J.34.d.5.5	"T" Form post - completed and camouflaged.	Position for one gun to 250^x in rear. 150^x North of SLAG HEAP.
No.32.	K.34.a.9.9.	"T" Form post, dug and camouflaged. Has a Field Battery in open, close in front and is near a Quarry.	
No.31.A.	J.28.a.8.3.	"T" Form Post dug and camouflaged.	One gun on West bank of Sunken Road at road junction J.28.c.75.55 to fire N.E. to S.W.
M.G. Post.	J.28.c.45.85.	M.G. Post for 1 Vickers is dug and has overhead cover, but is rather obvious.	Prepare alternative positions in Sunken Road near by.
No.31.	J.28.a.5.4.	"T" Form post completed and camouflaged. Faces North of Railway towards HERMIES but has no field of fire southwards.	One gun at cross roads J.28.a.0.6 fire East.
No.30.	J.22.c.0.4.	"T" Form post - completed and camouflaged.	One gun at 21.d.6.2.
No.29.	J.21.b.7.3.	"T" Form post completed and camouflaged. There is rather a big gap between 29 and 28A but there are several trenches and dug-outs in vicinity of 29 which could be manned.	One gun at 21.d.4.4.
No.28.	J.21.a.9.9.	"T" Form post - completed and camouflaged.	One gun at 21.c.5.7.
No.27.	J.15.c.2.1.	"T" Form post - completed and camouflaged.	One gun 20.b.9.3.

(2)

No. of Post.	Location.	Description of Post.	M.G. Emplacements.
No.28.	J.14.d.8.6.	T Form post, completed and camouflaged.	One gun 15.a.7.4.
No.25.	J.14.b.5.2.	T Form post, completed and camouflaged.	One gun 14.a.8.4.
No.24.	J.14.b.8.9.	T Form post, completed and camouflaged.	

Left Sector.

No.23.A.	J.8.c.8.1.	Half-moon shaped Post completed and camouflaged.	
No.23.	J.8.c.5.3.	Post shaped	One gun J.8.c.9.6.
No.22.	J.8.c.2.9.	-do-	One gun J.7.d.9.9.
No.21.	J.7.b.5.2.	-do-	
No.20.	J.7.a.9.9.	-do-	One gun in post.
No.19.	J.1.c.0.6.	-do-	One gun near post.
No.18.	I.6.d.6.5.	-do-	
No.17.	I.6.c.8.8.	-do-	One gun in post.
No.16.	I.5.b.9.4.	-do-	One gun I.5.d.2.5.

APPENDIX II.

DISPOSITIONS OF 11th. DIVISION.

LEFT BRIGADE.	RIGHT BRIGADE.
Brigade H.Q.　　　　J.20.c.6.7.	I.11.c.5.6.
"A" Battalion(H.Q.J.17.a.5.8) From K.1.a.0.2- J.6.d.4.0- DOIGNIES exclusive BEAUMETZ exclusive. to J.6.a.0.8- J.5.b.central- J.10.b.0.6- CAMBRAI Road inclusive.	"A" Battalion(H.Q.J.29.b.2.2) From K.31.b.5.3 - J.36.central - J.35.c.0.7 to K.14.c.7.8. J.18.d.0.2. J.22.a.0.7.
"B" Battalion(H.Q.J.4.c.8.0) Thence to D.22.d.5.5 - D.27.b.9.3- D.27.a.9.3- J.3.a.3.2.	"B" Battalion(H.Q.J.23.a.1.6) Thence K.1.a.0.2 - J.6.d.4.0 - DOIGNIES inclus BEAUMETZ exclus
"C" Battalion(H.Q.D.25.a.6.9) Thence to D.14.d.0.5- D.19.b.5.0- D.30 central- MORCHIES inclusive- I.10.central.	"C" Battalion(H.Q.J.34.b.3.3). In Reserve.
"D" Battalion(H.Q.C.30.d.2.7). In Reserve.	"D" Battalion(BEAUMETZ). In Reserve.
"A", "B", "C" Battalions each have three Companies in the front line and support, and one company in Battalion Reserve.	"A" and "B" Battalions each have three Companies in the front line and support and one company in Battalion Reserve.
"D" Battalion has two Companies along the road between Bn.H.Q. and J.1.d.2.3., One Company south of MORCHIES and in CHAUFOURS WOOD., One Company holding posts in the LOUVERVAL-LAGNICOURT Line.	"C" Battalion has two companies in the Sunken Road in J.34.b. and two Companies in Sunken Road in J.29.c. "D" Battalion has two Companies in the depression in J.21.b. and two Companies in J.20.c.

RESERVE BRIGADE holding BEAUMETZ-MORCHIES Line.
===

"A" Battalion (H.Q. LEBUCQUIERE).   From J.34.d.7.8
                                         To   J.8.d.0.0.

"B" Battalion (H.Q. I.12.a.2.6).   Thence to
                                                I.5.b.7.6.

"C" Battalion (H.Q. VELU).   Divisional
                                         In Reserve.

"D" Battalion (H.Q. FREMICOURT).   Divisional
                                         In Reserve.

"A" Battalion has 2 Companies in the BEAUMETZ-MORCHIES Line and 2 Companies in LEBUCQUIERE.

"B" Battalion has 3 Companies in the BEAUMETZ-MORCHIES Line and 1 Company in I.11.d.

"C" Battalion is in VELU with 2 Platoons detached as escort to guns in J.25.b.

"D" Battalion (less 2 Platoons) is in FREMICOURT. Two Platoons are detached as escort for guns in I.5.d.

Dispositions of other Units of the Division.
========

5th.Aust. D.A.H.Q., I.26.a.8.2.
  "A" Group.H.Q.   J.32.c.5.5.
  "B"   "   "   I.22.a.7.4.
  "C"   "   "   I.21.b.Central.
  "D"   "   "   J.13.d.8.2.
  5th. D.A.C.   HAPLINCOURT.
  S.A.A. Sec: HAPLINCOURT.

M.G. Coys.
  32nd.M.G.Coy.   VELU.
  33rd.   "   "   I.12.a.8.8.
  34th.   "   "   DELSAUX FARM.

A.D.M.S.   N.11.Central.
  33rd.Fd.Amb.   BEUGNY.I.21.b.2.5
  34th. "   "   LEBUCQUIERE.
                             I.30.b.0.6.
  35th. "   "   BAPAUME.
                             H.33.b.5.7.

Engineers.
  3.R.E.   N.11.Central.
  67th.Fd.Co.   I.30.a.7.7.
  68th. "   "   I.16.c.
  86th. "   "   I.20.d.2.7.

Divnl.Train.H.Q.   N.4.a.9.9.

D.A.D.O.S.   H.30.a.1.2.
A.P.M.   BAPAUME.
A.D.V.S.   N.11.Central.
22nd.Mob.Vet.Sec.   N.4.b.2.5.
Div.Supply Col.   G.17.b.5.9.

Pioneers.
  6th.E.Yorks R.   I.29.d.6.2.

APPENDIX III.

SUPPLY OF R.E. MATERIALS.

1. Divisional R.E. Dump has been established at Railway Siding N.E. of FREMICOURT (I.20.b.6.0). This Dump is filled at present by lorry and horse transport from BAPAUME Siding, to which point material is sent up by rail from Corps Workshops. Stores are also collected when transport is available from various dumps in back area. As accomodation on Railway is very limited only a certain amount of stores can be brought up and it is desireable that all units should be as economical as possible.

2. Stores may be drawn on indent signed by Headquarters R.E. or an Officer of Field Companies affiliated to Brigades (except certain reserve stores as under : -

   Huts (Nissen, Armstrong, Greenlees).
   Tarpaulins.
   Pumps.
   Horse Troughs.
   Timber.
   Tarred Felt.
   Canvas.

   Authority for issue of which must be obtained from Headquarters R.E.)

3. Units drawing stores must provide their own transport from Divisional Dump. A loading party is provided at the Dump. Transport should arrive if possible before 4 p.m. after which hour loading parties must be provided by Unit drawing.

4. In case of possibility of extraordinary demands for stores being anticipated, early information should be given to C.R.E. so that necessary arrangments may be made, as it takes a minimum of 48 hours to obtain stores from Corps Workshops.

APPENDIX IV.

Supply of Ammunition, Supplies, Water and Ordnance Stores.

SYSTEM OF SUPPLY OF S.A.A., GRENADES etc.

I. (a) Ammunition is taken to Divisional Dump at BEUGNY by Corps Ammunition Park Lorries or Light Railway on receipt of a wire by the Ammunition Park from D.H.Q.

Corps sanction is required for issue of special stores such as S.O.S. Rockets and Coloured Very Lights.

(b) An officer is in charge of Divisional Dump.
All No. 5 and No. 23 Grenades are detonated before being issued from the Divisional Dump.

(c) Ammunition etc., may be drawn on indent signed by H.Q. of Inf. Bdes. for Units of Bdes. or by O.C. of other Units, but indents for S.O.S. Rockets and Coloured Very Lights must be sanctioned by D.H.Q.

(d) Units will provide their own transport for drawing ammunition from the Dump.
A loading party is provided at the Dump.

SYSTEM OF SUPPLY OF RATIONS

DUMPED AT BAPAUME.

II. Supplies are drawn by Train H.T. and dumped at Refilling Point at H.30.a. & c. on BAPCOURT-BEUGNATRE ROAD.

Supplies are delivered from Refilling Point to the Transport Lines of Brigades in the Line by Train Transport. All other Units draw supplies from the Refilling Point with their own H.T.

WATER SUPPLY.

III. FREMICOURT.
Pumping station and storage tanks in I.19.d. North of Road. Piped supply to horse watering point and standpipes for water cart filling.

Several wells in village fitted with bucket and windlass.

VELU.
Borehole and air lift at J.31.a.1.9 reported to yield 12,000 gallons per hour. Large horse-watering point is being established here.

Other villages in the Area have small wells.

IV. Ordnance stores established at H.30.a.0.3 on BAPAUME-CAMBRAI ROAD.

Units draw stores from this point with their own H.T.

APPENDIX V

MEDICAL ARRANGEMENTS.

For the evacuation of wounded the main BAPAUME-CAMBRAI Road is taken as the dividing line between the right and left sectors. The right sector is cleared by 34th. Field Ambulance and the left sector by 33rd. Field Ambulance.

There is a Main Dressing Station for both sectors at BEUGNY (I.21.b.2.5) run by 33rd. Field Ambulance to which all lying down cases are taken and evacuated to C.C.S's by Motor Ambulance Convoy.

Right Sector.
    Regimental Aid Posts.- No.1 (R) J.29.b.2.2.
                           No.2 (R) J.17.a.6.6.
                           No.3 (R) J.12.a.05.80.
                           No.4 (R) J.34.b.4.2.

    Field Ambulance Posts:-

                No.1.   J.28.d.5.8 (HERMIES POST)
                      A horsed Ambulance Wagon is at this post.
                No.2.   J.16.c.5.5 (CRUCIFIX POST)
                      A horsed Ambulance Wagon stands in valley about J.15.d.9.5.
                No.3.   J.20.a.1.2 (BEAUMETZ POST)
                      A Ford Ambulance Car is at this post. In wet weather this will be replaced by a horsed Ambulance Wagon.

    Advanced Dressing Station:-   LEBUCQUIERE (I.30.a.8.8).

    Methods of Evacuation:-   From Regimental Aid Posts by hand carriage (or wheeled stretchers in dry weather) by Field Ambulance bearers to Field Ambulance posts as follows :-

                                 From Nos.1(R) & 4(R). R.A.P's to Field Ambulance Post at J.28.d.5.8.
From No.2(R). R.A.P. to Field Ambulance Post at J.16.c.5.5.
From No.3(R). R.A.P. to relay at No.2(R) R.A.P. and thence to Field Ambulance Post at J.16.c.5.5.
By horsed Ambulance Wagons from Field Ambulance Posts at J.28.d.9.8 and J.16.c.5.5 to Advanced Dressing Station at LEBUCQUIERE.
By Ford Ambulance Car from Post at J.20.a.1.2 (which collects from Reserve Battalions, Artillery etc. in the neighbourhood) to Advanced Dressing Station, LEBUCQUIERE.
From Advanced Dressing Station, LEBUCQUIERE, all serious and stretcher cases are evacuated to Main Dressing Station, BEUGNY, by Field Ambulance Cars.

Method of Evacuation (contd).

All walking wounded are evacuated to 35th. Field Ambulance, BAPAUME, by Field Ambulance Cars.

At each R.A.P. in the right sector there are 8 O.R., R.A.M.C.

Left Sector.

Regimental Aid Posts:-

No.1(L)	J.4.c.5.4.
No.2(L)	D.26.c.1.4.
No.3(L)	C.30.a.Central.

Relay Posts:-

No.1.	J.3.c.8.8.
No.2.	J.1.a.5.4.

Horsed Ambulance Post:- J.7.b.7.3.

Motor Ambulance Post:- I.17.b.Central.

Advanced Dressing Station:- I.12.c.9.5.

Methods of Evacuation:-

From Regimental Aid Post by hand carriage, by Field Ambulance bearers, via Relay Posts, to Horsed Ambulance Post.

The Relay Post for No.1(L) R.A.P. being at J.3.c.8.8, and the Relay Post for Nos.2(L) and 3(L) R.A.P's being at J.1.a.5.4.

From Horsed Ambulance Post at J.7.b.7.3 by horsed Ambulance Wagon to Advanced Dressing Station at I.12.c.9.5 and thence by horsed Ambulance Wagon to Post at I.17.b.Central, whence they are taken by Ford Ambulance Car to Main Dressing Station, BEUGNY, from where walking wounded are evacuated to 35th. Field Ambulance, BAPAUME.

At each R.A.P. in the left sector there are 4 O.R., R.A.M.C.

OPERATION ORDERS.

APPENDIX III

APPENDIX III (I)

"A" Form.
Army Form C 2121
(in pads of 100).

MESSAGES AND SIGNALS.

No. of Message...........

Prefix.....Code......m.	Words	Charge	This message is on a/c of:	Recd. at..........m.
Office of Origin and Service Instructions.			Operation Orders	Date 63
	Sent		Service.	From
	At......m.			
	To			
	By		(Signature of Franking Officer)	

TO:
- 32nd. Inf. Bde.
- 33rd. " "
- 34th. " "

6th. Corps "Q"
G.S.O.
Q.M.G.
A.D.M.S.

6th. Corps "Q"
A.P.M.
6th. E. Yorks.
11th. Div. Train
"Q" AAA

Sender's Number.	Day of Month.	In reply to Number.	
G.628.	11th.		

The Division less artillery will move as follows
today AAA 32nd. Brigade, 67th. Fd. Coy.,33rd. Fd. Amb.
to MAILLY MAILLET Area under orders of 32nd. Brigade
and to clear LOUVENCOURT by 7 p.m. AAA 33rd. Brigade
33rd. Fd. Amb. to VAUCHELLES, BATHONVAL and
LOUVENCOURT under orders 33rd. Brigade AAA 34th.
Brigade 86th. Fd. Coy. 34th. Fd. Amb. to LEALVILLERS
and ACHEUX under orders of 34th. Brigade AAA
Headquarters of Brigades will be CAMP JOURDAIN in
MAILLY 33rd. LOUVENCOURT, 34th. ACHEUX AAA Usual
march distances AAA 66th. Fd. Coy., 6th. E. Yorks
and C.A.M. Sec. D.A.C. will not move AAA Train Coys.
move under orders "Q" to be billetted by Brigades AAA
D.H.Q. close at MAILLY noon 12th. and open at
ENGLEBELMER same hour AAA ACK OTHERS.

From 11th.Divn. 3.30p.m. Major.
Place
Time

The above may be forwarded as now corrected. (Z)

Censor. Signature of Addressor or person authorised to telegraph in his name.

APPENDIX III (2)

SECRET.

Copy No. 23

18th. April.1917.

11th. Division Order No. 64.

Ref. 1/40,000 Map.
Sheet 57D.

1. (a) 11th. Division (less Divisional Artillery) will relieve the 5th. Australian Division (less Divisional Artillery) in their present positions, the relief being completed on the 21st. April.

   (b) 5th. Australian Division is at present in Reserve to 1st. ANZAC CORPS and is located as under :-

Divisional Headquarters	N.11.Central.
8th. Aust. Bde.	FREMICOURT.
14th. Aust. Bde.	THILLOY.
15th. Aust. Bde.	N.24. Central.

2. 11th. Division will move tomorrow the 19th. inst., in accordance with attached March Table to the Area OVILLERS-AVELUY - BOUZINCOURT - SENLIS. The usual intervals will be maintained.

3. Companies of the Train will billet with their Brigade Groups, and will march under orders to be issued by the A.A. & Q.M.G.

4. Units not mentioned in March Table will move under the orders of the A.A. & Q.M.G.

5. Divisional Headquarters will close at ACHEUX at 12 noon and re-open at BOUZINCOURT at same hour.

6. On arrival at 1st. ANZAC CORPS Area 11th. Division will come under the command of 1st. ANZAC CORPS.

7. ACKNOWLEDGE.

Issued at 3.30 p.m.

Lieut. Colonel,
General Staff, 11th. Division.

Copy No.	1. A.D.C. for G.O.C.	Copy No. 12.	A.D.V.S.
	2. G.S.O. I.	13.	A.P.M.
	3. C.R.A.	14.	11th.Div.Train.
	4. C.R.E.	15.	D.A.D.O.S.
	5. 32nd. Inf. Bde.	16.	Camp Commdt.
	6. 33rd. " "	17.	Vth. Corps "G".
	7. 34th. " "	18.	Vth. Corps "Q".
	8. 6th. E. Yorks Regt.	19.	1st. Anzac Corps "G".
	9. Signal Coy.	20.	1st. Anzac Corps "Q".
	10. A.A. & Q.M.G.	21.	5th. Aust. Divn.
	11. A.D.M.S.	22 - 23.	War Diary.
		24 - 25.	Office.

M A R C H   T A B L E.   Issued with Operation Order No. 64 dated 19/4/17.

TROOPS.	STARTING POINT PLACE.	STARTING POINT TIME OF PASSING.	ROUTE.	DESTINATION.	REMARKS.
32nd. Brigade Group. 32nd. Brigade. 67th. Fd. Coy. R.E. 35th. Fd. Amb.	Under Brigade arrangements.		AUCHONVILLERS - BEAUMONT HAMEL - BEAUCOURT STATION thence to AVELUY and OVILLERS.	OVILLERS HUTS and AVELUY.	No restrictions.
53rd. Brigade Group. 53rd. Brigade. 68th. Fd. Co. R.E. 53rd. Fd. Amb.	Under Brigade arrangements.		(a) ACHEUX - FORCEVILLE - HEDAUVILLE and (b) ARQUEVES = LEALVILLERS - VARENNES.	BOUZINCOURT and SENLIS.	(a) Not to enter ACHEUX before 10.30 a.m. (b) Not to enter LEALVILLERS before 10.45 a.m.
54th. Brigade Group. 54th. Brigade. 86th. Fd. Co. R.E. 54th. Fd. /mb.	Under Brigade arrangements.		HEDAUVILLE- BOUZINCOURT.	GABSTAND HUTS BRUCE HUTS. } W.10. MIDLAND HUTS }	To be clear of ACHEUX and LEALVILLERS, by 10 a.m.
6th. E. Yorks Regt.	ARQUEVES.	9.50 a.m.	LEALVILLERS - V. RENNES.	SENLIS.	

APPENDIX III (3)

SECRET.

Copy No. 22

19th. April '17.

11th. Division Order No. 65.

Ref. Maps 1/40,000
Sheets 57C. & D.

1. The 11th. Division (less Artillery) will move on the 20th. and 21st. April in accordance with attached March Table.

2 (a) The Field Companies and Pioneer Battalion of the 11th. Division on relieving the corresponding Units of the 5th. Aust. Divn. will carry on the works mentioned in paras 1 and 2 of Appendix I.

(b) The 34th. Infantry Brigade relieving the 14th. Aust. Inf. Bde. will relieve the working parties mentioned in paras 3, 4 & 5 of Appendix I on the 20th. inst.

(c) All other permanent working parties found by the 5th. Aust. Divn. under Corps Orders will remain for the present.

3. The Relief of all Medical Units will be carried out under separate instructions to be issued by the D.D.M.S., 1st. Anzac Corps

4. The following intervals will be maintained on the march :-

200 yards between Battalions.
200 yards between Transport and other Units.
100 yards between Companies.

There will be no "long" halts between POZIERES and BAPAUME.

5. Separate Administrative Instructions are issued in Appendix II. Units not mentioned in attached March Table will move under the orders of the A.A. & Q.M.G.

6. Divisional Headquarters will close at ACHEUX at 12 noon on the 21st. inst. and re-open at N.11.Central at the same hour.

7. ACKNOWLEDGE.

Issued at 2-30 p.m.

J. D. Coleridge   Lieut. Col.
General Staff, 11th. Division.

Copy No. 1 A.D.C. for G.O.C.
2 G.S.O. I.
3 C.R.A.
4 C.R.E.
5. 32nd. Inf. Bde.
6 33rd. "   "
7 34th. "   "
8 6th. E. Yorks Regt.
9 Signal Coy.
10 A.A. & Q.M.G.
11 A.D.M.S.

Copy No. 12. A.D.V.S.
13 A.P.M.
14 11th. Div. Train.
15 D.A.D.O.S.
16 Camp Commdt.
17 Vth. Corps "G".
18 Vth. Corps "Q".
19 1st. Anzac Corps "G"
20 1st. Anzac Corps "Q"
21 5th. Aust. Divn.
22 - 23 War Diary.
24 - 25 Office.

MARCH TABLE issued with 11th. Division Order No. 65 dated 19/4/17.

Date.	Unit.	From.	To.	Route.	Relieving.	Remarks.
April 20th.	54th.Brigade. 86th.Fd.Coy.R.E.	Huts in W.10.	THILLOY.	CRUCIFIX CORNER - VILLERS - LE SARS. BAPAUME.	14th.Aust.Inf. Brigade. H.Q., THILLOY.	March to be completed by 12.30 p.m.
	32nd.Brigade. 67th.Fd.Co.R.E.	OVILLERS. AVELUY.	BEAULENCOURT. RIENCOURT. Camps in N.11.	LE SARS - BAPAUME.	15th.Aust.Inf. Brigade. H.Q., SUCRERIE.	March to be completed by 11.30 a.m.
	33rd.Brigade.(a)	BOUZINCOURT and SENLIS.	(a) M.20 Camp. LE SARS.	(a) ALBERT-POZIERES	—	Not to reach POZIERES before 5.30 p.m.
	68th.Fd.Co.R.E.(b)		(b) OVILLERS HUTS.	(b) AVELUY-CRUCIFIX CORNER.		
	6th.E.Yorks Regt.	SENLIS.	SPRING GARDENS X.9.Central.	ALBERT-POZIERES.	—	To follow 33rd. Brigade. Under Orders of O.C. 33rd. Bri.Bde.
April 21st.	33rd.Brigade (a)	(a) M.20 Camp.	(a) FREMICOURT. HABLIECOURT. BANCOURT.	BAPAUME.	8th.Aust.Inf. Brigade. H.Q., FREMICOURT.	To be East of BAPAUME by 10.30 a.m.
	68th.Fd.Co. (b) R.E.	(b) OVILLERS HUTS.	(b) FREMICOURT.			
	6th.E.Yorks Regt.	SPRING GARDENS.	I.30.Central.	BAPAUME.	5th.Aust.Pioneer Battalion.	To be East of BAPAUME by 11.30 a.m. To march under orders of G.O.C. 33rd.Inf.Bde.

APPENDIX I.

Issued with 11th. D.O. No. 65.

Schedule of works to be taken
over from 5th. Australian Division.
======

By C.R.E.

1. **Field Companies:-**

    1 Company on Corps second line.
    1 Company on BAPAUME-GREVILLERS Road and dry-weather
      track at the side of BAPAUME.
    1 Company on Corps second line BAPAUME-LeTRANSLOY Road.

2. **Pioneer Battalion :-**

    2 Companies on BANCOURT Road.
    2 Companies on Divisional Support line under orders
      of C.R.E., 2nd. Australian Division.

By 34th. Inf. Bde.

3. 400 men under R.T.O. BAPAUME for unloading ammunition
      (two shifts come on 8 a.m. and 8 p.m.).

4. 1,000 men on transportation under Captain GREENLEES,
      4th. Canadian Railway Battalion (H.Q. at H.22.a.8.5).
    Half the above reports 8 a.m. daily I.19.b.2.7.
    Half the above reports 8 a.m. daily BAPAUME Station.

5. 1 Officer and 60 other ranks attached to First Anzac Corps
      Siege Park at FREMICOURT for unloading ammunition
      at Railhead I.20.

------ooOoo------

APPENDIX II.

ADMINISTRATIVE INSTRUCTIONS.
Issued with O.O.No. 65.

---

1. **Administration** - 1st ANZAC will administer the 11th Division from midnight 19th/20th April.

2. **Railheads.** - Railhead for 11th Division (less Artillery) will open at ALBERT on 20th. Railhead for 11th Division complete will open at BAPAUME on 21st.

3. **Ammunition.** - The 5th Australian Division will move out with ammunition echelons empty. All S.A A., Grenades, etc. in possession (including establishments of mobile echelons) will be handed over to the 11th Division, lists of stores handed over will be forwarded to Corps Q.

4. **Trench Stores.** - Any Trench Stores in possession of 5th Australian Division will be handed over to 11th Division - Lists of stores handed over will be forwarded to A.D.O.S., 1st ANZAC.

5. **Accommodation** - No Trench Shelters or tents will be moved out with the 5th Australian Division. All accommodation now occupied by the 5th Australian Division will be handed over to the 11th Division.

6. **Pack Saddlery** - No Pack-saddlery will be handed over to the 11th Division.

7. **Rations in Supporting Points** - Any rations now in Supporting Points on charge to the 5th Australian Division will be handed over to the 11th Division.

8. **Salvage.** - The 11th Divisional Salvage Company is at the disposal of 1st ANZAC Corps Salvage Officer for work from midnight 21st/22nd April.

War Diary APPENDIX III (24)

SECRET.

11th. Division Order No. 66.

22nd. April. 1917.

Copy No. 19

22nd. Apl. 1917.

Reference Map 1/40,000
Sheet 57C.

1. The 11th. Division (less Artillery) will relieve the 1st. Australian Division (less Artillery) on night 23rd/24th., 24th inst., and night 24th/25th. in accordance with the attached table.

2. (a) The boundary between Sub-sectors from 9 a.m. on 25th. inst. will be J.8.d.2.0 to BEAUMETZ (inclusive to the Right Brigade) and thence a line drawn from J.13.Central to I.31.Central.

   (b) The boundary between the 11th. Division and 20th. Division will remain as at present.

   (c) The boundary between the 11th. Division and the 2nd. Australian Division from 9 a.m. on 25th. inst. will be H.23.d.5.0 - I.14.Central - I.9.d.0.0 - I.10.Central - I.5.d.2.3 - C.30.Central - D.19.b.5.0 - D.14.d.5.0 - D.15.b.1.9.

3. Details of relief will be arranged by Brigade Commanders concerned.

4. The 34th. Brigade will be relieved of Corps Working Parties by the 3rd. Australian Brigade - details to be arranged by Brigade Commanders concerned.

5. Relieving Units will take over plans of work, photographs, documents and intelligence relating to future operations, and all huts, tents and shelters from the Units they are relieving.

6. Units will march with ammunition echelons full and will take over all surplus ammunition left by relieved units.

7. Instructions will be issued later regarding
   (a) Administrative matters.
   (b) Relief of Field Coys., Pioneer Battalion, Field Ambs. and Mob.Vet.Section.

8. The 5th. Australian D.A. will cover the front of the Division for the present.

9. Relief to be completed by 9 a.m. on 25th. inst. when Command will pass to G.O.C.,11th.Division.
   H.Q.,11th. Division will remain at N.11.Central for the present.

J.D. Coleridge Lieut. Colonel,

Issued at 1 p.m.

General Staff, 11th. Division.

Copy No. 1 A.D.C. for G.O.C.
2 C.R.A.
3 C.R.E.
4. 32nd. Inf. Bde.
5. 33rd.   "   "
6. 34th.   "   "
7. 6th. E. Yorks.
8. Signals.
9. "Q".
10. A.D.M.S.
11. Train.
12. 1st.Anzac Corps"G".
13. 1st.   "   "Q".
14. 1st. Aust.Div.
15. 2nd.Aust.Div.
16. 20th.Divn.
17. 3rd.R.F.C.
18) War
19) Diary.
20)
21) Office.
22 CRA 5th Aus Div

TABLE TO ACCOMPANY 11th. DIVISION ORDER No. 66.

Date.	Serial Number.	Unit.	To.	Relieving.	Remarks.
Night 23rd/24th.	1.	"A" Battalion 32nd. Brigade.	Right Sub-sector.	"A" Battalion 1st.Aust.Bde.	H.Q.Coys. and L.T.M.Bttys. of 32nd. and 33rd. Bdes. will relieve similar units of the 1st. & 2nd. Aust.Bdes. under Bde.arrangments.
	2.	"B" Battalion 33rd. Brigade.	Left Sub-sector.	"A" Battalion 2nd. "	
	3.	"C" Battalion 33rd. Brigade.	Left Sub-sector.	"B" Battalion 2nd. "	
24th.	4.	H.Q., 34th. Brigade.	J.25.c.3.0.	H.Q., 3rd.Aust.Bde.	Relief of 3rd. Aust.Bde. by 34th. Bde. to be completed by 9 a.m. on 25th. inst.
	5.	"A" Battalion 34th. Brigade.	BEAULETZ – MORCHIES Line. }	"A" Battalion 3rd. "	
	6.	"B" Battalion 34th. Brigade.	"	"B" Battalion 3rd. "	
	7.	34th. M.G. Company.	"	3rd. M.G. Company.	
	8.	34th. L.T.M. Battery.	"	3rd. L.T.M. Battery.	
	9.	"C" Battalion 34th. Brigade.	VELU.	"C" Battalion 3rd.Aust.Bde.	"C" & "D" Battns. 34th.Bde. will form the Divnl. Reserve.
	10.	"D" Battalion 34th. Brigade.	FREMICOURT.	"D" Battalion 3rd. "	
Night 24th/25th.	11.	H.Q., 32nd. Brigade.	BEAUMETZ.	H.Q., 1st.Aust.Bde.	
	12.	"B" Battalion 32nd. Brigade.	Right Sub-sector.	"B" Battalion 1st. "	
	13.	"A" Battalion 33rd. Brigade.	Left Sub-sector.	"C" Battalion 1st. "	"C" Battalion was previously located in the Right Sub-sector.

/14.

2.

Date.	Serial Number.	Unit.	To.	Relieving.	Remarks.
Night 24th/25th. (contd)	14.	"C" Battalion 32nd. Brigade.	BEAUMETZ	"D" Battalion 1st. Aust. Bde.	Bde. Reserve.
	15.	"D" Battalion 32nd. Brigade.	Sq.J.22.b.		
	16.	H.Q., 33rd. Brigade.	I.11.c.5.d.	H.Q., 2nd.Aust.Bde.	
	17.	"D" Battalion 33rd. Brigade.	Site S.E. of MORCHIES	"D" Battalion 2nd. Aust. Bde.	

NOTES:- 1. No relief forward of the BEAUMETZ - MORCHIES line will take place by day, but small advanced parties can be sent to the various posts by daylight if required.

2. By day movement in the open will be made in artillery formation.

War Diary

SECRET.   Copy No.........

ADMINISTRATIVE INSTRUCTIONS. NO 12.

Reference 11th Divisional Order No.66, dated 20/4/17.

I. Ammunition, rockets, flares etc.
(a) Great care should be taken in taking over all dumps. A return showing various items and quantities of each in the dumps, and giving map locations will be compiled as soon as possible and forwarded to D.H.Q.

(b) A Divisional Dump now exists at BEAULENCOURT.

(c) S.A.A. Sec., D.A.C. will be located at HAPLINCOURT.

II. Accommodation.
No accommodation will be removed from the present area. All huts, tents, and trench shelters will be transferred between Brigades and Units relieving each other.

III Supplies.
(a) Rations in Supporting Points will be taken over.

(b) Refilling Point after the relief will be at H.30.a.

(c) The Train will deliver supplies to the Transport Lines of Infantry Brigades holding the Line.

IV. Water.
Water Police will be posted on all sources of water supply. Reliable men only should be put on this duty.
Where necessary the R.A.M.C. personnel attached to Battalions for water-duties are to be employed in superintending and supervising the Water Supply for Human consumption.
Wells which have been marked "Dangerous" most of which have been battened down, are on no account to be used until declared fit by competent authority.

V. Trench Stores.
All Trench Stores will be taken over.

VI. Returns.
Returns showing all such and area stores given over or received will be forwarded to D.H.Q. as soon as possible after the relief.

All shortages of munitions, Trench and area stores especially those dealing with defence against gas attack will be reported to D.H.Q. and steps taken to replace or augment.

VII. Horse Lines.
In selecting horse and transport lines provision should be exercised that the sites should allow for long occupation. Natural drainage and good approaches are as essential as protection against weather.

D. F. Gordon.
Lieut. Colonel.
A.A. & Q.M.G., 11th Division.

20/4/17.

Copy No. 1 A.D.C. for G.O.C.
2 C.R.A.   8. Signals.   15. 2nd Aust.Div.
3 C.R.E.   9. "G".   16. 20th Divn.
4. 32nd Inf.Bde. 10. A.D.M.S.   17. 3rd.R.F.C.
5. 33rd "   "   11. Train.   18.) War
6. 54th "   "   12. 1st Anzac Corps "G". 19.) Diary.
7. 6th E.Yorks.   13. 1st   "   " "Q". 20.)
                  14. 1st Aust. Div.   21.) Office.
                                            22. C.R.A. 5th Aust.)
                                                            Divn.)

APPENDIX III (5)

S E C R E T.

Copy No. 14

25th. April 1917.

11th. Division Order No. 67.

Reference Map 1/40,000
Sheet 57C.

1. Gas Projectors are installed on the Divisional front in the neighbourhood of DEMICOURT in K.7.d.
    Objective: Enemy's position about Lock 6. Sq.K.3.a.
    Gas will be discharged at the first suitable opportunity when the wind is favourable.

2. The discharge will be supplemented by a brief Artillery Gas Shell Bombardment on the enemy trenches in Square K.3.a. and K.3.c. commencing at ZERO ─ 10 minutes.

3. ZERO hour will be 2.30 a.m.

4. The personnel of "H" Special Company R.E. on receipt of orders from 11th. Division H.Q. to carry out the operation will proceed at an appropiate time to the projectors and will discharge the gas as detailed in paras 1 & 3, unless :-

    (1) The wind prove unfavourable, at ZERO HOUR.

    (2) G.O.C., 32nd. Inf. Bde. on account of tactical developments or for some other reason, forbids the discharge.
    If he has no objection he will send the following "Priority" wire at 12 midnight to :-

    (i) C.R.A., 5th. Aust. D.A.

    (ii) O.C.,"H" Special Company R.E.

    (iii) 11th. Division H.Q.

    (iv) Right and Left Flank Brigades.

    (v) Battalions in his sector.

    "GOODS WILL BE DELIVERED".

    Before gas is discharged the O.C.,"H" Special Company will report to G.O.C.,32nd. Inf. Bde. and inform him where he can be found prior to ZERO hour.

5. All troops will be warned and those in the forward area East of a North-South line through LOUVERVAL-DOIGNIES will wear Gas Helmets in the alert position.

6. G.O.C.,32nd. Inf. Bde. will arrange (a) to withdraw all troops from posts in front of the Projectors to the rear of the Projectors from ZERO - 5 minutes to ZERO ─ 5 minutes, (b) to cover these posts by troops in rear during that time, (c) to re-occupy the posts immediately afterwards.

7. Hostile enemy artillery fire is to be anticipated in retaliation.

/8

8. Watches will be synchronised with Divisional Signals daily at 9 a.m. and 6 p.m.

9. Before the operation can take place projectiles and charges have to be carried up.

For this purpose, the following parties will be detailed to be in readiness each evening to proceed to the Rendezvous ordered :-

(a) O.C., "H" Special Company R.E. will apply to the G.O.C., 32nd. Brigade for any working parties he may require.

(b) 9 - G.S. Wagons with reliable N.C.O's to be detailed by "Q" 11th. Division to report at Headquarters "H" Special Company R.E. at LEBUCQUIERE (I.30.a.2.5) at 7 p.m. on the evening prior to ZERO hour.
Load up there and proceed to DEMICOURT.
This route must be reconnoitred at once.

<u>"H" Special Company to provide guides.</u>

The above parties will not proceed to their respective rendezvous until orders are received.
These will be sent from D.H.Q. every evening about 5.30 p.m. on the evening previous to ZERO hour.

10. ACKNOWLEDGE.

Issued at 7./pm

J. D. Coleridge Lieut. Colonel,
General Staff, 11th. Division.

Copy No. 1 to A.D.C. for G.O.C.
   2.   C.R.E.
   3.   32nd. Inf. Bde.
   4.   33rd. "   "
   5.   34th. "   "
   6.   6th. E. Yorks Regt.
   7.   Signal Coy.
   8.   "Q"
   9.   A.D.M.S.
   10.   Train.
   11.   1st. Anzac Corps.
   12.   2nd. Aust. Divn.
   13.   1st. "   "
   14.   "H" Special Coy. R.E.
   15.   C.R.A., 5th. Aust. Divn.
  16- 17   War Diary.
  18- 19   File.

APPENDIX III (6)

SECRET   Copy No. 15

11th Division Order No. 38.

Reference Map 1/40,000   27th April, 1917
Sheet. 57.C.

1. The 34th Brigade will relieve the 33rd Brigade in the Left Sector of the Divisional Front on the night 30th April/1st May.

2. All details will be arranged direct between Brigades concerned.

3. All necessary Trench Maps, Photographs, Stores and appliances will be handed over.

4. The relief to be completed by 6-0 a.m. May 1st.

5. Reconnaissance of the BEAUMETZ - MORCHIES Line by the 33rd Brigade, and of the Left Sector by the 34th Brigade should be begun at once.

6. ACKNOWLEDGE.

J. M. R. Harrison Maj
for Lieut-Colonel,
Gen. Staff, 11th Division.

Issued at 1.15 p.m.

Copy No. 1. A.D.C. for G.O.C.
        2. C.R.E.
        3. 32nd Inf. Bde.
        4. 33rd Inf. Bde.
        5. 34th Inf. Bde.
        6. 8th E. Yorks Regt.
        7. Signal Coy.
        8. "Q"
        9. A.D.M.S.
        10. Train.
        11. 1st ANZAC Corps.
        12. 2nd Aust. Div.
        13. 1st Aust. Div.
        14. C.R.A. 5th Aust. Div.
     15 -16. War Diary.
     17 - 18. File.

SECRET

APPENDIX III (7)

Copy No. 18

29th April, 1917.

11th Division Order No. 69.

Reference Map 1/40,000
Sheet 57.C.

1. Gas Projectors are installed about J.12.d.7.7.

    These will be discharged to-night 29th/30th if wind is favourable.

    Objective neighbourhood of LOCK 6.

2. ZERO hour will be 2-0 a.m.

3. The personnel of "H" Special Company R.E. on receipt of orders from 11th Division H.Q. to carry out the operation will proceed at an appropiate time to the projectors and will discharge the gas as detailed in paras 1 & 2. unless:-

    (1) The wind prove unfavourable, at ZERO Hour.

    (2) G.O.C. 32nd Inf. Bde. on account of tactical developments or for some other reason, forbids the discharge.
    If he has no objection he will send the following "Priority" wire at 12 midnight to :-

    (i) C.R.A., 5th Aust. D.A.

    (ii) O.C. "H" Special Company R.E.

    (iii) 11th Division H.Q.

    (iv) Right and Left Flank Brigades.

    (v) Battalions in his Sector.

    "RATIONS WILL BE ISSUED".

    Before gas is discharged the O.C. "H" Special Company will report to G.O.C. 32nd Inf. Bde. and inform him where he can be found prior to ZERO HOUR.

4. All troops will be warned and those in the forward area East of a North-South line through LOUVERVAL - DOIGNIES will wear Gas Helmets in the alert position.

5. G.O.C. 32nd Inf. Bde. will arrange (a) to wothdraw all troops from posts in front of the Projectors to the rear of the Projectors from ZERO - 5 minutes to ZERO 5 minutes, (b) to cover these posts by troops in rear during that time, (c) to re-occupy the posts immediately afterwards.

6. Watches will be synchronised with Divisional Signals at 6 p.m.

7. 4 G.S. wagons with reliable N.C.O's to be detailed by 'Q' 11th Division to report at Headquarters "H" Special Company R.E. at LEBUCQUIERE (I.30.a.2.5) at 7-30 p.m. this evening 29th instant. Load up there and proceed to DEMICOURT.

    "H" Special Company to provide guides.

8. ACKNOWLEDGE.

Issued at 1.45 p.m.

S.M.R. Harrison May
for Lieut-Colonel,
Gen. Staff. 11th Division.

Distribution see over.

SECRET   APPENDIX III 8.   Copy No 13.

11th Division Order No. 70.

30th April, 1917.

ESCORT for GUNS.

1.   Infantry Brigades in the line will provide escorts for all guns in their areas forward of the BEAUMETZ - MORCHIES Line.

These are at present "D" Group, 5th Aust. D.A. consisting of :-

   16th Bty. J.16.a.2.2.
   17th "   J.16.c.4.6.
   18th "   J.9.c.7.5.
   106th "   J.16.a.25.80.

in the DOIGNIES Area, and the escort will consist of 1 Platoon (to be found by Right Brigade), the O.C. of which will receive orders from and make his dispositions in conjunction with the Officer Commanding "D" Group, 5th Aust. D.A. Hd. Qrs. J.13.d.8.2.

2.   Escort for all batteries both Field and Heavy between the BEAUMETZ - MORCHIES and the YTRES - BEUGNY Line will be found by the Reserve Brigade.

These Batteries will be classified by localities into 3 Areas, with one escort for each Area.

 (i) The VELU Area.

  Field Artillery 7th Bty. J.34.a.2.1.
        8th "   J.28.d.15.15.
        9th "   J.27.d.15.80.
        103rd " J.34.c.6.1.

  Heavy Artillery 189th Bty. J.25.c.80.66.
        142nd " J.25.d.94.85.
        31st "   J.32.a.10.81.
        65th "   J.32.a.45.63.

Escort ½ Company (to be found by the Reserve Brigade) the O.C. of which will receive orders from and arrange his dispositions with O.C. "A" Group, 5th Aust. D.A. Hd. Qrs. J.32.c.5.5.

 (ii) The BEAUMETZ Area.

  Heavy Artillery 276th Bty. J.19.d.28.97.
        163rd " J.19.d.91.87.
        264th " J.19.b.48.37.
        78th "   J.13.d.46.03.

Escort 1 Platoon (to be found by the Reserve Brigade) the O.C. of which will receive orders from and arrange his dispositions with the O.C. 44th Heavy Artillery Group Hd. Qrs. I.30.a.6.5.

/ (iii)

(iii) The MORCHIES Area.

Field Artillery	49th Bty.	J.7.a.5.7.
	50th "	I.12.b.8.1.
	51st "	I.12.c.85.20.
	113th "	J.7.c.5.6.
	53rd "	I.5.d.5.2.
	54th "	I.6.c.4.9.
	55th "	I.5.d.69.45.
Heavy Artillery	26th Bty.	I.18.a.80.89.
	34th "	I.11.d.5.9.

Escort ½ Company (to be found by the Reserve Brigade) the O.C. of which will receive orders from and arrange his dispositions with O.C. "B" Group, 5th Aust. D.A. Hd. Qrs. I.22.a.7.4.

3. Artillery officers responsible for the various areas, will arrange that the O's C. their escorts will make their dispositions with due regard to those of Artillery escorts on their flanks.

4. O's C. Artillery escorts will get into touch with Artillery Officers Commanding their "Areas" at the earliest opportunity.

5. Please acknowledge.

J. D. Coleridge
Lieut-Colonel,
General Staff. 11th Division.

Issued at 1-45 pm

Copy No. 1. G.O.C.
2. 32nd Inf. Bde.
3. 33rd Inf. Bde.
4. 34th Inf. Bde.
5. C.R.A. 5th Aust. Div.
6. 'Q' 11th Div.
7. 1st ANZAC Corps 'G'
8. " " " 'Q'
9. G.O.C.R.A. 1st ANZAC Corps.
10. 20th Div.
11. 2nd Aust. Div.
12. 1st ANZAC Corps Heavy Arty.
13 & 14. War Diary.
15 & 16. File.

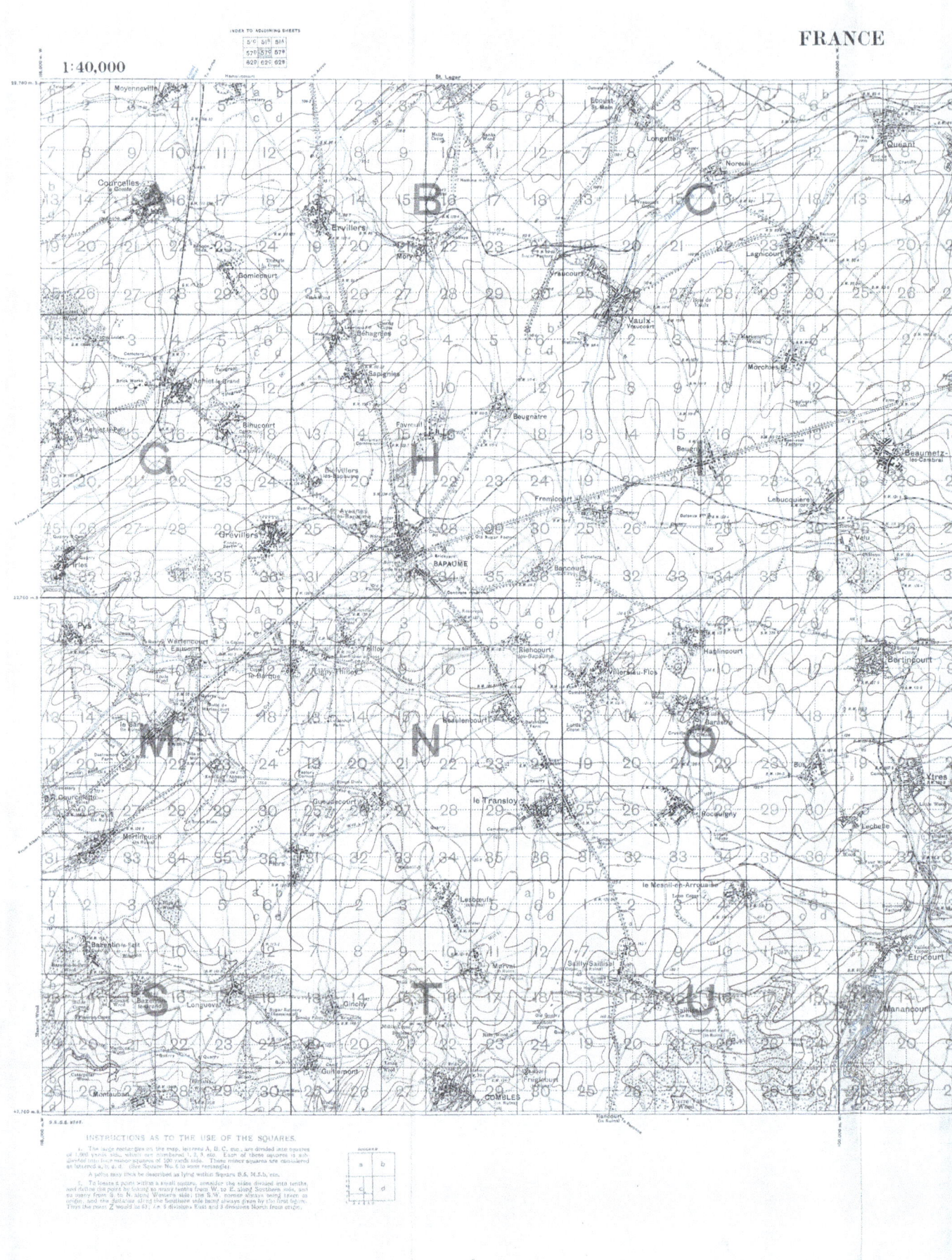

FRANCE

EDITION 2.   SHEET 57c

Scale 1:40,000
Contour Interval 10 Metres.

Ordnance Survey. March. 1917.

GLOSSARY.

Abbaye, Abⁿ	Abbey.
Abreuvoir, Abʳ	Watering place.
Abri de douanier	Customs-shelter.
Aciérie	Steel works.
Aiguille	Point(y).
Allée	Alley, Narrow road.
Ancien -ne, Ancⁿ	Old.
Aqueduc	Aqueduct.
Arbre	Tree.
„ éventail	„ fan-shaped.
„ décharné	„ bare.
„ fourchu	„ forked.
„ isolé	„ isolated.
„ penché	„ leaning.
Arbrisseau	Small tree.
Arc	Arch.
Ardoisière, Ardʳᵉ	Slate quarry.
Arrêt	Halt.
Asile	Asylum.
„ des aliénés	Lunatic asylum.
„ de charité	Asylum.
„ des pauvres	
„ de refuge	
Auberge, Aubᵉ	Inn.
Aune	Alder-tree.
Bac	Ferry.
„ à treille	
Bains	Baths.
Place aux bains	Bathing place.
Balise	Buoy, Beacon.
Banc de sable	Sand-bank.
„ vase	Mud-bank.
Baraque	Hut.
Barrage	Dam.
Barrière	Gate, Stile.
Bascule (à) Bascule	Weigh-bridge.
Bassin	Dock, Pond.
„ d'échouage	Tidal dock.

Bassin de radoub	Dry dock.
Bateau phare	Light-ship.
Blanchisserie	Laundry.
B.M. (borne milliare)	Mile stone.
Bᵉ (borne kilométrique)	
Bouchonnerie	
Fabⁿ de bouchons	Bolt Factory.
Bouée	Buoy.
Brasserie, Brasˢᵉ	Brewery.
Briqueterie, Briqᵗᵉ	Brickfield.
Brise-lames	Breakwater.
Bureau de poste	Post office.
„ de douane	Custom house.
Butte	Butt, Mound.
Cabane	Hut.
Cabaret, Cabᵗ	Inn.
Câble sous-marin	Submarine cable.
Calvaire, Calvᵉ	Calvary.
Canal de dessèchement	Drainage canal.
Canal d'irrigation	Irrigation canal.
Fabⁿ de caoutchouc	Rubber factory.
Carrière, Carrᵉ	Quarry.
„ de gravier	Gravel-pit.
Caserne	Barracks.
Champ de courses	Race course.
„ „ manœuvres	Drill-ground.
„ „ tir	Rifle range.
Chantier	Building yard.
Chantier de construction	Ship yard.
	Dock yard.
Chapelle, Chˡˡᵉ	Slip-way.
Charbonnage	Chapel.
Château d'eau	Colliery.
	Water tower.
Chaussée	Causeway.
	Highway.
Chemin de fer	Railway.
Cheminée, Chⁿᵉᵉ	Chimney.
Chêne	Oak tree.
Cimetière, Cimᵗʳᵉ	Cemetery.
Clocher	Belfry.
Cloutérie	Nail factory.
Colombier	Dove-cot.

Corons	Workmen's dwellings.
Cour des marchandises	Goods yard.
Couvent	Convent.
Crassier	Slag heap.
Croix	Cross.
Darse	Inner dock.
Démoli -e	Destroyed.
Détruit -e, Détʳ	
Déversoir	Weir.
Digue	Dyke, causeway.
Distillerie, Distⁿᵉ	Distillery.
Douane	Custom-house.
Bureau de douane	
Entrepôt de douane	Custom warehouse.
Dynamitière, Dynamᵗ	Dynamite magazine.
Dynamiterie	Dynamite factory.
Écluse	Sluice, Lock.
Éclusette, Eclᵗᵉ	Sluice.
École	School.
Écurie	Stable.
Église	Church.
Émaillerie	Enamel works.
Embarcadère, Embʳᵉ	Landing-place.
Estaminet, Estamⁱ	Inn.
Étang	Pond.
Fabrique, Fabⁿ	Factory.
Fabⁿ de produits chimiques	Chemical works.
Fabⁿ de faïence	Pottery.
Faïencerie	
Ferme, Fᵐᵉ	Farm.
Filature, Filʳᵉ	Spinning mill.
Fonderie, Fondᵉ	Foundry.
Fontaine, Fontⁿᵉ	Spring, fountain.
Forêt	Forest.
Forme de radoub	Dry dock.
Forge	Smithy.
Fosse	Mine, Pit.
Fossé	Moat, Ditch.
Four	Kiln.
„ à chaux	Lime-kiln.

Four à coke	Coke oven.
Ganterie	Glove Factory.
Gare	Station.
Garenne	Warren.
Garnison	Garrison.
Gazomètre	Gasometer.
Glacerie	
Fabⁿ de glaces	Mirror Factory.
Glacière	Ice factory.
Grue	Crane.
Gué	Ford.
Guérite	Sentry-box, Turret.
„ à signaux	Signal box (Ry.)
Halte	Halt.
Hangar	Shed, Hanger.
Hôpital	Hospital.
Hôtel-de-Ville	Town hall.
Houillère	Colliery.
Huilerie	Oil factory.
Imprimerie, Impʳⁱᵉ	Printing works.
Jetée	Pier.
Lamineries	Rolling mills.
Ligne de haute laisse marée	High water mark
„ de basse marée	Low „
Maison Forestière, Mᵒⁿ Fʳᵉ	Forester's house.
Malterie	Malt-house.
Marbrerie	Marble works.
Marais	Marsh.
Marais salant	Saltern, Salt marsh.
Marché	Market.
Mare	Pool.
Meule	Rick.
Minière	Mine.
Monastère	Monastery.
Moulin, Mⁿ	Mill.
„ à vapeur	Steam mill.
Mur	Wall.
„ crénelé	Loop-holed wall.

Nacelle	Ferry
Orme	Elm
Orphelinat	Orphanage
Osseraie	Osier-beds
Ouvrage	Fort
Ouvrages hydrauliques	Water works
Papeterie	Paper-mill
Parc	Park, yard
„ aérostatique	Aviation ground
„ à charbon	Coal yard
„ à petrole	Petrol store
Passage à niveau P.N.	Level crossing
Passerelle, Pass^lle	Foot-bridge
Pépinière	Nursery garden
Peuplier	Poplar tree
Phare	Light-house
Pilier, P^r	Pier
Plaine d'exercises	Drill ground
Pompe	Pump
Ponceau	Culvert
Pont	Bridge
„ levis	Drawbridge
Poste de garde	Coast guard station
Station „	
Poteau P^u	Post
Poterie	Pottery
Poudrière, Poud^re	Powder magazine
Magasin à poudres	
Prise d'eau	Water supply
Puits	Pit-head, Shaft, Well
„ artésien	Artesian well
„ d'épuise	Ventilating shaft
„ ventilateur	
„ de sondage	Boring
Quai	Quay, Platform
„ aux bestiaux	Cattle platform
„ aux marchandises	Goods platform
„ des „	
Raccordement	Junction
Raffinerie	Refinery
„ de sucre	Sugar refinery
Rāperie	Beet root factory
Remblai	Embankment
Remise (des Machines)	Engine shed
Réservoir, Rés^r	Reservoir
Route cavalière	Bridle road
Rubanerie	Ribbon Factory
Ruines / Ruines / En ruine / Ruiné e	Ruin
Sablière	Sand-pit
Sablonnière, Sablon^re	
Sapin	Fir tree
Saule	Willow tree
Saunerie	Salt-works
Scierie, Sc^ie	Saw-mill
Sondage	Boring
Source	Spring
Sucrerie, Suc^re	Sugar factory
Tannerie	Tannery
Tir à la cible	Rifle range
Tissage	Weaving mill
Tūlerie	Rolling mill
Tombeau	Tomb
Tour	Tower
Tourbière	Peat-bog, Peat-bed
Tourelle	Small tower
Tuilerie	Tile works
Usine à gas	Gas works
„ électrique / d'electricité	Electricity works
„ métallurgique	Metal works
„ à agglomérés	Briquette factory
Verrerie, Verr^ie	Glass works
Viaduc	Viaduct
Vivier	Fish Pond
Voie de chargement / „ „ déchargement / „ „ d'évitement / „ „ formation / „ „ manœuvre	Siding
Zinguerie	Zinc works

FRANCE.

SHEET 57°
EDITION 2.

INDEX TO ADJOINING SHEETS.

SCALE 40,000

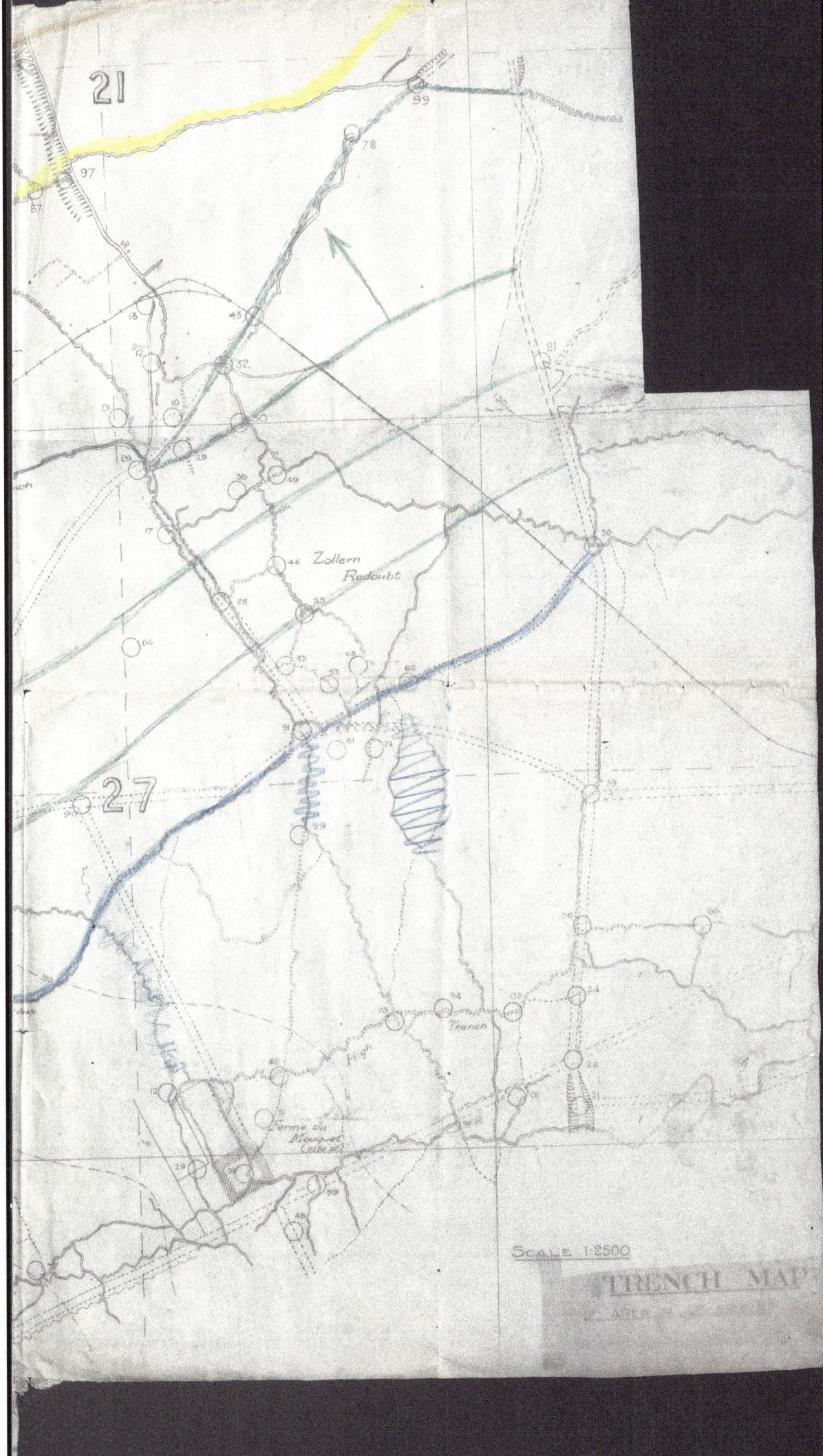